THE YOUNGER
CHILDREN'S
ENCYCLOPAEDIA

First published   1955
Revised editions 1960, 1964, 1966
Reprinted   1973

ISBN 0 600 70569 2

Published for Odhams Books by
THE HAMLYN PUBLISHING GROUP LTD.
London · New York · Sydney · Toronto
Astronaut House, Feltham, Middlesex, England

PRINTED BY
BUTLER AND TANNER LTD, FROME AND LONDON

THE YOUNGER CHILDREN'S ENCYCLOPAEDIA

Advisory Editors:

J. C. HILL, M.Sc.

M. G. RAWLINS

W. G. MOORE, B.Sc., F.R.G.S.

ODHAMS BOOKS

London · New York · Sydney · Toronto

WHAT THIS BOOK CONTAINS

HAVE you ever wanted a book which would explain the many puzzling things that you see and hear of as you grow up? If so, this book is just what you need, for it is a storehouse of interesting facts about all sorts of subjects.

To make it easy to find the facts you want, the entries have been arranged in alphabetical order. Sometimes while you are reading one entry you will come across a word printed in CAPITALS. Look it up, too, and you will find further facts about the subject which interests you.

At the end are three special sections on Arithmetic, English and Intelligence Tests. These will help you prepare for examinations and tests of all kinds.

ENCYCLOPAEDIA A TO Z

SUPPLEMENTS

The Publishers regret that the page references in the text to the colour plates are incorrect. The colour plates will be found four pages preceding the page mentioned and as listed below.

COLOUR PLATES

A

AARON, the brother of Moses who led the Israelites from bondage out of Egypt into the Promised Land.

ABBEY. MONKS live in a MONASTERY, and the largest monasteries were called abbeys. Nowadays there are many abbeys where services are held, such as WESTMINSTER ABBEY, but people do not live there.

ABBOT, the head of an ABBEY. See also CONVENT; NUNS.

ABDOMEN, the part of the body which contains the stomach, in which we digest our food. See DIGESTION; INTESTINE.

ABORIGINES are to be found in Australia. This race of brown-skinned people were there before the white man arrived. They keep very closely to their ancient tribal customs and way of life, and when not working for the Australian settlers are likely to be wandering in the "outback."

ABRAHAM, the father of Isaac and founder of the Jewish people. He lived about 1,500 B.C.

ACID, a sour liquid, like vinegar. There are several strong and dangerous acids which are used in chemistry for dissolving metals, and for other purposes. Hydro-chloric acid, nitric acid and sulphuric acid are the three most important ones.

ACORN, the fruit of the OAK tree.

Acorn.

ACRE, originally, the amount of land which could be ploughed by two oxen in one day. They could plough about 33 furrows. The furrows were about 2 feet apart. Hence an acre came to mean a piece of land a furrow long (a furlong, which is 220 yards) and 66 feet, or 22 yards broad.

Multiply 220 yards by 22 yards and you will find there are 4,840 square yards in an acre. Nowadays an acre can be any shape so long as it has 4,840 square yards.

ADAM, the name given in the Bible to the first man created by God; the first woman is called EVE. They lived in the garden of Eden. Their first son was CAIN.

Adder.

ADDER, or viper, a poisonous snake, found in heath land in Britain and over most of Europe.

ADJECTIVE, a word which describes a NOUN, so as to limit its meaning. "Horse" is a noun, and it can mean any horse. If we say "a black horse," "black" is an adjective which limits its meaning. Or we could say "The horse is small and black." "Small" and "black" are both adjectives.

ADMIRAL, rank and title of the commander-in-chief of a fleet of warships.

Westminster Abbey.

5

The Wright Brothers' aeroplane.

AEROPLANE, a flying-machine which is heavier than air. The blades of the propeller cut the air at an angle and pull the aeroplane forward. Then the pressure of the air on the wings causes the aeroplane to rise. In the "jet" aeroplanes the pressure of hot expanding gases provides the power to drive the machine. These gases escape in jets, the force of which pushes the aeroplane forward.

The first aeroplane which actually stayed up in the air was built by two Americans, Wilbur and Orville Wright, and the flight in 1903 lasted for just under a minute. See AIRPORT; FLIGHT; JET ENGINE; ROCKETS, and picture facing page 160.

AESOP, a Greek who wrote many FABLES. *The Dog and the Bone, The Fox and the Grapes, The Boy who Cried "Wolf,"* are three of them. Aesop was said to be a slave. He lived about 600 B.C.

AFRICA, one of the big CONTINENTS. The EQUATOR goes through the middle of it. Most of the land near the equator has heavy rainfall and great heat, so there are dense, tropical forests there.

In the African tropical forests, there are gorillas, monkeys, beautiful birds, and snakes. Elephants used to be found in most parts of the continent, but now they live chiefly in central Africa, and seem to prefer more open country. The valley of the upper NILE is particularly attractive to them. The forests are too dense for lions, antelopes or giraffes. These animals live in the tropical grass-lands north and south of the forests. The rhinoceroses also live there, and hippopotami are found near the rivers.

North of the tropical grass-land is the great SAHARA Desert, with the River Nile flowing to the east of it. The climates south of the equator are the same: tropical grass-land, then desert (the KALAHARI Desert where the ostrich and springbok are found), then the fruit-growing area in the south of SOUTH AFRICA.

North of the Sahara Desert, the land gets warm, dry, desert conditions in the summer, but has rain in the winter, and the trees which grow there store up the winter rain for their seeds. Hence we get fruits which have plenty of juice, and tough skins to prevent the fruit drying up in the hot summer, among them oranges, lemons, grapes, pomegranates. These fruits are grown in the north of Africa, on the MEDITERRANEAN coast (as well as in Spain, France, Italy and Greece, on the other side of the Mediterranean Sea). They are also grown in the south of South Africa, and we get wine from there too.

The great River Nile overflows its banks every year because of floods on the plateau of ETHIOPIA. The Blue Nile brings the extra water down and this makes the Nile flow over part of the Sahara Desert and the Nubian Desert. The fertile soil which is left behind when the floods subside gives the Egyptians good crops of wheat, cotton, maize, rice, and sugar. Other great rivers are the Zaïre, the NIGER and the ZAMBESI. Study the map of Africa and see how much you can learn. See also ALGERIA; EGYPT; SUDAN.

AGINCOURT (a-zhin-koor), a village in northern France, where the English king, HENRY V, defeated a French army much bigger than his own. The date of the battle is 1415. See also ARCHERY; BOW.

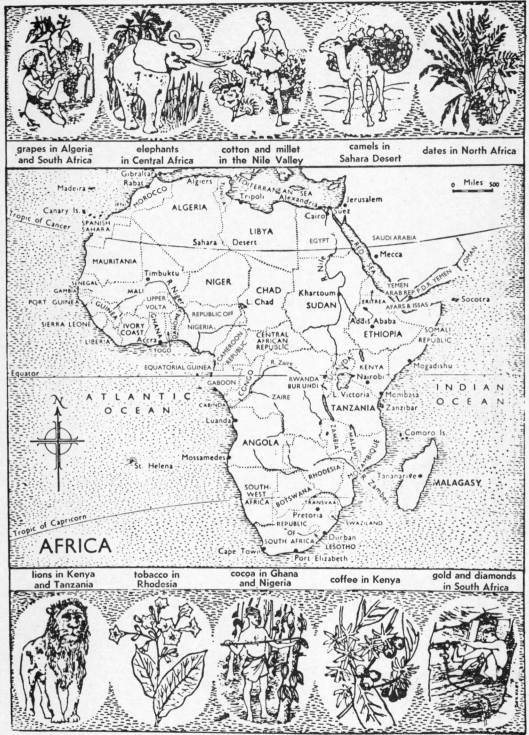

grapes in Algeria and South Africa

elephants in Central Africa

cotton and millet in the Nile Valley

camels in Sahara Desert

dates in North Africa

lions in Kenya and Tanzania

tobacco in Rhodesia

cocoa in Ghana and Nigeria

coffee in Kenya

gold and diamonds in South Africa

The African continent and some of the things found there.

AIR, the gases which surround the earth. Air is made up of one part OXYGEN and four parts NITROGEN, with very small quantities of other gases.

AIRCRAFT-CARRIER, a naval ship which carries many AEROPLANES. It has a large deck from which the planes can take off and land.

AIR-GUN, a gun which fires darts or small bullets by air pressure. A spring in the barrel is compressed, usually by bending the gun or by pulling a lever, and when this spring is released by pulling the trigger air is forced out and drives the bullet or dart out of the barrel. Air-guns can kill small animals or birds.

AIRPORT, a landing-place for airliners arriving from abroad, and a ground from which they can take-off to fly to other countries. It must have several long runways so that aeroplanes can land or take-off against the wind, whichever direction the wind is blowing from. An airport has a control tower, Customs offices, restaurants, petrol supplies, ambulances, fire-engines, and other arrangements for the safety and comfort of the passengers. See colour plate facing page 160.

AIR PUMP. A bicycle pump is one kind of air PUMP. There are several other kinds.

AIRSHIP, a big cigar-shaped balloon made of a metal frame covered with fabric. It is filled with HYDROGEN or HELIUM to make it rise, and has motors to drive it through the air.

ALASKA, the north-west part of NORTH AMERICA. It is one of the UNITED STATES OF AMERICA. It has good timber, and there are many fur-bearing animals, for it is very cold in winter and the animals need fur to keep

Airship.

them warm. The largest river is the YUKON. There are large numbers of salmon in the rivers, and the fish is exported in tins. Gold is also found. The Alaska highway is a motor-road 1,523 miles long, from British Columbia, CANADA, to Fairbanks, Alaska, and people can now travel there from the United States by motor-car. See map of CANADA.

ALBATROSS, a sea-bird found in the southern HEMISPHERE. There are several species, of which the Wandering Albatross is the best-known. It is powerful in flight, with a wing-spread of about twelve feet.

ALBERT, Prince, was born in 1819. He became the husband of Queen VICTORIA in 1840, but did not receive the title of Prince Consort until 1857. The Albert Hall, a large concert hall in London, is named after him. He died in 1861.

ALBINO, a person or animal without any dark colouring matter, or pigment, in hair, or skin, for example, white mouse.

An aircraft-carrier can store aeroplanes below the flight-deck.

ALCHEMY, the kind of chemistry which was studied in the MIDDLE AGES. The alchemists tried to find out how one could turn common metals into gold, and how one could live longer. They were not successful, but they learned some important chemistry by their experiments.

ALCOHOL, an intoxicating liquor which is the result of fermentation of grape-juice and other substances. There is alcohol in wine, cider, beer and other drinks. These drinks are very dangerous for young people.

ALEXANDER THE GREAT, the son of Philip of Macedon, was born in 356 B.C. His teacher was ARISTOTLE. He became king at twenty and died in 323 B.C. when he was thirty-two, but with his army he conquered most of the known world in these twelve years.

ALEXANDRIA, an important city and seaport in Egypt near a mouth of the Nile. It was founded by ALEXANDER THE GREAT in 332 B.C. See map of AFRICA.

ALFRED THE GREAT (born A.D. 849), became King of ENGLAND in 871, but had to flee from the Danes for a time till he gathered an army about him. Then he defeated them. Afterwards he rebuilt the community, trained the army, built a navy, and helped to educate the people. He died in 901 and was buried at Winchester.

ALGEBRA is a way of solving mathematical problems by using letters for quantities instead of numbers.

ALGERIA is a country in the north of Africa. It was part of the French Union but is now a republic. Grapes and dates grow there. See map of AFRICA.

ALICE'S ADVENTURES IN WONDERLAND, a book for children written by Lewis CARROLL. It tells of Alice, a little girl who dreams that she follows a White Rabbit down a rabbit-hole, and there meets with all kinds of strange adventures. She also meets some very odd characters—amongst them are the Ugly Duchess, the Cheshire Cat that was always grinning, the Mad Hatter and the March Hare who had a strange tea-party, the King and Queen of Hearts, and the Mock Turtle.

ALIMENTARY CANAL. This name is given to the digestive tube. It is about 30 feet long from the mouth to the anus. Juices which digest the food enter the tube at various points. See DIGESTION.

ALLEGORY, a story which has a deeper meaning than it seems to have at first sight, like a PARABLE in the New Testament. John BUNYAN'S story, *The Pilgrim's Progress*, is an allegory.

ALLIGATOR, a large REPTILE like the crocodile, but with a shorter, flatter head. True alligators are found only in the Mississippi Basin and southern China. Their near relatives, the caimans, are confined to tropical South America.

Alligator.

ALLOY. Two or more metals can be melted together to make a new substance called an alloy. Brass is an alloy made from copper and zinc. Bronze, stainless steel and solder are other examples.

ALPHABET, the signs a, b, c, d and so on, used to represent sounds. The two first letters of the Greek alphabet are "alpha" and "beta," and we got the name "alphabet" from these two words.

ALPS, the highest mountains in EUROPE. They stretch round the north of Italy and are part of the great wrinkle in the earth's crust which extends from the Pyrenees in Spain to Asia. This wrinkle runs east and west. The wrinkle in America is north and south. See EARTH.

ALSATIAN, a native of Alsace; also the name of a large wolf-hound formerly used in Alsace to protect sheep. The police train these dogs to catch criminals, and many people keep them as watch-dogs.

ALTO. This is the highest singing voice in a male choir. See also CONTRALTO.

ALUMINIUM, a light metal, useful for making aeroplanes and other things.

AMAZON. The largest river system in the world is that of the Amazon. It rises in the Andes, in the north of South America, near the equator, where there is plenty of rain, and it flows through an immense tropical forest. The river is about 4,000 miles long and has 200 tributaries.

AMERICA is the name given to one of the CONTINENTS. It is bordered by the Atlantic Ocean on the east and the Pacific on the west, and stretches from the Arctic in the north to the Antarctic in the south.

Nowadays geographers think of America as two continents—NORTH AMERICA and SOUTH AMERICA, linked by CENTRAL AMERICA, which is a neck of land between the Caribbean Sea and the Pacific. A canal called the Panama Canal has been cut between the north and south to allow ships to pass through.

Many people use the name America when they are talking about the UNITED STATES, which are in the northern part of the continent.

AMOEBA, one of the simplest forms of animal life. It is just a tiny blob of jelly, so small that we need a microscope to see it. This jelly is called protoplasm, and contains a thicker spot called the nucleus. Amoebas "breed" in a curious way. The nucleus merely divides into two parts, each surrounded by jelly, and so you have two amoebas where before there was only one. The amoeba has no legs but moves about

Amoeba dividing.

by putting out "false feet," which are projections of the protoplasm. It has no stomach, but seems to fold itself around its food and then absorbs it.

AMPHIBIANS. This name describes animals like the FROG, which begin life as a tadpole living in water, and breathing by means of gills; they later develop lungs, which means that they are able to live on land. NEWTS, toads and salamanders are amphibians.

AMSTERDAM is the capital of Holland. The painter Rembrandt lived here, and some of his pictures are in the Ryks Museum. The cutting and polishing of diamonds is an important industry. See also NETHERLANDS.

Anaconda.

ANACONDA, a very large snake, sometimes 30 feet long, which kills its prey by coiling itself around it and crushing it. It is found in the tropical forests of SOUTH AMERICA.

ANALYSIS means the breaking up of something into the various parts which make the whole. A chemist, for example, can analyse salt into two elements, sodium and chlorine; he can analyse the food from the stomach and find out what has made someone ill, or he can analyse a piece of rock and say if there is gold or silver or copper or lead in it, and how much there is.

ANATOMY is the study of the structure of the body. Doctors have to study the SKELETON very carefully to understand all about bones and joints, so that they can mend broken or twisted limbs. They must know where all the blood-vessels, nerves and muscles are so that they do not cut them when they are operating. See also ARTERIES, CAPILLARIES; NERVOUS SYSTEM; SURGERY; VEIN.

ANDERSEN, Hans Christian, was born in Denmark in 1805. He wrote poetry and fables, but is famous chiefly for his fairy tales. Two of the best-known are *The Emperor's New Clothes* and *The Ugly Duckling*. He died in 1875.

ANDES, part of the wrinkle on the earth's crust which stretches along the west coast of North and South America. In South America this tremendous mountain system, over 5,000 miles long, is called the Andes; it has many volcanoes. See ARGENTINE REPUBLIC; CHILE.

ANGLE. This is the amount of difference in direction between two straight lines which start from the same point. A protractor will show you the scale of degrees which we use in measuring angles. If an 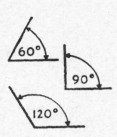 angle has less than 90 degrees it is called an acute angle. The one shown is an angle of 60 degrees, or 60° as we write it. If an angle has 90° it is called a right angle. Every right angle has 90°. If an angle has more than 90° but less than 180° it is called an obtuse angle. The one shown has 120°.

The scale for measuring angles was made by the Babylonian people, who divided the CIRCLE into 360 parts, or degrees, because they knew there were about 360 days in the year, and 360 divided better than any number near it.

Draw a circle, and keeping the same distance between the points of the COMPASS, mark off six points round the circumference as shown below.

You will find the compass makes exactly six marks in going round.

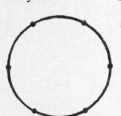

Now join the points as shown in the diagram. You then have six TRIANGLES, each 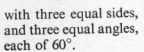 with three equal sides, and three equal angles, each of 60°.

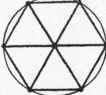

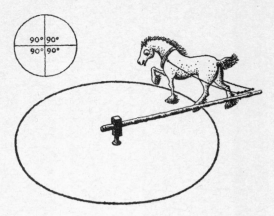

If this horse walks round the circle once, the beam of wood it pulls has travelled through 360°, or four right angles.

(Farmers used to churn milk this way to make butter.)

The earth travels round the sun in one year, so it travels through 360° in 365 days:

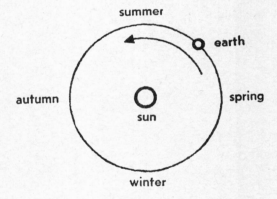

ANGLO-SAXONS. After the Romans left Britain (A.D. 410), the country was invaded by tribes called Angles, Jutes and SAXONS. They came from Northern Germany and from Jutland (which belongs to Denmark). The old inhabitants, the BRITONS, were driven into Cumberland, Wales and Cornwall, and some even sailed from Cornwall to Brittany in France.

ANIMAL. Every living thing is either a plant or an animal. All living things breathe, feed, get rid of waste products, and reproduce themselves in some way. All animals feed on plants or on other animals which live on plants. Birds, fish, and insects are all examples of animals. See also INVERTEBRATES; VERTEBRATES.

ANNE, Queen of Great Britain and Ireland from 1702 to 1714. The Parliaments of England and Scotland were joined in her reign by the Act of Union in 1707. Queen Anne was the last of the Stuart sovereigns. She married Prince George of Denmark and had seventeen children, but they all died in infancy.

ANNUALS, plants which grow from seed, flower and die, all in one year, like sweet peas and many other flowers. GRASSES, like wheat, oats, barley, and tropical grasses are also annuals.

ANTARCTIC, the region around the South Pole. There is a good deal of land below the masses of ice and snow and Antarctica is one of the CONTINENTS. The seas, although very cold, are rich in vegetable food, and fish, penguins, seals, and whales live here.

ANT-EATER. This animal is found in SOUTH AMERICA, and lives on ants and other insects. It has strong, curved claws on the front feet for breaking into ant-hills, and a very small head which tapers into an elongated snout. It does not need teeth, and has none, because it licks up the ants with its long sticky tongue.

Ant-eater

The Banded ant-eater is a rare animal which lives in Western Australia, and the Porcupine ant-eater (better-known as the echidna) lives in Australia and Tasmania, and New Guinea.

ANTELOPES are animals like deer. They are found chiefly in the tropical grass-lands of Africa, but a few live in Asia. Gazelles are small antelopes.

ANTENNAE are the "feelers" on an insect's head. These are believed to be very sensitive to smells, and the insect waves them about to detect delicate scents. They may have other uses as well. Look at the picture of ants on the opposite page. In the singular the word is antenna, and this is sometimes used of a long, slender wireless aerial, which detects or broadcasts radio waves.

ANTICYCLONE. Big circular eddies of air come to Britain, usually across the Atlantic Ocean. When the greater air pressure is on the outside this is called a CYCLONE. When the greater pressure is on the inside this is known as an anticyclone. When an anticyclone is over Britain the weather is usually warm and sunny or clear and cold. With a cyclone the weather is likely to be wet.

ANTIPODES. If a line were drawn through the centre of the earth from Britain it would come out near NEW ZEALAND and AUSTRALIA. We call these countries the Antipodes (meaning "against feet"), because the feet of the people there are, in a sense, opposite ours.

ANTISEPTICS are solutions of chlorine, iodine, carbolic acid and other substances which kill germs. One can buy antiseptics nowadays from any chemist. The first person to discover the importance of their use was Joseph LISTER, a British surgeon.

ANTONY, Mark. When Julius CAESAR was murdered in 44 B.C. Mark Antony and Octavian became rulers of ROME. They did not agree for long, however, and finally fought a sea battle at Actium in 31 B.C. Although Mark Antony had the help of CLEOPATRA, Queen of Egypt, he was defeated, and he left his sailors and sailed away with her to Egypt.

ANTS. Ants are wonderful little INSECTS which live together in colonies. They are found in most parts of the world, particularly in the tropics. There are males and females, and there are also workers, who build the ant-hills, dig out the galleries, get the food, look after the larvae or young ants, and fight enemies. Some ants keep and look after greenfly, or scale-insects, and get a sweet juice from them almost as we get milk from the cows we keep. On the right is a picture of the ants' home.

ANVIL, a heavy piece of iron on which pieces of metal can be laid and then hammered to the shape required. The heavy anvil moves very little under the hammer blows, and so the metal is squeezed between the hammer and the anvil. See also FORGING.

APE, a name given to those mammals which, with the MONKEYS, are most like man. These are the GORILLA, the orang-utan, the CHIMPANZEE and the gibbon. The gorilla lives in tropical Africa, and is bigger and heavier than the orang-utan, which builds a nest in the trees of the tropical forests of Borneo and Sumatra (islands between Asia and Australia). The chimpanzee is found in western and equatorial Africa, while the smallest of the apes, the gibbon, lives in eastern Asia.

APOSTLES, the twelve disciples whom JESUS sent out to preach the GOSPEL. They were Simon, called PETER, Andrew, James the son of Zebedee, John, Philip, Bartholomew, Matthew, Thomas, James the son of Alphaeus, Thaddaeus and Simon the Zealot. Judas Iscariot was one of the disciples until he betrayed Jesus.

APPRENTICE. When a boy leaves school and wants to become a joiner, plumber, or shipbuilder, for example, he usually becomes an apprentice first; that is, he agrees to work for about five years or so with a firm so that he can learn the trade. He usually gets a wage while he is learning, but not as much as he will get when he knows enough about his trade to do his work properly.

AQUARIUM, a large glass tank or bowl containing live fish or other creatures which live in water. It should have about two inches of sand or gravel at the bottom on which suitable water plants can grow. From time to time a little water is poured away and is replaced by fresh water, but

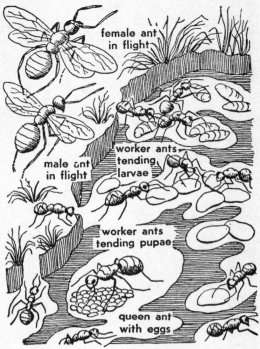

female ant in flight

male ant in flight

worker ants tending larvae

worker ants tending pupae

queen ant with eggs

Inside an ants' nest

it is never completely changed. See also GOLDFISH, and colour plate facing page 32.

AQUEDUCT. *Aqua* means water, and *duco* means I lead. The Romans built great stone aqueducts to lead water to their towns. We still use the Latin name which the Romans used.

ARABIA, a peninsula between the Red Sea and the PERSIAN GULF. The people who live here are called ARABS. It is a desert land like the Sahara, and has oases where the date-palm, grain and other vegetation grows. Horses, sheep and goats are reared, and it is here that you find the single-hump CAMEL. The best-known type is the fast riding camel, or dromedary, but there are others, including the more heavily built baggage camel. Arabia consists of a number of countries—Saudia Arabia is the largest, and contains MECCA, the holy city of the Moslems; Kuwait, on the Persian Gulf, is rich in oil. Other countries are Oman, Qatar, the Trucial States, the Yemen Arab Republic, and the People's

Democratic Republic of Yemen. The Bahrain islands form an archipelago in the Persian Gulf. We get dates, coffee, wool, hides, and spices from Arabia. See also ARABIC NUMERALS; ARABS.

ARABIC NUMERALS. The Moors invaded Spain from Africa, and it was from them we learned the figures 1, 2, 3, 4, and so on, which we now use in counting. The Moors had learned this way of counting from the ARABS, so the figures are called arabic numerals.

ARABS. In the MIDDLE AGES (about A.D. 1,000) the Arabs were a very clever people and knew more about mathematics, astronomy and medicine than other nations did. They invented ALGEBRA and the wonderful way of counting which we now use. See ARABIA; ARABIC NUMERALS.

ARCH. Any structure of the kind illustrated here is called an arch:

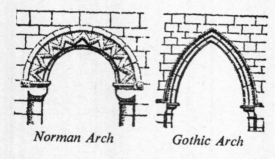

Norman Arch   *Gothic Arch*

When made of stone, the top stone (the centre one) is called the keystone, because it is the most important one. See also ARCHITECTURE; GOTHIC ARCHITECTURE; NORMAN ARCHITECTURE.

ARCHERY, the art of shooting with the BOW and arrow. This was an important weapon from 5,000 B.C., if not earlier, till fire-arms were used (about A.D. 1,500). English archers fought at AGINCOURT.

ARCHIMEDES was a famous Greek scientist who lived about 250 B.C. King Hieron had ordered a new gold crown, and he suspected that the man who made the crown had put some lead in the middle of it. The King asked Archimedes if he could find this out without cutting the crown. While in his bath Archimedes discovered how to do it, and ran home undressed shouting, "*Eureka! Eureka!* (I have found it! I have found it!)." He weighed the crown in air as usual, then weighed it when the crown was hanging under water. It then weighed less, of course, and the difference in weight was the weight of the water displaced. From this he could calculate how much heavier the metal was than water, and so find out if the crown had the same weight as pure gold or less. Gold is heavier than lead.

ARCHIPELAGO, a group of islands; originally, the islands off the coast of Greece in the Aegean Sea.

ARCHITECTURE, the art of designing and building houses, churches, bridges and so on. The pyramids of Egypt were built about 3,000 B.C. The Greeks built wonderful temples (like the Parthenon) and invented several different styles. They used flat blocks of stone supported by graceful pillars or columns. The Romans built the great Colosseum and many beautiful palaces, roads, aqueducts, bridges and houses. They knew how to make rounded arches and domes. The Roman style, mixed with other influences, became known as the Romanesque. The Normans introduced it into England, where it was called the Norman style. From the 12th century onward the Gothic style became popular, with its pointed arches, large windows and spires; buttresses supported the walls, and the vaulted roofs were held up by groups of thin pillars instead of single thick columns. The picture opposite shows you some of the differences between them. As time went by, other details were added to the designs, as in the Tudor and Renaissance styles. See also GOTHIC ARCHITECTURE; NORMAN ARCHITECTURE; WREN.

ARC LIGHT. When a current of electricity passes through two carbon rods which are close together, but not quite touching, there is a very bright light due

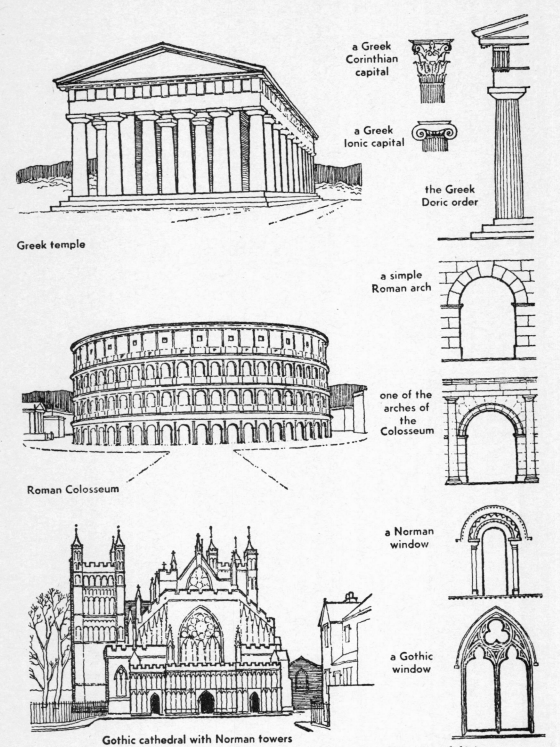

a Greek
Corinthian
capital

a Greek
Ionic capital

the Greek
Doric order

Greek temple

a simple
Roman arch

one of the
arches of
the
Colosseum

Roman Colosseum

a Norman
window

a Gothic
window

Gothic cathedral with Norman towers

Various styles of architecture, showing some of the details of design.

to the carbon points and carbon particles becoming intensely heated.

ARCTIC, the region around the North Pole. The ESKIMOS live there, chiefly in the north of CANADA and in GREENLAND. There are plenty of fish, seals, and some Polar bears. There used to be many whales (such as the huge Greenland whales), but so many have been killed recently that they are now scarce. Whaling ships now go to the ANTARCTIC, near the South Pole. See also NORTH.

AREA, the amount of surface a plane figure covers. This figure has an area of 1 square inch:

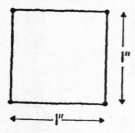

This figure, which is 3 inches long and 2 inches wide has an area of 6 square inches:

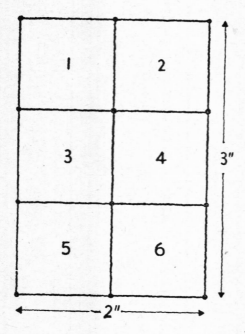

The area of a TRIANGLE is half the area of a RECTANGLE, having the same base and height:

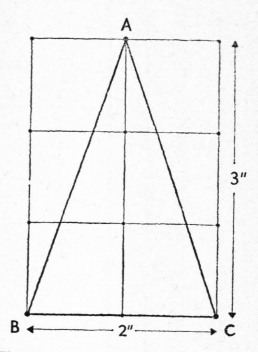

Thus, the area of triangle ABC is 3 square inches.

To find the area of a CIRCLE:

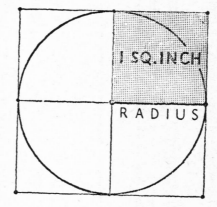

If the RADIUS is 1 inch, the area of the square on the radius will be 1 square inch. The area of the big square will be 4 square inches. The area of the circle is a little less than that. It is found to be $3\frac{1}{7}$ square inches. So if you know the radius of any circle, find the area of the square which has this side and then multiply this by $3\frac{1}{7}$ and this will be the area of the circle.

For example, if the radius of a circle is 7 inches, the area of the square on the radius will be 49 square inches. The area of the circle will be $49 \times 3\frac{1}{7}$ square inches.

$$49 \times 3 = 147$$
$$\text{and } \tfrac{1}{7} \text{ of } 49 = 7$$

Area of circle is 154 square inches.

ARGENTINE REPUBLIC, one of the large countries in SOUTH AMERICA. The mountain range of the ANDES forms a boundary between Argentina and CHILE. The northern part of the Argentine plain is called the Gran Chaco, and is woody and swampy; in the central plain there are few trees, but it is a grassy area, and it is here that great quantities of wheat, maize, and other crops are grown. It also provides grazing for enormous numbers of cattle, horses and sheep.

Beef, mutton, wheat, maize, wool and hides are exported from Buenos Aires, which is a port and also the capital. Other important ports are La Plata and Rosario. The estuary of La Plata was the scene of an exciting naval battle in the Second World War, when three British cruisers fought the German pocket battle-ship *Graf Spee*. This is called the Battle of the River Plate. See also ARMADILLO.

ARISTOTLE, a famous Greek scholar who was for a time tutor to ALEXANDER THE GREAT (he began in 342 B.C.). His books are still studied in universities.

ARITHMETIC. When the Egyptians started to count (about 5,000 B.C.), they counted on their fingers, and when they wrote down the numbers 1, 2, 3, they drew fingers, like this:

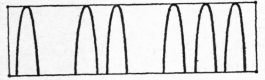

The Greeks and Romans, although so clever in many ways, could not count like us either. This is how they wrote the numbers:

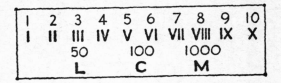

The number 314 had to be written like this: CCCXIV. You can see how difficult it could be to multiply this by, say, CXXXVI, so the Greeks and the Romans had to use either the abacus or a bag of pebbles for counting. You have done the same sort of thing in school, when you used a counting-frame and slid little coloured balls along the wires.

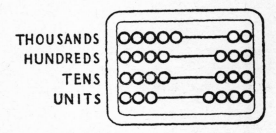

This person has marked up 2 thousands, 3 hundreds, 3 tens and 4 units.

Later on, people used Roman numerals and Arabic numerals together, like this:

M	C	X	I
3	2	4	6
1		3	7
4	6		9

Then someone made the wonderful discovery which enabled people to count without the fingers, or the abacus, or the bag of pebbles. He found that he could show thousands, hundreds, tens and units

17

by the place the figure was in, so instead of writing:

3 thousands
2 hundreds
4 tens
6 units
he just wrote 3246.

When there was no figure (see the last diagram on page 17) he had to put in an 0 to keep the place right, so the next number was written 1037, and the next 4609. Nowadays nearly every boy and girl can do sums quicker than Archimedes or EUCLID could. A short way of adding numbers together, instead of by counting them, is by MULTIPLICATION. Taking one number away

Armadillo.

from another is called SUBTRACTION. See also ALGEBRA; DIVISION.

ARMADA, a large number of fighting ships. The name is usually given to the Spanish Armada which attempted to conquer England in 1588. See DRAKE.

ARMADILLO. This animal lives in Patagonia (which is the southern part of Argentina) and in central America. It has a coat of "armour" on its back which is made of bone covered with horn joined by flexible bands of skin.

ARMOUR. In the days when soldiers fought with swords, spears, and bows and arrows, metal armour was very useful. It was also useful against bullets from the earliest muskets and pistols. But no soldier could carry about with him the heavy steel plates he would need to stop modern bullets, so metal armour is not used now. Recently bullet-proof vests have been made of nylon thread. There are many specimens of armour in the museums.

ART. The mind can make up pictures, which we call visual images, and the people who are able to reproduce the picture which is in their "mind's eye"—by painting pictures, perhaps, or in some other way—are called artists. The work they do is given the general name of art. Some artists make statues of marble or bronze, and they are called sculptors; others design houses and other buildings, and they are called architects. See also ARCHITECTURE; BALLET; MUSIC; PAINTING; POETRY; SCULPTURE; STONE AGE.

ARTERIES are the tubes which carry the blood from the HEART to all parts of the body. When you "feel your pulse" on the wrist, that is the pulse of the blood going along an artery to the hand. Arteries get smaller as they spread out, like the branches of a tree; then the VEINS receive the blood and take it back to the heart, where it is pumped into the LUNGS to

Knights used to wear heavy metal armour to protect themselves.

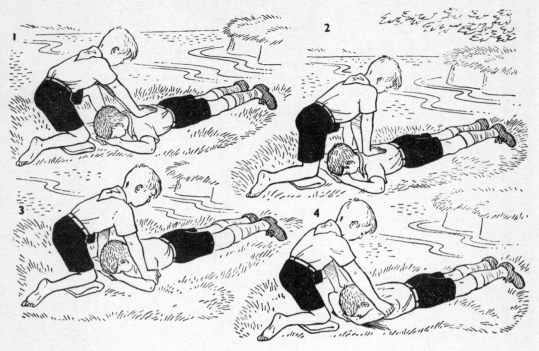

A life can often be saved if artificial respiration is given in time.

collect more oxygen. The blood returns along the veins steadily, not in pulses.

ARTIFICIAL RESPIRATION is a way of helping a person who has stopped breathing to start again, and it is used in saving the lives of partly-drowned or suffocated people. The pictures above show one method of artificial respiration:

First, lay the patient face down, and place his hands one on top of the other, under his forehead. Kneel on one knee at his head, place the other foot near his elbow. Give two slaps between the shoulder blades to make his tongue fall forward. Then place your hands on the upper edge of his shoulder blades, with arms extended and your thumbs on his spine (1). Rock forward, so that the weight of your body falls on your arms and exerts moderate pressure downwards (2). Slide your hands over the patient's shoulders, and grasp the upper arms near the elbows (3). Rock backwards, at the same time pulling the patient's arms upward to his shoulder level (4). Put the patient's arms back on to the ground. Replace your hands on his shoulder blades and repeat the movements until they restart the bellows action of the lungs.

ARTILLERY is the name given to all kinds of big guns that are too heavy to be carried and fired by a single soldier. See CANNON.

ASIA is the largest CONTINENT. It is separated from AFRICA by the isthmus of Suez and the Red Sea, and is bounded by the ARCTIC OCEAN on the north, the PACIFIC on the east, and the INDIAN OCEAN on the south. It has about 1,300 million people.

SIBERIA occupies the whole of northern Asia, Mongolia and CHINA are in the east, INDIA is in the south. Other countries include PAKISTAN, BURMA, MALAYA, IRAN, and TURKEY.

North of India is the great PLATEAU of TIBET, an enormous land, all of which is over 12,000 feet high. A peculiarity of the

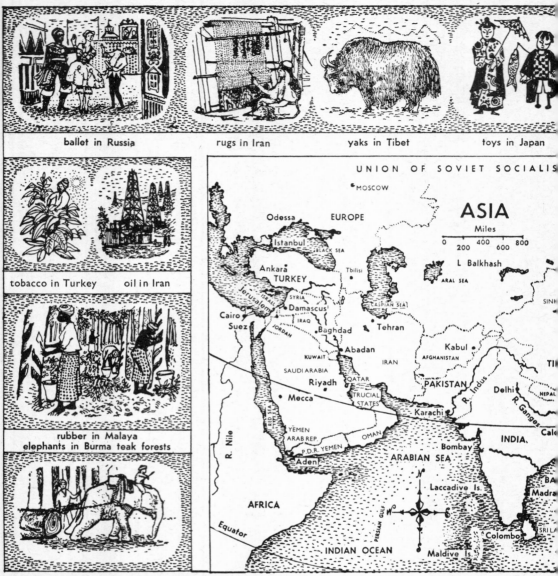

ballet in Russia   rugs in Iran   yaks in Tibet   toys in Japan

tobacco in Turkey   oil in Iran

rubber in Malaya
elephants in Burma teak forests

This map shows the countries of Asia. It is the largest of the continents. Over thirteen

climate in this part of the world is the season of the rains. In India rain falls between June and September and is known as the time of the MONSOON.

There are plenty of tigers in India and parts of China, and in the East Indian islands of Sumatra and JAVA, but hardly any lions. There are elephants in India, Sri Lanka and elsewhere, and many of them have been trained by man to work

for him. In Arabia there are camels and in Tibet there are yaks; wolves, reindeer and bears live in Siberia. See also ASIA MINOR; JAPAN; MALAY PENINSULA; RUSSIA; SUEZ CANAL.

ASIA MINOR is a south-west peninsula of ASIA and contains the greater part of the republic of TURKEY. It lies between the BLACK SEA and the MEDITERRANEAN. See also DARDANELLES.

gers in India   silk and tea in China

hundred million people live in this area.

ASSYRIANS. The Assyrian and Babylonian people both lived near the rivers EUPHRATES and Tigris. These rivers, like the Nile, overflow their banks every year, and leave silt which makes fertile soil. The Babylonian people were very clever in some ways. They built irrigation canals, as our experts do nowadays, and grew great crops of wheat, which helped to make them rich.

The Assyrians were a more warlike people, fonder of making raids than of digging canals, and their history is one of many battles. They built up a great Empire and then lost it, but they went to war again and built up a second Empire. They dominated Babylonia from about 1150 B.C. until the Persian king Cyrus entered Babylon about 539 B.C.

In spite of their warlike behaviour they also had artists who made glazed pottery, which they painted. They also made statues of bronze, and carved pictures in soft alabaster of military and religious subjects. These are called bas-reliefs. See also BABYLON.

ASTRONOMY is the scientific study of the STARS and planets. The SUN is a star, and there are millions of stars like the sun. A number of planets go round the sun, our EARTH being one of them. The planet nearest the sun is called Mercury, then comes VENUS, then the Earth, then MARS and others. If the earth were the size of a table-tennis ball, the sun would be a flaming sphere 9 feet in diameter, and the earth would be going round the sun at a distance of 350 yards. The MOON, circling the earth, would be the size of a small pea.

ATHENS is the capital of GREECE. It was founded about 1,500 B.C. and was the centre of Greek culture about 500 B.C. The remains of a beautiful marble building called the Parthenon are still standing in Athens, and there were many others equally wonderful.

Some sculptures from the Parthenon are in the British Museum. They are among the most wonderful pieces of sculpture the world has ever seen. Lord Elgin brought them to England and they are known as the Elgin Marbles.

ATLANTIC OCEAN, the great ocean between the west coasts of EUROPE and AFRICA and the east coasts of NORTH and SOUTH AMERICA. It is about two miles deep, but some places are shallower and some "deeps" are five miles or more below sea-level. There are two main OCEAN CURRENTS, one north of the EQUATOR and one south of the equator. Inside these great currents two masses of seaweed collect. The collection of seaweed in the northern hemisphere is called the Sargasso Sea.

ATMOSPHERE, the AIR around the earth. It puts quite a pressure on our bodies, but our bodies are so accustomed to the pressure that we do not notice it. But if people go up a high mountain where the air is less thick and pressure not so great, they find difficulty in breathing. It is not easy to make good tea at this height because the water boils before it is hot enough. This is because the pressure of the atmosphere is less, and the water can boil more easily.

ATOM. The smallest possible particle that you can have of any simple substance is called an atom. There are over 90 different kinds of atoms. Everything in the world is made up of these atoms, mixed or joined together in various ways. See also ATOMIC ENERGY.

ATOMIC ENERGY. If you break an ATOM you change it into another kind of atom. This is not an easy thing to do because the parts of an atom are very strongly held together. The force which holds them together is called atomic energy. If you *do* manage to break an atom up, this energy flies off as a flash of LIGHT and HEAT.

An atomic bomb is one which uses atomic energy instead of explosive chemicals. Certain rare kinds of atoms are liable to fly apart if too many of them are brought suddenly together, and this is what happens inside an atomic bomb when it goes off. The flash of atomic energy from a few pounds of uranium or plutonium is equal to many thousands of tons of high explosive.

AUSTRALASIA, a collective name given to Australia, New Zealand, New Guinea and other islands in the south-west Pacific.

AUSTRALIA, one of the CONTINENTS. It has a great DESERT in the centre, in the same LATITUDE as the KALAHARI Desert in South Africa. There are rich grass-lands on the eastern side, where cattle and sheep are reared. Grapes and other juicy fruits grow south of the desert. Gold, silver, and other metals are found.

Australia is the home of animals which carry their young in a pouch. The best-known are the KANGAROO and the koala —which is not a bear although it looks like one. A strange animal found in eastern Australia and in Tasmania is the duck-billed platypus. It is odd because it is an egg-laying mammal; there is only one other mammal

Koala

which lays eggs, as far as we know, and that is the echidna (also called the porcupine ANT-EATER), which lives in Australia, Tasmania and New Guinea.

There are several hundred kinds of bird, but if you were asked to name some, those you would think of first would probably be the emu, which looks like an OSTRICH, the kookaburra, whose curious laughing cry has earned it the name of "laughing jackass," and the LYRE-BIRD.

Platypus

Whales and sea-lions are found round the coast, and there are many crocodiles in the rivers of the north, where the climate is hotter because the north of Australia is nearer the EQUATOR. Australia is divided into different states, each with its own capital, but the capital of the entire country is CANBERRA. See also ANTIPODES.

AVALANCHE, a large mass of SNOW or ICE blowing or sliding into valleys from the mountains. Sometimes houses on the mountain-side are smashed to pieces.

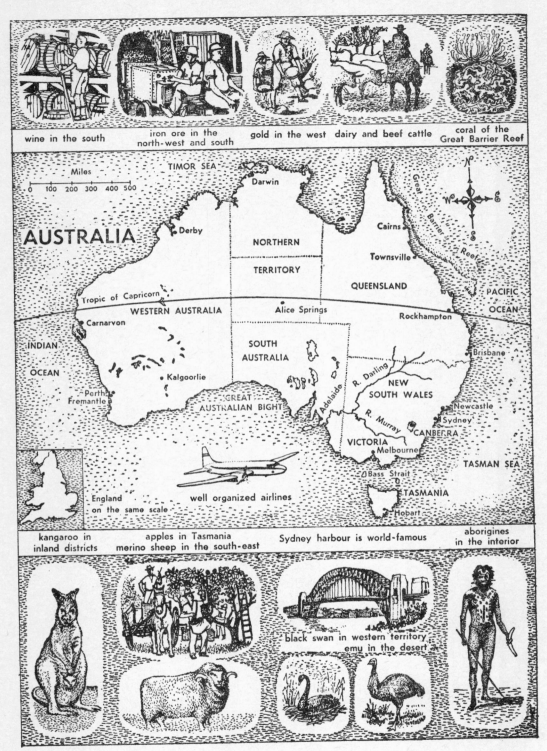

wine in the south

iron ore in the north-west and south

gold in the west

dairy and beef cattle

coral of the Great Barrier Reef

AUSTRALIA

Miles
0 100 200 300 400 500

TIMOR SEA

Darwin

Derby

NORTHERN

TERRITORY

Cairns

Townsville

QUEENSLAND

PACIFIC

OCEAN

Tropic of Capricorn

WESTERN AUSTRALIA

Alice Springs

Rockhampton

INDIAN

Carnarvon

OCEAN

SOUTH AUSTRALIA

Kalgoorlie

Brisbane

R. Darling

NEW SOUTH WALES

Perth
Fremantle

GREAT AUSTRALIAN BIGHT

Adelaide

Newcastle

R. Murray

Sydney

CANBERRA

England on the same scale

well organized airlines

VICTORIA

Melbourne

TASMAN SEA

Bass Strait

TASMANIA

Hobart

kangaroo in inland districts

apples in Tasmania merino sheep in the south-east

Sydney harbour is world-famous

aborigines in the interior

black swan in western territory emu in the desert

The Australian continent and some of the things found there.

23

B

BABOON, a type of MONKEY, usually about the size of a dog and with a face rather like a dog. Baboons live in thousands in Africa and are a serious nuisance to anyone who is trying to grow fruit. Some of them are very ugly with bright red or blue patches on their faces or hind quarters.

BABYLON. At one time an independent kingdom, Babylon became the capital of Babylonia about 2,000 B.C. This was during the reign of King Hammurabi, who drew up an important code of law to which he gave his name.

The fertile valleys of the EUPHRATES and the Tigris were particularly good for growing crops, and the Babylonians built

Hamadryad baboon and baby.

canals to irrigate the land and to drain the marshes. They grew a lot of wheat, and became very rich. Trade with other countries developed, and the canals became even more important as river boats were used to carry the merchandise.

Towns were built near the canals, and the population increased. The Babylonians were very clever; they developed MATHE-MATICS, and studied the stars. They also made pottery and sculpture, and planned beautiful buildings. See also ASSYRIANS; SEVEN WONDERS OF THE ANCIENT WORLD.

BACH, Johann Sebastian, was born in 1685 and became one of the great musicians; no man of his time could play the organ or harpsichord as well as Bach did. His wonderful compositions delight audiences today, although he died in 1750.

BACTERIA is another name for GERMS or microbes. They reproduce like the amoeba, by dividing into two, and some types do this so quickly that one germ may become about twenty million germs in a day. When the body detects any harmful germs, the white CORPUSCLES in the blood attack them.

BADGER, a thick-set, bear-like animal about three feet long, with coarse greyish hair and a white face with a black stripe on each side of it. It lives in deep burrows called sets, in banks or hillocks in forests and woods. It feeds on roots and fruits, snails, insects, and young rabbits.

BADMINTON is a game like tennis, but played with light rackets, and a shuttle-cock instead of a ball. The shuttle-cock has fourteen to sixteen feathers, each about two and a half inches long, which are stuck into a ball of cork.

BALLANTYNE, Robert Michael, was born in Scotland in 1825. When he was a boy he went to Canada and spent six years trapping animals in the lonely parts of the Hudson Bay Territory. He wrote about his adventures in *The Young Fur Traders*. He also wrote many other exciting books for boys, among them *Coral Island* and *Martin Rattler*. He died in 1894.

BALLET, a way in which a story is told by dance movement done to music but no words are spoken. Ballet dancers move very gracefully, and almost every movement is expressive and a pleasure to watch. Some good music has been specially written for the ballet, for example, the *Nutcracker Suite* by Tchaikovsky.

BALLOON, the name given to a bag which rises and floats when filled with a gas lighter than air. Balloons were sometimes filled with coal gas but now they are filled with hydrogen, which is very much lighter, or the scarce gas, helium, if there is danger of fire. During the Second World War barrage balloons attached to the ground by steel cables were used to hinder enemy aeroplanes. Balloons are used nowadays to take scientific instruments high into the atmosphere, where they get information on which weather forecasts are based. See also AIRSHIP.

BALLOT. There are various ways in which people can vote for something. The commonest ways are to raise their hands while somebody counts them, or to write their votes on pieces of paper which are collected and counted afterwards. The second way is called a ballot. In days gone by, when few could write, small coloured balls were used instead of pieces of paper. The ballot is sometimes called the "secret vote," because nobody sees what you are writing on your ballot paper, and nobody need know which way you are voting.

BAND. In mixed choirs there are sopranos, contraltos, tenors and basses. Women with the highest voices sing soprano, men with the deepest voices sing bass. So, too, in brass bands there are small cornets or trumpets to play the high notes, and big tubas to play the low notes,

An early balloon with sandbags as ballast.

and horns and trombones in between. Drums are added. Military bands are different, because they have flutes and clarinets in addition to the brass instruments. Usually they are regimental bands, but the description is given also to civilian bands which use the same musical instruments.

BANJO, once the favourite musical instrument of the negroes in the southern states of North America. It has a body like a tambourine, a long neck, and usually five or six strings.

BANK, a place which keeps people's money safe for them, and gives them the money back as they want it. When you bank your money you are really lending it to the bank which can then lend it to other people who must pay back more than they borrow.

BARCELONA, a Mediterranean seaport town in Spain with a university founded in 1430. Wine, olive-oil, and nuts are important exports.

BARITONE. A man singer with a high voice is called a tenor, one with a deep voice is called a bass. A baritone singer has a voice between these two.

25

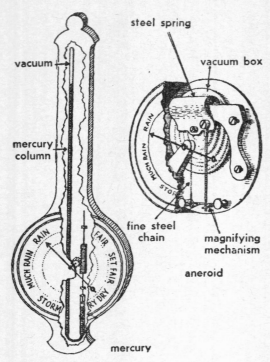

Barometers show changes in the weather.

BARNACLE, a relative of the crabs and shrimps. Ship-barnacles are attached by means of "stalks" to the bottom of ships and floating timbers; acorn-barnacles cling closely to rocks on the shore. Their LARVAE swim about freely and look like those of crabs. Barnacles feed on small floating animals.

BAROMETER, an instrument for measuring the pressure of the air. A simple type of barometer is a flattish circular box from which most of the air has been taken out. The greater the pressure the flatter it becomes, and levers are arranged to show these movements. This is called an aneroid barometer. The mercury barometer is more reliable.

BARRISTER. In the higher courts of LAW, over which a JUDGE presides, important cases are usually presented by barristers. They are engaged by SOLICITORS to appear on behalf of their clients.

BASS. Men singers who have deep voices are called bass singers. The bass fiddle is the very big one which plays the lowest notes. See ORCHESTRA.

BAT. Although the bat is a mammal which can fly, it is not at all like a bird. Its furry body is like that of a mouse, and its wings are not made of bone and feathers but of a very thin stretched skin. This skin stretches between the fore and hind limbs and is supported chiefly by the bony fingers.

Bats fly by night, and have a wonderful kind of "radar" arrangement which tells them what is ahead of them. They make a special high-pitched note, and echoes from anything in front are picked up by the fine nerves in their nose-leaves, and in their ears.

Bats sleep during the winter, hanging upside down in some sheltered place.

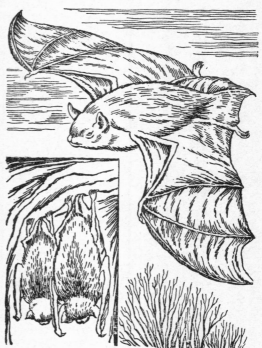

Bats hang upside down to sleep.

BATHYSCAPHE. This is a kind of metal chamber with windows used to explore the depths of the ocean. It is not suspended by a steel cable, as is the

26

A modern battleship compared with a wooden ship of Nelson's time.

BATHYSPHERE, but is made to sink down to the ocean depths by a heavy weight of steel held close to the bathyscaphe by an electro-magnet. When the current is switched off the magnet, the steel ballast drops away and the chamber, freed of the weight, floats up. A cigar-shaped tank filled with petrol is fixed to the top and floats in the water, in much the same way as a balloon floats in air.

BATHYSPHERE. This is used for DEEP-SEA EXPLORATION, and is a steel chamber, shaped like a ball, which is lowered into deep water by a steel cable. It has windows, which must be very thick, of course, and searchlights so that the men inside can see the kind of fish and plants which live in the deep seas.

BATTERY, ELECTRIC, a device by which chemicals can be used to make electricity. Two or three small ones joined together will ring a bell or light a torch; several big ones will drive a car.

In a dry battery a metal case (zinc) is filled with chemical in the form of a paste or jelly, and containing a carbon rod. It cannot spill, so it can be carried about. This kind of battery is used for pocket torches. A wet battery acts in the same way, but the chemical is liquid.

BATTLESHIP, once the most important type of warship, now largely replaced by AIRCRAFT-CARRIERS and SUBMARINES. It had thick plates and very long-range guns and used to form the kernel of the Fleet. Of the other kinds of warship, torpedo-boats are the smallest; these are fast little ships which launch torpedoes. Next are the destroyers, which carry small guns. Cruisers are fast big ships and they have some big guns. See also CONVOY; NAVY.

BAY. When the sea-coast curves inward and out again, it forms a bay. If the sea has scooped out a deep curve in the land, leaving high cliffs at each end, the bay gets more shelter from the wind than one which is only a gentle curve.

B.B.C. These letters stand for British Broadcasting Corporation. In Britain broadcasting is a public service, and the governors of the Corporation are chosen by the Crown. Its duties are to broadcast news, weather reports and educational programmes for school-children. Other programmes include foreign talks and light entertainment. See also TELEVISION.

BEAKS are the horny jaws of turtles and birds. The name is also used for the sucking-tubes of some insects. The beaks of birds are also called "bills."

BEAR. The biggest kind of bear is the grizzly, which lives in the Rocky Mountains in North America; also big are the Polar bear, which lives among the snows in the Arctic and feeds on seals and fish, and the brown or black bear which lives in the northern parts of Europe and Asia, and once lived in Britain also. There are smaller bears in North America, India, China, Siberia and other countries. Many bears can climb trees very well, and, although they live mostly on vegetable food, some of them are very dangerous animals if provoked.

BEAVER, an animal about two feet long, with webbed hind feet and a flat tail which help it in swimming. Beavers used to live in Britain but are now found in large numbers only in North America.

Beavers usually live together in colonies; they build a "lodge" by burrowing into the earth on the bank of a river, or on an island in the river. They dig out a cavity, or room, and make the floor on two levels —one just above water-level and the other a few inches higher. They take care to make a chimney, so that they get plenty of air. Beavers wait until after the first hard frost of winter before they plaster the outside of the lodge with mud; it then freezes hard and protects them against their enemies.

The floors of the lodge are a few inches above water-level, but the tunnels leading into them are underwater. This also is to keep their enemies away. If the level of the water is not as high as the beaver would like, it builds a dam across the river with sticks and mud. If a tree is leaning towards the

Male stag-beetle.

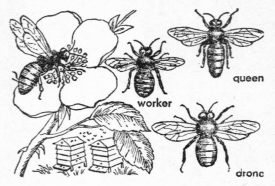

Bees are social insects.

river the beaver sometimes gnaws it through and lets it fall across to help in making the dam.

BEE, a winged insect which lives in colonies almost like nations of human beings. But a nation of bees has only one mother, the queen bee, who for two or three years lays her thousands of eggs in little cells of the waxen comb made by the worker bees, of which there may be 30,000 in a hive. There are also a few male bees, one of which must mate with a young queen before she can lay any eggs. When the eggs hatch there grows in each cell a tiny grub that later changes into a bee. The younger workers look after the grubs and feed them, and when they are older go foraging for the nectar which they store in the honeycombs. Bees have stings and will use them in defence of their hives or when annoyed. See also SOCIAL INSECTS.

BEETHOVEN, Ludwig Van (born 1770), one of the great composers. He was a brilliant pianist and while playing could compose music as he went along, but his best works took much thought and effort. It is sad to think that he wrote some of his best work after he had become deaf, and could only imagine how it sounded. Beethoven died in 1827.

BEETLE, an insect which usually has a hard pair of wing-cases to protect its wings. The ladybird is one type of beetle, the GLOW-WORM is another, and there are big beetles about three or four inches long

An aquarium is a glass tank in which various kinds of live fish can be kept. In this tank are the Paradise fish of Australia (top left), the Zebra fish of India and Sri Lanka (centre), the Jack Dempsey of Yucatan (bottom left), the Angel fish of Australia and the Bahamas (top right), and the Sword-tail of Mexico (bottom right).

Ballet is a form of art which combines music, drama, colour, and graceful movement. Music composed by Chopin is used in "Les Sylphides," one of the classic ballets.

Map of the British Isles with some of the things found there.

bears live in the forest

the beaver cuts
down a tree

the dam controls
the level of the water

the beaver feeds on
tree-bark, berries and roots

the lodge is made
of twigs and mud

D.H. Ralphs

Two of the best-known animals of North America are the bear and the beaver.

29

in South America. The Colorado beetle is disliked in North America because it destroys the potato crops; the Stag-beetle is the largest of the British beetles.

BELFAST is the capital of NORTHERN IRELAND. It is the centre of the Irish linen trade and has big shipbuilding yards. Over 350,000 people live there.

BELGIUM, a small country on the North Sea coast and bordered by the Netherlands, Germany, Luxembourg, and France. So many battles have been fought there that it has been called the "cockpit of Europe." The capital is Brussels. The port of Antwerp is one of the largest in Europe, and is very important; it is also famous for its diamond-cutting industry. Ostend, a fishing port, is a popular place for holidays. In the north Flemish is spoken, in the south French.

BELL, ELECTRIC. If you wind a piece of insulated wire round a poker, or a nail or any piece of soft iron, and attach the ends of the wire to a small battery, the poker will become a magnet. (The battery will run down quickly if you leave it connected.) A nail placed near our magnet will be pulled towards it. The poker is now an electro-magnet.

In the same way an electric bell has an electro-magnet, and when we press the push-button at the door, a current flows and the electro-magnet becomes magnetized and pulls a metal strip with a knob on it against a gong so that it strikes the gong. In so doing, the metal strip comes away from a screw and the current is cut off. At once the electro-magnet is no longer magnetized, and the metal strip flies back against the screw. This causes the current to flow again, the electromagnet pulls the metal strip, the knob hits the bell, and so on. This backwards and forwards movement of the knob occurs several times a second and so causes the ringing of the bell. See also CIRCUIT.

BENGAL, in Asia, is divided into two parts. West Bengal is in INDIA and East Bengal is in Bangladesh. River floods make much of the soil of Bengal very fertile, and rice, cotton, and cane sugar are grown. Tea comes from Darjeeling, but the biggest export is of jute. These and other goods are sent out through CALCUTTA, the chief port.

BEN NEVIS, in Inverness-shire, Scotland, is the highest mountain in Britain (4,406 feet.)

BERLIN, the capital of the German State from 1871 to 1945. It is now divided into two: East Berlin is the capital of East Germany, and West Berlin is a city of West Germany.

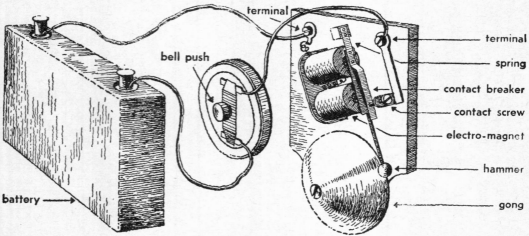

The ringing of an electric bell is caused by the action of an electro-magnet.

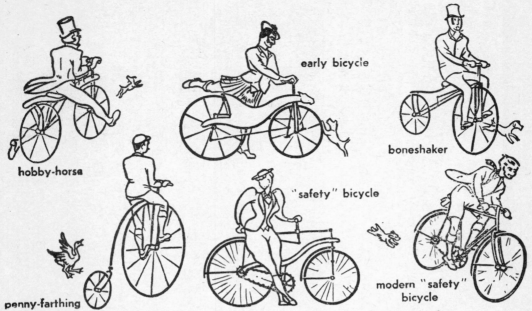

The design of a bicycle has changed a lot since the early hobby-horse.

BETHLEHEM, the village near Jerusalem in Palestine where JESUS was born.

BIBLE. The Bible is divided into the Old Testament and the New Testament. The Old Testament tells us the history of the Jewish people. The New Testament tells us about the life of JESUS and His wonderful work and of the work of his APOSTLES in founding the Christian Church.

BICEPS, the muscle which bends the arm. The triceps muscle can pull it straight again. These muscles have a little telephone arrangement with the brain to tell each other when to slack off, because if they both pull at the same time the forearm cannot move.

BICYCLE. A very early kind of bicycle was made with only two wheels and a cross-bar, and the rider had to push himself along with his feet on the ground. This was called the "hobby-horse" or "dandy-horse." When the "safety" bicycle was invented it was so much better that we have used it ever since.

A big driving wheel is not necessary for speed because the gear wheels make the back wheel turn two or three times with one turn of the pedals.

BIENNIAL. A plant which normally lives for about two years is called a biennial. Such plants store up food in their roots during the first year, and flower and fruit in the second. Examples are turnips and cabbages.

BILE, one of the juices which help in the digestion and absorption of food. It is secreted from the blood by the liver, and poured into the digestive tract, or INTESTINE, as required.

BINOCULAR, two telescopes or microscopes fitted together so that both eyes can see the object.

BIOGRAPHY, the story of someone's life. If written by the man himself it is called an autobiography. Boswell's *Life of Dr. Samuel Johnson* is one of the most famous of biographies.

BIOLOGY is the study of plants and animals and especially of their being alive and able to reproduce themselves. The study of plants by themselves is called botany, and the study of animals by themselves is called zoology.

31

BIRDS are warm-blooded animals with backbones. They are different from all other animals because they are covered with feathers. They have beaks instead of a mouth, and wings instead of hands and arms, to enable them to fly. Like men, they have two legs so they are bipeds. The legs are scaly. Most birds have four clawed toes on each foot.

There are some birds which are different from the general run: the OSTRICH is not able to fly, its wings being very undeveloped. DUCKS and SWANS, which are WATER-BIRDS, have webbed feet which make swimming easier. Some birds live in Britain all the year round, while others fly away to warmer climates when winter comes. This is known as MIGRATION. Young birds are hatched from eggs.

BIRD OF PARADISE, a bird which is rather like a crow in shape, but which has the most beautiful coloured feathers. It is found in New Guinea, a big island north of Australia, and in nearby islands. It feeds on wild fruits and insects.

cockle

mussel

oyster

Bivalves have hinged shells.

BIRDS OF PREY live on other birds and small animals. Eagles and falcons are two examples. An EAGLE can pick up a rabbit, or even a young lamb, and fly off with it. Falcons are smaller and kill lizards and small birds. See also HAWK; OWL; VULTURE.

BISCAY, BAY OF, an inlet of the Atlantic Ocean, on the west coast of France and the north coast of Spain. Storms here are severe.

BISON are a kind of wild cattle that used to live in great herds in the United States and Canada, where the Indians pursued them for food; later, Europeans came to hunt them with guns, and so many of the animals were killed that the herds nearly died out.

Although BUFFALOES are entirely different animals, the name is often given in America to the bison. William Cody was called BUFFALO BILL because he used to shoot bison as food for the men building the railways.

BIVALVES are shell-fish with two shells on a hinge, like oysters, mussels, cockles, scallops and clams.

BLACKBIRD, a type of thrush. The male has black feathers and an orange-yellow beak, and is a beautiful singer. The female is brown. The blackbird is common throughout the British Isles.

BLACK DEATH. This was the name given to a terrible plague which swept over Europe in the fourteenth century. It came to England in 1348–1349, and killed over a million of the four million people who lived in England at that time.

BLACK PRINCE. See EDWARD III.

BLACK SEA, a large inland sea in the south of Europe. It is bounded on the north by Russia, with the Crimean peninsula jutting into the sea, on the south by Turkey, with Rumania and Bulgaria on the west. Ships can sail from the Black Sea—by way of the Bosporus into the Sea of Marmora, then through the DARDANELLES into the Aegean Sea—into the Mediterranean.

BLAST FURNACE, a furnace that is made specially hot by blasts of dry air being blown through the burning material. It is used to get iron from the rock or ore in which it is found. The lumps of ore are mixed with limestone and coke and burnt in the furnace; the metal melts in the great heat and trickles out.

BLASTING. This is a method of breaking up masses of rock or stone or coal by the use of explosives.

BLIZZARD. A storm of wind and snow is described as a blizzard. In the United States and some other countries blizzards sometimes cause many deaths.

BLOOD, the fluid which flows from the heart through the arteries to all parts of the body. It returns to the heart through the veins. Blood would be a clear yellow in colour were it not for the millions of red CORPUSCLES in it which make it look red. These corpuscles are important because they carry oxygen through the body from the lungs (which get it when we breathe); we would die if we didn't get enough oxygen. There are also thousands of white corpuscles whose job it is to fight any harmful germs in the body.

Blood also carries digested food from the intestines to the muscles and brain and other parts of the body, and takes waste matter to the liver and kidneys. Some GLANDS pour their juices direct into

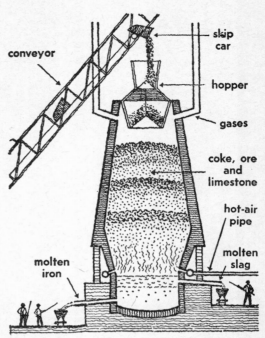

Iron is smelted in a blast-furnace.

the blood, and these juices are carried in the bloodstream to the parts of the body which need them.

BLOWLAMP, a lamp used by plumbers and others for melting lead, heating pipes, burning off paint, and so on. Air is pumped into the little tank of paraffin, and this compressed air forces the paraffin out through a heated nozzle, causing it to turn to vapour and burn fiercely.

BOA, or BOA CONSTRICTOR, a snake which belongs to the same family as the PYTHON. It is found in the tropical forest of South America and may be as much as fourteen feet long. It is called a constrictor because it kills its prey by coiling round it and crushing it to death. Boas usually feed on rats and mice, and birds. They swallow their victims whole.

BOADICEA, Queen of the Iceni in Britain, when Nero was Emperor of Rome. She led a revolt of the Britons against the Romans. London was burned down and many thousands of Romans were killed. She poisoned herself rather than fall into enemy hands (A.D. 62).

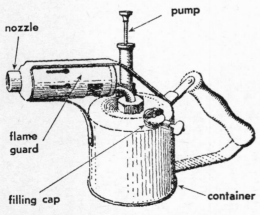

A blowlamp is used by plumbers.

33

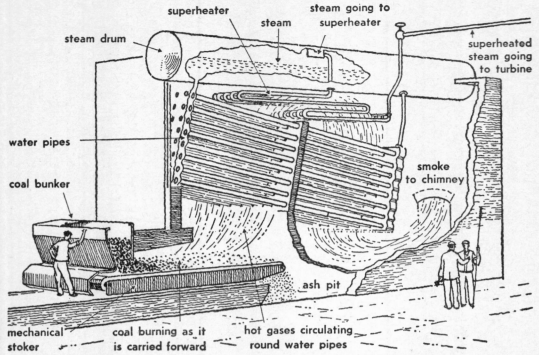

steam drum

superheater

steam

steam going to superheater

superheated steam going to turbine

water pipes

coal bunker

smoke to chimney

ash pit

mechanical stoker

coal burning as it is carried forward

hot gases circulating round water pipes

In this boiler the water circulates through tubes surrounded by hot flames.

BOILER, a tank for heating water. In a house we just want hot water, not steam; but for ship or railway engines we need a boiler strong enough to hold the pressure of water heated to steam and able to push the engine pistons which turn the propeller or wheels. Some engine boilers let the water circulate through tubes upon which the flames of the furnace play (water-tube boilers). Others have hollow tubes running through the water containers; and through these tubes the heat of the furnace is forced so as to heat the surrounding water (fire tube boilers).

BOILING POINT is the temperature at which a liquid turns into a gas and "gets all boiled away." For water this temperature at sea level is 100 degrees Centigrade. Some oils will not boil till the temperature is 200 degrees Centigrade. Chlorine, on the other hand, will boil even on a cold day and will soon change to gas. Boiling point temperatures, however, are greatly affected by atmospheric pressure—the weight of the air. So if you boil water on a high mountain, where the air pressure is less, the water will boil away long before it is hot enough to cook potatoes!

BOMBAY, the chief seaport on the west coast of India.

BONE is the hard material which makes up the skeleton of the body. A lobster or crab has its skeleton outside the body like a coat of armour; a man has most of his skeleton inside as his softer parts grow around it. But his skull is made of bone to protect the very delicate brain inside.

BOOMERANG. The Australian natives cut a piece of (-shaped wood in a clever way so that when it is thrown and fails to hit its mark it comes back towards

Boomerang.

the thrower in a circle. Thus it is close at hand for another try.

BORING, cutting holes in wood or metal, or in the earth when looking for coal, oil, or other minerals. Sometimes drills studded with diamonds are used for boring hard rock. Black diamonds are used, for they are equally hard and not very expensive.

BORNEO, a large island between Asia and Australia. The equator goes through the middle of it, so it has tropical forests. Coal and petroleum are found here, and teak wood and rubber are also exported. The elephant, rhinoceros and orang-utan live here. See map on page 21.

Shooting with a bow and arrows is called archery.

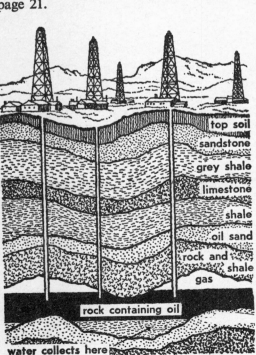

Boring an oil-well.

BOTANY is the name given to the study of plants. The study of both plants and animals is called BIOLOGY.

BOULOGNE is a town on the French coast. Fast steamers carry passengers and goods across the Channel, to Folkestone in England, in two hours. Napoleon assembled 180,000 men here when he was getting ready to invade England, but the Battle of Trafalgar (1805) put an end to that plan. See map on page 116.

BOW, a weapon for shooting arrows. The Egyptians, Assyrians and Persians all used bows and arrows. The English bow was made of yew or ash and was about six feet long.

BRAHMS, Johannes (born 1833), one of the great musicians. Born a German, he settled in Vienna. Like BEETHOVEN, he was a wonderful pianist. He wrote four symphonies, two concertos for piano and orchestra, two hundred songs, and many other works. He died in 1897.

BRAIN. The brain lies inside the skull. It is made up of nerve cells and is connected to the spinal cord, which lies inside the backbone (or SPINE). The brain and spinal cord form the telephone exchange of the body; they are connected to all parts of the body by nerves, which carry messages to and from the brain. All the movements of the body are controlled by nerves, but some nerves can act without getting a message from the brain.

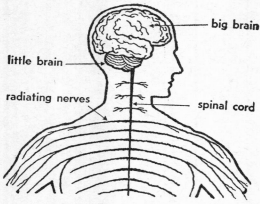

Nerves carry messages to the brain.

BRAKE. In the simplest bicycle brake two pieces of rubber are pulled against the rim of the revolving wheel to slow it down. Strong blocks of metal worked by compressed air are used to stop trains. You have to pull the lever yourself to brake the bicycle wheel, but the train brakes go on of their own accord if any of the carriages break loose. This is because air pressure is used to bring the brakes into operation. When the air tube, which runs the whole length of the train, is disconnected at any place, all the train brakes go on at once.

BRASS is an ALLOY of copper and zinc. It is a strong metal and does not rust.

BRASS INSTRUMENTS. The musical instruments made of brass (and sometimes silver) include the cornet, trumpet, horn, trombone, euphonium, bombardon and bass tuba. The bugle, too, is a brass instrument but plays only a few notes. These instruments all have to be sounded by a special use of the lips, and cannot be played by just blowing through them. See also MUSICAL INSTRUMENTS.

BRAZIL, the largest country in South America. The equator goes through the north of it, so this part has rain at all seasons and a tropical forest. The River Amazon flows through the forest. Rubber trees grow here, and it was from here that the seeds were taken to Kew Gardens, grown into little trees and planted in Ceylon, Malaya, Borneo and other East Indian islands.

The south of Brazil is a grassland area, and great herds of cattle are kept. Sugar, cotton, coffee, Brazil nuts and many fruits are grown. Brasilia is the new capital.

BREAKWATER, a wall of stone built to protect a harbour from the waves. Sometimes breakwaters built with enormous masses of concrete are smashed to pieces in a storm.

BRICK, a block of clay baked hard and used in building. The Egyptians dried their bricks in the sun, but bricks are now baked in ovens, called kilns.

BRICKLAYING is building with bricks, using cement or lime mortar to hold them together firmly.

BRIDGE. The earliest bridge was probably a tree trunk, lying across a river. Bridges are now built of wood, stone or steel. There are many types of bridges, of which you can see examples on page 37.

BRIGHTON is perhaps the most famous seaside resort on the south coast of England, about fifty miles from London. It gets lots of sunshine, and is protected from the cold north winds by high land behind it. The Pavilion was built (1784–7) for the Prince of Wales, later George IV, and is today a museum and art gallery. The Aquarium was founded in 1872.

BRISBANE, the capital of Queensland, in Australia. See map on page 23.

BRITISH COMMONWEALTH OF NATIONS, an association formed by nations that govern themselves but which recognize the Sovereign of the United Kingdom as the head of the Commonwealth. They include the United Kingdom,

LOG

MASONRY ARCH

GIRDER

STEEL ARCH

CANTILEVER

SUSPENSION

BASCULE

There are many kinds of bridges, from a simple log to the great steel arch of today.

Chieftain of the Ancient Britons.

Canada, Australia, New Zealand, India, Bangladesh, Sri Lanka, Hong Kong, Ghana, Tanzania, Uganda, Zambia, Malawi, Kenya, Sierra Leone, Nigeria, Malaysia, and Guyana, each with its own government. Others included in this term are the colonies and other territories which are those countries receiving the protection of Great Britain. The Commonwealth covers more than a quarter of the earth, and contains almost 900 million people.

BRITISH ISLES. This is the collective name for England, Scotland, Wales, Ireland and some small islands round the coast. All the land is part of the continent of EUROPE, and the seas around the British Isles are shallow seas compared with any ocean. England, Scotland, and Wales together form Great Britain; these three, with NORTHERN IRELAND, form the UNITED KINGDOM. The rest of IRELAND is an independent republic.

England has the best farmland, Scotland and Wales being much more mountainous. All three have minerals. In England and Wales the layers of rock are tilted as if the west coast had been pushed up slightly and all the newer rocks washed off. There was a wrinkle of the earth's crust north and south down the middle of England, and the remains of this wrinkle form the Pennine Chain.

In Scotland there were two cracks right across the country, and the middle part sank slightly. Parts of the layer of coal are still preserved in this low-lying part, and the coal is used to smelt iron for shipbuilding and other manufactures. Glasgow and Edinburgh (the capital) are in this "rift valley" as it is called.

Most of the people—over forty-five million—live in England. Scotland has about five million, Ireland about four million, Wales about two and a half million.

Ireland is mainly a farming country having few valuable minerals. It is famed for its cattle, horses and pigs. See map facing page 33.

BRITONS, ANCIENT, the people who lived in Britain before the Romans came in 55 B.C. They had less knowledge than the Romans, but they grew corn, made cloth, and dug up tin and other metals. After the Romans left (A.D. 410) the Anglo-Saxons invaded England (A.D. 449 and later) and the Ancient Britons were driven into Wales and Cornwall.

BROADCASTING is the use of RADIO for transmitting music or speech. For this purpose radio waves are sent out in all directions, and those with receiving sets can "tune in" and hear.

BRONTOSAURUS, one of the huge reptiles which ceased to exist millions of years ago. Parts of its skeleton have been found which show that it was about seventy feet long. It lived on vegetation, probably in swampy places.

BRONZE is an ALLOY of copper and tin. Weapons and tools were made of bronze by primitive people before anyone had learned to work iron. This period of history is sometimes called the Bronze Age. Nowadays bronze is used for making ships' propellers, large bells, and many other things.

BROWNIES, the youngest grade of GIRL GUIDES, for children who are between seven and a half and eleven years old.

BRUCE, Robert, the greatest of the kings of Scotland. EDWARD I, King of England, tried hard to conquer the Scots, but Bruce successfully resisted him. Later his son, EDWARD II, came north with a great army to conquer the country, but in 1314 he was heavily defeated by Bruce at Bannockburn, a small town near Stirling.

BRUSSELS is the capital of BELGIUM. It has many beautiful buildings and important manufactures, including the making of lace. Brussels lace has long been famous. Many battles have been fought around this town, including the Battle of WATERLOO in 1815.

BUCKINGHAM PALACE, a royal palace in London, facing St. James's Park. The Sovereign of Britain lives here.

BUD. The leaves, flowers and side branches of plants grow from buds which protect them until they are ready to develop.

BUDDHA was an Indian prince who lived about 500 B.C. He renounced his royal pleasures and left home to wander in search of Truth. When he found it, he spent the rest of his life serving mankind by his example and teaching. Those who

Some animals which no longer exist. The middle one is the brontosaurus.

Pony Express rider

EVENTS IN THE LIFE
OF BUFFALO BILL

shooting bison

follow his path are called Buddhists. See BUDDHISM.

BUDDHISM is the name given to the faith of those who believe that BUDDHA pointed out the straight path that leads to a man becoming perfect. Buddha taught that the cause of suffering was craving, but that we could get rid of suffering and gain the Highest Happiness by following the Noble Eightfold Path which he had discovered.

BUDGERIGARS are small beautiful birds, like little parrots. They live among the wild grasses in Australia and feed on the grass seed.

BUENOS AIRES is the capital of the ARGENTINE Republic in South America. It exports wheat and maize grown on the great fertile plains, and wool, meat and hides from the millions of sheep and cattle which are reared there.

BUFFALO. There are two kinds of buffalo, the Indian and the African. The buffalo which lives in the jungle swamps of India loves wet, muddy places, and so is sometimes called the water buffalo. It has a very bad temper, and will even fight a tiger. Some Indian buffalo have been domesticated, and used as pack animals, able to carry heavy loads. The African buffalo, on the other hand, is not domesticated, and is even more dangerous than the Indian beast; it will attack man as well as other animals. See also BISON.

BUFFALO BILL was a hero of the Wild West, whose real name was William Frederick Cody. He was born in 1846. When he was only fourteen years old he used to ride seventy-five miles a day in the Pony Express, which carried mail by relays of ponies nearly two thousand miles across the American continent. Cody became a scout and guide in the United States army; later he enlisted in the cavalry and fought until the end of the American Civil War.

He gained his nickname of Buffalo Bill in 1867, when the Kansas Pacific

touring Europe

Indian Creek

Railway was being built across the wilds of North America. He used to shoot BISON, to supply the workers with meat, and the Americans often call bison by the name of buffalo.

In the following years Buffalo Bill fought with the army against the Sioux and Cheyenne Indians, and in 1876 he killed the Cheyenne chief Yellow Hand in single combat at Indian Creek.

He founded a Wild West show in 1883, and brought it to Europe four years later. Buffalo Bill died in 1917.

BUGLE, a musical instrument made of brass, formerly used to give signals in battle. It is still used in the army in peacetime.

BULBS are formed out of a bud by many plants, to serve as food-stores. If the weather is too dry or if there is a lot of frost, the plant can lie buried in the earth, and get its food from the bulb, until it can flower in better conditions. Hyacinths, daffodils and lilies all grow from bulbs. Millions of tulip bulbs are grown in Holland. See also CORM.

BULKHEADS. All big ships are divided by partitions, so that if a hole is knocked in the ship the watertight doors in the partitions can be closed and the ship will still float. These partitions are called bulkheads.

BULL, the male of wild or domestic cattle. The name is also used for the male elephant, for male seals, and even for the male terrapin.

BULLETS are pieces of metal for firing from machine-guns, rifles, and so on. Bullets used to be round balls of lead, now they are shaped like a short piece of pencil. This shape goes through the air better. The barrel of a machine-gun or rifle has spiral grooves cut throughout the inside to give spin to the bullet as it starts its flight. This spinning movement keeps the more pointed end forward as it flies. We say the barrel is "rifled," and it is from this that the rifle gets its name.

BUNSEN BURNER, a form of gas burner designed to give more heat. If we light gas at the end of a pipe it gives light and smoke as well as heat. This is because particles of carbon in the gas are only heated in the flame and not fully burned. The famous chemist, Robert Bunsen, designed a burner which brought in more air,

Bunsen burner.

so that the carbon particles were burned up. The flame then gives more heat and neither light nor smoke.

BUNYAN, John, was born in 1628. He was a humble man, who had little education, yet he wrote one of the most famous books in the world—*The Pilgrim's Progress.* He was in prison at the time for preaching his religious views. He wrote his story in symbolical language; for example the load of sin on his mind is represented as a bundle on Christian's back, and the difficulties of life are represented by steep and stony paths. John Bunyan died in 1688.

BUOY. Sometimes in a wide river or shallow sea there is only one channel which is deep enough for ships to sail

Port-hand buoy and bell-buoy.

safely. This channel is marked with floating objects called buoys. Buoys are also used to mark the place where a ship has sunk, or where there are dangerous sandbanks or rocks. See NAVIGATION.

BURMA, a country adjoining the subcontinent of India, on the Bay of Bengal. Rangoon is the capital. It is a mountainous country, but ships can sail up the River Irrawaddy for eight hundred miles. Rice, sugar, tobacco and cotton are grown. There are many valuable minerals, including gold, silver, jade, precious stones (especially rubies), iron, marble and lead. Elephants, rhinoceroses, tigers and leopards are found there, and elephants are trained to carry heavy loads.

BURNING GLASS. This is any lens or magnifying glass which, when held at the perfect angle to catch the sun's rays, will

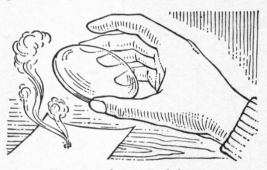

Focusing the rays of the sun.

concentrate those rays to a single point so hot that it will set fire to a piece of paper on which it is focused.

BURNS, Robert (born 1759), is the most famous of Scottish poets. He was a farmer, and not a very good one, but his poems describe the joys and sorrows of human beings so well, and with so much sympathy, that thousands of people still read them. Burns died in 1796, aged 37.

BUSHEL, a measure for wheat, barley, oats, and so on. It contains eight gallons.

BUTTERFLY, an insect with beautiful wings. The female lays a large number of eggs which become caterpillars, and these feed on leaves or other vegetation. The caterpillar then rests for a time inside a protective covering, develops, and emerges as a butterfly. See also INSECTS, and colour plate facing page 64.

C

CABLE, a strong rope or chain, such as is used to hold a ship at anchor. An *electric* cable is one or more copper wires enclosed in a protective covering.

CACAO. See COCOA.

CACTUS, a type of plant adapted to desert conditions. Water is stored in the stem, and the leaves are reduced to spines so that very little water is given off.

CAESAR, Gaius Julius, a great Roman general and ruler. He was born about 102 B.C., and was about forty-seven years of age when he invaded Britain. He was a statesman, an orator, an engineer and architect, as well as a great general. He was murdered by Brutus and Cassius in 44 B.C.

CAIN was the eldest son of ADAM and Eve. He killed his brother Abel. The story is told in the Bible (Genesis, Chapter IV).

CALAIS, a French port on the narrowest part of the English Channel. Fast steamers travel between Calais and Dover. Calais was captured by EDWARD III in 1347 and remained an English possession until 1558. See also HUNDRED YEARS' WAR.

CALCUTTA, a city in West Bengal, India, on the River Hooghly. It was the capital of India until 1912, when Delhi became the new capital. See map on page 156 and INDIA, REPUBLIC OF.

Julius Caesar invaded Britain.

CALENDAR. Days and years are measured by the movements of the earth. Months are measured by the movements of the moon. It took men a long time, however, to learn to measure time as exactly as we do now and to set it down in what we call a calendar.

CALIFORNIA is one of the UNITED STATES of America, and is on the Pacific coast. Part of it has the same climate as the Mediterranean countries, that is, warm, dry summers and some rain brought by the west wind in the winter, so the juicy fruits grow here, too, such as grapes, olives, oranges, peaches, pomegranates. It also has valuable minerals, especially gold and oil.

San Francisco is the chief port and is famous for the Golden Gate Harbour. Los Angeles is the name of the largest

Cactus plants can live in the desert.

city and of a district or county. It is famous for two reasons—as an oil-refining centre, and because it contains Hollywood, which is the centre of the film industry.

CALORIE, the amount of heat required to raise one gram of water one degree on the Centigrade thermometer. It is convenient to have a measure for heat, as it is convenient to have a measure for length or for weight.

CAMBRIDGE, an English county, and the name of its chief town. There is a famous UNIVERSITY in the town. The colleges are lovely old buildings with beautiful gardens.

CAMEL, an animal adapted to live in desert lands. Its feet do not sink in soft sand like the feet of a horse, and it carries a hump of fat on its back as reserve food. (Its backbone is straight.) It can also store extra water in the walls of its stomach. The fast riding-camel used by the ARABS is called a DROMEDARY. The Bactrian camel of Asia has two humps.

CAMOUFLAGE, colouring, whether natural or artificial, to enable something to blend with its background. Many animals have markings which make them almost invisible in the places where they live. This protects them from their enemies. The polar bear is white, and the Arctic fox and the mountain hare become white in winter, so that they can hide in the snow. The peacock, with its beautiful blue breast and long tail, is almost invisible to people or animals looking up at it in the tree tops, with the tropical blue sky overhead. Many fish and insects have similar protection. See also MIMICRY.

Camouflage is used in warfare, too. For example, a fishing-net covered with imitation leaves may be put over a gun to hide it from an enemy aeroplane; or a ship has white and black triangles painted on it to break up its well-known shape, and make it look like waves and sea.

CAMPING, living in tents or other kinds of shelter in places where there are no houses. Explorers must have camps. Boys or girls often go to lovely, quiet country places and camp there. They cook their own food on wood fires, or oil stoves, and sleep on the ground with waterproof sheets and blankets.

CANADA is part of the BRITISH COMMONWEALTH. It consists of most of the northern half of North America. Ottawa is the capital of the Dominion and it is also the headquarters of the Royal Canadian Mounted Police—better-known

The camel is of great value to nomadic Arab tribes, for riding, and as baggage-carrier.

rucksack

collecting wood

canvas bucket

lighting fire from windward side

camp fire

pitching a tent

D. H. Ralphs

Camping is fun, as long as everyone does his share of the work!

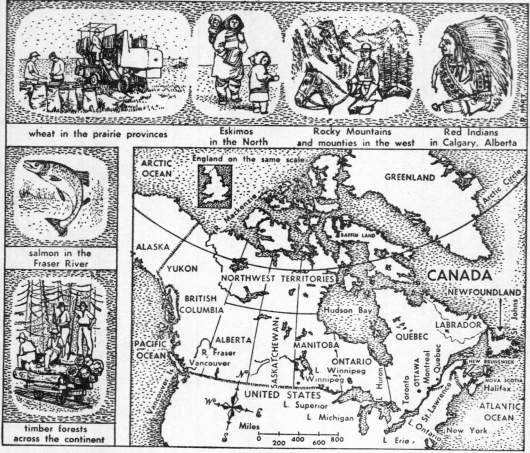

Map of Canada, showing the provinces, and some of the things found there.

as the "Mounties." Montreal, in the province of Quebec, is the largest city and port in Canada, while Quebec itself, the capital of the province, is also an important port.

Although it is as large as Europe and has enormous fertile plains and rich minerals Canada has only about twenty-one million people. Round the northern part of Hudson Bay the winter is very cold and only the Eskimos live there. And, of course, there are not many people in the Rocky Mountains in the west. But there are great wheat fields between these two parts; much of the wheat comes across the Great Lakes (Superior, Huron, Ontario, Erie, Michigan) and down the

St. Lawrence Seaway for export. Unfortunately this river freezes up in winter.

NEWFOUNDLAND, an island off the mouth of the St. Lawrence, has enormous quantities of fish, especially cod, in the seas around it.

Many of the valuable minerals (gold, silver, nickel, copper, lead, zinc and iron) are found north of the Great Lakes. There are great forests of valuable timber in many places. Some of it is exported as logs, and some is made into pulp for paper-making. There are also many dairy farms, especially around the St. Lawrence, and north of the Great Lakes.

On the western side of the Rockies the climate is milder. Vancouver is the chief

46

town of British Columbia. It is on the Fraser River, in which there are so many salmon that men stand in the shallow places and throw them on to the bank.

CANAL, an artificial waterway. The Egyptians cut canals so that the waters of the Nile would make more of the desert fertile. A big canal is cut between North and South America (the Panama Canal), so that ocean liners can sail through. Another big one is the Suez Canal, near the mouth of the Nile. Until the Six Day War in 1967, great ships could sail through it instead of going round Africa.

Unless the land is quite flat canals must have LOCKS to keep the water at different levels. This applies both to canals like the Panama, carrying big ships, and to canals which carry small river boats. There are no locks in the Suez Canal.

CANARIES, small birds which come chiefly from the Canary Islands. In the wild state they are olive-green, black and yellow, and the beautiful yellow colour we know so well is only obtained by careful breeding. Birds from the Harz Mountains in Germany sing very sweetly, but many people prefer the canaries which are bred in the Norfolk town of Norwich, in England.

CANBERRA is the capital of Australia as a whole. The Australian Parliament Building was built at Canberra so that the old cities of SYDNEY and MELBOURNE should not quarrel over which of them should be the capital. The population of the capital territory is over 150,000.

CANNON. Big guns of various kinds are called cannon. Some have long bar-rels and long range (guns). Others have shorter barrels and can fire higher, but not so far (howitzers). Some have very short barrels for throwing heavy shells into nearby trenches (trench mortars).

For a long time gunpowder was used as the EXPLOSIVE. Then cordite was found to be better. Dynamite cannot be used for firing a shell, because it would blow the whole gun to pieces.

CANOE, a light boat, usually driven by a paddle. It may be a hollowed tree trunk, or a frame of wood covered with skin, like the Eskimo's kayak.

CANUTE was the son of a Danish King, Sweyn, whose army came to England and conquered Wessex in 1013. Ethelred the Unready escaped to Normandy but returned after Sweyn's death in 1014. This time it was Canute's turn to fly from England. He sailed back with a Danish fleet in 1015 and his forces overran northern England. Ethelred died in the following year and Canute was elected king of part of England. But Ethelred's son, Edmund "Ironside," was the lawful king and he and his supporters fought a battle with the Danish invader at Assandune in

King Canute showed his flatterers they were wrong.

Essex. They lost this battle and a conference took place at Olney. It was agreed that Canute should rule over Mercia and the north, and Edmund should rule over Wessex, East Anglia and London. When Edmund died in 1016 Canute was acclaimed as king of all England. He succeeded to the throne of Denmark also, when his brother Harold died in 1018.

Canute was a good and strong ruler. He was admired so much that people said he had only to command the tide to stop coming in and it would obey him. It is said that he really did go down to the shore and order the waves back, just to show his flatterers how foolish they were to suggest that he could work miracles. He died in 1035 and was buried at Winchester.

CANYON. When a river flows over land it cuts its bed deeper and deeper, but at the same time the surface of the land is gradually being washed away by the rain. In certain parts of the world, however, there is no rainfall, and the rocks are as high as they were thousands of years ago.

A canyon is a deep, narrow valley.

If a river flows through this area it goes on cutting its bed deeper and deeper below the surface. The Colorado River, which flows into the Gulf of California, has cut its bed over a mile down through the solid rock. This great deep valley is called the Grand Canyon of the Colorado.

CAPE HORN is the southernmost point of South America. Ships travelling between the Atlantic and Pacific can cut through the MAGELLAN Strait, a little farther north.

CAPE OF GOOD HOPE, the cape just south of Cape Town. See map of AFRICA.

CAPE TOWN, an important town in South Africa, near the Cape of Good Hope. The South African Parliament meets here.

CAPILLARIES, the small blood-vessels which link the ends of the ARTERIES with the beginnings of the VEINS.

CAPSTAN. A capstan is like a large bobbin standing upright on a strong axle. The bobbin part can be turned by steam or electric power; it has a rope or cable wound round it so as to lift anchors or pull the ships close to the quay once they have fastened the rope to the shore. There is a ratchet at the foot so that the capstan will not turn the wrong way.

CAPTAIN. This name comes from the Latin word *caput*, meaning head. The man in charge of a ship is called the captain; so is an officer who commands a company of infantry. The name is given also to a leader of games, such as the captain of a cricket eleven.

CARBON. Soot from the fire is nearly pure carbon, and so is the lead of a lead pencil, and, strangely enough, a diamond. If we burn soot, the lead of a pencil or a diamond, we get a compound of carbon and oxygen called CARBON DIOXIDE.

CARBON DIOXIDE. When coal or coke burns, carbon dioxide is formed. This is a compound of carbon and oxygen. When there is not enough oxygen, another gas called carbon monoxide is formed. It has only half as much oxygen as carbon dioxide (*mono* means one, and *di* means two). Carbon monoxide is a poisonous gas, and has no smell.

CARBON MONOXIDE. See CARBON DIOXIDE.

CARBURETTOR, a device which supplies and controls the mixture of air and petrol in an internal combustion engine. When the piston partly withdraws from the cylinder (see page 94) it sucks some petrol through a fine jet in the carburettor. This spray of petrol is mixed with enough air to make it explosive, and it is then passed into the cylinder to be fired by the sparking-plug. The quantities of petrol and air passed through the carburettor are controlled by the driver's "accelerator."

CARICATURE, a drawing, usually of a person, in which his less attractive features are exaggerated for fun. If a man has a big nose, for example, someone might draw a picture making his nose even bigger than it is. If a man is always talking about his strength someone might draw him with great bulging muscles, and people who knew him would be amused.

CARNIVORES are animals which live on the flesh of other animals. Lions and tigers, for example, are carnivorous animals. Animals which live on grass or other vegetation are called herbivorous animals. See also CAT.

CARNIVOROUS PLANTS. See INSECT-EATING PLANTS.

CAROL, the type of song people sing at Christmas time. "Good King Wenceslas" is a carol.

CARPENTRY is the craft of building things with wood. The carpenter does the heavy work, like laying wooden decks on ships, or building the framework of a big wooden shed. A joiner does the lighter work, like fitting doors and windows in houses.

CARROLL, Lewis, was born in 1832. He was the author of ALICE'S ADVENTURES IN WONDERLAND, *Through the Looking-glass* and other books. He was a lecturer in mathematics at Oxford University, and

Lewis Carroll wrote the story of Alice.

his real name was the Reverend Charles Dodgson. He died in 1898 but his books are still read today.

CARTHAGE, one of the most famous cities of ancient times. It was in northern Africa, opposite the island of Sicily. The Carthaginians captured Corsica, Sardinia, and other islands, and fought many battles with the Greeks in Sicily. Their most famous general was Hannibal. His father (Hamilcar) had conquered part of Spain, and Hannibal marched from Spain over the Pyrenees, across the River Rhône, over the Alps into Italy, and fought many successful battles with the Romans in their own country. He set off on that march with 90,000 foot soldiers, 12,000 horsemen and 40 elephants.

CARTILAGE, or gristle as we sometimes call it, forms the flexible bone of the

49

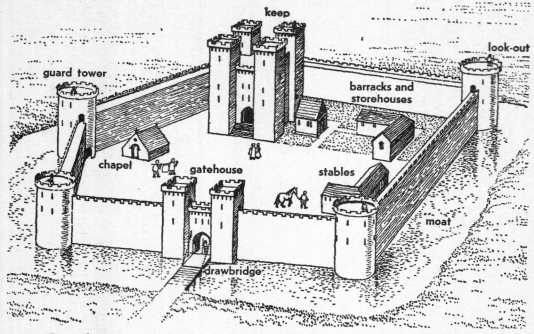

In earlier times castles used to be a strong defence against enemy attack.

nose. There is also a covering of cartilage on the ends of bones where they make a joint. See also SPINE.

CARTOON. Today a cartoon is either a drawing which shows some event of the day in a humorous and unfriendly light, being often a sort of CARICATURE of some politician or political manoeuvre, or it is a film made out of coloured drawings, like the Walt Disney cartoons.

CASPIAN SEA, the largest inland lake in the world. Although the greatest river in Europe (the River Volga) flows into it, the Caspian Sea has no outlet. The water evaporates quicker than the rivers replace it, so this sea is gradually drying up.

CASSOWARY, a bird that cannot fly; it lives in forest land in AUSTRALASIA. See also EMU; KIWI; OSTRICH.

CAST IRON. Iron which has been melted and poured into moulds to cool is called cast iron. Many common objects, such as fire-grates, lawn-mower wheels and garden rollers are made of cast iron. In cooling, the iron forms tiny crystals which make it brittle, so that cast iron is unsuitable for making tools. Iron can be made tough by heating it and then hammering it, but in this state it is called wrought iron.

CASTLE, a strong residence which could be defended easily against an enemy. Sometimes it was on a steep hill, and sometimes it was surrounded by a moat filled with water. The walls were always very thick and had loopholes through which the defenders could shoot arrows. The bridge over the moat to the door of the castle could be drawn up (the drawbridge). Modern artillery, of course, could pound a castle to pieces, so it is no longer much of a defence.

Historic castles in Britain include Stirling, Caernarvon and Walmer. The Tower of London is a castle, and Windsor Castle is still a royal residence, as it has been since there was a FORTIFICATION there in the time of William the Conqueror.

CAT. Lions, tigers and leopards are all members of the cat family. Like them, the

leopard

lynx

lion

lioness

cheetah

tiger

All members of the cat family are flesh-eating animals, or carnivores.

household cat lives on flesh and enjoys hunting animals and birds. Most of the cat tribe can climb trees with their claws and they can all draw in their claws and walk silently on the pads of their feet. They all see very well in dim light, and often hunt at night. See also CARNIVORES.

CATARACT, a waterfall. The best known is NIAGARA Falls, over which an enormous amount of water falls about 160 feet. But the VICTORIA FALLS, on the Zambesi River, in Africa, are higher—the whole river falls over 300 feet. There are many beautiful waterfalls in the mountainous parts of the British Isles, and in Norway, Switzerland, and other countries. The force of the falling water is often used nowadays to make electricity.

CATHEDRAL, a large and beautiful church. The name comes from the Latin *cathedra*, meaning a chair, and a cathedral is a church which contains the throne of a bishop.

CATTLE, a general name for cows and bulls of various kinds. Some are well-known because they produce good meat —the black Aberdeen-Angus is one breed which provides that lovely Scotch beef for which Britain is noted. Highland cattle are hardy and have shaggy brown hair to keep them warm. Jersey, Sussex and South Devon cattle live in better conditions and the cows are famous for the quality of their milk. The South Devon, particularly, provide a lot of very rich milk which is used to make the thick Devon and Cornish cream.

Other countries often import cattle from the British Isles to improve and strengthen their stock. Shorthorns are very adaptable and are found in most parts of the world.

CAVALRY, troops who fight on horseback. They had a very important place in all wars until motor-cars were invented. Now tank corps do the work.

CAVE, a hollow in a cliff or rock which extends beneath the surface of the earth. The sea and shingle beat against the rocks and the weakest parts get worn away. Sometimes only a little hollow is made but sometimes these caves are like big rooms. One may lead into another for quite a long way underground.

The men of the Old STONE AGE lived in caves. Sometimes the entrance got blocked up and the cave was not found again for thousands of years. Then interesting discoveries were sometimes made. In caves in France and Spain remarkable draw-

The earliest cave-men drew wonderful pictures of animals.

Growing coffee in Central America.

ings were found which had been made by the earliest men. We find also the remains of animals which no longer live in the country.

CAXTON, William, was the man who introduced printing to England. He had seen it, probably at Cologne, and when he returned to England he set up a printing press and printed many books. The date of his birth is believed to be 1422, and he died in 1491.

CELLO. This is the shortened name of the violoncello. It is something like a violin only much larger. It has four strings and a very deep tone. The player sits down and holds the cello between his legs and plays it with a bow which is drawn across the strings. See also ORCHESTRA.

CENSUS, the official counting of the population in a country. In the British Isles a census is taken every ten years. The last one was in 1971.

CENTIPEDE, a small animal like an insect, but with many pairs of legs. The name means "a hundred feet."

CENTRAL AMERICA, a neck of land which connects NORTH and SOUTH AMERICA. It lies between the PACIFIC OCEAN on the west and the Caribbean Sea on the east. The states of Central America are Costa Rica, Guatemala, Honduras, Nicaragua, Panama, Salvador, and the colony of

British Honduras. Exports are bananas, cocoa, COFFEE and timber. See also AMERICA; ARMADILLO; WEST INDIES.

CEYLON, now Sri Lanka, is an island in the Indian Ocean, near the southern tip of India. It is part of the BRITISH COMMONWEALTH OF NATIONS. Rice, tea, and coconut are grown and rubber trees (see BRAZIL) produce much valuable rubber. Beautiful timber, such as ebony, rosewood, and satinwood is grown in the forests, and rubies, sapphires, and other precious stones are found. At Kandy, in the hills, is the Temple of the Tooth, a famous Buddhist shrine. Colombo is the capital and chief port.

CHAIN, a length of 22 yards. A metal chain of this length, made with a hundred links, is used by surveyors when they are measuring land. See ACRE.

CHALK is a soft, white rock, formed by the chemical deposits of minute sea animals. All chalk was formed at the bottom of the sea, but earth movements sometimes push it up. The white cliffs at Dover and Calais, and the North and South Downs are remains of a bed of chalk which was forced up into a ridge.

CHAMELEON, a kind of LIZARD. It can change its colour according to its sur-

Tea is grown in Sri Lanka.

Cavaliers and Roundheads fought bitterly in the time of Charles I.

roundings, which is very good CAMOU-FLAGE against its enemies. Another peculiarity is its tongue, which is very long, and sticky at the tip. The chameleon shoots out its tongue with terrific speed to trap insects for food.

CHAMOIS, a type of antelope, rather like a goat, which lives among the mountains of Europe and is very difficult to catch. What we call chamois leather is usually made now from the skin of sheep.

CHANNEL ISLANDS, a group of islands in the English Channel, near the coast of France. They belong to Great Britain. Jersey and Guernsey are the two largest islands, and they are popular holiday resorts. They export potatoes, tomatoes and other vegetables to Britain, because, since their climate is milder, their crops are ready earlier. See map on page 116.

CHARCOAL is impure carbon. It can be made by heating wood in a retort, as coal is heated in a gas-works. Charcoal is used for making gunpowder, for filtering and purifying water, for making black paint, and other purposes.

CHARLES I, King of Great Britain and Ireland, came to the throne on the death of his father, JAMES I (James VI of Scotland) in 1625. In the same year he married Henrietta Maria of France. His wife was a Roman Catholic and many people were afraid of the influence this might have on the King.

Charles was a good man but he believed that God had made him King and that he could rule the country as he liked. For some years he ruled without a parliament at all. But the way Charles dealt with religious problems, money difficulties, and Parliament annoyed the people and soon there was CIVIL WAR. The King's followers were called Cavaliers; the rebels were called Roundheads, because they wore their hair short. The Roundheads were skilfully led by Oliver CROMWELL, and the royalist forces were defeated. The King was beheaded in 1649 and the country became a republic. See also CHARLES II.

CHARLES II, son of CHARLES I, ruled as King of Great Britain and Ireland from 1660 to 1685. He had two coronations. Soon after Charles I had been beheaded in 1649, Charles II was proclaimed King in Scotland and was crowned at Scone in 1651. Then he marched into England at the head of a Scottish army to fight against Oliver CROMWELL. He was defeated at Worcester but escaped capture by hiding in an oak tree, and then fled to France. In 1660, two years after Cromwell's death, Charles was asked to return to England, and this is known as the Restoration. He was crowned at Westminster in 1661.

During his reign London suffered a terrible plague (1665) and was afterwards partly destroyed by the Great Fire (1666).

Although King Charles is remembered best because he had a sense of fun, and loved theatres and gay times, he had a serious side too; he loved the sea and knew a lot about navigation, so the Royal Observatory was built at Greenwich in 1675 for the study of navigation and nautical astronomy. It has since been moved to Hurstmonceux, in Sussex. He also founded the Royal Hospital, Chelsea, for invalid soldiers; but the building was not finished until seven years after the King's death in 1685.

CHARLIE, Bonnie Prince. His real name was Charles Edward Stuart, and he was born in 1720, the grandson of JAMES II. He was also called the Young Pretender, because he claimed the throne of Britain. He came to Scotland in 1745 to lead a rebellion against the forces of GEORGE II, and fought several successful battles, but he was finally defeated at Culloden Moor, in 1746. With the help of Flora Macdonald he escaped to France. He died in 1788.

CHART. A map for the use of sailors is usually called a chart. It shows depth of

The Great Fire of London was a tragic event in the time of Charles II.

55

Chaucer's book, "The Canterbury Tales," tells some entertaining stories.

water, dangerous rocks, good harbours, and so on. We also speak of weather charts and temperature charts.

CHAUCER, Geoffrey, was the first of the great English poets; the date of his birth is believed to be about 1340. He was a friend of RICHARD II and the courtiers of that time. His best known work is *The Canterbury Tales*. These are a number of stories supposed to have been told by a group of people going on a pilgrimage to Canterbury. Chaucer died in 1400, and was buried in Westminster Abbey.

CHEMISTRY. This is the name given to the study of the composition of substances and the changes which take place

Chinese temple

rice fields

when different substances are combined with, or separated from, one another. See also ANALYSIS.

CHILE, a country in South America. It stretches along the west coast, with the great ANDES mountains on the east. Part of it is in line with (in the same LATITUDE as) the southern points of Africa and Australia, and like them has a Mediterranean type of climate, so that grapes, oranges, peaches and other juicy fruits are grown. Large quantities of silver, copper and nitrates are exported, and gold, lead, iron and other metals are also found. Santiago is the capital, and Valparaiso the chief port.

CHIMNEY. A brick or metal tube to carry away the smoke of a fire is called a chimney, and the hole through the middle of it is called the flue. In olden times the fire was lit in the middle of the floor for fear of setting the wooden walls alight, and then the smoke escaped through a hole in the roof. When the hearths were moved to a wall at one side of the house, a sort of groove was made in the wall to conduct the smoke to the roof-hole. Then somebody thought of making this groove very deep and bricking it up, and so the chimney was invented.

CHIMPANZEE, a very intelligent APE, like the gorilla, but not so big or so strong. It walks upright quite easily, and builds a kind of nest in the trees. It lives in Central and West Africa. See also MONKEYS.

CHINA. One of the first civilizations began in the fertile river valleys of the Hwang Ho and Yangtze Kiang. We learned from the Chinese how to make silk, paper, and the cups and saucers we still call china. Now the great country called China has more than 700 million people, nearly a quarter of the population of the whole world. The people live chiefly on rice, and much wheat is grown in the north, but with so many to feed there is little grain to export.

Canton is an important port, and the goods which are sent out to the rest of the world include silk, tea, soya beans and cotton. There are great quantities of coal, iron, oil and other minerals which may be used when more railways are built.

Peking is the capital, and other important towns are Shanghai and Nanking.

CHINA, GREAT WALL OF. The Egyptian civilization flourished because there were natural barriers round it, but the Chinese had to build a great wall in the north to keep the savage tribes from stealing everything they had. The wall was built more than two thousand years ago

Great Wall of China

port of Canton

57

and much of it still stands. It is high and wide and is used as a road. It extends from the sea near Peking westward to the deserts of central Asia.

Pottery is made from china clay.

CHINA CLAY. When granite rocks are gradually dissolved by rain a white clay is carried down by the rivers. This is collected and used for making china. Very good clay of this kind is found in China, in Germany (Dresden china is famous) and in England at St. Austell in Cornwall.

CHOPIN, Frederic, was born in 1810. He became a famous composer. Like Beethoven and Brahms he was a brilliant pianist, and much of his delightful music was for the piano. He died in 1849.

CHRISTIANITY is the religion of those of us who follow JESUS CHRIST and believe in His teachings, as told in the New Testament. See BIBLE; GOSPELS.

CHRISTMAS, the festival of the Christian Church, observed on 25 December every year in memory of the birth of Christ.

CHROMIUM is a metal which can be used like silver for electroplating. Steel which has some chromium in it is very hard and tough.

CHRONOMETER, an accurate watch or clock, used by ships in calculating their position at sea, and for other purposes.

When the spring of a watch is heated by a warm climate it becomes less springy, and the watch begins to go slow. A chronometer has a mechanism which prevents this from happening.

CHRYSALIS, the second stage in the growth of an insect, during which it neither eats nor moves, but just changes slowly into its complete form. A chrysalis (or pupa) is often enclosed in a light, silken envelope called a cocoon.

CHURCH, a building in which we worship God. A large and beautiful church is sometimes called a CATHEDRAL, and a small church is sometimes called a chapel. See also ABBEYS.

CHURCHILL, Sir Winston Spencer, was born in 1874 at Blenheim Palace. One of his ancestors was the first Duke of Marlborough who won the battle of Blenheim in the reign of Queen ANNE. Churchill became one of the greatest men in British history. In his early years he was a soldier in India and the Sudan, and was captured by the Boers in South Africa while he was a war correspondent. Later he became a Member of Parliament and Cabinet Minister; and during the First World War he was for a time First Lord of the Admiralty. After the outbreak of the Second World War he was made

Sir Winston Churchill.

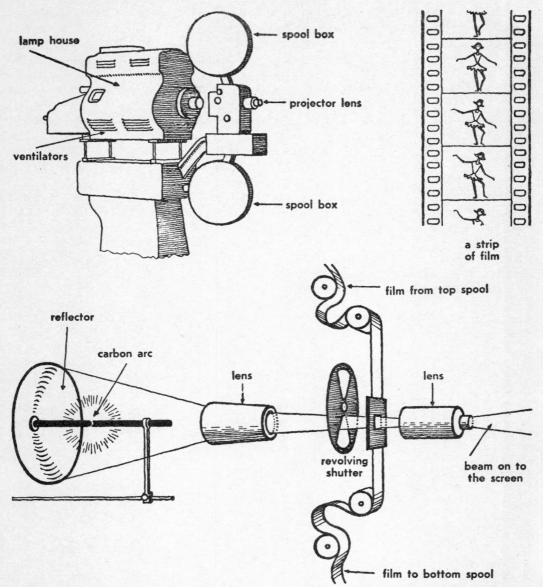

Labels in the diagram:

lamp house

spool box

projector lens

ventilators

spool box

a strip
of film

reflector

carbon arc

lens

lens

film from top spool

revolving
shutter

beam on to
the screen

film to bottom spool

The pictures on a strip of film are thrown on to a screen by a cinematograph projector.

Prime Minister (in May, 1940) and proved to be an inspired and inspiring leader both of the British and of the peoples of many nations who were fighting for freedom. He was again Prime Minister from 1951 to 1955 and was knighted in 1953.

As well as being a statesman and soldier, Churchill has written books on both the World Wars. He died in 1965.

CINEMATOGRAPH. The cine camera, as it is sometimes called, takes pictures rapidly, one after the other. When these are thrown on a screen by a projector we get the impression of movement. Speech and other sounds are recorded, too, and transmitted to a loud-speaker behind the screen, and it seems to us that the people in the pictures are speaking. See also FILM.

59

CIRCLE, a figure like a wheel. A line drawn from the centre to the circumference is called a radius; all such lines are equal. A line drawn through the centre and right across the circle is called a diameter. The circumference of any circle is three and one-seventh times the length of the diameter.

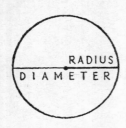

CIRCUIT. Electricity travels along a circuit. If you accidentally connect the two terminals of a battery with a piece of copper wire you will make a "short circuit." The electricity will rush from one terminal to the other and the battery may lose its strength very quickly. When, however, you include a small electric light in the circuit, the wire within the bulb becomes part of the circuit. It is a special

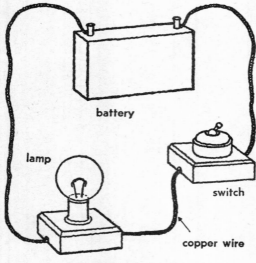

Electrical circuit

kind of wire through which the current cannot race so easily; the wire becomes white hot, and we have light.

CIRCULATION OF THE BLOOD, the flow of blood from the HEART through the ARTERIES to all parts of the body, and its return to the heart through the VEINS.

CIRCUS, a show of skill in horsemanship, acrobatics, performances of trained animals and so on. The Roman circus was a much more elaborate affair than the present-day entertainment. One circus building could hold a quarter of a million people, and there were chariot races, games, and fights between wild animals. The modern circus has jugglers and clowns to amuse everybody, and the ring is more circular in shape. It is often a travelling show given in a tent.

CIVIL ENGINEER, a man who designs roads, bridges, tunnels, canals and work of this kind.

CIVIL SERVICE. All persons employed and paid by the State to look after its affairs belong to the Civil Service. They see to it that the laws which have been passed by Parliament are carried out. When special problems arise in a department or questions are asked in Parliament, the Minister deals with them according to the information he is given by the people who work in that department.

Some of the chief government departments, in alphabetical order, are the Department of Trade and Industry, Foreign and Commonwealth Office, Home Office, Ministry of Defence, Scottish Office, Treasury, Welsh Office. Various Ministries, also part of the Civil Service, include Education and Science, Health and Social Security, and Employment.

CIVIL WAR is the name given to a war which is fought between people of the same country. The American Civil War was fought between 1861 and 1865. In England a struggle for power between CHARLES I and Parliament went on from 1641 to 1648. See also Oliver CROMWELL.

CLARINET, the woodwind which plays the higher notes in orchestral music. See MUSICAL INSTRUMENTS.

CLAW, the nail on the finger or toe of an animal, especially when it is sharp and curved as in birds and cats. The word is also used for the hooks at the ends of insects' legs, and for the pincers of crabs

brimstone

South American Butterfly

common blue

purple emperor

peacock

Queen of Spain fritillary

red admiral

swallow-tail

orange tip

Richmond Birdwing Australia

All of these butterflies can be seen in Britain except the first and the last.

The circus is an exciting entertainment, with its acrobats, clowns and performing animals.

and lobsters. The very stout claws of birds-of-prey are called "talons." Cats, including the lions and tigers, are able to withdraw their claws into sheaths when they do not wish to use them.

CLEOPATRA was a queen of Egypt who was greatly admired by Julius CAESAR and Mark ANTONY. Antony was so much in love with her that he stayed at her court for long periods when he should have been helping to govern Rome. At the naval battle at Actium she brought her fleet to help him, but sailed away during the battle, and Mark Antony left his men and sailed away after her.

CLIMATE, the kind of weather a country usually gets. Along the equator countries usually have hot, wet climates, but high up on the ANDES mountains it is cold even at the equator. Deserts like the Sahara have hot, dry climates. Countries like Britain and New Zealand have temperate climates, with not very much change between winter and summer. In the middle of Russia it is very hot in

Cleopatra was a queen of Egypt.

summer and very cold in winter (land surfaces do not collect and store the heat so well as the oceans do). Around the North and South Poles it is always cold. As a rule, the nearer the country is to the equator the warmer the climate is.

lion

partridge

domestic cat

South American harpy

leg of beetle (greatly magnified)

Animals use their claws as grappling-hooks, or as weapons of attack.

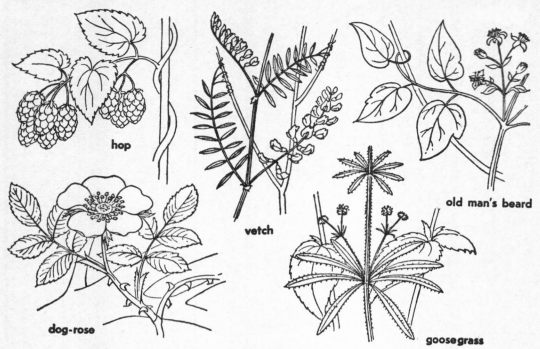

Climbing plants can get support in various ways while they grow.

hop

vetch

old man's beard

dog-rose

goosegrass

CLIMBING PLANTS are plants which hold on to trees or other supports as they grow upwards. Some just wind round the support as they grow, others grow tendrils, or leaf-stalks, or hooks, or prickles with which to hold on.

CLOCK, a machine for showing the time. The wheels are turned by a weight or a spring. A PENDULUM, or an oscillating balance wheel, keeps the wheels turning at an even rate. A special kind of clock, called a CHRONOMETER, is used by ships at sea.

CLOUD. When you blow out your breath on a cold day you can sometimes see a little cloud. The warm air in your lungs can hold some moisture, but when you breathe it out into the cold atmosphere the moisture becomes visible as tiny drops which together appear as the little cloud. Big clouds are made in much the same way. For example, warm air which has taken up moisture from the sea rises over mountains, cools and forms clouds which may drop some of the moisture as rain.

CLUTCH, the part of a motor-car which connects the engine to the wheels. It is not convenient to stop the engine for a few seconds, at traffic lights, for example, and then start it again. It is simpler to let the engine continue to run slowly and break the connexion with the wheels of the car. We can do this either by putting the gears in neutral or by letting out the clutch.

CLYDE, an important river in Scotland. It flows through Glasgow to the Firth of Clyde. Glasgow is a port, and there are big shipbuilding yards at Clydebank.

COAL is a kind of fossilized material in the earth. At one time masses of vegetation covered Britain and other countries. This decayed and chemical changes took place. With the sinking of the land and volcanic disturbances of the earth the vegetation was covered over by other materials like sand and mud. In the end, pressure, heat and further chemical changes turned it all into a hard rock-like substance which we call coal.

Miners go underground to dig out the coal from the rock face. Some of the coal-fields of Britain are in Durham, Derby, Lancashire, and South Wales.

COBRA, a very poisonous SNAKE which kills thousands of people in India every year. It is also found in other parts of southern Asia. When it is getting ready to bite it raises its head and spreads out the skin on its neck so that it looks rather like a hood.

COCKATOO, a bird like a parrot, but usually rather larger, and with a crest on its head. It is found in Australia and the East Indian Islands.

COCKROACH, commonly called the black BEETLE. It belongs to the family of insects which have horny shields to protect the wings, although in some kinds the wings are absent and only the hard case remains. The cockroach came to Britain from a hot climate, so it likes to find warm places in which to live.

COCOA, the powdered beans of the cacao tree, from which we make chocolate and the drink called cocoa. The trees grow in tropical countries like Mexico, Brazil, West Africa, and Sri Lanka.

COCONUT. The coconut grows on a tropical palm-tree fifty feet high or more. The kernel is eaten both ripe and unripe; it is also dried and exported as "copra," from which coconut oil is obtained. The nut is enclosed in an enormous husk, the fibres of which are used for making ropes and matting.

COCOON. See CHRYSALIS.

COFFEE, a drink made from the seeds of an EVERGREEN shrub. It was grown originally in Arabia and Abyssinia, but is also grown now in Brazil, Central America, Southern India and elsewhere. The beans are roasted and ground into the brown powder we call coffee.

COKE. When we heat wood or coal, useful gases are given off, then a light liquid, then a tarry liquid, and finally a solid remains. With wood, the solid is charcoal; with coal, the solid is coke. In a gas-works all these products are made.

COLERIDGE, Samuel Taylor, an English poet and philosopher, was born in 1772. He was a great friend of WORDS-WORTH, and shared his idea that poetry should be written as simply as possible so that everyone could understand it. He wrote some very original poetry—*The Rime of the Ancient Mariner* is particularly well-known. Coleridge died in 1834.

COLLECTING. This means keeping as many things of one sort as you can find—coins, rocks, wild flowers, shells and so on—and then arranging them. If they are all alike you can only arrange them to make pretty patterns, but if they are different in detail you can sometimes arrange them so that they tell part of their own story. Thus, you may collect stamps and arrange them according to their countries and dates, or books and arrange them according to their authors or subject.

COLOUR. Sunlight can be broken up into light of many colours. This happens when it passes through a PRISM, or in the

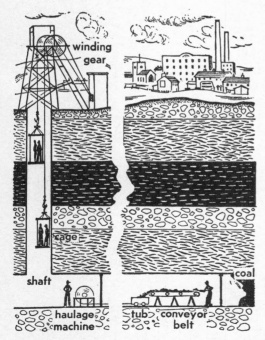

Men go down a coal-mine to dig out coal.

63

RAINBOW. A film of oil on water also breaks up light into its coloured parts. A red dress or red roses absorbs most of the colours and reflects only the red rays.

COLOUR BLINDNESS. About four per cent of men and one per cent of women cannot distinguish red from green. They could not, without looking carefully, find a red coat lying on a green lawn. A smaller number of people cannot distinguish blue from yellow, and a few cannot see any colour although their eyes seem normal.

COLUMBUS, Christopher, the Italian sailor and explorer who discovered America. The date of his birth is believed to be about 1446. He was at sea from his boyhood and knew a lot about ships, and he tried to convince people that as the world was round we ought to get to India by sailing across the Atlantic Ocean. For a long time no country would give him ships to try the experiment, but at last the King of Spain gave him three small vessels and off he went in 1492 on his great voyage. He did not get to India, for it was much farther than he realized, but he discovered land and thought he had got to India. He called the natives Indians

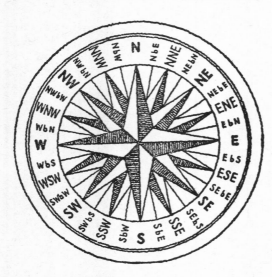

Mariner's compass.

and the islands the West Indies, and we still use these names. Columbus died in 1506.

COMET, a body which travels round the sun like a planet. As it gets near the sun it often sheds small particles which form a long tail behind the comet. The path it takes is much more an elongated oval than the short ELLIPSE in which a planet moves. Halley's comet, for example, flies round the sun in a few months and then goes off into space for another 75 years. It is due to come back in 1986. See also SOLAR SYSTEM.

COMMERCE. At first men lived on the food they found around them, or could grow. Later they exchanged food and other things with other people. The PHOENICIANS brought cloth to Britain, for example, and went away with furs and tin. This was a system of "barter."

We do much the same thing today, except that we pay money for the goods we get from other countries. Then we sell our own goods to earn money ourselves. This is still an exchange of goods, but if one country has not got what we want, or cannot supply as much as we want, we are able to try somewhere else. This is called commerce.

COMMONWEALTH OF NATIONS, a term widely used among the sovereign and equal self-governing countries which together form an association more usually known in Britain as the BRITISH COMMONWEALTH OF NATIONS.

COMMUNISM is the idea that all wealth, work, service, skill and knowledge should belong to the people or the community as a whole, and not be used for private gain. Russia and China are the most important countries which aim at transforming capitalist societies into Communist ones.

COMPASS. If a bar-magnet or a magnetized needle is suspended at the centre one end turns towards the North Pole. This enables ships and aeroplanes to find their way over the great oceans. In the mariner's compass magnetized needles are fixed to a round card which shows the compass points, and the card itself can be turned as well. The whole compass can be suspended in a liquid so that it is always horizontal whichever way the ship rolls.

COMPASSES. A pair of compasses is a device for drawing a circle of any desired size. It consists of two arms hinged together at one end so that the distance apart of the other two ends may be varied. One of these arms ends in a needle-point; the other arm carries a pencil which is screwed into it. When you stick the point in any surface and rotate the other arm, the pencil draws a perfect circle with the needle-point marking the centre.

COMPRESSED AIR is used for working pneumatic hammers and drills, for keeping water out of tunnels, raising sunken ships and many other purposes.

CONCERTO, a piece of orchestral music with an outstanding part for a solo instrument. In a piano concerto, for example, a first-class pianist plays this special part.

CONCRETE, a mixture of granite chips, Portland cement, sand and water which is used for building houses, sewer pipes and so on. With rods of steel inside it, it can be made very strong (reinforced concrete), and is used to build bridges and similar structures.

CONE, a solid figure with a circular base, tapering to a point. See CONIC SECTION; MENSURATION.

CONGO, now Zaïre, is a great river in tropical Africa. It gave its name to the Congo, that part of west Africa formerly controlled by Belgium. David LIVINGSTONE explored the river in an attempt to find its source, and another explorer, Henry Stanley, continued to trace its course and discovered Stanley Falls.

CONIC SECTION. If a wooden cone were standing on its base and someone took a saw and cut horizontally through it, the shape of the top of the cone would be a *circle*. If the cut were made at an angle, the top of the cone would be an *ellipse*. If the cut were made vertically downwards from one side, the shape left would be a *hyperbola*. If the cut were made parallel to one of the sides, the shape left would be a *parabola*. These shapes are known as conic sections.

Conic sections have different shapes and different names.

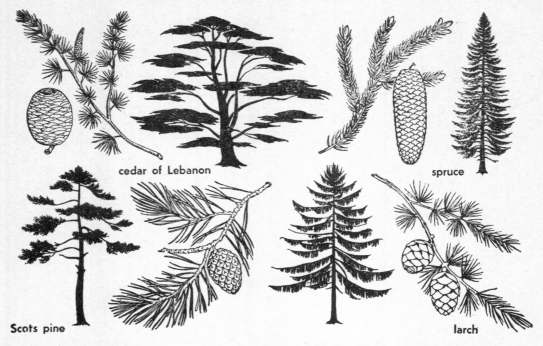

cedar of Lebanon

spruce

Scots pine

larch

Most conifers are evergreen, and do not shed their leaves in the autumn.

CONIFERS are woody PERENNIAL plants which bear cones. The seeds grow in these. The trees are usually EVERGREEN —like the pine, fir, and cedar of Lebanon. The larch, also, is a conifer; it is the only one which is DECIDUOUS.

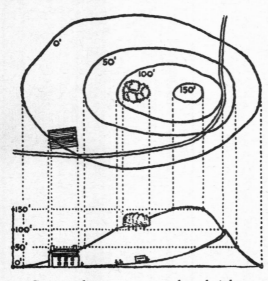

Contour lines on a map show height.

CONSERVATIVE, the name of a political party in Britain. People who feel that the country is running reasonably well, and that reforms should be carried out slowly and carefully, tend to be Conservative. See POLITICS.

CONSTABLE, John, was born in 1776, and became a famous landscape painter. He made his living painting portraits, but he was much happier painting pictures of country scenes in Suffolk, where he was born. Constable died in 1837.

CONTINENT. The land masses known as Africa, America, Antarctica, Asia, Australia and Europe are often referred to as continents. Many geographers think of America as two continents because North America and South America are two large land masses joined by a narrow neck of land.

CONTOUR LINES are lines drawn on a map to join places of the same height. From the diagram (*left*) it will be seen that when the lines are close together the slope is steep.

66

CONTRALTO. This is the lowest singing voice among women.

CONVENT. A community of NUNS who live together to worship God live in a convent. Some convents send the nuns to help the poor and the sick people in the neighbourhood.

CONVEX. The outside of a saucer is convex, the inside is concave. A magnifying glass is a convex lens.

CONVOY, a number of ships with cargoes, under protection of warships. In both World Wars, for example, British ships were sunk by enemy submarines or aircraft, and it was thought to be safer if the slower cargo boats sailed together in a fleet, with a few fast ships such as corvettes and destroyers with them to keep a look-out for enemy attack.

COPERNICUS was the great astronomer who first discovered that the earth and the other planets went round the sun. He was born in Poland in 1473 and died in 1543. See SOLAR SYSTEM.

COPPER is a metal of great importance. It is a good conductor of electricity and is used for telegraph wires, cables, and so on. Brass is an ALLOY of copper and zinc; bronze is an alloy of copper and tin.

COPYRIGHT. Laws of copyright prevent the copying or publication of what an author has written, or a musician has set down on paper, without his consent. Copyright continues as long as the author lives, plus 50 years following his death.

CORAL, a tiny sea animal which builds a skeleton from the lime in sea water. Masses of them live together, and the skeletons form coral reefs.

CORM, an underground stem in which food is stored, for use by the plant in the winter. The crocus grows from a corm. See also BULB.

CORMORANT, a sea bird which dives and swims with great power when chasing fish, even under water. The Chinese train cormorants to catch fish for them.

CORN. This word really means any small hard seed, and includes the pepper-corn, but it is generally used for the grains of cereal grasses like wheat, barley, oats and rye. In America it means chiefly maize or "Indian" corn.

CORPUSCLE, a very small body or "cell" found floating in large numbers in the BLOOD. There are two kinds of corpuscles, red and white. The red corpuscles are shaped like coins, and they carry oxygen from the lungs to the other parts of the body. The white corpuscles are like little blobs of jelly which are able to stick out "fingers" in all directions, and they capture and destroy any germs which get into the body. The corpuscles cannot be seen without a microscope, for there are about 20 billion (million million) of them in the blood of a grown man.

CORROSION. This is the slow destruction of any substance by a weak acid or anything else which will attack or dissolve it. The word corrosion is used especially of the eating away of metals or stone by the oxygen and weak acids in the

Cormorants are taught to catch fish.

67

air. Examples are the rusting of iron and the verdigris found on copper.

CORRUGATED IRON is often used for roofing huts and temporary buildings. It is sheet iron which has been specially treated to protect it from CORROSION. The iron is given a coating of zinc and then put through a powerful press to bend it into a series of ridges.

CORSICA, an island in the Mediterranean. It is a French possession. NAPOLEON BONAPARTE was born in Ajaccio. which is the capital.

COTTON. Some plants make little white parachutes for their seeds so that they are carried away by the wind. The dandelion does this. In the cotton plant there is so much of this white stuff that one could quickly gather a big handful of "cotton wool," as we call it. The fibres are spun into threads, and from the threads cotton cloth is woven.

Cotton is grown in the south of the United States, and in India, Egypt and the south of Russia.

Cranes lift heavy goods.

CRAB, a sea animal which is a CRUSTACEAN because it has a hard shell to protect its soft body. It has ten legs, of which the front two are developed into strong pincer-like claws which can crack other shellfish.

CRANE, a machine for moving goods which are too heavy to shift in any other way. Ships' cargoes, for example, are sometimes loaded and unloaded by a crane. A common type is shown in the picture. The arm, or jib, can be raised or lowered; it has a pulley wheel at the top, and a wire rope goes over the pulley wheel to the steam or electric winch in the car. A special kind of crane is used in building also.

CRICKET, a national game of England. Two teams, with eleven men in each, take part. One side goes in to bat, the other side fields in turn. There are two umpires to see that the rules are kept.

The cricket pitch is a length of ground marked off by a wicket at each end. A wicket consists of three stumps of wood stuck upright in the ground, with two pieces of wood called the bails lying across the top.

The bowler tries to make the bails fall by bowling a hard leather ball at the wicket. The batsman defends the wicket by hitting the ball; if he hits it far enough he has time to dash along the length of ground, to change places with the batsman at the other end, and is said to have scored a "run." There are many ways a batsman can be "out," including when the bails fall, or if a fielder catches the ball after he has hit it. If he is out before he has made a run he is said to be out for a "duck." If he makes a hundred runs he has scored a "century."

The fielding positions vary, according to the style of bowling (that is, whether the bowler sends down very fast balls, or slow balls with spin on them) and also according to the style of the batsman (who may be known as a hard-hitter who sends the ball long distances into the field).

orthodox bowling grips

D. H. Ralpho.

swinger

leg-break

correct stance

jumping out to drive

left-arm bowler

the back cut

back defensive stroke

forward defensive stroke

Cricket is a favourite summer game. Here are some basic strokes.

69

Oliver Cromwell.

CRIMEA, a peninsula in the Black Sea, linked to the mainland of Russia by the isthmus of Perekop. See CRIMEAN WAR; Florence NIGHTINGALE.

CRIMEAN WAR, a war fought from 1854 to 1856 by Russia against Britain, France and Turkey. The famous Charge of the Light Brigade, about which Lord TENNYSON wrote a poem, took place at Balaclava. See also Florence NIGHTINGALE.

CRINOLINE, a dress worn by women about the time of Elizabeth I and James I, and again about a hundred years ago. It had a very wide skirt, kept out by whalebone or steel hoops.

CROCODILE, a dangerous REPTILE with powerful jaws found in the rivers of Africa, India and elsewhere. The young crocodiles hatch out of EGGS, just as chickens do, but crocodiles' eggs are round, and have soft shells.

CROMWELL, Oliver. The son of a farmer in Huntingdon, Oliver Cromwell was born in 1599. He became a Member of Parliament three years after CHARLES I came to the throne; when civil war broke out, Cromwell led a troop of volunteers which he had trained, and played an important part in the defeat of the royalist forces. He was such an able man that he soon became leader of the Army.

After King Charles was executed in 1649 the country became a republic. Cromwell was a member of the Council of State which was set up, and in 1653 he was asked to act as the ruler of England. He was called the Lord Protector of the Commonwealth. When he died in 1658, his son Richard took his place until CHARLES II was restored to the throne.

CRUSADES, wars which were undertaken to free the Holy Land from the Turks. They were fought between the years 1096 to 1291. Pilgrims to Jerusalem were being badly treated by the Turks, and this aroused so much indignation in Christian countries that several armies of people set off without proper military training to help fight the Turks. Most of these people died before they got there, for no proper arrangements had been made for their feeding and care on the route.

Jerusalem was captured in the First Crusade (1096 to 1099), but was recaptured in 1187 by Saladin, the leader of the Moslems in the Second Crusade.

Many nobles went on the Crusades.

RICHARD I of England (Richard the Lion-Heart) led one of the armies himself, in the Third Crusade (1189 to 1192), and the organization of food supplies was much better.

CRUSTACEAN, a member of a group of sea animals which includes the CRAB, LOBSTER, and SHRIMP. They all have hard shells to protect them. The wood-louse, although it lives on land, is a crustacean.

CUB SCOUTS, junior Boy Scouts between the ages of eight and eleven. They are trained in woodcraft, camping and other useful activities, and are taught how to behave, how to help others, how to save life, and how to be good citizens. Badges are given to those who do well in the various branches of training. See also GIRL GUIDES; SCOUTING.

CUCKOO, a bird which comes to Britain in April. It is about the size of a pigeon, and the male bird makes the sound which gives it its name. The female lays an egg in another bird's nest which has eggs in it, taking one of the eggs away in her bill when she leaves the nest. Then she lays another egg and puts it in another nest, until she has distributed about six eggs in this way.

When the young cuckoo is hatched out by its foster parents, who are often meadow pipits, it pushes any other eggs or young birds out of the nest so that it will get all the food and attention itself.

The cuckoo leaves Britain in July or August to spend the winter in warmer climates, but the young ones do not go till about a month later. How they know where to go nobody can tell.

CURRANTS are small grapes which are dried naturally in the sun. They come from the islands of Greece and get their name from Corinth. These fruits are not the same as the black, red and white currants which are picked from bushes.

CYCLING is an easy and cheap means of travelling. People who could not walk more than about twenty miles in a day

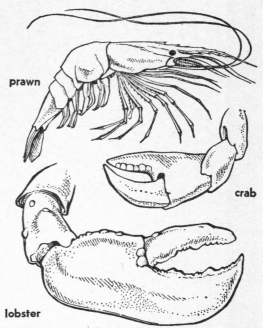

prawn

crab

lobster

Crustaceans have pincers as weapons.

can do a hundred miles on a BICYCLE, and expert racing cyclists can travel two hundred miles in a day.

CYCLONE. Originally the word meant a violent storm in the tropics, and it is still used in this sense. But when it is used in weather reports it means the movement of eddies of air which, in the southern HEMISPHERE, travel in the same direction as the hands of a clock. In the northern hemisphere the air travels in the opposite direction to the hands of a clock. See also ANTICYCLONE.

CYLINDER. A tin can is a cylinder. Make one from a sheet of paper and you will see how to measure the area of it. (See MENSURATION.) In motor or steam engines the cylinder is the chamber in which the explosions take place, to drive the piston backwards and forwards.

CYMBALS, two hollow plates of brass which are used in bands and orchestras.

CZECHOSLOVAKIA, a republic in Central Europe. It was created after the First World War. The capital of the country is Prague.

D

Hoover Dam.

DAM, a barrier built across a river or lake to control the flow of water. The great dam at Aswan, for example, holds back some of the flood waters of the NILE till water is needed for the crops. Some dams can be opened to let the river water rush through when it is required to make electricity. Others are built to hold back the water until the river is deep enough for boats to sail. A river must be dammed or diverted when men are laying the foundations of a new bridge. Dams are also built to form reservoirs to store drinking-water for great cities.

DANCING. We have different ways of showing emotion, and one way is in the way we move about. When children are happy they skip along rather than walk.

Most tribes and nations have dances by which they express happiness, love, sorrow, anger and other emotions.

Dancing is encouraged in schools because it is good exercise for the body, and teaches you to move gracefully all the time, whether dancing or walking. Children usually learn country dances, but if they are going to be BALLET dancers when they grow up they have special training for this.

DANUBE, an important river in Europe. It rises in the Black Forest in Germany, and flows across Europe to the Black Sea. See map on page 124.

DARDANELLES (called in ancient times the Hellespont), a channel one to four miles broad, leading out of the Sea of Marmora to the Aegean Sea. It is part of the route taken by ships sailing from the BLACK SEA to the Aegean. The Persian king, XERXES, built a bridge of boats across this channel and sent a million men over it to invade Greece in 480 B.C.

DARK AGES. The wonderful Roman civilization collapsed in A.D. 476 soon after the Vandals had plundered Rome. For about five hundred years after that art, science, literature and learning of all kinds had very little place in the lives of the people. That is why this period is sometimes called the **Dark Ages.** See also MIDDLE AGES.

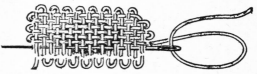

Darning is a way of repairing holes.

DARNING, a method of mending a hole in cloth or knitted material by weaving new thread into it. A row of threads all running in the same direction is first worked in with a darning-needle, and then a second row is put in to run across the first, the second threads going alternately under and over the first threads.

DARWIN, Charles, a scientist who is known all over the world. He was born in Shropshire, England, in 1809. As a boy he was not considered very intelligent because he was always studying worms, or collecting beetles, or studying rocks, instead of learning what other people wanted him to learn. H.M.S. *Beagle* had to go on a surveying voyage round the world, and Darwin got the chance of going with it. The voyage lasted from 1831 to 1836; this gave him wonderful opportunities of studying plants, animals and rock formations, and he kept full notes of all he saw. The idea that all forms of life were related, and that even men had evolved from simpler creatures is spoken of as the

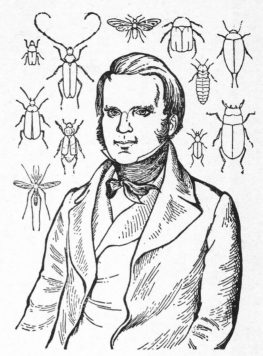

Charles Darwin.

"Theory of Evolution," and Darwin wrote a book about it called *The Origin of the Species by Natural Selection.* He died in 1882.

DATE-PALM. This palm tree shoots straight up to sixty feet or so without any branches, and then grows leaves and fruit at the top. In North Africa dates are the chief food of some of the ARAB tribes. The date-palm is also grown in Iran, Israel, and ARABIA.

DAVY, Sir Humphry, was born in 1778. He became a distinguished chemist, and made some very important discoveries. He invented the Davy lamp, which prevented many fires and explosions in mines in the days before miners had electric lamps. He died in 1829.

DAY, the time the earth takes to turn round on its axis once. If you put a mark on a ball to represent Britain, and turn the ball round slowly in front of a fire or light, you will see why we get day and night in each complete turn.

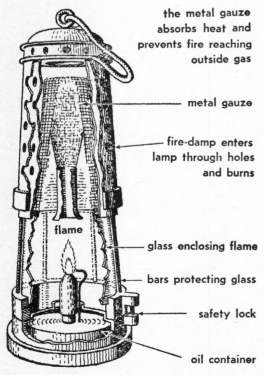

the metal gauze absorbs heat and prevents fire reaching outside gas

metal gauze

fire-damp enters lamp through holes and burns

flame

glass enclosing flame

bars protecting glass

safety lock

oil container

Davy safety-lamp.

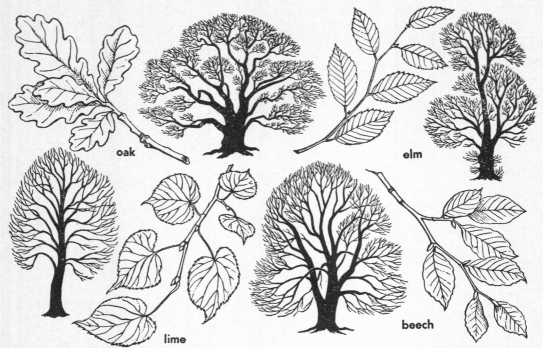

In autumn deciduous trees shed their leaves and remain leafless until the spring.

DEAD SEA, a lake between Israel and Jordan. It is thirteen hundred feet below sea-level, and is so salt that no life exists in it.

DEAD SEA SCROLLS. Papyrus and leather parchments discovered in caves near the Dead Sea between 1947 and 1951 and containing all the books of the Old Testament of the Bible except the Book of Esther. The documents, which date from approximately A.D. 130, are the oldest surviving manuscripts of the Bible, and represent one of the most exciting archaeological discoveries of modern times.

DEBUSSY, Claude (1862–1918). French composer, and creator of musical "Impressionism" through his highly original harmonic style and tonal effects. He was thus a major influence on the development of 20th-century music.

DECIDUOUS TREES are trees which shed their leaves in autumn, like the oak, beech, elm. The larch is the only CONIFER which is deciduous. See EVERGREEN.

DECIMALS. Because men had ten fingers they first counted in tens, 10, 20, 30, 40, and so on, and later they learned to write 10, 100, 1,000 and so on. It is sometimes convenient to count the other way, too, in multiples of ten, that is, 100, 10, 1, ·1, ·01, ·001. ·1 is $\frac{1}{10}$, ·01 is $\frac{1}{100}$, ·001 is $\frac{1}{1,000}$.

$$·25 \text{ is } \frac{25}{100} = \frac{1}{4}.$$
$$·50 \text{ is } \frac{50}{100} = \frac{1}{2}.$$
$$·75 \text{ is } \frac{75}{100} = \frac{3}{4}.$$

$\frac{1}{4}$, $\frac{1}{2}$, $\frac{3}{4}$, etc., are called vulgar fractions. ·25, ·5, ·75, etc., are decimal fractions.

DEEP-SEA EXPLORATION. Many ships have helped to map out the floor of the ocean. SOUNDINGS have been taken and from these we know of shallow banks, and great deeps nearly seven miles down. This information is valuable, but much more romantic is the underwater exploration by deep-sea divers.

Sometimes these men go down in an ordinary diving suit, sometimes they wear special suits which look rather like steel armour. Some of the treasures of the sea for which they search are coral, sponges,

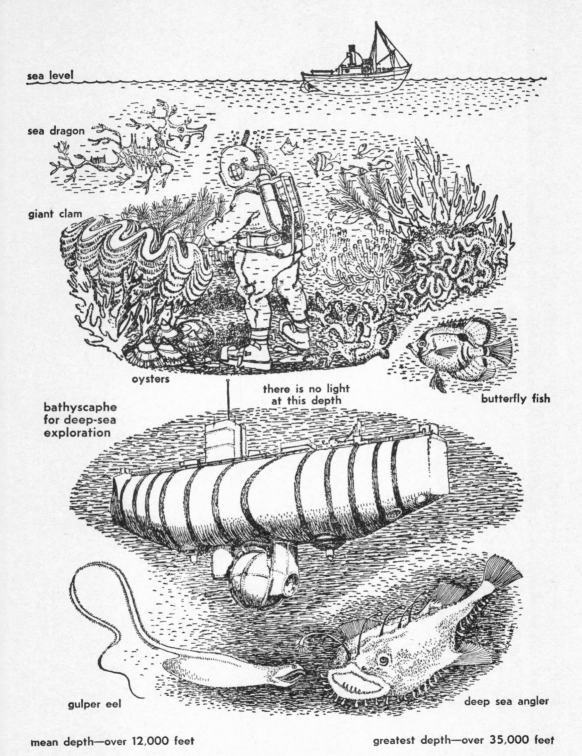

sea level

sea dragon

giant clam

oysters

butterfly fish

there is no light
at this depth

bathyscaphe
for deep-sea
exploration

gulper eel

deep sea angler

mean depth—over 12,000 feet

greatest depth—over 35,000 feet

Deep-sea exploration can be carried out by divers or in specially-built vessels.

Red Deer of the Highlands.

and pearl oysters. The Great Barrier Reef of Australia is a famous hunting-ground. Although the tropical seas are warm and colourful, they are also dangerous, and divers run the risk of being attacked by sharks, or trapped by the Giant Clam.

The greater depths of the ocean have been explored by men who go down in specially-built machines. Dr. William Beebe, an American scientist, was the first to use the BATHYSPHERE. A new machine was brought into use in 1953 called the BATHYSCAPHE, and with it new records were set up for deep-sea diving. See also DIVING.

DEER, large animals found in most countries but not in Australia and seldom in Africa. Herds of Red Deer are found in the Scottish Highlands and Fallow Deer are sometimes kept half-tame on large English estates. The people in Lapland keep REINDEER as we keep cattle and horses. Males carry branching horns (antlers) but the females do not, except in the reindeer. Both male and female reindeer have antlers. See also ANTELOPE.

DEFOE, Daniel, was born in London in 1660. He was the author of *Robinson Crusoe* (1719), one of the first English novels. A sailor called Alexander Selkirk had lived alone for four years on one of the Juan Fernandez Islands, and Defoe

cast away on a desert island

Crusoe sews a goatskin jacket

Man Friday is saved from the savages

The story of "Robinson Crusoe" was written by Daniel Defoe.

wrote an account of all this in such a way as to try to make you believe that it had actually happened to his hero.

Defoe wrote a great deal and two other books which we still read are his *Colonel Jack* and *Journal of the Plague Year*. Although he mixed a lot of fiction with his facts, he makes you feel that it is all as true as a diary, and we read him to discover what these times were like. He died in 1731.

DEGREE. The circle is divided into 360 degrees. A right-angle has 90 degrees. The earth is a sphere and is divided into degrees for measuring LATITUDE and LONGITUDE. The North Pole is at latitude 90 degrees North. London is about latitude 51½ degrees North. Degrees of longitude are measured East and West from Greenwich, London.

DELTA. In the course of their journey from their source to the sea, great rivers carry down much fine sand or mud. Sometimes this forms an island at the mouth of the river and blocks the exit. This deposit is known as silt and the island it forms is called a delta. The river is forced to branch off into channels to get to the sea. The Nile and the Ganges have large deltas.

DEMOSTHENES, the most famous orator of ancient Greece, was born about 384 B.C. He had a slight stammer, but he overcame this difficulty and made many wonderful speeches. He tried to warn the Greeks that King Philip of Macedon was a dangerous enemy to their freedom, and even after they were at war he continued to attack the King in a series of speeches which have gone down in history as the *Philippics*. Demosthenes took poison in 322 B.C. to avoid capture by his enemies.

DENMARK, a kingdom of northern Europe, between the North Sea and the Baltic. The people who live there are called Danes. Copenhagen is the capital and nearly a million people live there. Although much of the soil is not very

River deposits form a delta.

fertile, there are many good farms from which we get butter, eggs and bacon. A famous naval battle was fought off Jutland in the First World War, between the British and the Germans.

DESERT, a place in which little vegetation, or no vegetation, can grow, either because there is too little rain, as in the Sahara, Kalahari, and Australian Deserts, or because of the intense cold, as in most of Greenland, and the Arctic and Antarctic wastes. CACTUS plants can grow in desert land, because they are adapted to store water. Some of them produce beautiful flowers, but these do not live for long.

DESTROYER. This is a small, light and very fast warship which acts as a scout for the larger ships, and protects them from torpedo attacks. It is also called a torpedo-boat destroyer. See also CONVOY; NAVY.

DEW. The air contains moisture, and the warmer the air is the more moisture it can hold. When the air gets colder at night it cannot hold so much moisture and it falls out as dew, just as the hot air in your bathroom gives up its moisture against the cold window pane. When the sun comes out the air gets warmer and takes up the moisture again as an invisible vapour.

DIAMETER, a straight line drawn from side to side of a CIRCLE through the centre. It divides the circle into two equal parts.

DIAMOND, a precious stone obtained from mines in Africa, Brazil, and other places. It consists of pure carbon, like ordinary soot or charcoal, but in the rare form of a transparent crystal. Diamond is the hardest substance known, so that small diamonds are used for cutting glass and for boring holes in very hard rocks. Diamond dust is also used for cutting larger diamonds into the brilliant shapes required for jewellery.

DIAPHRAGM, a thick sheet of muscle separating the chest from the ABDOMEN. This word is also used to describe a thin metal disk. See DICTATING MACHINE; GRAMOPHONE.

DICKENS, Charles, was born in 1812, and became one of the great English novelists. Some of his stories are very sad in parts but there are always lots of funny things happening as well, and you will have a lot of fun sharing the adventures of Mr. Pickwick in *Pickwick Papers,* or Mr. Micawber in *David Copperfield.*

Charles Dickens.

Other good books include *Nicholas Nickleby, Great Expectations* and *A Tale of Two Cities.* Dickens died in 1870.

DICTATING MACHINE, a machine which is very useful in offices as it records the human voice. You can dictate letters to the machine, and, when the typist is ready to type them, the machine is turned on and reproduces the words. It works in much the same way as a gramophone. Sound waves on a DIAPHRAGM make a needle vibrate on a revolving wax sleeve and cut grooves in it. A needle going over the grooves gives out the same sounds again, and with modern electrical equipment it is easy to amplify the sounds.

DICTIONARY. This is a book that explains the meaning of words. The words are arranged according to the letters of the alphabet, the words beginning with the letter A coming first.

DIGESTION is the preparation of food so that it can be absorbed into the body. It is chiefly a chemical process. Saliva from the salivary GLANDS in the mouth, gastric juices from the walls of the STOMACH, the BILE from the liver, and other juices all help to make the necessary chemical changes as the food goes down through the stomach and INTESTINES. The nourishment is then absorbed by the body and the waste products passed out.

DIGIT. Any of the figures 0, 1, 2, 3, 4, 5, 6, 7, 8, 9, is called a digit. The word means "a finger," and as people first counted on their fingers the word came to be used for these numbers.

DILEMMA. We speak of being "in a dilemma," or "on the horns of a dilemma," when we have to decide between two courses of action, neither of which we like. If, for example, the engine of an aeroplane stopped and the pilot had to decide whether to land among the tree-tops or in the sea, he would be in a dilemma.

DINOSAUR, the name of a group of REPTILES which lived millions of years ago, before there were any men in the world, or monkeys or elephants, or sheep or lions. We find skeletons of the dinosaurs preserved in the rocks (see FOSSILS). Some are a few feet long, but others are nearly one hundred feet long. Most of them lived on vegetation, but a few were flesh-eaters, as lions and tigers are nowadays. See also BRONTOSAURUS.

DISLOCATION. If the bones of a joint get out of their proper positions they (or the joint itself) are said to be dislocated. Dislocation usually locks the joint, and some force has to be used to get the bones back into place. This should never be attempted except by a doctor.

been separated from the water. There are other ways of distilling, but this is the simplest method. See also BOILING POINT.

DIVING. Men go down under water to recover valuables from ships which have sunk, to examine the foundations of bridges and so on. Sometimes they go down in a diving bell, sometimes in a diving suit. They cannot go down very deep, of course, for the pressure of water would kill them, but with special care some divers can go down two hundred feet for a short time. See also DEEP-SEA EXPLORATION.

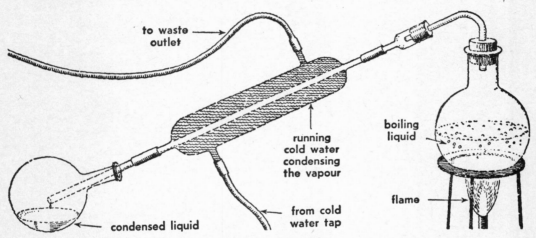

to waste outlet

running cold water condensing the vapour

boiling liquid

from cold water tap

flame

condensed liquid

Simple apparatus used for the distillation of liquids.

DISTILLATION is a way in which liquids are separated by boiling. They have to be turned into vapour and then changed back into liquid. Wine is made from grapes, and contains both alcohol and water. If wine were carefully heated in a kettle the vapour to come off first would be chiefly alcohol vapour, because alcohol boils at a lower temperature than water.

The diagram shows the kind of apparatus a chemist uses. A long glass tube is fixed to the neck of a boiling-jar and slopes downwards to lead into another glass jar. The vapour which comes off passes into the tube (which is cooled by water) and turns to liquid again to flow into the second jar. In this way the alcohol has

DIVISION. We can divide twelve things into two lots of six each, or three lots of four each, or four lots of three each, or six lots of two each. If we divide 12 by 6 we get 2; if we divide 12 by 3 we get 4, and so on. If we write it down as a sum in ARITHMETIC we usually do it like this:

$$\frac{12}{6} = 2; \quad \frac{12}{3} = 4.$$

But for large numbers we use a division sign, for example, $540 \div 270 = 2$ or $9{,}000 \div 5 = 1{,}800$.

DOCKS, places where ships can rest for a time, while cargoes are loaded or unloaded. Cargo docks have CRANES to lift the cargo and warehouses in which to store it. If ships need repair or repainting

Dogs make devoted pets, but some of them are trained to do different kinds of work as well.

dachshund · poodle · terrier · cocker spaniel · Welsh collie

they go into DRY DOCKS. These have gates which can be closed, and the water can be pumped out. A very big ship may go into a FLOATING DOCK, which is built with hollow walls so that it can be filled with water to make it sink far enough to let a ship float into it, and then emptied in order to rise and lift the ship out of the water.

DODO, a bird, about the size of a swan, which became extinct about 1681. People sometimes say "as dead as the dodo."

DOG. Dogs are kept as pets, and to guard homes or sheep or cattle against thieves or wolves. St. Bernard and New-foundland dogs will attack wolves; BLOODHOUNDS and ALSATIANS can track criminals; GREYHOUNDS can catch hares or rabbits; TERRIERS can kill rats; and sheep-dogs and collies collect the sheep for the shepherds.

Greek, B.C. · English, about 1700 · Victorian, about 1860 · German, late 18th century · Bohemian, 19th century · French, early 18th century

For thousands of years dolls have been

DOGGER BANK, a great sandbank in the North Sea. It is only fifty feet below the surface in places, and as the sunlight gets through the shallow water the sea plants grow very well. These provide food for the small sea creatures, and the large FISH, like cod, come to feed on these. It is a good fishing-ground for trawlers.

DOLLS, toy figures made to resemble human beings, usually babies. Children of all countries have played with dolls for many thousands of years. The oldest dolls known were played with by Egyptian children four thousand years ago.

DOVER, STRAIT OF, the narrow channel between England and France. There are white CHALK cliffs on each side because the Wealden uplift stretched across the Channel to France.

DOYLE, Sir Arthur Conan, a doctor who became a writer. He invented the famous detective, Sherlock Holmes, and wrote many interesting stories about him. He also wrote historical novels, but these are not as well-known. Conan Doyle was born in 1859 and died in 1930.

Dragonfly and larva.

DRAGONFLY, a large insect with a movable head, large compound eyes, a long body and two pairs of long, finely-veined wings. It catches smaller insects with its long legs while flying, and chews

h" doll   American,   German,   Danish,   Japanese,   Chinese,   Victorian paper   Italian,
century   1820   1810   1800   modern   modern   doll   modern

'baby' doll, modern

favourite toys. Sometimes they are dressed in the fashion of the day.

them with powerful jaws. The dragonfly LARVA lives in stagnant ponds, where it preys on other small water-animals.

DRAKE, Sir Francis, born about 1540, was one of the great English admirals in the reign of ELIZABETH I. He sailed round the world in just under three years—from 1577 to 1580—"singed Philip of Spain's beard" by burning some of his ships in Cadiz harbour, and helped to defeat the ARMADA in 1588. When the Spanish galleons were sighted in the English Channel Drake was playing bowls on Plymouth Hoe. The English fleet put the Spaniards to flight; Drake, in the *Revenge*, led the chase. This great victory made England, for a time, supreme on the sea. Drake died on board his ship, during a voyage to the West Indies, in 1596.

DRAMA is the telling of a story on a stage, in action and in speech. Since the time of Ancient Greece we have had PLAYS of one kind or another. The Greeks did not act as we do today, but told their story in long speeches, with a chorus to explain or comment.

People have tried to teach religion and good citizenship by means of plays. There are also amusing little plays to make us laugh and keep us happy.

SHAKESPEARE is the greatest man of the theatre. He died in 1616, but his plays are still popular today. See also THEATRE.

DRAWBRIDGE. When CASTLES were protected by a moat or ditch, the bridge across could sometimes be pulled up by chains inside the castle. This bridge was called a drawbridge.

DRAWING. There are two kinds of drawings: those which are made for men who have to build things—plans of ships, engines, bridges, houses, and so on, and those which are made by artists to delight the eye. The first must be an exact record of all the measurements of the thing planned. The second is less restricted and more imaginative: the scene or person that the artist draws is transformed into a delightful pattern quite different from a photograph. Sometimes it is like an improvement on the reality!

DREAMS. The meaning of dreams was discovered by Sigmund FREUD, a Viennese scientist who is now world-famous. Dreams usually represent wishes which we do not like to express. Thus, a boy who is not good at games may dream he is a brilliant footballer. A girl may dream that a fairy prince came and took her away to the ball, like Cinderella.

DREDGING. Rivers bring down mud, and this may settle in places and block the channel for ships. Special ships, called dredgers, dig out this mud and it is taken away in barges. The mud is either pumped up through pipes, or a chain of buckets is let down from the ship to

Special ships are used for dredging.

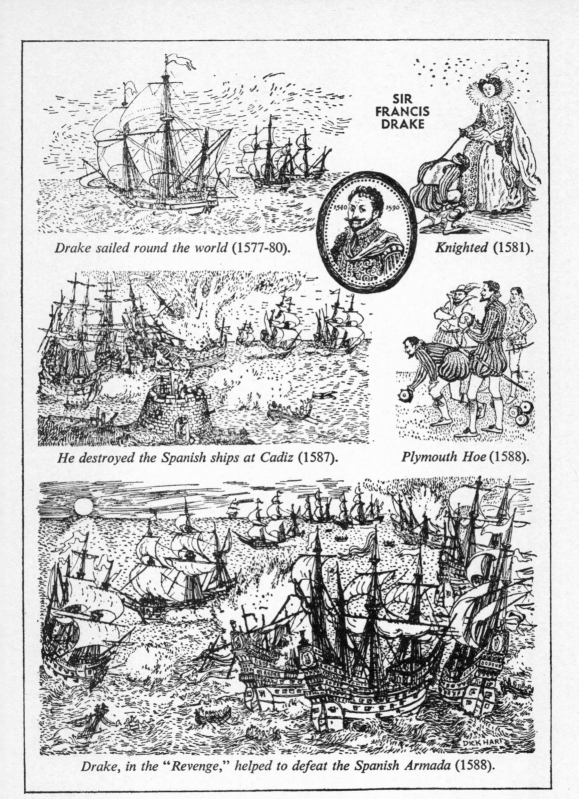

SIR
FRANCIS
DRAKE

Drake sailed round the world (1577-80).

1540 1596

Knighted (1581).

He destroyed the Spanish ships at Cadiz (1587).

Plymouth Hoe (1588).

DICK HART

Drake, in the "Revenge," helped to defeat the Spanish Armada (1588).

scoop it up, as shown in the picture on page 82. The entrances to harbours often have to be cleared of sand swept in by the waves.

DRILL, a tool for boring holes in wood, metal, rock, and so on. Different kinds of drill are required for each substance. The drill may be rotated by air pressure, or by an electric motor. Sometimes air pressure is used to hammer a hole, as we see men doing who break up the road to mend gas-pipes or drains. See also COMPRESSED AIR.

DROMEDARY, a special breed of the Arabian or one-humped CAMEL. It is used for speed, rather than for carrying heavy loads. It can carry a man sixty or eighty miles a day across the desert.

DRUIDS were the priests who had a great influence over the Britons at the time Julius CAESAR invaded the country. Like the priests in Egypt, they had scientific and other knowledge which the common people did not have, and this helped them to keep their power over the people.

DRUM. This is a MUSICAL INSTRUMENT, sometimes shaped like a cylinder, with a stretched skin covering each end; sometimes shaped like a bowl, with a stretched skin covering the open end. The drums used in orchestras can be tuned accurately by means of screws.

DRY CELL. Electricity can be made by putting two different metals, such as zinc and copper, into a jar of weak acid. This is called a wet cell, and it is very inconvenient as it cannot be carried about easily without getting spilt. A dry cell is a similar device in which a thick paste or jelly is used instead of a liquid, and two or more such cells form a dry battery of the kind used in pocket torches. See BATTERY, ELECTRIC.

DUBLIN, the capital of the Republic of IRELAND, and seat of the Irish Parliament (the Dáil). Over 500,000 people live here. Situated on the River Liffey, Dublin is also a busy port.

DUCK. Most birds which spend a lot of their time in the water have webbed feet, so that they can swim easily. Ducks, geese, and swans are like this. They all have broad beaks with saw-like edges so that they can separate insects and other food from water and mud. Many of the wild ducks and wild geese MIGRATE across Britain. See also WATER BIRDS.

DUMAS, Alexandre, the French novelist, was born in 1802. He wrote *The Three Musketeers*, and many other good stories. His name is on over a thousand books, but it is known that he had other people writing for him. He died in 1870. His son was also a famous novelist.

DUNKIRK is a seaport town in the north of France. In the Second World War the British Army in France was forced to fall back on this town, and it looked as if they would all be captured by the Germans. But the weather was fine and the sea calm, and hundreds of little English ships went over and brought most of the soldiers safely home.

DUST, the small particles of matter which are in the air and which settle on the furniture in a room and elsewhere. Volcanoes throw out masses of dust, and this and other kinds of dust circulate in the upper atmosphere and cause the blue sky, the red and golden sunsets, and, to a large extent, the twilight. See LIGHT.

DYEING, the art of colouring dress material, curtains, and so on, so that the colour is not easily faded or washed out. The early Britons got a blue dye from the woad plant, the Mexican people made lovely scarlet and crimson colours from the cochineal insects. In 1856 an English chemist called Perkin discovered how to make beautiful colours from coal TAR, and most dyes are now obtained in this way.

DYKE, a ditch which directs the flow of a river, or an embankment built to prevent the flooding of land, as in the NETHERLANDS. In Scotland, a dyke is a rough stone wall built as a boundary between fields.

E

EAGLE, a large bird of prey which flies very high and swoops down on birds or animals it wants to kill for food. The golden eagle is probably the best known, but is now rare in the British Isles. Some still nest in Scotland. It is a noble-looking and courageous bird, and for this reason it has often been used as a war standard or as a symbol. Julius Caesar's army had a golden eagle on their standard. An eagle was also chosen to represent the German Empire and the American nation.

EARTH, the planet on which we live. It travels round the sun, taking about 365

Golden Eagle.

days to go round (a year). It is also turning on its own axis and takes twenty-four hours to do this (a day). The earth is like a spinning top leaning over at $23\frac{1}{2}$ degrees. When the North Pole is leaning towards the sun, as it is during the British summer, the land and sea between the North Pole and latitude $66\frac{1}{2}$ degrees can get sunshine for twenty-four hours on some days. See also ERATOSTHENES; EROSION.

EARTHENWARE. See POTTERY.

EARTHQUAKE, a movement of the surface of the earth. It may be so slight that we hardly notice it, or so great as to shake a city to pieces or flood the land with an ocean wave. When we realize that great ridges of mountains like the Rockies and the Andes were thrown up by movements of the earth's crust it is not surprising that there are occasional ripples on the surface, due to the many changes that are always taking place. These are brought about by cooling, transfer of silt by rivers, mountains crumbling away, internal explosions, and so on.

EARTHWORM. This is the worm we see in the garden. It has no eyes or teeth. It swallows soil, takes the nourishment out of it, and leaves it behind as worm-casts. See also WORM.

EAST. If you face north, the direction on your right hand will be east. The sun rises in the east and sets in the west.

EASTER. Good Friday is kept as a holy day in memory of the crucifixion of Jesus. Easter Sunday is kept as a holy day in memory of His resurrection.

EAST INDIES, the name formerly given to the whole group of islands stretching from Malaya to Borneo. Excepting parts of Timor and New Guinea, these islands

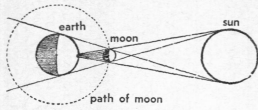

Eclipse of the sun.

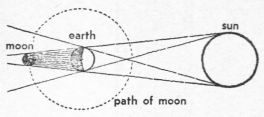

Eclipse of the moon.

were formerly Dutch colonies, which were formed into the independent republic of INDONESIA in 1950. Sabah (N. Borneo) became part of Malaysia; rubber, timber, and copra are exported from Borneo, and from Sarawak we get rubber and oil. The south-eastern part of New Guinea, Papua, is controlled by Australia. New Guinea will be self-governing by 1976.

EBONY is a very hard wood, sometimes jet black, found in Sri Lanka and other tropical regions. Many beautiful carvings are made from ebony. It is also used to make the black piano keys.

ECHO. Sounds are reflected from hard surfaces in the same way as light is reflected from a mirror, or as a ball bounces back from a wall. Sound takes only about five seconds to travel a mile, so if we shout loudly and there is something solid like the wall of a cave some way off to reflect the sound back to us, we can hear the sound repeated. This repetition is called an echo.

ECLIPSE. The earth goes round the sun, and the moon goes round the earth. Sometimes the moon comes between the sun and the earth and then we cannot see the sun, and the earth becomes dark and cold for a short time. This is called an eclipse of the sun. Sometimes the earth comes between the sun and the moon, and then the moon gets no sunlight, so we cannot see it for a time. This is called an eclipse of the moon. Usually it is only part of the sun or moon which is eclipsed.

EDINBURGH, the capital of Scotland, is a beautiful city near the Firth of Forth. Many of Scotland's historic treasures are kept in the famous castle, a mighty stronghold standing on Castle Hill. When Scotland had kings of its own, they lived in the Palace of Holyroodhouse in Edinburgh. It was originally an abbey.

EDISON, Thomas Alva, born in 1847, was a famous American inventor. He began work as a poor boy with little education, but he invented one of the first electric lights, an electric railway, and the phonograph. He also helped to improve the telegraph system and the telephone. He died in 1931.

EDWARD THE CONFESSOR was the son of Ethelred the Unready and Emma of Normandy. He became King of England in 1042 on the death of Hardicanute, second son of CANUTE. He was

Thomas Alva Edison.

called the Confessor because he was very religious. The foundations of WESTMINSTER ABBEY were laid during his reign but the building had not been finished when he died in 1066.

EDWARD I was one of England's greatest kings, and he reigned from 1272 to 1307. During his reign Wales first became united with England, and his son Edward was the first son of an English king to become Prince of Wales. The King hoped to unite Scotland and England but was unsuccessful. (See BRUCE.) Edward I made the rules for the first really good parliament (the Model Parliament, 1295) and got all the laws put into proper order. His tomb is in WESTMINSTER ABBEY.

EDWARD II, King of England from 1307 to 1327, was the son of EDWARD I. Before he became King he was the Prince of Wales—the first son of an English king to hold this title. He was a weak and worthless king, more fond of pleasure than of ruling his country. After the death of Edward I, the Scots, led by Robert BRUCE, recaptured the castles held by the English and defeated the army of Edward II at the battle of Bannockburn in 1314. In 1326 Edward was made a prisoner by his wife Isabella, and was forced to give up the throne in favour of his son in 1327. He was murdered in Berkeley Castle later the same year.

EDWARD III was made King of England before the death of his father, EDWARD II, and ruled wisely and well from 1327 to 1377. There was hostility between France and England for several reasons, one of which was Edward's claim to the French throne. This resulted in a war which went on for over a hundred years, although, of course, there were periods of peace in between. This is known as the HUNDRED YEARS WAR. In 1346 the English won the battle of Crécy and shortly afterwards took CALAIS. England's troubles were added to when the BLACK DEATH swept the country in 1348. In 1356 his son Edward the Black Prince, who had dis-

tinguished himself at Crécy when only sixteen years old, defeated the French at Poitiers. Edward III died in 1377.

EDWARD IV was King of England from 1461 to 1483, and was the first of the "Yorkists," or kings descended from the dukes of York. The followers of Lancaster were his enemies, but he defeated them at Mortimer's Cross, at Barnet, and in other battles. Through the last years of his reign he kept England at peace, ruling without much help from Parliament. An important event of his reign was the setting up of the first English printing-press. See CAXTON; Wars of the ROSES.

The Princes in the Tower.

EDWARD V, son of EDWARD IV, was only twelve years old when he became King on the death of his father in 1483. His uncle Richard, Duke of Gloucester, was his guardian, but instead of protecting the young King he shut him up in the Tower with his brother, and had himself crowned as RICHARD III. It is believed that the two princes were murdered in the Tower shortly afterwards.

EDWARD VI, son of HENRY VIII and Jane Seymour, became King of England in 1547 when he was only nine years old. His uncle, the Duke of Somerset, ruled for him in the early part of his reign, and the Duke of Northumberland in the last part. They were both bad rulers. Edward VI was fond of study and founded several Grammar Schools; the first English Prayer Book appeared in his reign. He died in 1553 at the age of fifteen.

EDWARD VII was the eldest son of Queen VICTORIA, and reigned as King of Great Britain and Ireland from 1901 to 1910. He was called the "Peacemaker" because he prevented a serious quarrel with the German Kaiser, came to a peaceful understanding with the Czar of Russia, and made friends with France. This friendship became known as the *Entente Cordiale*. His wife, Queen Alexandra, was a princess of Denmark, and was very beautiful.

Most animals develop from eggs.

EDWARD VIII, eldest son of GEORGE V, became King of Great Britain and Northern Ireland in 1936. After reigning for less than a year he gave up the throne and his brother, the Duke of York, became GEORGE VI. Edward was given the title of Duke of Windsor. He died in 1972.

EEL, a fish, rather like a snake, found in rivers, lakes and ponds all over the world. When eels are a certain age (five years old or more) they leave the ponds in which they live to travel to the sea. They will even wriggle through the fields to get to the nearest river, down which they make their way to the sea. Then begins an extraordinary journey across the Atlantic Ocean to the Sargasso Sea near Bermuda. There they breed deep down in the ocean, lay their eggs and apparently die. When the young fish (or elvers, as they are called) hatch out they set out for the ponds and rivers again, the European elvers going to Europe, and the American elvers going to America. Nobody knows how these little fish know the way for their two thousand to three thousand miles journey. It takes them two years or more. See also ELECTRIC FISH; METAMORPHOSIS.

EGG. The simpler forms of life, like GERMS, or the AMOEBA, reproduce by dividing into two equal halves. Others produce their young from special cells which we call eggs. Fish reproduce by the splitting of a large number of eggs (fish roe). Pigs, rabbits, cats, and other animals, split off only a few eggs resulting in a litter of young ones; cattle, whales, elephants, and human beings usually split off only one egg at a time which gives rise to one baby.

Birds and crocodiles provide a mass of food for the little cell or egg, and a shell to protect it. This hatches out to a chick, or a little crocodile. FROG eggs hatch out to tadpoles, and these change into frogs later. In sheep, whales, elephants, monkeys and human beings the egg develops inside the mother's body and is born as a little baby like the mother, and fed with milk from the mother's body. See also FERTILIZATION.

EGYPT is a very hot country in north Africa through which flows a great river, the Nile. Much of the water dries up in the dry season, but every year the Blue Nile from ETHIOPIA becomes flooded with melted snow and MONSOON rains, and pours this mass of extra water into the Nile at Khartoum. This makes the Nile overflow its banks and causes it to leave a layer of fertile mud along its banks, in which maize, wheat, cotton, rice and sugar-cane grow easily. In this strip of land along the banks of the Nile lives the population of Egypt. Cairo is the capital and the chief ports are ALEXANDRIA and Port Said. The SUEZ Canal runs from Port Said to Suez and joins the Mediterranean to the Red Sea. The canal is controlled by Egypt.

Because of the surrounding deserts it was difficult for enemies to attack Egypt, and one of the earliest civilizations began here. The people had food, clothing, plenty of mud for bricks and a hot sun to bake them, and so had time to make beautiful ornaments for their kings, and some wonderful monuments which still exist. The PYRAMIDS, for example, were built about 3,000 B.C. See also AFRICA; CLEOPATRA; SPHINX.

EINSTEIN, Albert, a famous scientist, was born in 1879. He made wonderful contributions to mathematics, physics and astronomy. He gave scientists new ideas about time and space, and Einstein's theory is known as the "Theory of Relativity." He died in 1955.

EIRE. See IRELAND, Republic of.

ELBA, a small island between Italy and Corsica. NAPOLEON BONAPARTE was sent to live there in 1814, but he escaped in 1815, gathered the French soldiers around him again, and fought the battle of WATERLOO, in Belgium.

ELECTION. This means the choice of one person to carry out a certain task,

Albert Einstein.

from a number of people who want to do it. For example, members of Parliament are elected by the people, who vote for one person they want to represent them. See POLITICS.

ELECTRIC BELL. See BELL.

ELECTRIC FISH. A South American EEL, and a few other fish, store up enough electricity in their bodies to give anyone who touches them an electric shock.

ELECTRICITY is a power created by millions of millions of ELECTRONS all moving in the same direction. Electricity can be made to flow along a metal wire, and that is the form in which we best know it. We learn about electricity by watching what it does to other things. For example, an electric current flowing along a wire will make a nearby compass needle move. It will also warm the wire along which it is flowing, a fact which we make use of in the electric fire and electric light. If, by accident, we touch a wire with a strong current flowing in it, we will get an electric shock, which may be very dangerous. We can make electricity in a generator, and can control it by turning it on or off at will at any one point, much as we turn the tap on and off over the kitchen sink. See also BELL; CIRCUIT; ELECTRIC LIGHT; ELECTRIC MOTOR; ELECTRO-MAGNET; and page 91.

ELECTRIC LIGHT. When an electric current flows along a wire, that wire gets warmer. If we use a special wire, along which the current can only travel with difficulty, then the struggle of the current to get along the wire makes the wire very hot. If we use wire which gets red-hot, we make an electric fire. If we use wire which gets white-hot, we make an electric light. Next time the electric light is on, notice the white-hot piece of wire inside the bulb. See also CIRCUIT; ELECTRICITY; FUSE.

ELECTRIC MOTOR. When an electric current flows along a coil of wire, the coil of wire acts like a magnet and will make a nearby compass needle move. An electric motor has two coils of wire, each coil of wire being wound round an iron core in order to make it act more powerfully.

Iron cores with wire wound round them are called ELECTRO-MAGNETS. One electromagnet is fixed, the other is free to turn round an axle. When the current is switched on, it flows through both coils of wire and makes them both magnets. The fixed one attracts the one free to move, and so starts it spinning round. A clever arrangement makes this spinning go on all the time the current is flowing. The spinning magnet can be used to turn machinery, as in a vacuum-cleaner, washing machine, electric train, hair-dryer, and other things. See also ELECTRICITY.

ELECTRO-MAG-NET. If you wind wire round a strip of steel or iron, such as a poker or a nail, and join the ends of the wire to a torch battery, then the strip of steel or iron becomes a magnet,

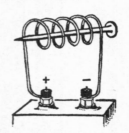
Electro-magnet.

able to attract other pieces of steel or iron to itself. It is best to use a piece of iron, as the iron ceases to be a magnet as soon as the current stops flowing through the wire. If the loops of wire wound round touch each other, then the wire must be insulated, that is covered with rubber or cotton to keep metal from touching metal.

Electro-magnets are used in the electric BELL. They look like tiny reels of cotton, but they are really covered wire wound round an iron core. When a current flows through the wire, the electro-magnet becomes a magnet. Electro-magnets are also used in the ELECTRIC MOTOR.

ELECTRON. Electricity is a power created when millions of millions of electrons all move in the same direction, usually along a metal wire. The electron is thus the smallest particle of this electric power.

Everything in the world, solid, liquid or gas, animal, vegetable or mineral, is made up of tiny pieces called atoms, and each tiny atom has electrons whirling round in it. The number of electrons whirling round in the atom is different for different substances. Thus the atom of lead has a different number of electrons from the atom of gold. See also ATOMIC ENERGY.

ELEMENTS are substances like oxygen, hydrogen, carbon, sulphur, iron or copper, which cannot be divided up (or, as we say, "broken down") into anything simpler than themselves. A substance which is not an element is called a *compound*. Common salt, for example, is a compound and can be broken down into sodium and chlorine. But sodium and chlorine are elements for they are made up of nothing but themselves.

ELEPHANT, the largest MAMMAL except the whale. The African elephant is larger than the Indian elephant and has much bigger ears. It is not easy to tame, but the Indian elephant is trained to carry logs and do other work for man. It is the Indian elephant which is used in processions. The elephant's long trunk has developed from the nose and upper lip and his great tusks have developed from the upper teeth. We get IVORY from the tusks.

ELGAR, Sir Edward, born in 1857, was a great English composer. Some of his best music is difficult to understand, but *The*

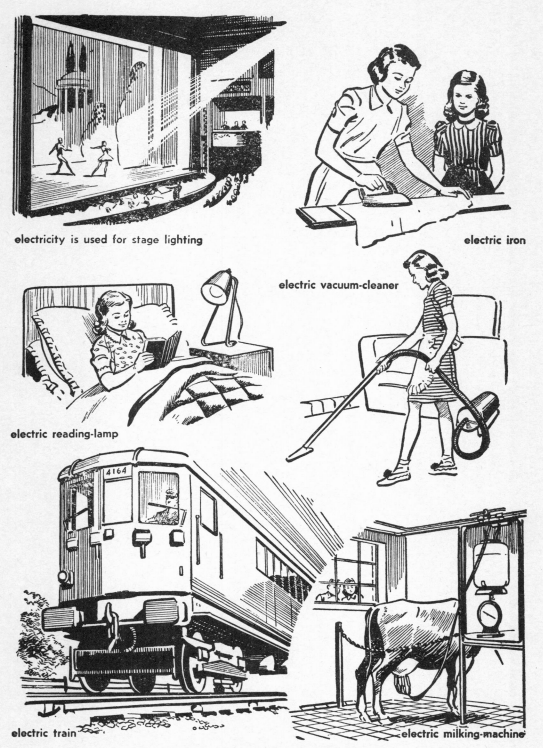

electricity is used for stage lighting

electric iron

electric reading-lamp

electric vacuum-cleaner

4164

electric train

electric milking-machine

Electricity can be used in many different ways.

The reign of Elizabeth I was a time of revival in trade and in learning.

Dream of Gerontius and *The Enigma Variations* are very popular with music lovers; most boys and girls know the tune *Land of Hope and Glory* which is part of Elgar's march *Pomp and Circumstance No. 1*. He died in 1934.

ELIJAH, one of the prophets of ISRAEL. He lived about 850 B.C.

ELIOT, George, the name under which Mary Ann Evans wrote her novels. The best known are *Adam Bede*, *The Mill on the Floss* and *Silas Marner*. The writer was born in 1819 and died in 1880.

ELISHA, the prophet who succeeded ELIJAH. He had been one of his disciples. He lived about 800 B.C.

ELIZABETH I, daughter of HENRY VIII and Anne Boleyn, was Queen of England from 1558 to 1603. This was a wonderful period in English history. DRAKE, Hawkins and RALEIGH were among the famous company of sailors who made England a great sea-power. They sailed all over the world and later defeated the great Spanish ARMADA. William SHAKE-SPEARE was writing his wonderful plays. Spenser, Marlowe and Philip Sidney were writing poetry. With increased trade, greater influence abroad, the revival of learning and other causes, the fame of England spread throughout the world.

MARY, QUEEN OF SCOTS had come to England in 1568, after rebellion by the Scottish nobles had forced her to give up the crown to her son. She was a cousin of Queen Elizabeth and the nearest heir to the English throne. Mary was a Roman Catholic and Queen Elizabeth was the head of the Protestant Church of England. There were many Catholic plots against Elizabeth, and finally Mary was accused of being concerned in a plot against the life of the English Queen. Mary was put to death in 1587, but her only son became King of England when Elizabeth died. He was James VI of Scotland, so the two countries were united under his rule. The two Parliaments were not united until 1707, in the reign of ANNE. See JAMES I.

ELIZABETH II. Elizabeth Alexandra Mary, elder daughter of GEORGE VI, was born in 1926. She married the Duke of Edinburgh, formerly Prince Philip of Greece, in 1947 and succeeded to the British throne on the death of her father in 1952. Her son, Charles, Prince of Wales, was born in 1948 and is heir to the throne; his sister, Princess Anne, was born in 1950. Prince Andrew was born in 1960 and Prince Edward in 1964.

ELLIPSE. Fix two pins on a piece of paper and put a loop of thread or string over them. Put a pencil point inside the loop and draw round with the pencil as shown in the diagram above. The figure

drawn is called an ellipse. The closer the pins are to each other, the nearer the ellipse is to a circle.

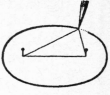

Ellipse.

EMBROIDERY, decoration done with a needle and thread, usually in coloured silk. Coloured borders and little rosettes of flowers are among the simplest subjects for embroidery; other kinds of work include "cut work," in which small pieces are cut out of the material, and complete needlework pictures.

EMIGRATION means leaving one's own country to seek a new life in another. Throughout the last two centuries many people have left the crowded countries of Europe for less populated lands where it seemed they would have a better chance to find work in which they could make a good living. See also IMMIGRATION.

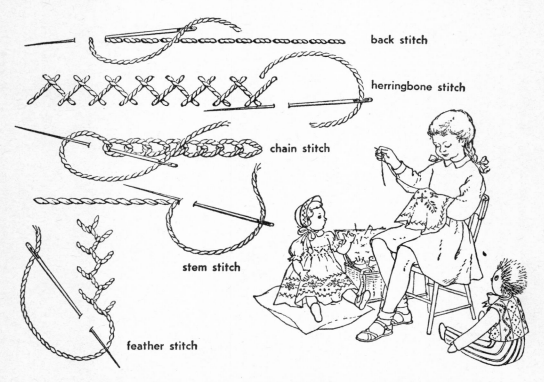

back stitch

herringbone stitch

chain stitch

stem stitch

feather stitch

Simple embroidery stitches make decorative patterns and are easy to do.

93

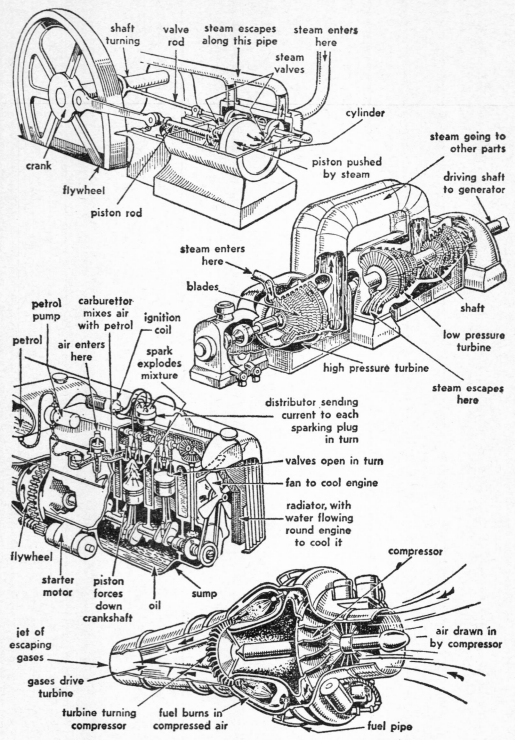

shaft turning

valve rod

steam escapes along this pipe

steam enters here

steam valves

cylinder

crank

flywheel

piston rod

piston pushed by steam

steam going to other parts

driving shaft to generator

steam enters here

blades

shaft

low pressure turbine

high pressure turbine

steam escapes here

petrol pump

carburettor mixes air with petrol

ignition coil

petrol

air enters here

spark explodes mixture

distributor sending current to each sparking plug in turn

valves open in turn

fan to cool engine

radiator, with water flowing round engine to cool it

flywheel

starter motor

piston forces down crankshaft

oil

sump

compressor

air drawn in by compressor

jet of escaping gases

gases drive turbine

turbine turning compressor

fuel burns in compressed air

fuel pipe

Heat provides the power to drive different kinds of engines.

94

EMU, a bird like the OSTRICH. It lives in AUSTRALIA, on the plains.

EMULSION. Oil and water will not mix, but if they are shaken up together very violently the oil breaks up into minute globules which will float about in the water for a long time, giving it a milky appearance. This is called an emulsion.

ENGINE. There are many kinds of engine, but they all do the same thing. They all use heat in such a way that it will make the wheels go round. In a STEAM ENGINE the heat is used to turn water into steam, and the hot steam pushes a PISTON, first forward, then backward; this moving piston can push round a wheel. In a *steam turbine* the hot steam goes through a wheel with a number of blades in it; as it pushes against these blades it turns round the wheel. In a motor-car engine (INTERNAL COMBUSTION ENGINE), the heat is made inside a cylinder; a mixture of air and petrol vapour is exploded and the hot gases from the explosion push down the piston inside the cylinder. The moving piston turns the wheels. In a *gas turbine*, a stream of hot gases goes through a wheel fitted with blades, and by pushing on the blades it turns the wheel. In the JET ENGINE, a stream of hot gases inside the engine can get out at the back, and it comes out as a fierce jet. But it cannot get out at the front, so it pushes the front of the engine away from it and makes it move forward.

ENGINEER, usually a man who works with engines. He may drive a LOCOMOTIVE, or look after the engines of a ship, or the dynamos of a power station. But there are also CIVIL ENGINEERS who build bridges, dig tunnels, and so on.

ENGLAND, the most populated country in the BRITISH ISLES. Over forty-five million people live here. For nearly one thousand years the seas around it have saved England from invasion. NAPOLEON would have invaded the country in 1805, and Hitler in 1940 if they could have got their armies over the sea. Before the country had a good NAVY, however, it was invaded by the Romans, the Angles, Jutes and Saxons, the Danes, and the Normans.

England has a variety of rocks, and this gives it different kinds of scenery. The Cotswold Hills are part of a ridge of limestone, the Chiltern Hills are part of a ridge of chalk.

In many places the layer of coal comes near the surface, where it is easily mined. Coal and the STEAM ENGINE have helped greatly in the development of the country. Cotton, woollen and iron goods of all kinds are made and exported. Great ships are built for many nations. Millions of motor-cars, motor-cycles and ordinary bicycles are sent abroad every year. In exchange for these and other goods other countries send wheat, wool, meat, dairy produce, fruit and so on, which the people in England want. See also COMMERCE. See colour map facing page 33.

ENGLISH CHANNEL, the narrow sea which separates England from France. Fast steamers travel between Dover and Calais, and between Folkestone and Boulogne.

ENGRAVING. An engraving is a copy of a picture made first by scratching or cutting the design into a metal plate with a sharp tool. To print a copy of the picture you must ink the plate. When next you wipe it clean some of the ink stays in the grooves and scratches of the picture. The whole plate is then pressed against a sheet of paper which gets the imprint of this engraved picture. See also ETCHING; WOOD-ENGRAVING.

ENTOMOLOGY is the study of insects.

ENVIRONMENT is another word for the surroundings, or the conditions, in which plants and animals live. Living things are adapted to their environment. Whales and seals have great layers of fat to keep them warm in the cold seas; ducks and swans have webbed feet for swimming in the water, and oil on their feathers so that the water runs off them; giraffes have long necks so that they can reach the leaves on the tall trees, and so on. Plants are adapted to their environment in similar ways; the CACTUS, for example, is adapted to desert conditions. See also EVOLUTION.

EPIC, a poem reciting the adventures of a great hero and his followers—one who belongs to the distant past and whose life was bound up with the fate of a nation. Thus for Britain King Arthur was such a hero, and Tennyson's *Idylls of the King* is such a poem.

EPIGLOTTIS. There are two passages down the throat, one for air and one for food. The one for food is behind the other, and the epiglottis is a lid which covers the top of the air-passage when food or liquid is being swallowed. If someone makes you laugh while you are swallowing, the epiglottis is pushed up and some crumbs or drops of liquid go down the windpipe, and then you start coughing violently to get them out.

EPSTEIN, Sir Jacob, a famous sculptor, lived from 1880 to 1959. His portrait busts are greatly admired, but some people do not understand or like his more symbolical work. Just as a child will draw someone with a big ear to mean he is listening, or will draw someone with a very long arm, to mean he can easily catch you, so some artists make pictures or statues to represent Strength, or Sorrow, or Motherhood, and so on, and in these works the proportions are not true to everyday life. Some of Epstein's work has been the subject of much argument between those who understand symbolical art and those who do not.

EQUATION. In mathematics an equation is a statement that two things are equal. In arithmetic, for example, $1 + 2 + 6 = 3 \times 3$, and $1 + 3 + 5 + 7 = 4 \times 4$. In algebra symbols are used, for example $(x + y) \times (x - y) = (x \times x) - (y \times y)$. If x is 3, and y is 2, work out this sum and prove that this is true. It is true whatever numbers you give to x and y.

EQUATOR. We imagine lines drawn on the surface of the earth so that we can say where places are. The one drawn round the middle, and dividing the earth into a northern hemisphere and southern hemisphere, is called the equator. It goes through the middle of Africa, the north of South America, and the East Indies.

EQUINOX. On 21 March and 23 September the earth is in the positions shown in the diagram below.

You can see that in June the north gets more sun than the south, while in December the south gets more sun than the north. On 21 March and 23 September, however, all places on the earth get twelve hours in the sun and twelve hours in the dark. These times are called the equinoxes. The word means "equal night."

ERATOSTHENES, a Greek astronomer who was born about 276 B.C. and lived until about 196 B.C. He calculated the size of the EARTH. He knew that at Aswan, a town on the Nile, the sun was directly overhead on a certain day, and he found the angle of the sun on the same day at Alexandria, 450 miles north of Aswan. The angle was $6\frac{1}{2}$ degrees from the overhead position. Therefore the circumference of the earth is $\dfrac{450 \times 360}{6\frac{1}{2}}$ and this works out to just about 25,000 miles.

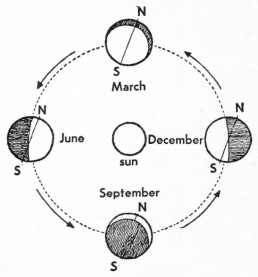

Equinox means "equal night."

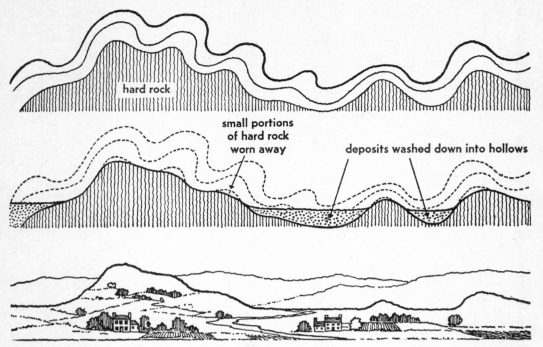

hard rock

small portions
of hard rock
worn away

deposits washed down into hollows

Erosion is a weathering process which wears down the earth's surface.

EROSION. The earth's crust is gradually being worn away by rain, rivers, the sea, the wind and frost. In a million years all the Alps will be washed away into the sea, and more land will be lifted up somewhere. Scotland, for instance, was washed down to a plain, then the plain was lifted up, then rivers cut a great many valleys, and now only a number of peaks all about four thousand feet high remain to show where the plain once was. The rift valley in the middle was a piece of Scotland that sank down.

ESKIMOS are people who live mainly in Greenland, northern CANADA and ALASKA. Many of them live in tents in the summer, and build snow HOUSES when making journeys in the winter. They are expert at catching fish and seals, and they can enjoy very big meals of raw meat and fat. They have Eskimo dogs to pull their sledges, and little canoes which they paddle in the icy waters.

ESPIONAGE is getting information about another country by secret methods. Every country has its own spy service and counter-spy service. In wartime spies are shot.

ESSAY, a short piece of writing explaining some topic from a personal point of view, or giving information about something. Thus R. L. Stevenson wrote papers, or essays, about *Walking Tours* and *Books which have influenced Me,* and other subjects. Charles Lamb, in *The Essays of Elia,* wrote of his personal experiences, and recollections of childhood, and other famous men who wrote essays include Francis Bacon, Joseph Addison, Sir Richard Steele, Matthew Arnold, John Dryden and Alexander Pope.

ETCHING is a certain way of ENGRAVING a picture. A metal plate is covered with wax, and lines are drawn on it with a sharp tool; this exposes parts of the metal. The plate is then put into a bath of *acid,* and the acid eats into the exposed metal, leaving grooves. Then the plate is taken out of the bath and the wax protecting the rest of the plate is removed.

The plate is covered with ink and wiped carefully, but some ink remains in the grooves which have been made by the acid. If we put a piece of paper on the plate and put both through rollers, some of the ink is transferred to the paper, and we get a print of the picture.

Sometimes the lines are cut by a hard steel needle, and no acid is used. This type of etching is called *dry-point*.

ETHER. This is the name of an anaesthetic, or drug, which deadens pain. If you go into hospital to have an operation you may have a whiff of chloroform or of ether, which puts you to sleep for a while. When you wake up the operation is over and you know nothing about it!

ETHIOPIA, a country in the northeast of Africa. It has high lands and deep valleys where cotton, coffee, grain, and fruit are grown. Addis Ababa is the capital. The Blue Nile rises in Ethiopia, and it is this river which causes the floods in EGYPT.

ETHNOLOGY is the study of man's origin and development. From the few remains we have of primitive men it seems that men and APES were once even more similar than they are now. Men have developed in one direction, apes in another.

ETNA, a great VOLCANO on the island of Sicily. Although there have been many eruptions and much loss of life, people still live around it, and grow grapes, olives and other fruits on the fertile soil at the foot. It is ten thousand feet high, and the top is always covered with snow.

EUCALYPTUS, an Australian gum tree which grows to a great height. The koala feeds on the leaves, and Eucalyptus oil is made from the gum.

EUCLID, a Greek mathematician who lived about 400 B.C. He gathered together in thirteen volumes much of the mathematical knowledge of the Greeks, and made many original contributions. Boys and girls doing geometry usually begin by studying adaptations of Euclid's work.

EUPHRATES, a river which flows into the Persian Gulf. Mesopotamia means "the land between the rivers," and the rivers are the Euphrates and the Tigris. As there was plenty of water and good soil this area became one of the early centres of civilization. See BABYLON.

EUREKA, a Greek word, meaning "I have found it." See ARCHIMEDES.

EURHYTHMICS, training the body to move to music. Many infants' schools exercise the children in walking, running, and skipping to music of different kinds, and this is elementary eurhythmics. Emile Jacques Dalcroze, of Geneva, developed the work much further.

EUROPE is the second smallest CONTINENT, Australia being the smallest. So much of it is surrounded by the sea that it is like a peninsula from ASIA. The Ural mountains in the east form part of the boundary between the two continents. Other mountain ranges include the Carpathians, the Alps and the Pyrenees. The Alps are the highest and many of the rivers rise there, such as the Rhine, the Rhône and the Po. The Danube and the Volga are the longest rivers.

In the north it is very cold in winter. In the south the countries are on the Mediterranean Sea, and have mild winters with plenty of rain, and hot dry summers. So we get oranges, lemons, grapes and other fruits which store up moisture inside a tough skin so that the seeds will be well supplied with it. In countries far from the sea, like RUSSIA, it is very hot in summer and very cold in winter. In countries like Britain which are near the sea the summers are not very hot and the winters not very cold.

Wheat, maize, oats, barley and other crops are grown in many countries and there are forests of good timber. Europe is rich in mineral wealth, too; oil is obtained in RUMANIA and in Russia, while the largest coalfield is in the Ruhr, an important industrial centre in Germany. Countries in Europe include the BRITISH

shipbuilding in Britain | lace-making in Belgium | good food and wine in France | dairy produce and bacon in Denmark

coal and steel in the Ruhr, Germany | olives in Italy | timber in Sweden | agriculture in the Balkans

windmills and tulips in Holland | oranges in Spain | ski-ing in Switzerland | marble in Greece

The countries of Europe and some of the things found there.

99

The summit of Mount Everest was first reached in 1953.

ISLES, BELGIUM, CZECHOSLOVAKIA, DEN-MARK, FRANCE, GERMANY, HUNGARY, ITALY, NETHERLANDS, NORWAY, PORTUGAL, SPAIN, SWEDEN, SWITZERLAND.

EVAPORATION. If a liquid is heated sufficiently it will change into a gas or into vapour. This is called evaporation. Boiling is the quickest way to make a liquid evaporate.

If there is rain on the pavement and the sun comes out, the heat rays soon change the water into vapour. Similarly some of the water in the seas and rivers is always evaporating. The vapour forms clouds, from which we get rain on the land again. See also BOILING POINT; DISTILLATION.

EVE is the wife of ADAM, in the Bible story of the beginning of the world.

EVEREST, Mount, the highest mountain peak in the world. It is over 29,000 feet high and is in the HIMALAYAS, the great mountain mass round the north of India. See also NEPAL.

Although many people had tried to climb to the summit of Everest, no one succeeded until Colonel Hunt led the expedition of 1953. Then Edmund Hillary, a New Zealander, and a Sherpa porter called Tensing, reached the top on 29 May.

Colonel Hunt and Hillary were both knighted.

EVERGREENS. Fir trees, cedar trees, holly bushes and other plants have leaves on them at all seasons of the year, and so are called evergreen. They shed old leaves after the new ones are formed. See also DECIDUOUS TREES.

EVIDENCE. In a court of LAW, all the facts which help the court to find out the truth are called the evidence. They are often disclosed by persons (called witnesses) who have seen or heard something important. Evidence can also take the form of objects, like pieces of clothing, which have been found by detectives. See also BARRISTER; JUDGE; JURY; SOLICITOR.

EVOLUTION is the process which produces gradual changes in the make-up of all living things. Since no two individual plants or animals are exactly alike, there are always some with certain things about them that make them better able to survive than others.

For example, creatures with long legs are likely to live longest because they can run faster than their enemies; their offspring will have long legs, and in time a species may develop with longer legs and greater speed than their parents. If food grows scarce on the ground and a creature has to take to eating leaves from the trees, although that creature may look like an antelope, its descendants, in order to survive, may have to grow long necks, like the giraffe.

DARWIN believed that such changes are caused through every species which survives having had to adapt itself to its surroundings. There is plenty of evidence to support this view. The deer has the same number of bones in its neck as the long-necked giraffe. Ostriches have the remains of wings, showing that they once could fly; whales the remains of legs showing that they once lived on land and have taken to the sea. It seems as though all living plants and animals began as very simple forms and changed through multitudes of years to meet the needs of changes in the world around them. See also ENVIRONMENT.

EXPANSION. Most solids, liquids and gases take up more space when heated. Gases expand more than liquids and liquids expand more than solids. Railway engineers allow a little space between the lengths of rail. Then when the metal gets hot in the sun the rails have room to expand a little. If there were no space the rails would bend and the train would come off the line.

EXPERIMENT. Scientists are always making experiments to see what happens in certain conditions. Boys and girls learning CHEMISTRY and other sciences have to repeat experiments to help them to understand the science. It is much more interesting and instructive to do the experiments oneself than simply to read about them or to watch someone else do them.

A witness about to give evidence in a court of law swears to tell the whole truth.

Marco Polo was received by the Great Khan: 1275

Columbus sighted the West Indies: 1492

Vasco da Gama sailed to India: 1497

Captain Cook landed at Botany Bay: 1770

Peary hoisted the American flag at the North Pole: 1909

Amundsen reached the South Pole, December 1911

Scott arrived at the South Pole a month after Amundsen

Exploration of the unknown is a story of danger and of achievement.

EXPLORATION. Many people have an overpowering desire to explore unknown places, and will even risk their lives for this interest. In 1271 MARCO POLO left Venice and travelled through Persia, Afghanistan and northern Tibet, to China. In 1519 MAGELLAN sailed from Spain across the Atlantic, round South America into the Magellan Straits, then into the Pacific Ocean and on to the Philippines, where he was killed. His crew went on to India, then round the Cape of Good Hope and home. This was the first ship to sail round the world. You will see the names of other famous explorers on the opposite page. See also COLUMBUS; DRAKE; POLAR EXPLORATION.

EXPLOSIVES are substances which, when they are heated as by the friction of a knock, will change instantly from small grains of solid to large volumes of gas. The small grains of solid occupy very little space while the hot gases into which they suddenly change need a great deal of space. The gases making room for themselves *is* the explosion: everything in the way gets blown up with a bang. See also EXPANSION.

Explosives are set off by "detonators"; these contain chemicals with mercury or lead in them. The slightest shock will make the detonators go off, and this in turn causes the main explosion.

The first known explosive was gunpowder. Guy Fawkes tried to blow up Parliament with gunpowder (see GUNPOWDER PLOT), and it is also used in fireworks.

Different kinds of explosives are used for different tasks, such as BLASTING rocks, or in coal-mines, or in warfare for propelling shells or bullets from guns.

EXPORTS AND IMPORTS. This is the description given to an exchange of goods between various countries. In Britain, for example, the amount of food grown is not enough to feed all the people who live there (there are about fifty-five million), so meat, grain, dairy produce, and other food is brought in from other countries. In exchange, goods such as ships, motor-cars, tools, materials made from wool or cotton, and so on, are sent out from Britain.

Goods brought into our country are called *imports*; we buy them. Goods sent out of our country are called *exports*; we sell them. See also COMMERCE.

EYE, the organ of the body by which we see. It is, in many ways, like a camera. It has a *lens*, through which come light rays from the object we are looking at. The lens bends these light rays so that they fall on to the *retina*, which is the back part of the eye. On the retina, there is an upside-down image of what we are looking at. A nerve goes from the retina to the brain, carrying a description of what is on the retina, and the brain thereby understands what is in front of the eye, making you see things the right way up.

In order to protect the retina from too much light, there are special muscles which control an opening, called the *pupil*, over the lens of the eye. Thus the pupil closes slightly in bright light, but opens wider in poor light.

Fish, birds and rabbits have an eye on each side of the head, and so have very wide vision. Cats, dogs, monkeys and human beings have eyes which are connected up together and work together. This arrangement enables them to judge distances accurately. The two eyes linked in this way form a range finder.

See also NERVOUS SYSTEM.

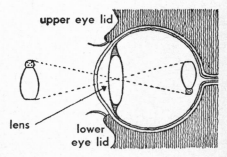

The eye works like a camera.

F

FABLE, a short story about animals, which really teaches a lesson to man. The animals in this kind of story speak and behave like human beings. AESOP, a Greek slave, told many delightful fables, for example, *The Fox and the Grapes, The Hare and the Tortoise, The Dog and the Bone.*

FACTOR. 2 × 2 = 4. We say that 2 is a factor of 4. 2 is a factor of all even numbers (2, 4, 6, 8, and so on). 3 is a factor of 9, 12, 15, 18, and so on. 4 is a factor of 8, 12, 16, 20, and so on. The figures 2, 3, 4, 5, 6, 10, 12, 15, 20, 30 are all factors of 60.

FAHRENHEIT, Gabriel Daniel, a German scientist who improved the THERMOMETER by using mercury instead of alcohol, and by arranging a new and very convenient scale. Scientists now use the Centigrade thermometer, but for many purposes, such as recording body temperature, the Fahrenheit thermometer is still considered more convenient.

FAIR. In the MIDDLE AGES a fair was a great market, held once or twice a year, where merchants sold their goods to the people who came in from the surrounding countryside. They could also hire labourers to work on the farms and house servants. There were side-shows, too, to entertain people, such as boxing matches, and jugglers, and even actors playing in travelling theatres. Through the centuries, as transport improved and people no longer depended on the annual trading centre, the fair lost its business side and became more important as a pleasure-ground, with roundabouts and swings, and coconut shies.

FALCON, a BIRD OF PREY. The Peregrine falcon is the best-known; others in the

A medieval fair had side-shows.

same family are the buzzards, EAGLES, harriers, HAWKS, and kites.

Falconry, or hawking, used to be a popular sport in the Middle Ages, when the birds were used to strike down other birds such as the partridge or the magpie.

FAMILY, a group of people consisting of father and mother and their children; the word is sometimes used in a wider sense to include all their ancestors as well. A diagram showing whom their ancestors married and what children they had is called a "family tree."

FANGS, two special poison teeth which some SNAKES have. The poison comes from glands in the mouth, down a groove in the tooth, or down the centre of the hollow tooth in some species, into the wound which the tooth has made. The ADDER is the only poisonous snake in Britain. See also COBRA; RATTLESNAKE.

FARADAY, Michael, born in 1791, was a great English scientist. He made many important discoveries both in electrical work and in chemistry. He was also a brilliant lecturer and interested thousands of people in science. He died in 1867.

FARMING. Thousands of years ago men used to get their food by going hunting. If there was nothing to be had they had to go without. Then men learned to use the land on which they lived to grow enough crops to feed themselves.

Farmers today grow crops and breed animals to feed themselves and other people.

Some farmers grow lots of wheat (as in Canada), some have sheep-farms (as in Australia). Farmers also keep cattle to get milk and beef, and pigs to get bacon and pork, and chickens to get eggs.

Work on a farm became much quicker when machinery was invented to help the farmer. See also ROTATION OF CROPS; TRACTOR.

FATHOM. When sailors threw a weight overboard to find out how deep the sea was in which they were sailing, they measured the rope by the full stretch of the arms. This length was called a fathom. Nowadays a fathom is six feet.

FATS are produced by animals and plants as a reserve store of food. The

A modern fair, with roundabouts and switchbacks, is an entertainment-ground.

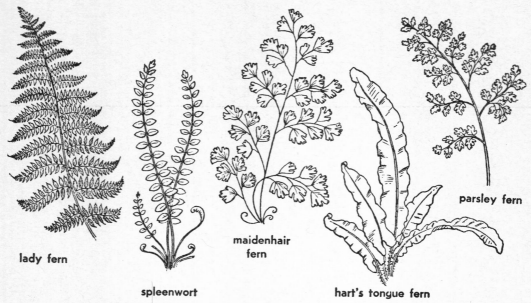

lady fern

spleenwort

maidenhair
fern

hart's tongue fern

parsley fern

Ferns grow in damp, rocky places, in woodland, and in open moors.

body uses food as fuel to produce heat and energy, and when men and animals are well-fed, they put on layers of fat which helps them if food becomes scarce. WHALES, for example, have a layer of fat all round the body. The CAMEL stores his fat in his hump. These are animal fats.

Plants produce vegetable fats such as olive-oil, castor-oil, and palm-oil. This kind of fat is also used to make things like soap and candles.

FEELING. If we put our fingers on a hot place we feel pain, and jerk the hand away. The little nerve cells in the finger-tips send a message along other nerves to the brain, saying this heat will damage the skin. Down comes another message along other nerves to the muscles of the arm telling them to contract at once and pull the hand away. See NERVOUS SYSTEM; SENSES.

FEMUR, the thigh bone. It is joined to the hip by a ball-and-socket joint.

FENCING. Before pistols were invented some people carried light swords, or rapiers, with which to defend themselves against attack. Nowadays fencing is a sport. Protective coverings are worn, and different kinds of swords are used; these are the foil, the epée and the sabre.

FENDER, a metal guard placed round the fire to prevent pieces of hot coal or wood falling out and setting fire to the wooden floor or the carpet.

A ship's fender is a mass of rope hung over the side to soften the bump when the ship touches the landing-stage.

FERMENTATION. The juice of grapes, apples, pears, and other fruit changes, if left in certain conditions, and some ALCOHOL is formed. Thus we get wine from grape juice, and cider from apple juice. This chemical change is brought about by tiny forms of life floating in the air, and is called fermentation.

FERNS are plants which have roots and leaves but no FLOWERS. On the underside of the leaves there are spore-cases containing spores. These spores form little plant structures which produce eggs and sperm, and these unite to make new fern plants. See also REPRODUCTION.

FERRY, a small boat which carries passengers across a river or lake. There are also large boats that take passengers and motor-cars across a short sea-route.

FERTILIZATION, the first step in the life of a new plant or animal. In most plants the pollen grains containing the male cells of a flower fall on to the pistil, or female part, of the same or another flower. There, a pollen grain unites with a female cell, or "ovule," which then develops into a seed. Very often pollen is taken from flower to flower in the fur of an insect's body, such as the BEE. In animals, the male germ-cell, or "sperm," takes the place of the pollen grain, and the female egg, or "ovum," takes the place of the ovule. No ovum can develop into a new animal until it has been fertilized by a sperm. See REPRODUCTION; SEEDS AND FRUITS.

FEUDAL SYSTEM. In most European countries during the MIDDLE AGES, land was owned only by the king. He would grant estates to lords or barons to hold in return for some form of service. Usually they had to provide men to fight for him when necessary. To do this, the barons let some of their land to sub-tenants, who promised to serve the baron faithfully. In their turn, the sub-tenants kept some of the land granted to them, and let the rest to the peasants, or "villeins." Instead of paying rent for this, the peasants worked on the lord's land as well as their own.

FIBRES. There are many useful fibres, such as, COTTON, wool, SILK, FLAX, hemp, the fibre on the coconut shell, and asbestos. Cotton is seed hair, like the hair of the dandelion seed; wool is the FLEECE which keeps the sheep warm; silk is spun by the silkworm, to form a cocoon; flax is the fibrous layer on the stem of the plant; hemp is fibre from another plant; and asbestos is a mineral. We make linen from flax, ropes from hemp, doormats from coconut fibres, and fireproof clothing and theatre curtains from asbestos. We also manufacture artificial fibres very like silk and make clothing from them.

FIBULA. Between the knee and ankle there are two long leg-bones, the fibula and the tibia. The fibula is the thin one.

FICTION is the name given to a story in which the author has invented the people and the events he describes. See also NOVEL.

FIELD-GLASSES, a short double TELESCOPE in which both eyes are used. It need not be so long as a telescope because the rays of light are refracted from PRISMS inside.

FIELD-MOUSE. Sometimes called a "wood-mouse," the long-tailed fieldmouse is slightly larger than a housemouse. It is reddish-brown above and white below, and has a long tail. It lives in woods, fields, hedgerows and gardens, feeding on seeds, nuts and corn. It nests in a burrow, often storing food in the ground.

FILM, a thin sheet of transparent PLASTIC like celluloid, on which a substance which is sensitive to light has been painted. Films are, of course, made in the dark, so that when you take a picture with your camera the light affects the film and the picture will be recorded. It then has to be developed and fixed before it is safe to bring it into the light again. See CINEMATOGRAPH; PHOTOGRAPHY.

FINGAL'S CAVE, a cave on the Island of Staffa in Scotland. A great sheet of lava once spread over Skye, Mull, Staffa and the plateau of Antrim in the north of Ireland. As it cooled it cracked into pillars with six sides. One can walk on the top of these pillars at the Giant's Causeway in Antrim, and the waves have smashed a great cave in the side of the Island of Staffa, where the pillars are seen.

FINGERPRINTS, the impression left by the pads of the fingers and thumb on glasses, cups, and so on, or on paper when ink has been placed on the pads. No two people have the same fingerprints, and they do not change with age, so this is an easy way to identify people. The POLICE take the fingerprints of all criminals, and keep them in a special file for reference, in case they commit fresh crimes after release from prison.

FINLAND, a country between the north of Russia and Sweden. Over four million people live there. Timber, wood-pulp, and paper are the chief exports. The northern part of Finland is called Lapland. For two months of the year the sun never sets in Lapland, but for nine months there is very little sun and the weather is very cold. The Lapps live on their herds of REINDEER, which feed on a special kind of moss which grows there in great quantities.

FINS are used by fish for swimming, balancing the body, and for steering. The fin on the back is called the *dorsal* fin (some fish have two). There are usually two pairs of fins on the underside—the first pair, the *pectoral* fins, are important as balancers—and one single fin. The powerful tail-fin is used for steering, and propelling the fish through the water.

Certain MAMMALS have fins, too. Dolphins and PORPOISES have a single fin in the middle of the back, and so has the Fin-back, or Rorqual, whale. The tail-fin of the whale is not really a fin, but a modified pair of limbs.

FIRE BRIGADE, a body of men trained to put out fires with the use of FIRE-ENGINES, and to rescue people from burning buildings. Their engines and FIRE-ESCAPES are kept at Fire Stations, where there is always somebody on duty. See the colour page facing page 128.

FIRE-ENGINE, a large motor-vehicle carrying ladders and machinery for pumping water to a great height. It is used by the FIRE BRIGADE.

FIRE-ESCAPE, a long ladder mounted on wheels, used to rescue people from the upstairs windows or roof of a house on fire. Some buildings are fitted with an iron staircase outside the walls, by which people may escape in case of fire. This also is called a fire-escape.

FIREFLY, a winged insect of the BEETLE family. Like the GLOW-WORM, it gives out light. In South America and the West Indies there are fireflies which give out enough light for people to read by. Natives sometimes put a few in a bottle to light the room.

FIRE OF LONDON, a great fire which destroyed two-thirds of LONDON in the year 1666.

FIRST AID is the attention given to an injured person while he is waiting for the doctor to arrive to make sure he does not get any worse. If he is badly hurt he should not be moved, but help should be sent for at once. If the patient is suffering from shock he should be kept at rest, and warmly wrapped in blankets. If possible, hot-water bottles should be given, and if he is conscious and can swallow, hot sweet tea may be given him to drink. See also ARTIFICIAL RESPIRATION.

FISH. Even in the coldest areas there is plenty of plant life in the sea, and fish and other sea creatures are found everywhere.

In Britain the HERRING fisheries are very important. Herring swim in shoals near the surface and are caught in drift nets. Cod fisheries are also very important. Cod like shallow banks, such as the Newfoundland banks, or the DOGGER BANK, where plants grow on the bottom of the sea. Haddock are also caught there. Many herring are split and smoked to make kippers, and many haddock are split and smoked to make smoked haddock.

Halibut, turbot, sole, plaice and skate are flat fish which live near the bottom of shallow seas. They are caught by trawl nets. When these fish lie on the bottom they merge with the sand. The eye which should be underneath comes up on top beside the other as the creature grows, but these eyes still work separately, as in the case of cod, herring, birds, and rabbits. They are not like the two eyes of cats, dogs, and human beings, which work together like a range-finder.

SALMON are born and grow up in rivers. They go out to the sea to feed and grow fat, then come up the rivers again to leave their eggs (or spawn).

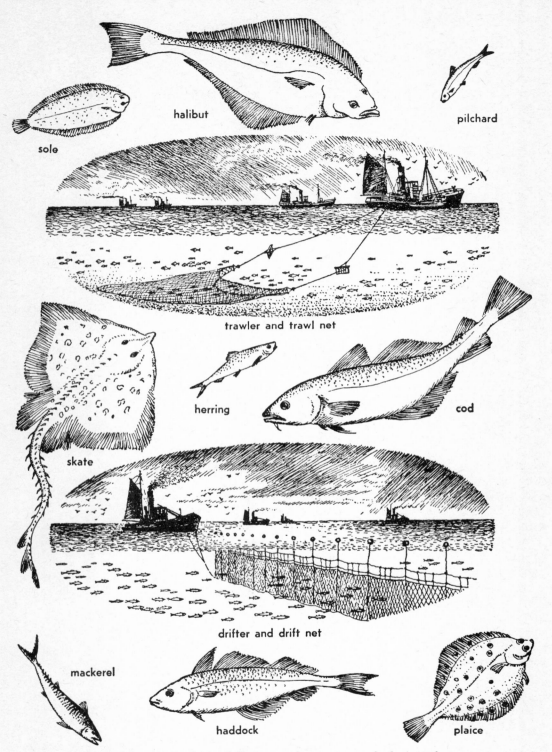

halibut

pilchard

sole

trawler and trawl net

skate

herring

cod

drifter and drift net

mackerel

haddock

plaice

Some fish are caught in drift nets, others are caught by trawl nets.

109

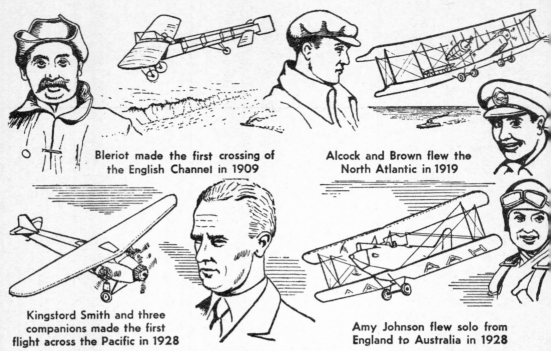

Bleriot made the first crossing of the English Channel in 1909

Alcock and Brown flew the North Atlantic in 1919

Kingstord Smith and three companions made the first flight across the Pacific in 1928

Amy Johnson flew solo from England to Australia in 1928

The first successful flight in an aeroplane was made by Orville Wright in 1903. *Above*

FLAG OF TRUCE, a white flag waved during a battle to signal to the enemy to cease fighting in order to discuss terms of peace. It is the flag of surrender.

FLAGS. Flags are used by armies, chiefly as a symbol. The Romans marched to battle under the Roman Eagle. The Normans had flags when they invaded Britain. All regiments still have flags which they display on occasions, and most ships fly distinctive flags. Countries, too, have their flags. The British flag is the Union Jack. Soon after James VI of Scotland became also JAMES I of England (1603), the red cross of St. George of England and the white cross of St. Andrew of Scotland were combined. This alteration was formally confirmed in the Act of Union in 1707. When IRELAND became part of the United Kingdom, in 1801, the thin red cross of St. Patrick of Ireland was combined with the other two to make the Union Jack.

FLAMINGO, a bird with a very long, supple neck, and legs like stilts; its plumage is rosy-white, black and scarlet. Flamingoes live together in large flocks in marshy districts, in Europe, Asia, Africa and India. There is an American species which is scarlet.

FLAX, the plant from which we get the fibres to make linen, and from the seeds of which we get linseed oil. The fibres come from the outer layer of the stalk of the plant. Linseed oil is used for making paints and varnishes, and the crushed seeds are made into linseed cakes for feeding cattle.

FLEA, a wingless INSECT which lives by sucking the blood of live animals. A flea's body is flattened from side to side, and it has very long legs for jumping. It lays its white, oval eggs among the fur or feathers of its "host," as the animal on which it is living is called. When the eggs presently drop to the ground and hatch, the wriggling, legless grubs hide in the dirt where they feed mainly on small particles of animal refuse. A few species will live on man. See also LARVA.

Lindbergh made a record non-stop flight from New York to Paris in 1927

Bert Hinkler flew solo from England to Australia in 1928

Wiley Post and Gatty made the first round-the-world flight from New York in 1931

Amelia Earhart flew solo from Hawaii to the U.S.A. in 1935

re some of the pioneers whose achievements helped the progress of aeroplane design.

FLEECE, the entire coat of wool covering a sheep. Wool is a kind of soft curly hair, of which each fibre is covered with scales which make the fibres cling together. See also FIBRE.

FLIGHT. Today we take for granted the aeroplanes that can travel faster than sound, and the great airliners that fly all over the world. Yet they were developed in less than fifty years from the time that the first aeroplane was invented.

Many experiments were made before that, however, to enable men to fly. Two brothers, Joseph and Etienne Montgolfier, achieved success in 1782, when they were experimenting with a hot-air BALLOON, but the first passenger flight did not take place till the following year. In 1785 a gas-filled balloon crossed the Straits of Dover, from England to France. Then came the development of the AIRSHIP, with a steam-driven ENGINE. Henri Giffard made the first flight in 1852. The invention of the petrol-driven engine led to improved designs. The first Zeppelin, completed in 1900, was named after the German designer Ferdinand, Count von Zeppelin.

Meanwhile, Otto Lilienthal, after years of experiment, built the first passenger-carrying GLIDER in 1891. Octave Chanute and John Montgomery were responsible for important developments in this field, and the Wright brothers built their most successful glider in 1902. Then they turned to AEROPLANE design, and in 1903 they made the first aeroplane by fitting a motor-car engine to a glider rather like a box-kite. See also AIRPORT; HELICOPTER; JET ENGINE.

FLINT, a hard bluish-grey rock found in lumps, usually in chalk. It breaks easily and the fragments have sharp edges.

FLINT IMPLEMENTS. Half a million years ago men chipped flints to make rough tools. It was not until about 10,000 years ago that they learned how to polish the flints, and to use them to make axes, hammers, spear-heads, arrow-heads, gimlets, fish-hooks, and so on.

The very long first period is called the

Old STONE AGE, and the short second period before men learned to use bronze and iron is called the New Stone Age.

FLOWER, the part of a plant which contains the organs for creating new seeds. The *pistil*, or female part, is formed of the stigma, the style and the ovary. (The ovary is made up of female organs called carpels, and inside each carpel are the egg-cells, or ovules.) The *stamens* are the male parts. Each stamen is made up of a stalk with an anther at its head. Pollen grains are produced inside the anther. A new seed is formed only if the pollen grains unite with the ovule. This is called FERTILIZATION, or pollination.

Some flowers have no carpels, others have no stamens. Most have both. In some flowers the pollen fertilizes its own ovule. In most flowers the pollen of the flower fertilizes the ovule of another similar flower. The pollen is spread by the wind or by insects. The insect may be attracted to a flower by the bright colour of its petals or by its perfume. The base of the flower is called the receptacle, and from it grow the sepals to protect the bud.

FLOWERS. We grow many beautiful flowers in our gardens, and choose them for their lovely colours and their scent. There are many more which grow wild in meadows, in woodland and hedgerows, in mountains and moors, and by ponds and streams. You can see pictures of some of them in the colour page facing page 129.

FLUTE, a wood-wind instrument. The player blows across a hole in the side and near the top and so makes air vibrations which form a musical note. By means of stops, or keys covering the holes, many different notes can be played.

A RECORDER is a kind of flute, but the player blows down the tube from the top. See MUSICAL INSTRUMENTS; ORCHESTRA.

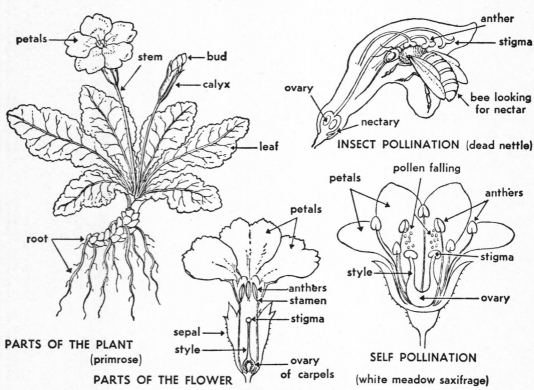

PARTS OF THE PLANT (primrose)

PARTS OF THE FLOWER

INSECT POLLINATION (dead nettle)

SELF POLLINATION (white meadow saxifrage)

Flowers are the parts of a plant that form seeds and so produce new plants.

FLY, an INSECT with transparent wings. The house-fly has hairy feet with suction pads that enable it to walk upside down on a ceiling. These hairs also collect germs from the dirty places that flies visit. They spread disease very easily, so we should keep our food where flies cannot get at it. See also MOSQUITO.

FLYING-FISH, a fish usually about the size of a herring. It has large fins and can fly or glide in the air for a hundred yards or so when trying to escape from other fish, or from dolphins.

FLY-WHEEL, a heavy wheel, usually made of cast-iron, with most of the weight in the rim. It is usually part of an engine, which pushes it round. Once the heavy fly-wheel is set spinning, its heavy rim will go on turning and provide a smooth and even source of power.

FOCUS. When the sun's rays are brought to a point by a convex LENS (or BURNING GLASS), the point is called a focus. Light from objects is focused by the lens in the EYE. For clear vision the focal point should be on the retina at the back of the eye.

FOG. In cold weather one's own breath makes a little fog. The air in the lungs is warm and can hold a good deal of moisture. When the air is breathed out it gets cold and cannot hold so much moisture, and some appears as very small drops of water. When warm winds meet the cold air rising from cold ocean currents, fog is formed. This happens very often near Newfoundland, and ships have to be careful. In the autumn the air gets hot during the day and takes up a good deal of moisture. But the nights become rather cold and then some of the moisture is deposited as minute drops of water which hang about and cause a fog. Then the sun warms up the air again, the water is again absorbed, and the fog disappears.

FOG-SIGNALS. Ships and trains cannot see the warning lights when there is fog, so sound signals are used. Many lighthouses have fog-horns with distinctive

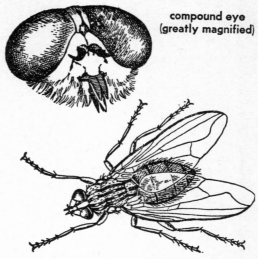

compound eye (greatly magnified)

A fly has only one pair of wings.

notes, and ships sound their sirens when sailing through fog. Nowadays ships are fitted with RADAR to detect danger ahead. On the railways explosives are sometimes put on the line. These go off as the train runs over them and the driver of the train knows whether it is safe to go on. They are rather outdated now because most main lines are equipped with fully-automatic colour-light signalling.

FOLK-LORE. Long before there were any books to read, people in many different countries made up tales about fairies and giants and goblins. They also told stories about all kinds of things that happened where they lived—about a great storm, or a flood, or about strange animals and birds they saw, or about real people. These stories were usually told in verse because verse was much easier to remember; parents repeated them to their children and they became known as the stories of the people, or folk-lore. See also ROBIN HOOD.

FOLK-SONGS. These were made up in the same way that people all over the world used to make up stories which we call FOLK-LORE. Sometimes these songs told a story, and sometimes they were used to help people to do their work. Sailors used to sing sea-shanties because the rhythm of the song helped the crew to keep in time when they were doing a special job all together, like hoisting the sails or hauling in the anchor.

FOOT, the lower part of the leg. There are twenty-six bones in the foot to make it strong and supple.

The foot was used as a measure of length. It is now a definite length, and is divided into twelve inches.

FOOTBALL, a very ancient game, which was played by the people of early times. It has been played in Britain for many centuries. For a long time it was played as an amusement, without many rules, but as the matches became more and more popular, and lots of people came to watch them, rules had to be made.

Referees see that these rules are kept. Three types of football are played in Britain: Rugby Union football, where there are fifteen players on each side, and the ball may be taken up in the hands; Rugby League football, with thirteen players a side; and Association football, where there are eleven players on each side, and the ball must not be touched by the hands, except by the goalkeeper.

Forging a horse-shoe.

FORCEPS, instruments like pincers. Some are made for pulling teeth, some for taking pieces of metal or stone out of wounds, some for picking up the tiny little screws and springs of watches, and so on.

FORECASTLE (pronounced fok'sel). A ship needs a high deck at the bow to keep the waves out. In merchant ships the sailors usually sleep and eat underneath this deck in the forward part of the ship.

FORESTRY, the science which helps us to know how to make the best use of trees. In some places trees would not grow again if they were once cut down. Climates sometimes change. The trees in a forest keep the sun from drying up the soil, and the roots of the trees bind the soil together, so that even if the rainfall has become irregular the trees continue to grow. But young trees, without this protection, would just wither away. Parts of Canada and France have lost their forests in this way, and the soil has become useless. A knowledge of forestry helps us to preserve our forests. The great tropical forest along the west coast of India would not grow again if all the trees were cut down. There are now too many hot months without rain. There must have been more regular rainfall here when the forest began.

FORGING, shaping hot metal by hammering it. One could forge a sword by hand hammering, but for forging the propeller of a big ship a steam hammer would be used.

FORTH BRIDGE, a great railway BRIDGE over the River Forth in Scotland. It is over a mile long, and one hundred and fifty feet above the water. A bridge built in the way the Forth Bridge is built is called a cantilever bridge.

FORTIFICATION. To fortify means to make strong, and a fortification is the name given to a building or structure which is made strong to protect a town or country against enemy attack. In Roman Britain walls were built to keep the Picts out; the Normans built castles with thick walls, moats and drawbridges; the people of Paris built bulwarks, or boulevards, which have now become wide streets encircling the city. Soldiers dig trenches for themselves, and put belts of barbed wire in front of them so that they can shoot the enemy soldiers while they are delayed by the wire. After the First WORLD WAR the French built a chain of forts with guns which were supplied with ammunition from underground stores by hydraulic power. It was called the Maginot Line and was thought to be a strong defence. But it failed to protect the country in the Second WORLD WAR.

FOSSILS, the remains or imprints of plants and animals preserved in the rocks. A piece of vegetation, or a dead animal, may fall to the bottom of a river and be covered up with the mud the river is bringing down. Millions of years later this layer of mud may have become a layer of SLATE. As men split the slate and cut it into convenient sizes for the roofs of houses, for example, they are always coming across the imprints of vegetable or animal life. Sometimes they find a shell-fish in solid stone: as the shell-fish gradually crumbled away, the space was filled in by deposits of calcium, or other salt, from solution, in the same way as STALACTITES and STALAGMITES are formed in a cave.

From the type of fossils found, geologists can tell how old the rocks are. See GEOLOGY.

FOUNDATION. Before designing a house or bridge, the architect or engineer studies the foundation on which it is to be built. If it is solid rock, as in New York, high buildings can be put up with safety. If the foundation is sand, even a one-storey house may not be safe. Sometimes one sees builders driving great piles of wood or concrete down into the earth. These are hammered down so far by a pile-driver that they cannot be removed. Then the builder puts a thick concrete

Casting molten metal in a foundry.

floor on top of the piles and builds the house on that.

FOUNDRY, a place where IRON, steel, and other metals are melted and run into moulds of various shapes to make different articles. See also BLAST FURNACE.

FOUNTAIN, a jet, or jets of water, forced up to a height. A fountain makes a pleasant ornament in a city square, for example, Trafalgar Square, in London. Rome, Paris, and other cities and towns also have beautiful fountains.

FOWL. We sometimes speak of "wild fowl" or "water fowl," meaning wild birds or WATER BIRDS, but "fowl" usually means the ordinary farmyard birds. They were developed from the jungle fowl, found in India and countries near it. POULTRY keepers breed fowls for good egg production and good birds for the dinnertable, just as racehorse owners breed to get horses that can run at greater speeds, and farmers breed cattle from the cows which give the most milk.

FOX, a wild animal with a bushy tail. It belongs to the dog family. It is very cunning and very destructive, sometimes killing all the poultry in a hen-house, although it can only carry away one hen at a time.

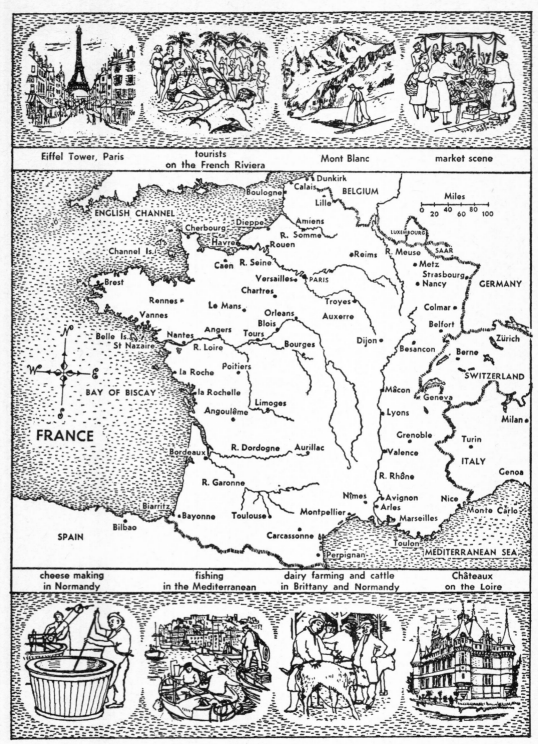

Eiffel Tower, Paris   tourists on the French Riviera   Mont Blanc   market scene

cheese making in Normandy   fishing in the Mediterranean   dairy farming and cattle in Brittany and Normandy   Châteaux on the Loire

France and some of the things which are found there.

FRACTION, a small part of something. For example, if a cake of chocolate is divided into four equal pieces, one can take one piece, two pieces, three pieces or four pieces. One piece would be $\frac{1}{4}$; two pieces would be $\frac{2}{4}$, or $\frac{1}{2}$; three pieces would be $\frac{3}{4}$; and four pieces would be $\frac{4}{4}$, or 1, that is, the whole cake. $\frac{1}{4}$, $\frac{1}{2}$, $\frac{3}{4}$ are known as fractions. Expressed as DECIMAL fractions they would be ·25, ·5, ·75.

FRACTURE means a break, or crack, especially a broken bone in the body.

In grown-ups the bone snaps right across if over-strained. In young children the bones are more flexible, and sometimes a bone is bent and only partly breaks, as a green stick breaks. This is called a *greenstick* fracture. When the broken bone breaks through the skin it is called a *compound* fracture, and care must be taken that no further damage is done to the flesh by the sharp broken ends.

FRANCE is the country nearest to Britain. It is more than twice as large, but has only about fifty million people, or five million more than England alone.

France is a very fertile country. A great deal of wheat is grown, especially in the valley of the River Seine around Paris; but much of the country is ploughed land. On the more rainy western side orchards and grass grow best, and butter and fruit are produced. In the river valleys the vine is grown, usually on the slope facing the sun, and France makes the best and the most wine of any country in the world. Champagne comes from the Marne valley, claret from the valleys of the Garonne and Dordogne, and burgundy from the valley of the Saône.

Where the rivers Seine and Marne meet stands Paris, the capital of France; a beautiful city with nearly three million inhabitants. Where the Garonne and Dordogne meet stands Bordeaux, an important seaport, exporting wine and other goods; where the Saône and Rhône meet stands Lyons, a town which is famous for its silk production.

Marseilles is a very important seaport on the Mediterranean coast. A little farther east is the naval station of Toulon, and east of that again is the beautiful Riviera coast. The manufacturing towns are in the north, around Lille.

France has had some exciting and troublesome times. Under Louis XIV, Louis XV, and Louis XVI, the country got seriously into debt, and the poor were so badly treated that finally they rebelled. The French Revolution began in 1789, when the people stormed the great Paris prison called the Bastille. The King and his Queen, Marie Antoinette, were put to death in 1793, and France became a REPUBLIC. Then a very successful general called NAPOLEON BONAPARTE took control of the country and ruled it very well on the whole; but he was so aggressive towards other countries that they combined against him. After many successful battles he was defeated at the battle of WATERLOO in 1815, and sent to St. Helena. Since then the French have fought against the Germans in the Franco-Prussian war in 1870, and the First and Second WORLD WARS.

FREE TRADE. Taxes, or duties, are sometimes charged on goods coming into a country to be sold there. The Government may put on the taxes because it wants the money, or to keep out certain foreign goods by making them too dear to buy, or to encourage people to make them in the country. When no such taxes are charged, trade is said to be "free."

FREEZING. When water changes from a liquid to a solid we say it is freezing. Most substances contract as they cool, and water does this until it is nearly at its freezing point (which is 0 degrees Centigrade or 32 degrees Fahrenheit), and then it expands slightly as it forms ICE. See also FROST.

FRENCH REVOLUTION. See FRANCE.

FRETWORK, a form of woodwork in which designs are traced on to thin wood such as three-ply, and the unwanted

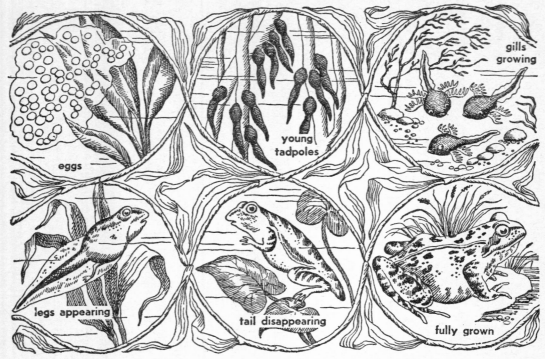

The way in which tadpoles turn into frogs is called metamorphosis.

parts are cut out by means of a very fine saw held in a spring frame. Parts can be cut out of the centre of the wood by drilling a small hole and threading the saw through it.

FREUD, Sigmund, born in Moravia in 1856, was a scientist who became world-famous. He was specially interested in the mental illness known as hysteria. He found that it was often caused by mental worry, and in trying to find the mental worries of his patients he made remarkable discoveries about dreams, and about the importance of the early years of a child's life, especially the first five years. His discoveries have had a great influence on the treatment of certain mental illnesses, and on the upbringing and education of children. Freud died in 1939.

FRICTION, the force which hinders or prevents one object from sliding smoothly over another. When the brake-blocks of a bicycle press against the rim of the wheel, it is friction which causes the bicycle to stop. Friction can be reduced by oiling and by the use of ball-bearings. If friction is forcibly overcome, as it is when you go on rubbing your hands together in cold weather, it is converted into heat. Primitive man obtained fire by the heat from friction when two pieces of wood are rubbed together.

FROEBEL, Friedrich, born in 1782, was a German teacher who realized that the best way to teach young children was to let them play with many useful toys and objects, as children do in good homes. Our present happy infants' schools are largely due to Froebel's inspiration. He died in 1852.

FROG. The frog lays its eggs in water, where they hatch out as tadpoles. The tadpole breathes through gills. Soon it grows hind legs, then forelegs, while the tail becomes smaller. Lungs begin to grow inside its body to replace the gills. At last the tadpole turns into a little frog, which leaves the water to live on land. It can now breathe air through its skin and its lungs.

The frog's tongue is fastened to the front of the mouth and folded back inside. When an insect comes near its mouth the frog flicks out its tongue with its sticky tip and catches the insect in this way. See also AMPHIBIANS.

FROST. When the temperature of the air is below freezing-point (0 degrees Centigrade or 32 degrees Fahrenheit), we say there is frost. If the temperature is —2 degrees Centigrade we sometimes speak of "two degrees of frost." When air with moisture in it is cooled, DEW is formed, but if the temperature is below 0 degrees Centigrade *hoar frost* is formed.

FRY, Elizabeth, born in 1780, was an Englishwoman of good family whose love spread beyond her own family to all the poor and needy, even to the criminals in prisons. When she saw the terrible con-ditions in which the women prisoners were living in Newgate prison, she went in to look after their children, got her friends to make clothes for them, then helped all the prisoners to get food and clothing and keep themselves clean. This terrible prison became so well conducted and the prisoners became such well-behaved people that the whole world was impressed. She died in 1845.

FUNGUS. Toadstools, mushrooms, mildews, moulds, yeast, and the dry rot in timber, are all fungi. This type of PLANT can only develop as a PARASITE on other plants, or on decayed vegetation or other organic matter. MUSHROOMS are edible, yeast is used in brewing beer and in making bread, but many other types of fungi are very poisonous.

A biologist called Alexander Fleming found that a fungus had grown on part of a plate on which he was developing germs,

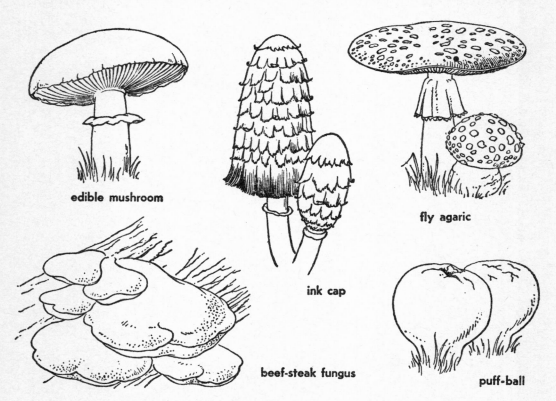

edible mushroom

ink cap

fly agaric

beef-steak fungus

puff-ball

There are many kinds of fungi. Some are very poisonous.

119

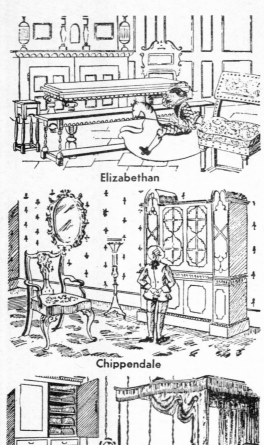

Elizabethan

Chippendale

Hepplewhite

Sheraton

Periods of English furniture.

and that the fungus had killed all the germs near it. He followed up this discovery, and obtained the drug penicillin from the fungus. Penicillin not only kills many kinds of germs, but does not usually harm the human body, hence it can be used in human beings. This discovery has proved of great importance for mankind.

FUR. Many animals, especially those which live in cold countries, have soft hair covering the skin. Primitive men wore these warm skins as clothing, and people still find fur coats the best protection against cold. Seals, bears, wolves, foxes, rabbits, and other wild animals provide fur for fur coats.

FURNACE, a large and very hot fire. There are BLAST FURNACES for smelting IRON and other metals, furnaces for heating steel so that it can be shaped into the steel plates and bars used in shipbuilding, and many other types.

FURNITURE. The history of furniture tells us much about the history of the world. In the museums there is furniture which was made in Egypt five thousand years ago, and we can guess the tools the workmen must have had to make it. We know the kinds of furniture made by the Babylonian people, and by the Greeks and Romans.

Furniture tells us much about the period in which it was made. Elizabethan, Jacobean (named after James I), Queen Anne and other designs are all distinctive.

There were three famous English makers of furniture. Their names are Chippendale, Hepplewhite and Sheraton. They lived in the eighteenth century, but some of their beautiful chairs and other creations are still in use.

FUSE. Boilers have safety valves so that too much steam will not burst the boiler. A fuse is the safety arrangement in an electric circuit. When too much CURRENT is flowing, the fuse melts and the current is broken, so that no damage is caused to the house. See also ELECTRIC LIGHT; ELECTRICITY.

G

GALILEE, Sea of, a lake in ISRAEL. The River Jordan flows through it and goes on to the DEAD SEA. The Jordan valley is a rift valley. The Sea of Galilee is seven hundred feet below the level of the Mediterranean, and the Dead Sea is thirteen hundred feet below it.

GALILEO, born in 1564, was one of the most distinguished of the early scientists. He was a professor of mathematics at Pisa in Italy, but he was also a great experimental physicist. He saw a lamp swinging in Pisa Cathedral, noted from his own pulse rate that it swung regularly, and saw how to use a swinging PENDULUM for measuring TIME. He worked out the rate at which bodies fall to the ground. (He had the great leaning tower of Pisa to experiment from.) He improved the TELESCOPE, used it to study the moon, and discovered four of the moons which go round JUPITER. These and other discoveries upset the monks, who thought his views contradicted what the Church taught, and Galileo was tried and put in prison. He was soon released, however. He died in 1642.

GAMES, forms of amusement in which two or more people try to discover which of them is the most skilful. There are indoor games like badminton, dominoes, snakes-and-ladders, chess, and card games, and there are outdoor games, like CRICKET, FOOTBALL and TENNIS. Sports contests are sometimes called athletic games, the OLYMPIC GAMES being of this kind.

GANGES, a great river which rises in the HIMALAYA Mountains and flows along the north-east of India to the Bay of Bengal. The wet summer monsoon sweeps up the Bay of Bengal, swings round the

Galileo.

mountains and up the Ganges valley, making all the land fertile, and providing water which can be stored and used in the dry season.

GAS MANTLE. A scientist called Welsbach was trying to find a new filament for the electric light. He was using cerium and other metals. Suddenly he saw a very bright spot glowing on his Bunsen burner. He collected the substance and examined it. It was a piece of cerium oxide. He made a little net of this, put it over the Bunsen, and it made a very bright light. He had discovered the gas mantle, which was superior to all electric lights for years.

GAS WORKS. Gas can be made by heating coal in retorts. Besides the gas, a light liquid and a tarry liquid are formed. From the former we get ammonia and other chemicals, from the latter dyes and disinfectants. The residue is coke. This is done at a gas works.

GEARS are toothed wheels which transmit power and motion to other

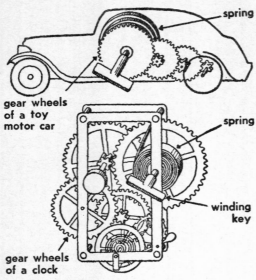

gear wheels
of a toy
motor car

spring

spring

winding
key

gear wheels
of a clock

Gears transmit power and motion.

wheels, and can regulate the speed and movement of the part being driven.

When a motor-car has to climb a steep hill the driver puts the engine in bottom gear; the engine goes fast and the car goes slowly, but with great climbing power. On a wide, clear and flat road, when climbing power is not needed, the driver changes to top gear, and the car travels fast.

You can see gear wheels at the back of a watch. The same balance wheel makes the minute hand rotate once in an hour, and the hour hand rotate once in twelve hours. The gear wheels do this.

GENESIS, the first book in the BIBLE. It gives the early history of the Jewish people and tells the story of how the Jews thought the world began.

GEOGRAPHY is the study of the earth's surface and its relation to living things. CLIMATE makes a lot of difference to the way in which men live, and the kinds of plants that grow in different parts of the world. Dense forests grow in the TROPICS where the rainfall is heavy and it is hot; where the rain is less heavy there are tropical grass-lands, and where there is little or no rain there is barren desert

land. The ARCTIC and the ANTARCTIC are very cold lands.

Changes are brought about in the earth's surface by the action of wind and rain, and frost; rivers may carve deep courses, so that valleys and CANYONS are formed.

Another branch of geography is the study of the particular countries in which different nations live. See also EARTH-QUAKE; EQUATOR; EROSION; MAPS.

GEOLOGY is the study of the ROCKS, how they were formed and changed, and what kind of life existed at various times. Geologists can tell the age of the rocks by the imprints of animals and plants, or by FOSSILS, found in the rocks. See also IGNEOUS ROCKS.

GEOMETRY is a branch of MATHE-MATICS. Pythagoras, who died about 500 B.C., had discovered that in a right-angled triangle the square on the largest side is equal to the sum of the squares on the other two sides. One can see this from the illustration below. EUCLID, who lived

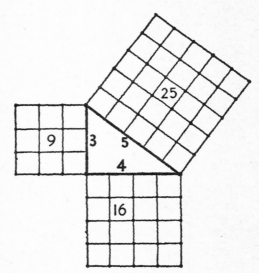

Pythagoras' theorem.

about 300 B.C., collected and arranged thirteen books of geometry problems. These books still exist, and much of this knowledge is taught to school children.

ARCHIMEDES, who died in 212 B.C., explained in his books how to calculate the circumference and the area of a CIRCLE, and the surface and volume of a sphere, if one knew the diameter (see MENSURATION). He was so pleased with his discovery that the area of the surface of a sphere is the same as that of the cylinder which fits round it (without the ends), that he asked that this figure should be put on his tombstone, and it was. Descartes invented co-ordinate geometry.

GEORGE I, who was the ruler of Hanover, in Germany, became King of Great Britain and Ireland in 1714. Though his mother was a granddaughter of JAMES I, his father was German and he could not speak a word of English. He reigned for thirteen years, but spent half that time in Hanover, where he was buried in 1727.

GEORGE II, son of GEORGE I, came to the throne in 1727 and reigned for thirty-three years. He spoke English, but with a strong German accent, and like his father he relied a great deal on the advice of his ministers. He also valued the opinions of his wife, Caroline, of whom he was very fond. He died in 1760.

GEORGE III, grandson of GEORGE II, was King of Great Britain and Ireland from 1760 to 1820. He began his reign by trying to increase his power as a king. He was unwise in this, and in many other matters, but he was popular because of his homely ways in private life. The people called him "Farmer George," and he had a family of nine sons and six daughters. Towards the end of his life he suffered from spells of madness which made him unfit to reign, so that his eldest son ruled in his place. This period is known as the Regency and Prince George was called the Prince Regent.

GEORGE IV, after reigning for about nine years as Prince Regent for his ailing father, GEORGE III, became King in 1820. He was not a successful ruler, and his extravagant and reckless ways made him very unpopular. His pleasure-loving companions called him "the first gentleman of Europe," but he has also been described as "a bad son, a bad husband, a bad monarch, and a bad friend." He died in 1830.

GEORGE V, who reigned from 1910 to 1936, was the second son of EDWARD VII. Before he came to the throne he served for many years in the Royal Navy, so was later called the Sailor King. During his reign the HOUSE OF LORDS lost its power to cancel laws made by the HOUSE OF COMMONS, women were given the right to vote for Members of Parliament, and the first National Insurance Act was passed. The First WORLD WAR against Germany and her allies was fought from 1914 to 1918, and King George often visited his soldiers fighting in France.

GEORGE VI came to the British throne in 1936 when his brother EDWARD VIII abdicated. When he was Duke of York he set up the Boys' Summer Camps, and was President of the National Playing Fields Association; even after he became King, his interest in the welfare of children never failed. He was a good King, and much loved. When he died in 1952 his elder daughter came to the throne as ELIZABETH II.

GERM. A disease germ is a very simple form of life. It consists of a single cell similar in many ways to a plant-cell. Though germs belong to the vegetable kingdom some of them are able to move or swim about. They are all much too small to be seen with the naked eye, but through a powerful microscope some look like little round balls, some like short rods, and others like curved sausages, while several kinds have long, whip-like hairs which they wave about. Germs multiply rapidly by simply growing bigger and then splitting into two. They may do this every half-hour or so. See BACTERIA.

GERM THEORY OF DISEASE. Louis PASTEUR, a French chemist, discovered that certain diseases in plants and animals

coal in the Ruhr   Black Forest scene   scientists   the beergarden

GERMANY EAST & WEST

BALTIC SEA

NORTH SEA

Kiel

Rostock

Wilhelmshaven

Frisian Is.

Lubeck

Hamburg

Groningen

Oldenburg

Bremen

R. Elbe

Szczecin (Stettin)

POLAND

Amsterdam

Osnabruck

Hanover

GERMAN DEMOCRATIC REPUBLIC

R. Oder

Rotterdam

Munster

Brunswick

BERLIN

Potsdam

HOLLAND

Essen

Ruhr

Magdeburg

Dusseldorf

R. Weser

Dessau

BRUSSELS

Cologne

Halle

Leipzig

BELGIUM

Bonn

Dresden

Wroclaw (Breslau)

Liege

Coblenz

FEDERAL REPUBLIC OF GERMANY

Mainz

LUXEMBOURG

Frankfurt

Darmstadt

R. Rhine

PRAGUE

Saar

Heidelberg

Nuremberg

CZECHO SLOVAKIA

Miles

FRANCE

Karlsruhe

Stuttgart

0 20 40 60 80 100

*Part also of Federal Republic

R. Danube

Augsburg

R. Isar

Munich

Linz

L. Constance

Oberammergau

Salzburg

AUSTRIA

SWITZERLAND

Zurich

castles on the Rhine   Nuremberg toys   lens manufacture   a medieval town

East and West Germany and some of the things found there.

The alarm is given.   *The call is received.*   *Fire engines race to the rescue.*

Fire-brigade at the scene of the fire a few minutes after an alarm is given.

poppy

MEADOW

heartsease

dog daisy

buttercup

clover

bell heather

gentian

gorse

MOORLAND and MOUNTAIN

golden saxifrage

lesser celandine

sweet violet

WOODLAND and HEDGEROW

wild rose

red campion

wild daffodil

bluebell

Flowers grow wild in many kinds of soil, brightening the landscape with vivid colours.

were caused by germs. Then Joseph LISTER, a British surgeon, found that cleanliness and an antiseptic spray made operations very much safer. Soon it was realized that many illnesses were caused by germs getting into the body. The body can fight germs if there are not too many of them. See also CORPUSCLE; MEDICINE.

GERMANY, a country in central EUROPE, with a population of over seventy-six million. Following the Second WORLD WAR Germany was divided into four zones occupied by the Western Powers, Britain, France, and the United States, and by Russia. In 1949 a new Constitution came into force, and the Federal Republic of Germany was formed from the three western zones, with Bonn as the capital. In Eastern Germany the Russians set up the German Democratic Republic with East Berlin as the capital.

Germany is quite a rich land; half of it is cultivated, and a quarter is under forests. Rye is the chief crop, wheat the second. Very good wines are made from grapes grown on the sunny slopes of the River Rhine, and its tributaries the Neckar, Main and Moselle.

The Ruhr coalfield is one of the greatest in the world, and there are great iron and steel industries, and big manufacturing towns, in this area, such as Cologne, Dortmund, and Essen. (The Ruhr is a small river which joins the River Rhine at Duisburg.) Farther east is the coalfield of Saxony, also an important industrial area. Dresden is famous for its china, and carved toys come from Nuremberg. Cameras are made in Munich, also beer.

There are big shipyards at Bremen and Hamburg. See also WORLD WAR.

GERMINATION. When a SEED gets enough moisture and warmth it begins to swell and grow. The young root pushes out and grows downward, and the shoot pushes out and grows upward. This development of the seed into a seedling is called germination.

GEYSERS are hot water springs, found in Iceland, in the North Island of New Zealand, and in the Yellowstone National Park in the United States of America.

GHANA, a country of tropical West Africa, formerly known as the Gold Coast. It is a member of the BRITISH COMMONWEALTH OF NATIONS. Ghana produces gold, diamonds, manganese, timber, and most of the cocoa used in the world. Accra is the capital. See map of AFRICA.

GIBRALTAR, Strait of, a sea passage between Spain and Africa, which connects the Atlantic and the Mediterranean. At the eastern end of the strait is the Rock of Gibraltar, a town and fortress which belongs to Britain. It is important as a refuelling and repair port.

GILBERT AND SULLIVAN. W. S. Gilbert wrote a number of light-hearted plays and Arthur Sullivan set the words to music. These musical plays were called comic operas. Two of the best-known are *The Mikado* and *The Pirates of Penzance.*

The giraffe has a long neck.

GIRAFFE, an animal with a very long neck and long, slender legs. It lives in Àfrica. The giraffe feeds chiefly on leaves, and its great height (eighteen feet sometimes) is very useful for this purpose. It can feed too on the grass of the tropical grass-lands, but it has to spread out its long forelegs or its head could not reach the ground. Its spotted coat is a good CAMOUFLAGE from its enemies when it is among the trees of the forest.

GIRL GUIDES, a youth movement founded by Lord Baden-Powell and his sister in 1910. Girls from seven and a half to eleven years old can join the Brownies, those from eleven to sixteen become Guides, and those from sixteen to twenty-one are called Rangers.

Girl Guides meet every week, and go camping once a year. They are trained in cookery, dress-making, child-nursing, first-aid, and other useful activities, and can gain badges for good work. Like the Boy Scouts they are taught a code of behaviour which makes them into good citizens. See also SCOUTING.

GLACIAL EPOCH. See ICE AGE.

GLACIER, a river of solid ice which moves slowly downwards. In Greenland the glaciers slide into the sea, where great pieces break off and form ICEBERGS.

GLADIATORS, men who fought, usually to the death of one of them, to entertain the people of ancient Rome.

GLANDS, organs of the body which make special substances the body needs. There are salivary glands to supply digestive juice to the mouth, lachrymal glands to supply tears to wash the eyes, mammary glands to supply milk to babies, and so on. There are also ductless glands which have no duct or tube leading out, but put their secretions direct into the blood-stream. The thyroid gland in the neck, and the suprarenal glands act in this way. See also DIGESTION; PERSPIRATION.

GLASGOW, the largest city in Scotland, and one of the largest in Britain. It is a great seaport, with shipbuilding yards on each side of the River CLYDE for miles down, and manufactures of many kinds in the city and neighbouring towns. At the mouth of the River Clyde there are many delightful seaside places, and some of the

service
map reading
signalling
stalking
first aid
wood craft
international friendship

Girl Guides are always willing to help other people if they can.

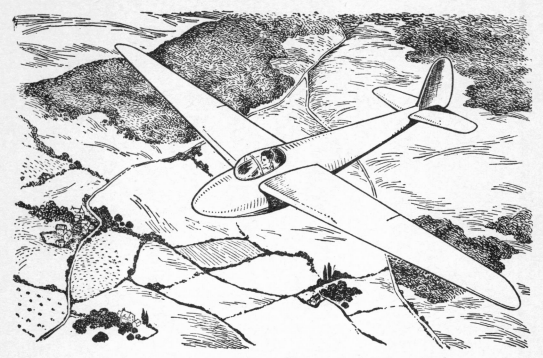

A glider uses the power of air currents to climb high in the sky.

most beautiful Scottish scenery is within easy reach of the city.

GLIDER, an AEROPLANE without an engine. It is either pulled into the air by an ordinary aeroplane, or catapulted from the ground, and then flies by itself. Skilful glider pilots, by taking advantage of air currents in the way birds do, can sometimes rise thousands of feet and fly two hundred miles or more.

GLOBE. As the earth is almost a sphere it is easier to represent the surface of the earth correctly on a globe than on a flat map, and many globes are made for mariners and for schools.

The earth makes a complete turn every twenty-four hours. If the equator is divided into twenty-four equal parts each part will represent a twenty-fourth part of the earth's turn, that is, the amount it will turn in one hour. One twenty-fourth of 360 degrees is 15 degrees. On a globe or a map the lines of LONGITUDE are sometimes marked every 15 degrees, that is, every hour. See also LATITUDE.

GLOW-WORM, an insect of the BEETLE type. The female is like a small caterpillar with a green light at one end. The males fly about at night and the lights attract them to the females. See also FIREFLY.

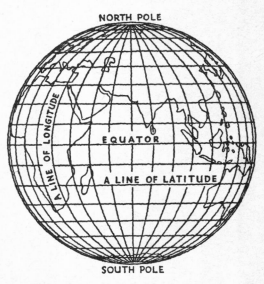

A globe is a spherical map of the earth.

GNU, or wildebeest, an animal of Africa, belonging to the ANTELOPE family. Once upon a time there were big herds in South Africa, but only a few now remain. The brindled gnu is common in East Africa.

GOAT, an animal like a sheep, but bolder, and more agile. The wild goat (such as the Alpine Ibex) lives in mountainous regions. The hair or wool of certain goats is used to make fine materials such as cashmere and mohair. Morocco leather is made from the skin. In some countries goats are kept for milk as we keep cattle.

GOLD is one of the precious metals. It can be hammered into sheets thinner than paper, or drawn into the finest wire. By itself it is rather too soft for making watches and other jewellery, and usually a small amount of another metal is added to make a hard ALLOY.

GOLD COAST. See GHANA.

GOLDFISH are ornamental fish, bred originally in China and Japan. They have to be carefully bred to keep their golden colour, for their natural colour is greenish, and in large ponds they are likely to change back to their original colour.

GOLDSMITH, Oliver, was born in 1728. He was a delightful Irishman, but rather happy-go-lucky, and he worried relatives and others with his debts and his

The Alpine Ibex is a wild goat.

unsettled behaviour. Yet he became a famous man because of the wonderful books and poems he wrote. Dr. Johnson got him £60 for his novel, *The Vicar of Wakefield*, to keep him out of prison for debt. This book has been reprinted over a hundred times and is still being reprinted. His poem *The Deserted Village* is a first-class poem, and *She Stoops to Conquer* is a first-class play. Yet when Goldsmith died in 1774 he was £2,000 in debt. Crowds of poor people whom he had helped came to his funeral.

GOLIATH. We are told in the first Book of Samuel, chapter seventeen, that when the Philistines were fighting the Israelites a very big man called Goliath challenged anyone in the Israelite army to fight him. Little David accepted the challenge and killed him with a pebble from his sling.

Goliath was "six cubits and a span" in height. Taking a cubit as eighteen inches that would make Goliath about nine and a half feet tall.

GOODWIN SANDS are very dangerous sand-banks about four or five miles off the coast of Kent, near Deal. There are four light-ships to warn sailors, yet ships

David defeated Goliath.

still make mistakes, or are swept by wind and tide, and run aground there.

GOOSE, a bird rather like a large DUCK. The domestic goose feeds chiefly on grass. See also WATER-BIRDS.

GORDON, Charles, born in 1833, was a famous British soldier. He was a brave and efficient officer who fought in the CRIMEAN WAR and in China, and was Governor of the SUDAN from 1877 to 1880. He was sent back to the Sudan in 1884, when a wild prophet, called the Mahdi, started a serious rebellion among the desert tribes. The rebels surrounded Khartoum and, although General Gordon defended the town successfully for ten months, they captured it, and he was slain (1885). Two days later a relief force arrived from England.

GORILLA, the largest APE. It lives in the equatorial forests of Africa, and is as tall as a man but very much stronger. It lives on fruits and other vegetation, and sometimes makes a nest in the trees, like a hammock.

GOSPELS, the first four books of the New Testament. They are four separate accounts of the life of JESUS, told by ST. MATTHEW, ST. MARK, ST. LUKE and ST. JOHN. Jesus was about thirty when he began his mission, and it lasted only two or three years. The Gospels tell us about it. Although all the recorded sayings of Jesus could be read in a few hours, yet this was the beginning of Christianity which has spread the gospel of love throughout the world. See also APOSTLES; BIBLE.

GOTHIC ARCHITECTURE. The GOTHS, the Huns and the Vandals were the three savage tribes who conquered Rome. All these names came to mean uncultured or vulgar people; they were barbarians, and this was a term of contempt. Later, a style of ARCHITECTURE was described as Gothic, not in contempt, but to indicate that it was not in the classical style of Greece and of Rome. Architects soon found that the Gothic style of building, with its pointed arches, was a very useful and beautiful style, and it was soon developed in various ways.

GOTHS, an ancient tribe of people who lived along the Black Sea and lower Danube. About A.D. 250 they began to challenge the Roman Empire, and in A.D. 409 they invaded Rome and sacked the city.

GOUNOD, Charles François, a French composer, was born in 1818. He wrote symphonies and church music; one of his best-known works is the opera *Faust*. Gounod died in 1893.

GOVERNOR. In the BRITISH COMMONWEALTH this title is given to a representative of the Crown who acts as the head of the administration of affairs. In the self-governing nations of the Commonwealth which are not republics he is a diplomatic representative, and is in this case given the title of Governor-General.

GOVERNOR, an arrangement for controlling the speed of an engine. It regulates the amount of steam or petrol admitted, so that the engine runs at a constant rate.

There are also governors on gramophones to keep the records turning at a definite speed.

Gothic style of architecture.

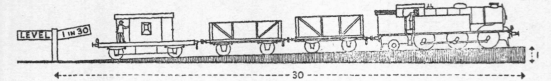

This indicator shows the gradient of a railway line (it is not drawn to scale).

GRADIENT, the slope, of a railway line for example. The picture above shows a train going up a gradient of 1 in 30. Electric trains can climb steeper tracks, and Alpine railways, with cog wheels working in a rack, or with a cable attached, can climb up gradients of 1 in 4.

GRAIN. Men have developed grasses which have big seeds, like maize, rice, wheat, oats, barley and rye. All these seeds which are grown for food are called grain.

GRAMMAR involves a knowledge of the right way to use words so that we can form them into proper sentences. We must know the kind of work that words do. Some words are names of people and things (*nouns:* chair, Tom, crowd, victory); other words are used instead of names (*pronouns:* I, me, you, he, she, it, him, her, we, us, they, them). Some words describe people and things (*adjectives:* red, many, my, which, that). Some words are doing-words (*verbs:* go, walks, is loving, has seen, will think, played); others tell us something more about the verb, how often, or where, or in what way the thing happens that the verb is telling us about (*adverbs:* soon, quickly, here). Other words join (*conjunctions:* and, for, but); while a few words express pain, surprise or pleasure (*interjections:* oh, ah, eh). Here is a sentence showing the work of the different words:

Girls love pretty flowers for
noun verb adjective noun conjunction
they often go into fields
pronoun adverb verb preposition noun
and pick them.
conjunction verb pronoun

GRAMOPHONE. Sound travels through the air in a series of waves, not unlike the bumps which travel along a goods train when the engine hits the first truck. These waves make a thin disk, a diaphragm, move backwards and forwards rapidly, that is, the disk vibrates, and different sounds cause different vibrations. These vibrations can be recorded on a revolving plate of wax, forming a groove with uneven sides.

A record can be made with the same grooves in it. When this record is put on to a gramophone and played, the needle put into the groove now vibrates and these vibrations influence an electric current, which works a loudspeaker in the same way that a radio loudspeaker is worked.

GRANITE, a type of ROCK which has been melted by great heat below the

wheat

oats

barley

maize

Grain is grown for food.

130

surface of the earth, and compressed into a mass of crystals, usually felspar, mica and quartz. It may be very old rock, or it may be later rocks which went into the earth's furnace, as it were, and came out again as granite. The Alps, Pyrenees and other mountain ranges are made of granite, and so are many of the mountains of Scotland. Where the granite is near the sea, as at Peterhead (red granite) and Aberdeen (grey granite) it is shipped to other towns to be used for building. It is a very durable stone. The PYRAMIDS of Egypt are made of granite. See also IGNEOUS ROCKS.

GRAPEFRUIT, a fruit like an orange, but larger, and with a smooth skin. It has a slightly bitter taste. It flourishes in the West Indies and Florida and in other tropical and sub-tropical climates like those of South Africa and Israel.

GRAPH. A temperature chart is one kind of graph. The chart below is one for a little girl who was in hospital. The following graph is of a train travelling at fifty miles an hour. One can find out from the graph how far the train will go in fifteen minutes, thirty minutes and so on, without doing any sums.

Straight line graphs can be used for

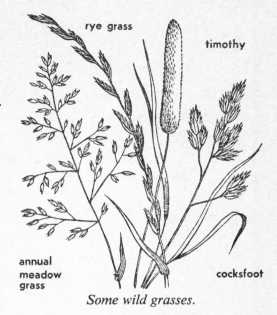

Some wild grasses.

calculating wages, or for changing inches to centimetres, and so on.

GRASSES are plants which grow quickly when there is rain and sunshine, and preserve their life in tough little SEEDS which can survive droughts for years if necessary, and still grow when conditions are favourable again. A field of grass is the commonest crop of all. The tropical forests have grasslands north and south

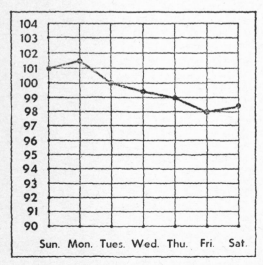

A temperature chart is one kind of graph.

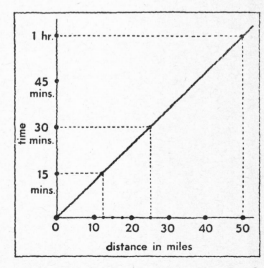

Graph to show the distance a train travels.

131

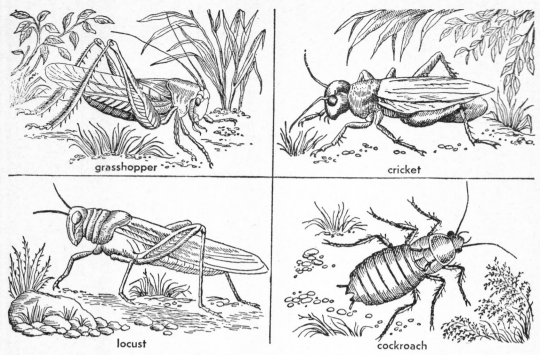

The grasshopper, cricket and locust are all more agile than the cockroach.

of them. The EQUATOR gets rain at all seasons, but the land north and south of the equator has periods of rain and periods of drought every year.

Maize, rice, wheat, oats, barley, rye, sugar canes and bamboo are all grasses, as well as the grasses which grow wild.

GRASSHOPPER, an INSECT of the same type as the COCKROACH and the locust. It has very long and slender hind legs which enable it to jump remarkable distances in the grass. The chirping noise grasshoppers make is caused by the males rubbing the outer edges of their wing cases against the file-like ridges on the inner surfaces of their hind legs.

GRAVITY. This is a force which causes all free objects to move towards each other. We see it at work whenever an object falls to the ground, and this is because the gravitation of that very large body, the Earth, makes smaller objects move towards it quite quickly. The force with which they are thus pulled earthwards is usually called their "weight." It is the gravitation of the Earth which keeps the Moon from flying away into space, and the gravitation of the Sun which holds the Earth and all the other planets in their orbits.

GRAY, Thomas, an English poet, was born in 1716. The best-known of his poems is the *Elegy Written in a Country Churchyard*. Gray died in 1771 and was buried at Stoke Poges, in Buckinghamshire.

GREAT BRITAIN. See UNITED KINGDOM.

GREECE is a small country in south-eastern Europe, on the Mediterranean Sea. There are many Greek islands in the Aegean Sea, of which Crete is the biggest. Over half a million people live in Athens, important both as capital of the country and as an international airport.

From the early civilizations of EGYPT, BABYLON and Phoenicia, knowledge spread to Greece, and the Greek civilization became in some ways the most wonderful the world has ever known. The people of

sports stadium about 400 B.C.

warriors, about 500 B.C.

dancers

theatre, about 400 B.C.

the Parthenon

dress, about 450 B.C.

The people of ancient Greece knew a great deal, and we have learned a lot from them.

133

Hunting the Greenland whale in the cold Arctic Ocean.

ancient Greece made many discoveries in ARITHMETIC and GEOMETRY, in MEDICINE, education, philosophy and other branches of knowledge; and their sculpture and literature have never been surpassed. See also ARCHIMEDES; ARCHITECTURE; ARISTOTLE; DRAMA; ERATOSTHENES; EUCLID; GYMNASIUM; OLYMPIC GAMES; PLATO; SOCRATES; SPARTA.

GREENLAND, an island north-east of Canada. It is like a great ice-desert. The ice slides down slowly into the sea, and pieces break off to form ICEBERGS. The inhabitants (mostly ESKIMOS) live round the coast in the south, and depend chiefly on fish, seals, and whales for their food. Greenland is Danish territory. See also WHALE; WHALING.

GREENWICH, a borough of London, which contains the National Maritime Museum and the Royal Naval College. In 1675 CHARLES II founded the Greenwich Observatory, which became world-famous. It has since been moved to Herstmonceux, in Sussex. The longitudes of all places are calculated from the Greenwich meridian of LONGITUDE; for example, the south of Sweden is fifteen degrees east of Greenwich (noon there is an hour earlier than it is at Greenwich). New York is about seventy-four degrees west of Greenwich (noon there is five hours later than at Greenwich).

GRENADIER, originally a foot-soldier who threw grenades, that is, small explosive shells. Now the Grenadiers or the

Grenadier Guards are the first regiment of Household Infantry. Household regiments are those whose special duty is to protect the Sovereign. See Brigade of GUARDS.

GREY, Earl Charles. When Charles Grey was born, in 1764, the HOUSE OF COMMONS represented only the wealthy part of the nation. Working people believed that if they were represented too they would be better treated, so they began to agitate for the reform of Parliament. Grey, as a young man, supported the reform movement in the House of Commons. At long last, in 1831, after great opposition, a Reform Bill was passed by the Commons, only to be thrown out by the HOUSE OF LORDS! It was Earl Grey, now Prime Minister, who persuaded the Lords to accept it, and it became law in 1832. The first step had been taken to make Parliament really represent the people. Grey died in 1845. See also REFORM ACTS.

GREYHOUND, the fastest type of dog. It is bred for speed and can run down hares and other game.

GROUSE, a name given to several different kinds of large, moorland birds, which are shot for sport and food. The chief grouse are the ptarmigan, blackcock, capercailzie and red grouse. The red grouse is the most common in Britain, especially on the moors and hills of Scotland; and it is also one of the very few British birds which are not found wild in any other part of the world.

GUARDS, Brigade of. The Guards were formed in the reign of CHARLES II, and their chief duty was to guard the King. There are now three regiments of horse guards—the 1st and 2nd regiments of the Life Guards and the Royal Horse Guards. They are collectively known as the Household Cavalry. The Royal Horse Guards are also known as "the Blues." The five regiments of foot guards are the Grenadier, the Coldstream, the Scots, the Irish, and the Welsh Guards.

A greyhound can run at great speed.

GUINEA-PIG, a RODENT from South America. It is sometimes kept by children as a pet. The name is probably a corruption of "Guiana pig." Guyana is north of the Amazon forest. See map of SOUTH AMERICA.

GULF STREAM, a warm OCEAN CURRENT which flows from the Gulf of Mexico across the Atlantic Ocean to Britain. Once it leaves the American coast

Royal Horse Guard.

135

it soon slows down to three miles per hour, then to one mile per hour, so that it is only a drift as it nears Britain, and it is not much warmer than the rest of the sea.

GULLIVER, Capt. Lemuel, fictitious hero of *Gulliver's Travels*, a book written by Jonathan Swift. Gulliver was shipwrecked on a strange island called Lilliput where all the people were only six inches high. To them Gulliver was a giant and he had many unusual adventures. He captured the enemy fleet of fifty ships by tying them together and dragging them out of the harbour behind him like little toy boats. On another journey he came to Brobdingnag, the land of giants, where he was only a few inches high by comparison with his captors. Here he was frightened by wasps as big as sparrows and dogs as big as horses, and had a fierce battle with a rat. At last Gulliver escaped and came back to England.

GUN, a general name for weapons which fire missiles by means of explosive charges. Battleships and forts have enormous guns firing shells, and sportsmen carry small guns to shoot duck or pheasants. See also ARTILLERY; CANNON; EXPLOSIVE.

traditional search of the cellars

Guy Fawkes was arrested in 1605

"Please to remember the Fifth of November!"

The failure of the Gunpowder Plot is still celebrated on Bonfire Night.

Gypsies are wandering folk who get a living in many different ways.

GUNPOWDER. See EXPLOSIVES.

GUNPOWDER PLOT (1605). JAMES I had been only two years on the English throne when some Roman Catholics plotted to blow up the King and the members of Parliament. Thirty-six barrels of gunpowder were smuggled into a cellar below the House of Lords, and it was arranged that Guy Fawkes should explode it on 5 November, when the King would be opening Parliament. The plot was discovered and the conspirators were executed. It has been a traditional ceremony ever since to search the cellars of Parliament, and to burn a dummy of Guy Fawkes on Bonfire Night.

GYMNASIUM. The GREEKS believed in having "a sound mind in a sound body." The gymnasium was the public building in which the young men developed strong and beautiful bodies by games and exercises of various kinds. Many modern schools have gymnasia.

GYMNASTICS, exercises which are designed to make the body strong, supple and generally healthy. Swedish and other exercises use and develop all the muscles in the body.

GYPSIES, a race of people who probably came from India to Europe. They have olive skins, black hair and eyes, and very white teeth. They wander from place to place, living in caravans, making mats and baskets, telling fortunes, and doing odd jobs such as fruit-picking.

GYROSCOPE, a heavy, rapidly spinning wheel, which tends to keep its spindle (the rod through the middle) always pointing in the same direction. Because of this fact, the gyroscope can be made to work as a compass if it is placed with the spindle pointing in the right direction. A very heavy gyroscope can be fitted into the bottom part of a ship, where it spins with its spindle pointing up. Each time the ship begins to roll to one side, the gyroscope wheel (which wants to stay level) will help to steady the ship.

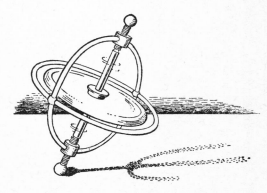

This is a simple kind of gyroscope.

H

Handel playing the clavichord.

HAIL. If rain falls through a very cold layer of air it will freeze into little round pieces of ICE. This is one kind of hail. But bigger hailstones are quite common. In hot climates it happens occasionally that hailstones as big as tennis balls come battering down and do considerable damage.

HAIR helps to keep the body warm. Our savage ancestors probably had much more hair on their bodies than men have nowadays. Each hair grows from a pit in the skin, and each pit has a bundle of muscle fibres and nerves; oil-glands open into the hair-pit and keep the hair soft and smooth.

When we are frightened, or cold, the muscles contract and make the hair stand on end, and we get goose-flesh. Animals such as the dog, cat, and lion look much bigger and fiercer when their fur is fluffed out. See also ALBINO.

HAMSTER, an animal, little bigger than a mouse. It is a member of the RODENT family. The golden hamster is often kept as a pet.

HANDEL, George Frederick, one of the great musicians. He was born at Halle, in Germany, in 1685, but lived most of his life in England. His father did not want him to become a musician, but when the boy was discovered secretly practising the clavichord in the middle of the night his father let him have some lessons. He was only seven at the time. He later learned to play the violin, the oboe and the organ, was composing music at ten years of age, and playing the organ in the cathedral at Halle at sixteen. Handel's music pleases almost everyone, and can be heard again and again without one becoming tired of it. The *Messiah* is his best-known work. He became blind in 1752, but continued to compose music until his death in 1759.

HANDICAPPING. There would be no fun in running friendly races unless the slower runners were given a start, thus handicapping the faster ones. In some games, like golf, the handicapping can be accurate, because each player plays his own ball, and many shots are played. Handicapping is more difficult in tennis, for the strong player can play many shots that the weak player cannot return.

HANNIBAL was a very successful general of the Carthaginian army. He lived from 247 B.C. to 183 B.C. He led his army from the north of Africa, through Spain, across the Pyrenees, across the Rhône and over the Alps to attack Rome. When he set out he had 90,000 foot soldiers, 12,000 horsemen and 40 elephants, and although he lost more than half his army in getting to Rome, he defeated the Romans in several battles. See CARTHAGE.

Hannibal invaded Italy by leading his army over the Alps.

A harbour gives shelter to ships.

HARBOUR, a sheltered part of the coast where ships are safe even in rough weather. It may be a natural harbour, like Southampton Water, or Milford Haven, or the estuaries of the Thames or the Clyde; or an artificial harbour, like the one at Madras in India, or the one built quickly for the landing of the Allies in France in the Second WORLD WAR. Many harbours are partly natural, partly artificial.

HARE, an animal like a big rabbit. It does not burrow underground, but can run very fast. Few dogs except the greyhound can catch it. The mountain hare is found in places that have plenty of snow in winter, when its coat turns white, making the animal less easy to see.

HARMONY. A simple tune is a melody. But two melodies played together become

Mountain hare.

a harmony. If a soprano, CONTRALTO, tenor and BASS were all singing parts which were not the same, but which all fitted in with one another, this would be called harmony. In complicated music, like symphonies, the whole range of strings, of woodwinds, of BRASS INSTRUMENTS and of PERCUSSION INSTRUMENTS may all be playing at once, making many different sounds, which all blend, or harmonize with each other, to give a richer meaning. See MUSICAL INSTRUMENTS; ORCHESTRA.

HARP, a stringed instrument, played by plucking the strings with the fingers. The Egyptians, the Assyrians, the Hebrews and the Greeks all used it, and it is still a popular instrument in Wales. Modern orchestras sometimes use one or two harps.

HARPSICHORD, a musical instrument like a grandpiano. The wires in it, however, are not hit by hammers but are plucked by little quills. In the seventeenth century,

A harp is played by plucking the strings.

early 20th century—Edwardian

Ancient Greek

15th century—Edward IV

late 19th century—Victorian

early 16th century— Henry VIII

late 18th century—George III

early 19th century—George IV

late 16th century—Elizabeth I

early 18th century—George II

late 17th century—Charles II

early 17th century—Cromwell

Throughout the ages hats have been part of fashionable dress.

before pianos were invented, the harpsichord was an important instrument. It is still played occasionally.

HARVEY, William, born in 1578, became famous as the English physician who discovered how the blood circulates in the body. He was physician to James I and Charles I and was with King Charles at the Battle of Edgehill in 1642. Harvey died in 1657.

HAT. A hat is a covering worn on the head to protect it. Hats have a very ancient history. They are worn to-day with a crown and a brim, a style which

Hawks and other birds of prey are the fierce hunters of the air.

was begun by the ancient Greeks. The Romans had a felt hat with a high crown and broad brim, and in the twelfth century such hats were worn by the rich people in England. These hats were brightly coloured and became taller and taller until the fifteenth century, when there was a sudden change to flat velvet hats like "tam-o'-shanters." In Elizabeth I's reign the "pot" hat came in; this was like an inverted pot with an upright feather. In Cromwell's time high crowns and broad brims reappeared, but the crowns became low again in Charles II's reign, when a great many feathers were worn. Next came the three-cornered or "cocked" hat, and

about the time of the French Revolution these gave place to "beavers," which were like top-hats decorated with strings and tassels. The black silk top-hat came in during Queen Victoria's reign, but was gradually replaced by the hard felt "bowler," the soft felt "Homburg" and "Trilby," and the felt "pork-pie."

HAWK, a BIRD OF PREY. In the Middle Ages hawking was a popular sport, and the Peregrine falcon was often used. The sparrow hawk is found over most of Europe, and is common in the British Isles. The kestrel, however, is the best-known of the hawks in Britain. It hovers in the air, looking for prey, then dives down at great speed to grip a mouse or bird in its powerful claws. Another member of the family is the common buzzard, found in Scotland and Wales and in parts of England.

HAY. When grass grows tall and is in flower it is often cut, dried and stored for feeding cattle, and horses. This dried grass is called hay.

HAYDN, Franz Joseph, born in Austria in 1732, became a famous composer. He wrote many symphonies, and several operas, oratorios and string quartettes. He came from a poor family and had a difficult time for some years, even playing in the street to get some money. Fortunately his genius was recognized, and he had a happy and comfortable later life. Haydn died in 1809.

HEAD. In the worm there is very little head, just the mouth and a few extra nerve-cells. The snake has a small head, with many nerve-cells in the brain; the dog has a bigger head, with more nerve-cells; the ape's head is still bigger in proportion to its body, and man has the biggest head of all, with a brain bigger than that of any other animal. The body needs a "telephone service," just as a city does, and the brain and the spinal cord act as a kind of telephone exchange. Delicate nerve-fibres act as telephone wires, and carry messages from all parts of the body to the brain. The big brain is helped by a smaller telephone exchange called the little brain, and instructions are sent out to different parts of the body by the nerve-fibres. See also BRAIN; NERVOUS SYSTEM; REFLEX ACTION.

HEART, the muscular organ which pumps BLOOD through the body. It has four cavities with valves which open and shut to prevent the blood from going the wrong way. The blood returns along the VEINS from all parts of the body, and pours into one cavity (the right auricle). The blood is then passed through a valve into another cavity (the right ventricle).

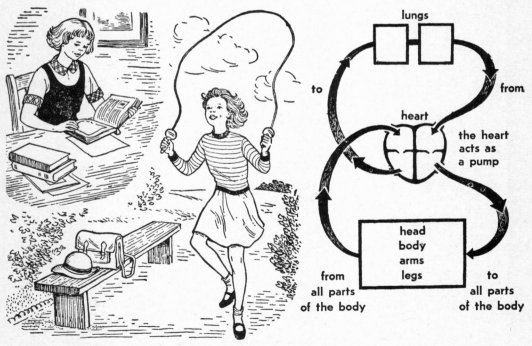

The heart pumps blood to the brain, and to the muscles and organs of the body.

143

From there it is pumped to the LUNGS to collect more oxygen and to give up some of its carbon dioxide. The blood then returns to another cavity (the left auricle), from which it passes through another valve to the left ventricle, from where it is pumped to the main artery, called the aorta, and from there through the ARTERIES to all parts of the body.

HEAT is a form of energy. It usually produces a change of temperature, or a change of state (for example, water into steam), or an expansion of the substance which is heated. Gases expand most with heat, liquids not so much, and solids least of all.

Some substances can hold much more heat than others. Water, for example, holds a great deal of heat. Sand, or mercury, hold very little. It is because the land gets hot quickly and cools quickly, and the sea gets hot slowly and cools slowly, that we get MONSOONS, and LAND AND SEA BREEZES.

Heat can be produced by burning fuel, or by friction, or by means of an electric current.

Hedgehog and young.

HEATING, The earliest method of heating a house was to have a fire in the middle of the earthen floor. Some Roman houses had a fire underneath the house, the hot air warming the floor and coming up hollow spaces in the outside walls. There were no chimneys, however. Chimneys began to be built in England in the reign of Henry VII (about 1500).

Heating by hot-water pipes was first used for greenhouses (about 1800), so that there would be no fumes to kill the plants; but the method soon spread to houses and theatres, and is widely used everywhere today.

HEBREW, the language of the Jews (or Israelites, or Hebrews). The Old Testament was written in Hebrew, and the language is still studied by the Jewish people as part of their religious training.

HEDGEHOG, a small MAMMAL, covered with spines. When an enemy is near he rolls himself into a ball with his spines out in all directions,

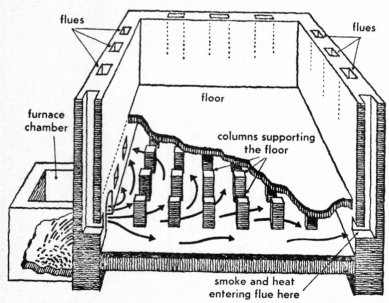

Roman houses had a form of central heating.

144

and then few animals like to touch him. The hedgehog lives on fruits, roots and insects, cockroaches and beetles for example, and likes to feed well before he goes to sleep for the winter. See also HIBERNATION.

HELICOPTER, a flying machine which has a large propeller (or rotor) above, rotating horizontally. By altering the inclination of the rotor blades the machine can be made to move forward or backward, that is, by "feathering" each blade for part of the turn. There is a smaller propeller on the tail to stop the machine being turned round by the movement of the rotor. The helicopter can rise straight up into the air, so there is no need for the long runway necessary to most aeroplanes.

HELIUM, a gas, rather heavier than HYDROGEN, but much safer because it does not catch fire. It is used in AIRSHIPS. See also BALLOON.

HELMET, a protection for the head. Helmets were used in battle until fighting with swords became obsolete, then they were not used for many years. But in the First WORLD WAR, when soldiers fought in trenches, the head was the most exposed part, and flat helmets, made of thin, but very tough steel, were found to prevent many casualties. Now these "tin hats," as the soldiers call them, are always worn in the battle area.

Firemen need helmets to help to protect them in their dangerous work; and racing motorists, motor-cyclists, and policemen wear them.

HEMISPHERE is half a sphere. We speak of the northern hemisphere, or the southern hemisphere, meaning that part of the world which is north of the EQUATOR, or that part which is south of it.

HENRY I, who reigned from 1100 to 1135, was the fourth son of WILLIAM THE CONQUEROR. He was made KING in the absence of his elder brother Robert, and

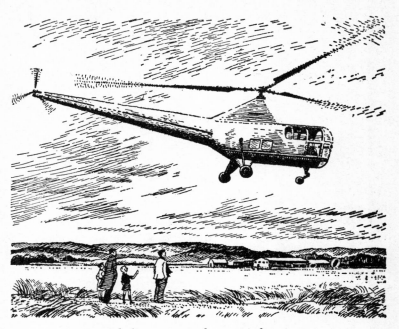

A helicopter can hover in the air.

his first task was to control the unruly Norman barons. His only son, William, was drowned in the English Channel when the White Ship foundered, and he left the throne to his daughter Matilda (or Maud), but she was never crowned QUEEN.

HENRY II, who came to the throne in 1154, found England in the power of the barons. Though only twenty-one years old he proved an energetic and able ruler. In order to make sure of his kingly power he pulled down more than a thousand of the barons' castles. He wanted the common law to apply to the clergy, instead of their being tried by courts set up by the Church, but he did not succeed in this. He quarrelled with Thomas à Becket over it, and

145

Becket left England. After his return six years later, Becket was murdered in Canterbury Cathedral. Ireland was made part of the Kingdom for the first time in Henry II's reign, which ended with the King's death in 1189.

HENRY III, King of England from 1216 to 1272. Though he reigned for more than half a century, Henry III was a weak and foolish king. He allowed his foreign relatives to take all the important positions in the state, and so upset the barons, and he failed to keep the terms of the Magna Carta which his father, King John, had agreed to. The barons rebelled, and were led by Simon de Montfort, who restored order to the country but was later killed at the battle of Evesham, 1265. Towards the end of his life Henry III allowed control of the state to pass to his son, who later succeeded to the throne as EDWARD I.

HENRY IV, or Henry Bolingbroke, was the first king of the House of Lancaster, and he reigned from 1399 to 1413. There were many rebellions during his reign, and Scotland, Wales and France all attacked him. These troubles weakened his power, and to obtain support from the Church Henry made a cruel law by which persons who did not believe the Church's teaching could be burnt.

HENRY V, son of HENRY IV, came to the throne of England in 1413, and soon showed himself an able ruler. He was, however, a harsh man, and had been known in his youth as "Madcap Harry" on account of his reckless ways. As a king he was both adventurous and wise. He renewed the war against France and won the battle of AGINCOURT in 1415. He died in France in 1422. See also HUNDRED YEARS' WAR.

HENRY VI, son of HENRY V, became King of England in 1422 when he was only nine months old, and during his childhood the country was ruled by a council. In this reign the French Army, led by JOAN OF ARC, defeated the English at Orleans, and England lost all her French possessions except Calais.

Henry VI loved scholarship, and Eton is among the schools and colleges he founded. He was also a good and gentle man, but he suffered from spells of madness. At such times the Duke of York was Protector of the Realm. In 1455 the Duke of York, who thought he had a better right to the throne than Henry, decided to fight for the crown, and so began the Wars of the ROSES. In 1461 Edward, son of the Duke of York, dethroned Henry VI and became the first king of the House of York. Henry VI was put to death while in prison in 1471.

HENRY VII became King of England in 1485, when RICHARD III was slain at the battle of Bosworth Field. He was descended from the House of Lancaster but married Elizabeth of York, and so the two Houses were at last united, and the Wars of the ROSES came to an end. His reign, the first of the House of Tudor, was troubled by the "pretenders" Lambert Simnel and Perkin Warbeck, each of whom claimed to be the rightful heir to the throne. Henry VII was a strong king who made the country wealthy and the Crown powerful. He died in 1509.

HENRY VIII, the second of the Tudor sovereigns, and father of the next three: EDWARD VI, MARY I, and ELIZABETH I. He reigned from 1509 to 1547. He was obstinate, and anyone who angered him risked the executioner's axe. But he helped to make England strong, and strengthened the navy. He persuaded Parliament to make him Head of the Church in England and to close the monasteries. Most people remember that he had six wives.

HERACLES, the legendary hero of Ancient Greece, famed for his great strength and mighty deeds. The Romans called him Hercules.

HEREDITY. The seeds of plants grow up into similar plants, and kittens, puppies and babies all grow up like their parents. This passing on of qualities to the next

Catherine of Aragon.   Anne Boleyn.   1509   HENRY VIII   1547   Jane Seymour.   Anne of Cleves.

Katherine Howard   Catherine Parr.

Great feasts were held at Hampton Court.   Hawking was a favourite sport.

Princess Elizabeth was born in 1533.   The monks were expelled from the monasteries.

Tyndale translated the Bible. Henry loved ships; he founded the Royal Docks at Woolwich.

generation is called heredity. Hens which lay many eggs tend to hatch chickens which will later lay many eggs; cows which give much milk tend to breed other cows which give much milk, and so on.

HEREWARD THE WAKE, one of the Englishmen who refused allegiance to WILLIAM THE CONQUEROR. He held land in Lincolnshire and took part in a Danish attack on Peterborough Abbey. He resisted the King in the Isle of Ely, and when the King at last took the isle in 1071 Hereward is supposed to have escaped,

HERON, a bird with long legs and a long beak to help it to fish in shallow water. It has been known to collect the goldfish out of ornamental ponds in gardens, but usually it fishes in streams, ponds, marshes and lakes, for fish, frogs, and other small creatures.

HERRICK, Robert, born in 1591, was a clergyman who wrote some lovely little poems, some of which have been set to music. He wrote about religious subjects and about life in the country. Herrick died in 1674.

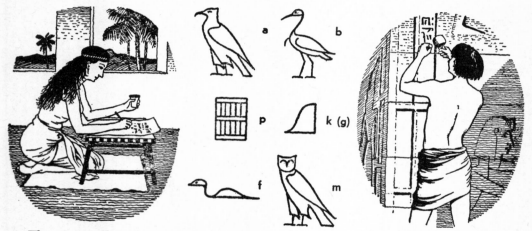

The ancient Egyptians wrote on papyrus, or carved hieroglyphics on stone tablets.

but nothing more is known of him for certain. Popular legend suggests that he was later pardoned and his lands were returned to him.

HEROD THE GREAT was King of Judaea from 37 B.C. to 5 B.C., the year in which JESUS CHRIST was born, according to recent discoveries by archaeologists. According to the old story, when King Herod heard that the child Jesus had also been called a king, he ordered the slaughter of all the children born in the neighbourhood of Bethlehem. The child Jesus escaped, for his parents had been warned in a dream to take him to Egypt, and they did not return until after Herod's death. The Herod to whom Pilate sent Jesus in A.D. 30 was the son of Herod the Great.

HERRING, a fish found in enormous shoals in all parts of the North Atlantic ocean. It is a valuable food, because it is rich in oil.

HIBERNATION. When food becomes scarce in winter some birds and animals migrate to warmer regions, but others get into as comfortable and safe a place as possible and hibernate, or go to sleep, for some months. Hedgehogs, tortoises, bats and frogs all do this.

HIEROGLYPHICS, the earliest form of writing. We use something like hieroglyphics for the signs for motor-cars (see ROAD SIGNS). Just as we learn what the motor-car signs mean, the Egyptians learned what their signs meant, and could send messages to each other. Soon they

Black bear of the Himalayas.

had signs for all they wanted to say.

Until 1799 we could not understand the Egyptian hieroglyphics, but in that year a stone was found at Rosetta, a town at the mouth of the Nile, and on it was an inscription written in three ways. Two were forms of Egyptian writing, and the third was Greek. Because they knew the Greek language, scholars were able to work out the meanings of the hieroglyphics, and now they can read almost anything in ancient Egyptian.

HIMALAYAS, a vast group of mountain ranges in central Asia, on the borders of India and Tibet. It contains many of the highest mountains in the world, including Mount EVEREST. The black bear that lives in the wooded regions of the Himalayas is much smaller than the American bear.

HINDUISM, the religious system of the HINDUS. Brahma is worshipped as the Supreme God, and Vishnu and Siva are next in importance; many Hindus pay tribute to other gods as well. They all share the belief that the cow is a sacred animal.

HINDUS, followers of a religious system known as HINDUISM. The greater number of people in the republic of INDIA are Hindus.

HIPPOPOTAMUS. The name means "the river horse," but the hippopotamus is more like a great pig, weighing three or four tons. It lives in and around the Zambesi and other rivers in Africa, south of the equator. At night the hippopotamus may wander far afield to find food, and causes great damage to crops.

HOCKEY, an outdoor game played on a field by two teams of eleven players each, the object of each team being to knock a hard ball through the other team's goal by means of curved, wooden sticks.

HOLLAND. See NETHERLANDS.

HOMER. The *Iliad* and the *Odyssey* were considered wonderful epic poems by the Greeks, and by every civilized nation since that time. New translations of them are still being published. It is believed that both poems were written by Homer, who is said to have been a blind minstrel. He lived about 800 B.C.

HONGKONG, a British Crown Colony consisting of the Kowloon peninsula, on the south-east coast of China, and the island of Hongkong. It has a fine natural HARBOUR and is an important port and naval base. Victoria is the capital.

HORIZON. This name is given to the line where the land or sea appears to meet the sky in the distance. It is a level line which makes a complete circle round you

Hippopotamus.

149

Ancient Britain

Ancient Rome

Malaya

Papua

Mongolia

Russia

Arctic

America

D.H.Ralphs.

Different men have built different kinds of houses.

150

at a distance of something like three miles, if you are standing about six feet above sea-level. The higher you happen to be the wider does the horizon become, and from the top of a cliff one hundred feet high it appears to be twelve miles away.

HORN. The horn of a cow (or ram, or buffalo) is hollow and one can make a musical instrument from it on which a loud note can be blown. The name is also given to a brass instrument in an orchestra, the French horn. A little metal trumpet gives a high note; a metal trumpet ten feet long gives a low note. As it is not convenient to carry or use a straight trumpet ten feet long, it is coiled. (See ORCHESTRA.) By the use of stops and other arrangements all the required notes can be played but this complicated orchestral instrument is still called the horn.

HORSE. There are two main types of horse; the fast Arab type, from which racehorses have been developed, and the Clydesdales and Shires, which can pull heavy loads. Horses have been used by man for over four thousand years. They have ploughed the fields, carried goods, fought in battle and generally have helped man greatly in his march towards civilization. MOTOR-CARS, TRACTORS, TANKS and other mechanical vehicles have now taken over much of the work horses used to do.

HORSE-POWER. When it became necessary to have a definite unit for measuring the amount of work done by engines, James WATT suggested that a useful unit would be the amount of work a horse can do. This suggestion was adopted, and called one horse-power. It is the power to lift thirty-three thousand pounds one foot in one minute; for example, if a weight of one thousand pounds was on the ground, and an electric motor lifted that weight thirty-three feet in one minute, the motor would be doing one horse-power of work. It was found later that Watt had overestimated the power of a horse, for even the best horses cannot work at this rate.

HOSPITAL. This word used to mean an inn, where travellers could get shelter, food and rest. Later it came to mean a place where the poor and sick were cared for. Today, a hospital provides sick people with medical or surgical attention which cannot be given at home.

HOUSE OF COMMONS. The affairs of the British nation are now conducted chiefly by the House of Commons. At one time the King had great power, but CHARLES I was beheaded (1649) and JAMES II was deposed (1688) for trying to hold that power too long. Then the HOUSE OF LORDS used to have more power than the House of Commons; but as more and more people were allowed to vote, the House of Commons gradually obtained more control over the affairs of the nation. There are 635 elected members. The chairman is called the Speaker, because he was the man who in days gone by had to speak to the King, and tell him what the views of the Commons were. See ELECTION; POLITICS.

HOUSE OF LORDS, part of the British Parliament. The members of the House of Lords are not elected and consist of about 1070 peers. These include the Royal peers; the Archbishops of Canterbury and York and 24 Bishops; all hereditary peers of England, Scotland, the United Kingdom or Great Britain; life peers and peeresses; peeresses in their own right and nine Lords of Appeal in Ordinary.

The Lords consider all new laws, and either agree to them, or suggest changes. In difficult LAW cases the House of Lords is the final appeal.

HOUSES. Primitive men took shelter in caves, but once men settled down to live in definite places, houses of one kind or another were built. The Egyptians had plenty of mud and made mud houses; then they made bricks with the mud and built houses with bricks. Beautiful stone houses were built by the Babylonians, the Phoenicians, the Greeks and the Romans. In New Guinea men build houses on stakes in the water; in the East Indian Islands they build houses in the trees. In parts of North America and parts of Russia, where trees are plentiful, houses are built with logs. ESKIMOS still build houses with snow when they go on long journeys.

See also ARCHITECTURE.

HOVERCRAFT, a new type of vehicle which travels on a cushion of air just above water level. The cushion of air is caused by a large fan in the centre of the vehicle.

HUMMING-BIRDS are beautiful birds which are found in North and South America, chiefly in the warmer areas. They are so small, and their wings beat so quickly, that they make a humming noise, just as the bee does. Some humming-birds are not much bigger than a bee; others are nearly as big as a wren. The lowest note we can hear is about sixteen vibrations per second, and if a humming-bird did not beat his wings at least sixteen times a second we should not hear any hum. See SOUND, and the colour frontispiece of birds.

HUNDRED YEARS' WAR. England was at war with France for over a hundred years, from 1338 to 1453. EDWARD III had some claim to the French crown and took his army over to France to assert his claim. He conquered much of France, but could not hold it.

Then in 1415 HENRY V took his army over, defeated the French army at AGIN-COURT, and over-ran most of the country. It was agreed (1420) that Henry should marry the French Princess Catherine and succeed to the French throne. Henry died in 1422, however, so he never achieved his ambition. Then the French people, who had been badly organized and badly equipped, were roused to enthusiasm for their country by JOAN OF ARC, and under this inspiration they recaptured all France except the town of CALAIS. They recaptured that town a hundred years later (1558).

HUNGARY, a republic in Central Europe. Most of it consists of the fertile plain of the River Danube, and agriculture is the chief occupation. Wheat and maize are the most important crops, and cattle, pigs and horses are reared. Vines also are cultivated. Budapest is the capital.

HYBRID. The young which arrive when a female of one species mates with the male of a different species. Hybrids are most easily obtained where the two species are closely related, as in the mule, which has a male ass and a female horse (mare) for parents. Plants form hybrids much more readily than animals do.

HYDROGEN, the lightest of all gases. It is an ELEMENT, that is, it cannot be broken down into anything simpler. If two volumes of hydrogen and one volume of oxygen are mixed, and a light applied, there will be an explosion, and the *three* volumes of the two gases will have become *two* volumes of steam, or a few drops of water. Hydrogen combines with nitrogen to give ammonia gas, and with chlorine to give hydrochloric acid gas. Both of these gases are very soluble in water and give liquid ammonia and hydrochloric acid.

HYENA, a flesh-eating animal with powerful teeth and jaws. The lion attacks and kills, say, a deer. He eats about sixty or seventy pounds of meat and walks off. Hyenas come later, often at night, to finish the rest, and not even a bone is left. The hyena can crack and eat the thigh bone of an ox. Hyenas live in South Africa, India and other parts of Asia.

HYGIENE, a set of rules followed by people who wish to keep healthy. Public hygiene deals with such things as the supply of clean water, keeping streets clean, and the disposal of refuse and sewage. There is also home hygiene, making for cleanliness in the home, and personal hygiene, which includes washing, cleaning the teeth and anything else which helps to keep the body healthy. The word "hygiene" comes from the name of the Greek goddess of health, Hygieia.

ICE. If water is cooled till it reaches nought degrees Centigrade it turns into ice. As it cools it first contracts steadily until the temperature is four degrees Centigrade. Then it gradually expands, until by the time it becomes solid ice, it occupies nine per cent more space than it did when it was water. This expansion causes water-pipes to burst when they freeze, and rocks to be split apart when the water in the cracks becomes ice.

ICE AGE. Around the North Pole there is a cap of ice which never melts. In the history of the world there have been times when this ice-cap came farther south. About ten thousand years ago it seems to have been as far south as the River Thames. The causes of these cold periods are not fully understood. They happen in both HEMISPHERES.

ICEBERGS. As GLACIERS slide down into the sea from Greenland and similar places, enormous pieces break off and float away on OCEAN CURRENTS. These are

There are volcanoes in Iceland.

icebergs. Eight-ninths of the icebergs are always out of sight under the water, making them a great danger to shipping. The *Titanic*, a beautiful new ocean liner, racing across the Atlantic on her first voyage in 1912, suddenly struck a very large iceberg. It ripped the bottom of the ship, which sank in a few hours.

ICE HOCKEY, a game similar to HOCKEY but played on ice with a hard rubber disk called a puck instead of a ball. The players wear skates, and there are six on each side. Ice hockey is the national game of Canada, though it was played as "bandy" in the Fen country of England more than a hundred years ago.

ICELAND, an island REPUBLIC in the North Atlantic Ocean, rather larger than Scotland and Wales together. The country is mountainous, and ice and snow cover

Icebergs are dangerous.

The Boston Tea Party, 1773.

The War of Independence begins, 177

France, Spain and Holland support America, 1778–1780.

British surrender at Yorktown, 178

much of the high land. There are many VOLCANOES and hot springs, and EARTH-QUAKES sometimes occur. Most of the men are sea fishermen or sheep farmers. The capital is Reykjavik. See also GEYSERS.

IGNEOUS ROCKS. Two miles below the surface of the earth the temperature is about the BOILING POINT of water. At fifty miles down even the ROCKS melt. LAVA, that is, molten rock, is thrown up on the top of the earth at times, leaving for example, the granite mountains of Scotland, and the granite in the Alps and Pyrenees. These rocks which have been melted below the surface of the earth are called igneous rocks.

ILIAD, a long story poem by the Greek poet HOMER. It tells the story of the siege of the town of Troy by the Greeks, who came to rescue Helen, who had been carried away by a Trojan prince named Paris. The war lasted for ten years and the Greeks won by a clever trick. They hid some soldiers inside a huge wooden

horse which was dragged into the town by the Trojans. At night the soldiers crept out, opened the gates and let in the main army of the Greeks, who captured the town. Achilles, the chief champion of the Greeks, killed Hector, the Trojan hero. Helen was taken back to Greece.

ILLITERACY is the state of being unable to read or write, for the word means "the state of being without letters." A person may also be said to be illiterate when he cannot read or write *properly*.

ILLUSTRATION. When a man wrote a book he would try to make what he said as clear as he possibly could, so that people reading the book would understand him. To make something clearer he would give examples which might be a description or a little story. These examples were called illustrations. Then it was found that pictures helped to make things described or related very much easier to follow, and so pictures were added to the books and were called illustrations. So an illustrated

Declaration of Independence, 1776.

George Washington becomes President, 1789.

book or magazine is one that has many pictures.

IMMIGRATION occurs when people come from abroad to settle in your country. It is the opposite of EMIGRATION.

IMPORTS. See EXPORTS AND IMPORTS.

INCOME TAX is the money paid to the government of a country out of the wages people earn or from the profits of their shops or businesses; it is used to help to pay the cost of running the country (see TAXATION). It was first imposed in Britain in 1799 to meet the cost of the Napoleonic Wars, but it was dropped after Waterloo. It was revived in 1842 and has been continued ever since, and greatly increased. In the United States of America two lots of taxes are paid, one to the Federal Government and one to the State Government.

INDEPENDENCE, WAR OF. In the eighteenth century the British colonists in North America quarrelled with the British Government for interfering with their free-dom to trade with other nations and for imposing taxes on them. A tax on tea stirred them to action in 1773. Colonists dressed as Red Indians went aboard some ships in Boston Harbour and emptied the tea-chests into the harbour. This came to be known as the Boston Tea Party.

Fighting between the colonists and British troops broke out at Lexington in 1775, and was followed by the Battle of Bunker Hill in June of that year. Shortly afterwards George Washington became Commander-in-Chief of the forces against the British soldiers. Thomas Jefferson drafted the Declaration of Independence proclaimed in 1776. It demanded that the thirteen colonies should be free and independent. The war ended with the surrender of Lord Cornwallis at York-town in 1781, and Britain signed the treaty in 1783. The colonies combined to form a single federal republic three years later, and in 1789 George Washington became the first President of the United States of America. Independence Day is cele-brated throughout America on 4 July.

INDIAN SUBCONTINENT, a part of ASIA which is divided into three countries, India (see INDIA, REPUBLIC OF), Bangla-desh, and PAKISTAN; the first two are members of the BRITISH COMMONWEALTH OF NATIONS. These three countries and the independent states of NEPAL and Bhutan are often discussed as a single *geographical* unit.

The subcontinent is separated from the rest of Asia by a range of mountains called the HIMALAYAS; three important rivers flow from these mountains: the INDUS, the GANGES and the Brahmaputra. One of the earliest civilizations was in the fertile valleys of the Ganges and the Indus, and this is still the most densely populated part of the subcontinent.

The Ganges brings much water from the Himalayas, and the wet summer MONSOON swings round the Bay of Bengal, goes up the Ganges and brings more water. The Indus valley is also well-watered. It does

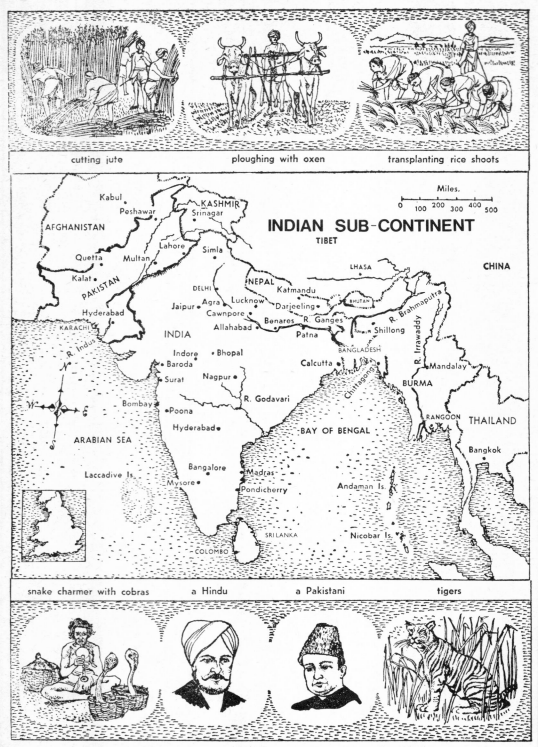

cutting jute ploughing with oxen transplanting rice shoots

INDIAN SUB-CONTINENT

Miles.
0 100 200 300 400 500

TIBET

AFGHANISTAN
Kabul
Peshawar
KASHMIR
Srinagar

CHINA
LHASA

Quetta
Multan
Lahore
Simla

Kalat
PAKISTAN

Hyderabad

KARACHI

R. Indus

DELHI
Jaipur
Agra
Cawnpore
Allahabad

NEPAL
Katmandu
Lucknow
Darjeeling
Benares
Patna

BHUTAN
R. Brahmaputra

R. Ganges
Shillong

BANGLADESH
Chittagong

Mandalay

INDIA

Indore
Baroda
Bhopal
Surat
Nagpur

Calcutta

BURMA

R. Godavari

R. Irrawaddy

Bombay
Poona
Hyderabad

ARABIAN SEA

BAY OF BENGAL

RANGOON

THAILAND

Bangkok

Bangalore
Mysore
Madras
Pondicherry

Laccadive Is.

Andaman Is.

SRI LANKA
COLOMBO

Nicobar Is.

snake charmer with cobras a Hindu a Pakistani tigers

The Indian subcontinent and some of the things found there.

156

Comet

hangars

runways

control tower

A jet aircraft flies over the airport before preparing to land.

LIGHT from the sun is made up of all the colours of the rainbow; these make up the spectrum

when the sun shines on rain the rays of light are bent; raindrops reflect the light, now separated into the colours of the spectrum, so forming a RAINBOW.

splitting-up of light by a glass prism

REFRACTION makes the brush look broken

a REFLECTION is seen when light rays are sent back just as they come.

spin a disk coloured like the rainbow and it will seem white

the PRIMARY colours in paints are red, blue and yellow; all the other colours are mixtures of these

Some things you should know about light and colour.

American Indians used to go on the warpath against the white man.

not get so much of the monsoon rain, but the river has five big tributaries all bringing water from the mountains and there are good IRRIGATION schemes. Great quantities of rice and wheat are grown in these two valleys and elsewhere, but there are over 650 million people in the subcontinent to be fed, and much grain is also imported. Rice, jute, tea and cotton are important exports.

There are many interesting animals in India, such as elephants, tigers and leopards. Poisonous snakes are a problem. They kill twenty thousand people every year, and if it were not for the little MONGOOSE, which is kept as a pet and kills any snake that may come into the house, many more people would be killed.

Important seaports and manufacturing towns include Calcutta, Bombay, Madras and Karachi.

There are many different forms of religion in this vast subcontinent, and many different languages. One of the earliest religions was that of BUDDHA, who lived about 500 B.C. Disagreement between the HINDUS and the MOSLEMS was one of the reasons for the division of the subcontinent into two countries. See also BUDDHISM; HINDUISM.

INDIA, REPUBLIC OF, a part of southern Asia. With PAKISTAN, Bangladesh and the states of NEPAL and Bhutan, it forms the INDIAN SUBCONTINENT. Most of the people who live in the republic are HINDUS. The Ganges and the Brahmaputra are the two chief rivers, and Delhi is the capital. See also HINDUISM.

INDIAN OCEAN, the great ocean which lies south of INDIA, and between Africa and Australia and the East Indian Islands. It extends south to about latitude forty degrees.

INDIANS, AMERICAN, natives of the American continent. COLUMBUS first used the name Indian to describe the people of the West Indies, because he thought he had reached India.

Nowadays American Indians, or Redskins, live peacefully in special reservations in Canada and the United States, but less than a hundred years ago they often went on the warpath. When the great herds of bison of the American plains began to die out, the Red Indians began to raid cow herds to get food; they held up stage-coaches and attacked lonely ranches. Cowboys and soldiers sometimes joined forces to fight them. The Cheyenne and the Sioux were very brave and good fighters. See also BUFFALO BILL.

INDO-CHINA is the name given to that part of south-east Asia which includes THAILAND, Laos, Cambodia, and Viet-Nam. Rice is the chief product; others include teak, pepper, sugar, tea and coffee.

INDONESIA is a republic in south-east Asia. It is made up of a group of islands lying along the equator and between south-east Asia and Australia; they make up most of the East Indies. Most of these islands were under Dutch rule (except for Timor, New Guinea and Sabah), but in 1949 these colonies became the United States of Indonesia with the Dutch Sovereign at the head, and in 1950 Indonesia became an independent republic. It includes the Sulawesi, Sumatra, Java and part of Kalimantan.

The climate is equatorial, something like that of Central Africa and the Amazon valley in South America. Rubber trees from the Amazon valley have been planted in some of the islands and in the Malay peninsula, and much rubber is exported. Other exports include copra, spices, sugar, tea, petroleum and tin. Rice is the chief food, and a lot of it is grown in Java. The name of the chief port is Djakarta (Batavia).

INDUS, a river in Pakistan. It has five important tributaries, the Beas, Jhelum, Chenab, Ravi and Sutlej; this land of the five rivers is called the Punjab, which means "five rivers."

INFANTRY. Soldiers who march and fight on foot are called infantry to distinguish them from the horse-soldiers or CAVALRY, and from the gunners or ARTILLERY.

INFECTION occurs when GERMS or microbes get into the body, where they multiply and produce poisons. When a disease such as an ordinary cold, or measles, spreads from one person to another it is called an infectious disease. A disease spread by touch is called *contagious*. See also BACTERIA.

INFLAMMATION is marked by a swelling and redness of a part of the body; the inflamed part is hot and painful. It is swollen and red because an extra supply of BLOOD flows to the affected place in order to fight the GERMS there. See also CORPUSCLES.

INFRA-RED RAYS. The ear can hear only a certain range of sounds, and the eye can see only a certain range of light rays: that is, violet, blue, green, yellow, orange, red. Violet rays have the shortest wave-length and red rays have the longest. Beyond the violet rays are the ultra-violet rays, which cannot be seen by the eye, although affecting a photographic plate. Beyond the red rays are the infra-red rays which also cannot be seen by the eye, but which likewise affect a photographic plate. The infra-red rays are next to heat rays. See LIGHT. Infra-red rays are in some ways more powerful than ordinary rays of light. Photographs taken through an infra-red ray filter show up the details much more clearly than do photographs taken in the ordinary way.

INOCULATION. This is putting a substance into the body of a person (through the skin), either to prevent or to cure a disease. When GERMS produce poisons (toxins) in the body, the body soon produces chemicals (anti-toxins) to fight against the poison. Anti-toxins can be obtained from a body that has already had the disease, and can be injected into the person who needs their help.

puppets used in Wayong shadow-show Java

girl dancers, Bali

lady of the Manankabau tribe, Sumatra

ships in Sulawesi harbour

native of Papua

copra in Sabah

palm-oil in Sarawak

Michael Ross

Some of the things found in Indonesia and other parts of the East Indies.

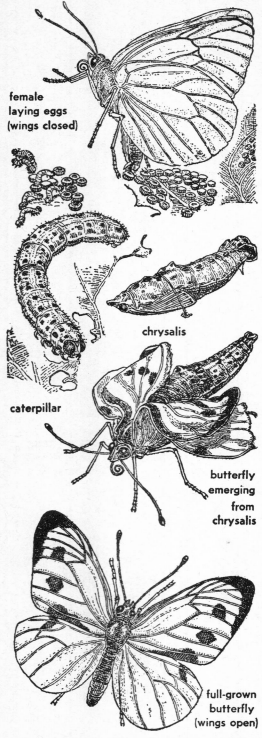

female laying eggs (wings closed)

caterpillar

chrysalis

butterfly emerging from chrysalis

full-grown butterfly (wings open)

Many insects go through a metamorphosis.

Sometimes a dose of the germs of the disease itself are put in to produce a mild form of the disease. This encourages the body to make its own chemicals to destroy the poison, and prevents a much more serious illness. Doing this is called VACCINATION.

INSECT. Scientists know over half a million different kinds of insect, and most of them breed at a remarkable rate. The name comes from the Latin word *insectum* meaning "cut into," and the body is divided into three parts. The first is the *head*. This carries the compound and simple eyes, one pair of feelers (antennae) and the mouth parts for biting and sucking or piercing and sucking.

The second part is the *thorax*, or front part. It carries three pairs of legs, and, in the flying insects, two pairs of wings. All insects have six legs. (The spider has eight legs and is not an insect.)

The third part is the *abdomen*, or hind part. It sometimes carries a sting.

Insects breathe through a series of openings along each side of the body. Air is then carried to all parts of the body by branching air-tubes

The development of many insects is through a change of form known as a *metamorphosis*. First, a larva hatches from an egg. This creature feeds and grows, and sheds its skin as it gets too big for it. This happens several times. When it has finished growing the creature usually becomes a pupa (see CHRYSALIS). It does not move about, or eat, but rests until it has changed into its complete form. Then the fully-grown insect comes out of the pupa.

Some insects develop a little differently. The BEETLE does not build a chrysalis and others like the DRAGONFLY, GRASSHOPPER, and earwig look like their parents (except that they have no wings) as soon as they come out of the eggs. They are then called nymphs. They grow and moult until they reach the adult stage. See also ANTS; BEE; BUTTERFLY; FLY; INVERTEBRATES; LOCUST; MOTH; SOCIAL INSECTS.

INSECT-EATING PLANTS. In addition to making their own food by photosynthesis, some PLANTS catch and digest insects as well. Some insect-eating plants found in Britain are the sundew, bladderwort, and butterwort. There are many kinds of pitcher-plant found in tropical countries.

The sundew has sticky tentacles on its leaves, which curl round the insect; digestive juices pour out, and dissolve the soft body of the insect so that the leaf can absorb it. The pitcher-plant has a different kind of trap. It is smooth inside, and the insect falls into a pool of digestive juices at the bottom of the pitcher.

INSULATOR. Electricity can flow along copper but it can hardly flow at all along glass. We call glass an insulator. The telegraph wires carry electrical messages. If we nailed the wires on to the wooden poles the electricity would spread over the pole when it was wet and into other wires, and then no one could read any of the messages. So all these wires are attached not directly to the posts but to knobs of grooved china, which is a very good insulator. In the house the wires are insulated by being covered in rubber fabric. Rubber is another good insulator.

INSURANCE is a way of guarding against loss, or damage to life or property. For example, if you insure your bicycle for £20, the insurance company will pay you £20 if it is stolen or gets smashed in an accident. A man who has a family often has a life insurance so that his family will get some money if he dies suddenly. Of course, the insurance company will not do this for nothing, but requires you to pay an agreed sum of money—called a premium—at regular intervals. This payment may be made weekly, monthly, or yearly. The agreement with the company is called a policy.

INTEREST. If a man asked his banker to lend him £100 for a year he might or might not get it, depending on how reliable a person he was, but if he got it he would have to pay back about £105 at the end of the year. The extra £5 is called the yearly interest. Many people want to borrow money to extend their business, or to help them over a difficulty; most of them are honest and successful and repay it. Occasionally someone cannot repay the money, or disappears and does not try to repay it. Bankers and others who lend money must have a little extra to make up for these losses, and to pay for the time and trouble they have to take in arranging the loan.

INTERNAL COMBUSTION ENGINE. Internal combustion engines are those which burn their fuel right inside the ENGINE instead of outside it under a boiler. The best example is an ordinary petrol engine, in which a mixture of air and petrol is exploded inside the cylinders, so forcing the pistons to turn the crankshaft. The diesel engine, which is used to drive some lorries, buses, locomotives and motor-ships, is an internal combustion

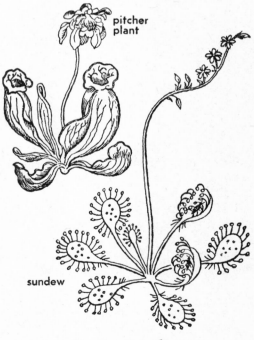

Insect-eating plants.

161

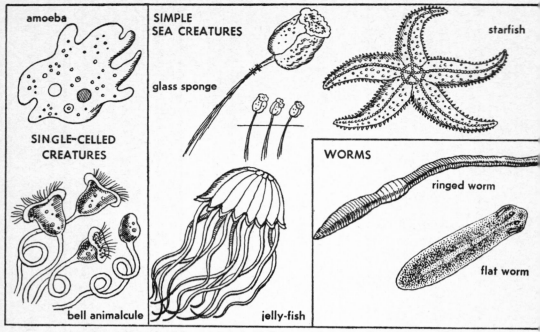

amoeba

SIMPLE SEA CREATURES

glass sponge

starfish

SINGLE-CELLED CREATURES

WORMS

ringed worm

flat worm

bell animalcule

jelly-fish

Animals without backbones are called invertebrates; they are arranged in groups

engine which burns heavy oil instead of petrol. ROCKETS, JET-ENGINES and gas-turbines are also internal combustion engines since they all burn their fuel inside. See also CARBURETTOR, SPARKING PLUG, VALVE.

INTERVAL, in music, is the distance between two notes. From C to D is called a second. C, D, E are three notes, and from C to E is called a third. C, D, E, F are four notes, and from C to F is called a fourth, and so on. Or, expressed in the sol-fa notation, doh to ray, or ray to me, is a second; doh to me, or ray to fah, is a third; doh to fah, or ray to soh, is a fourth, and so on.

INTESTINE, the long, narrow tube into which the contents of the stomach pass. Its walls are plentifully supplied with blood-vessels and nerves, as well as digestive glands, and they are strengthened with two layers of muscle. The intestine completes the digestion of food, absorbs nourishment to be passed on to the rest of the body, and carries off the waste matter. See also BLOOD, NERVOUS SYSTEM.

INVERTEBRATES. This is a convenient term for all animals which do not have backbones. These include all the insects and spiders, the crabs and lobsters, the slugs, snails and octopuses, the worms, starfish, jellyfish, sea-anemones and sponges. You can read about these under their own headings. See also AMOEBA; MOLLUSC; VERTEBRATES.

INVOICE, a list of articles which have been bought, with their prices marked beside them, or a description (including the cost) of some work which has been done to order.

IONA, an island of the Inner Hebrides, Scotland. Saint Columba, a missionary from Ireland, landed here in A.D. 563 and founded a monastery.

IRAN. See PERSIA.

IRAQ (Mesopotamia), a country in south-west Asia. The name Mesopotamia means "the land between the rivers," and the rivers are the EUPHRATES and the Tigris. These rivers bring down fertile mud, just as the Nile does in EGYPT. This area was one of the early civilizations. (See

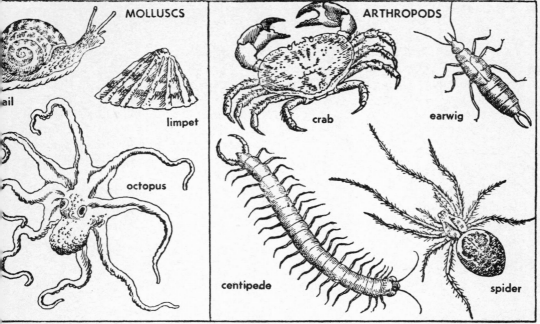

MOLLUSCS ARTHROPODS

ail

limpet

octopus

crab

earwig

centipede

spider

of which the arthropods form the largest. The name means "jointed feet."

BABYLON.) Dates are an important crop, but the chief export is oil. Over 800,000 people live in Baghdad, the capital.

IRELAND is one of the BRITISH ISLES. The north-eastern part of the island is part of the UNITED KINGDOM (see NORTHERN IRELAND). The rest of Ireland forms a self-governing republic, independent of Britain. (See IRELAND, REPUBLIC OF).

The rocks of Ireland are a continuation of those in Scotland and England, but there are differences. The layer of lime-stone, which is tilted up in England and makes the Cotswold Hills, is lying flat in the middle of the country, and the layer of coal which used to cover it has been almost completely washed off. A little of the coal remains at Carlow.

The mountains are round the edge of the country, but while there are great fields of lovely grass, and many fields of potatoes and oats, much of the land is too boggy to be useful. There are many inland lakes.

Most of the people live in small farms. Cattle, pigs, and dairy produce are exported. Dublin, Belfast and Cork are the largest towns. The Shannon, the Liffey and the Boyne are the chief rivers.

IRELAND, REPUBLIC OF. The country has a mild, rather wet, climate more suitable for grass than wheat, and cattle and dairy produce are exported. Potatoes and oats are grown to feed the people. There is very little coal in Ireland, so it is imported, and the river SHANNON is used to develop hydro-electric power. DUBLIN is the capital, and over 550,000 people live in the city. Dublin is also an important port: others include Cork, Galway, and Waterford. Most of the people living in the republic are Roman Catholics. See also IRELAND ; NORTHERN IRELAND.

IRISH SEA, a sea between Ireland and England. It is connected with the Atlantic Ocean to the north by the North Channel, and by Saint George's Channel to the south. It contains the ISLE OF MAN and some smaller islands. See the colour map facing page 33.

IRON is the most important metal. It is dug out of the ground in the form of iron ore, which has other materials in it, and the iron has to be separated from these materials.

The ore is melted in a BLAST FURNACE, and the impurities are skimmed off. This scum is called slag. The melted iron runs into moulds and when it has set hard is called pig-iron.

Cast-iron is made by melting pig-iron in a FOUNDRY; it runs into moulds of the shape of the article which is to be made. There is a small amount of carbon left in cast-iron after smelting, and this has to be taken out to make wrought-iron.

STEEL is an ALLOY of iron. It has less carbon than cast-iron, but more than wrought-iron.

IRON AGE, the third stage in the development of civilization of prehistoric man. The first two were the STONE AGE and the Bronze Age (see BRONZE).

IRRIGATION is the use of artificial ways of keeping the land supplied with water when there is not enough rain. Egypt, India, China and Mesopotamia all had arrangements of one kind or another for irrigating fields, as far back as we have any records of these lands. Water-wheels, for example, are still used in places, but people have since learned to build DAMS, to store water until it is needed, like the great dam at Aswan, on the Nile, or Boulder Dam, on the Colorado river in America. See also CANAL.

ISAIAH was one of the greatest of the Hebrew prophets. He lived about 760 B.C. to 700 B.C. Some of his prophecies are given in the Old Testament, in the Book of Isaiah. He foretold the coming of JESUS CHRIST.

ISLAND. Any land completely surrounded by water is called an island. It may be a little island in a lake, or a huge island like Australia. Islands like the Isle of Wight are just bits of the mainland separated by drowned valleys (drowned river valleys in this case). Islands like St. Helena were caused by volcanic eruptions in the middle of the ocean.

ISLE OF MAN, an island in the IRISH SEA. It is part of the UNITED KINGDOM but has its own Parliament, called the Tynwald. When laws have been approved by the British Sovereign they are read aloud on the Tynwald Hill, in English and in the ancient Manx language.

ISRAEL. This is the name which the BIBLE says God gave to JACOB at Bethel. The story is told in chapters thirty-two and thirty-five of the book of Genesis. The name soon came to be used for all Jacob's people, and to mean the Jews or Hebrews. The new Jewish country which was founded in 1948 by dividing PALESTINE into two countries is called Israel. It is a republic, and its capital is JERUSALEM.

ITALY. This country is a long peninsula, shaped like a leg, with the toe kicking the island of Sicily. ROME, with its wonderful history, is the capital. Round the north of Italy are the ALPS, and some of the beautiful lakes are in Italy. The Apennine chain of mountains runs down the middle of the peninsula. Between the Alps and the Apennines is the fertile plain of Lombardy, with the River Po flowing through it.

The usual Mediterranean fruits grow in Italy: oranges, lemons, olives, grapes, peaches and apricots.

Many of the mountain streams generate electricity used in manufacturing silk and cotton goods, chiefly in the plain of Lombardy.

Italy has some towns that are world famous: Rome, Venice, Naples, Florence, Genoa and others, and many of the most famous names in literature, art, music and science are Italian: Dante, Boccaccio, Leonardo da Vinci, Verdi, GALILEO, Torricelli; MARCO POLO, one of the greatest explorers, was also an Italian.

IVORY, the hard white, or cream, substance of which elephants' tusks, and the teeth of the hippopotamus and other big animals, are made. It is used for making beautifully carved ornaments, and for pianoforte keys, and knife handles.

J

JACOB, the son of Isaac, and the grandson of ABRAHAM. He was also called Israel, and it is from him that the Israelites got their name. The story of Jacob is told in the Bible, in the Book of Genesis. See also JOSEPH.

The jaguar is very strong.

JAGUAR, a member of the CAT family, found in Central and South America. It looks very like a leopard, but is bigger. The jaguar is a powerful animal. It can pull down a horse or a deer, climb trees like a cat, and swim across a river. See also CARNIVORES.

JAMAICA, one of the islands of the WEST INDIES. Christopher COLUMBUS discovered it in 1494, on his second voyage across the Atlantic. The climate is almost tropical, and the forests provide valuable woods. Pineapples, bananas, oranges, lemons, sugar, coffee and maize all grow well, and Jamaica is noted for its rum. Kingston is the capital and chief port.

JAMES I, son of MARY, QUEEN OF SCOTS, was proclaimed James VI of Scotland in 1567. On the death of ELIZABETH I of England the two kingdoms were united under his rule, and he reigned as James I, King of Great Britain and Ireland, from 1603 to 1625. (The Parliaments of England and Scotland were not united until the reign of Queen ANNE.)

James ruled at times as if Parliament had no importance, and the quarrels began which resulted later in his son, CHARLES I, being executed.

James authorized a new translation of the Bible, and this is still known as the "Authorized Version." Other important events during his reign were the GUNPOWDER PLOT, and the sailing of the PILGRIM FATHERS to America.

JAMES II. When CHARLES II died in 1685 his brother James, Duke of York, became King. He seemed to forget that his father, CHARLES I, had lost his life through defying Parliament, for he tried to defy it too. In 1688 Parliament deposed him and invited his daughter Mary and her husband William, who ruled in Holland, to come and rule Britain. James escaped to France with his wife and son, and WILLIAM III and MARY II ruled together. James died in exile in 1701.

Banana plantation in Jamaica.

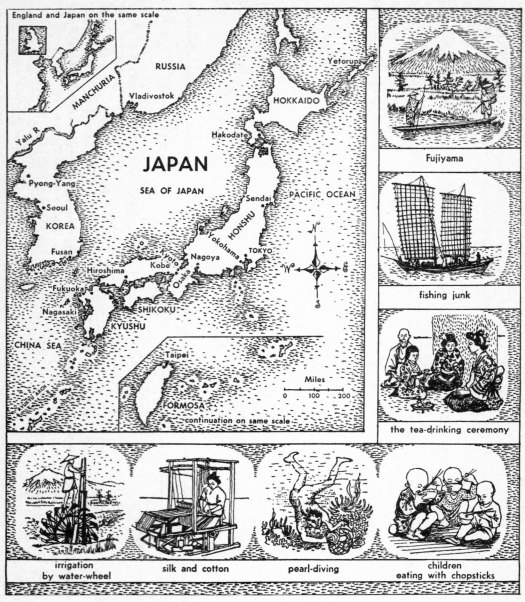

Japan, and some of the things found there.

JAPAN, a country off the east coast of ASIA. It is made up of four large islands—Honshu, Hokkaido, Kyushu, and Shikoku—and many small islands in the North Pacific. It is very mountainous and has many volcanoes. Mount Fujiyama is the sacred mountain of Japan.

Japan has a population of over 100 million, with over eleven million in the capital town, Tokyo. Rice is the chief food. Many Japanese are farmers or fishermen, but many more work in the factories.

Exports include cotton and rayon goods, machinery, ships, canned fish, chemicals, and a wide variety of manufactured goods, such as toys, cars, radios, and cameras. Yokohama, Kobe, and Nagasaki are the chief ports.

JAVA, an island in the EAST INDIES forming part of INDONESIA. Nearly three million people live in Djakarta, the capital. Exports include rubber, tea, coffee, and sugar. There are many interesting wild animals, such as the rhinoceros, tiger, panther, wild hog, and crocodile.

JELLY-FISH are sea animals which are just like pieces of transparent jelly. Their bodies are largely made of water. The shape of jelly-fish varies, but a typical example is like an umbrella with long, thin, trailing tentacles. Minute stinging-cells cover the surface of the body, and there are at least four thicker tentacles from the mouth. These have stinging-cells at the end. See INVERTEBRATES.

JERUSALEM, one of the oldest cities in the world. It is also known as the Holy City. Formerly the capital of PALESTINE, Jerusalem was divided into two parts until the end of the Six Day War in 1967—the Arab "Old City" and the Jewish "New City." It is now entirely under Israeli control. See also ISRAEL; JORDAN.

JESUS CHRIST was the founder of Christianity. His purpose was to teach people about the love and power of God and to show them how to live a good life by the way He lived His own. He was born in Bethlehem, a village near JERU-SALEM, but His mother, Mary, and her husband Joseph, had their home in Nazareth, and Jesus lived there until He was about thirty years old. Then He began to preach. He chose twelve people to help Him, so that they could continue to spread His teaching throughout the world after His death. (See APOSTLES.)

The story of His life is told in the Bible, in the NEW TESTAMENT. See GOSPELS.

JET ENGINE. A jet ENGINE has three principal parts. In front is an opening through which a powerful fan or "compressor" sucks in great quantities of air and packs it in tight or "compresses" it. In the middle are the combustion chambers where this compressed air is heated by jets of burning oil. The air expands as it gets hot. At the rear is the large exhaust-pipe or "nozzle," through which the hot expanded air and the exhaust gases rush out at enormous speed. On their way out they blow round a light fan or turbine, which is joined to the compressor in the front of the engine, so turning the compressor. The gases blow out of the nozzle at a speed equal to that of a rifle bullet, and the engine itself behaves like the rifle firing the bullet—that is, it recoils in the opposite direction. The recoil of a rifle is felt as a slight kick against the shoulder, but the recoil of a jet engine is a continuous push well able to drive an aeroplane forward. The first jet-aeroplane was developed as a result of experiments made by Sir Frank Whittle in 1930. See also AEROPLANE and the colour plate facing page 160.

Joan of Arc rallied the French forces.

JOAN OF ARC, born in 1412, was a French peasant girl, who lived at the time when England had conquered most of France. (See HUNDRED YEARS' WAR.) She was a highly imaginative girl, who sometimes heard voices and saw visions, and she felt that God was telling her to go to the aid of the rightful King of France and to help to restore the confidence of the French soldiers. Joan was about seventeen at the time. She dressed as a soldier and inspired the French army to raise the siege of Orléans in 1429. In the same year the Maid of Orléans, as she was known, attended the coronation of Charles VII at Reims. In 1430 she was taken prisoner, and the following year was burned as a witch, while only a girl of eighteen. She died bravely. It was a wonderful contribution she made to her country, for her life and death restored the courage and morale of the whole French nation. She was declared to be a saint in 1920.

JOHN, King of England from 1199 to 1216. Though he was called "Lackland" he received many rich gifts of land in both England and France, but he also quarrelled with the French and lost Normandy. He was a weak, vain and selfish king, and fought against his own barons. In 1215 they forced him to set his seal to the Great Charter, or MAGNA CARTA, which laid down just laws for the king to follow in ruling the people.

King John set his seal to Magna Carta.

JORDAN is an Arab country in the NEAR EAST (that is, the area to the east of the Mediterranean); it includes most of the fertile valley of the River Jordan. It is a kingdom, and its capital city is Amman. See also ISRAEL; JERUSALEM.

JOSEPH, one of the sons of JACOB and brother of Benjamin. Joseph's other brothers were jealous and sold him to some slave-dealers who took him to Egypt. Here he was imprisoned, but was sent for by Pharaoh to interpret a dream. Pharaoh was so impressed that he made Joseph deputy ruler. When a famine arose his brothers came to Egypt to buy corn, and Joseph forgave them and invited his whole family to come and live in Egypt. The story is told in the BIBLE, in the Book of Genesis.

JUDGE. A judge is an officer of the LAW appointed to hear criminal or civil cases brought to a court of law. He sees that each trial is fairly conducted, that the law is being used properly, and that the JURY understands thoroughly what the trial is about. If a person is found guilty the judge orders a suitable punishment as set out in the law of the country.

JUPITER is the largest planet. The EARTH has one moon, but Jupiter has four large moons, which were discovered by GALILEO in 1610, and several very small ones, which have been discovered since 1892.

Jupiter has three hundred times more mass than the earth, and has not cooled down yet as the earth has. But if it had a crust, and men lived on the crust, they would be very different people from us. The force of gravity would be so great that men would need very thick and strong legs to keep them up, and if a man lay down on the ground he could hardly get up again. See also SOLAR SYSTEM.

JURY, a group of ordinary persons appointed to listen to the EVIDENCE in a court of LAW, and then to decide if the person being tried is guilty or not. Their decision is called the verdict. See JUDGE.

K

KALAHARI, a desert in SOUTH AFRICA, corresponding to the Sahara desert in North Africa, and in the same latitude as the Australian desert. Ostriches live here, and springboks. These gazelles (members of the antelope family) are found in various parts of South Africa, and large herds are seen in the Kalahari desert. The springbok gets its name from the great leaps it can make.

KANGAROO, an animal found in AUSTRALIA. There are various kinds, some as small as a hare, some as big as a man. All of them, however, have huge hind legs which enable them to bound along in a series of big jumps. The females all have a pouch on the tummy, in which they keep their young; the baby kangaroos feed on milk from the mother's body, and as they grow bigger they come out of the pouch occasionally to explore the world on their own. If there is any danger they bolt in again, and the mother bounds off.

The wallaby is a small kangaroo. There are many species and they are found in Australia and Tasmania. See also MAMMALS.

KAOLIN, or china clay, is a pure white clay used for making porcelain and POTTERY. The Chinese were the first to make fine porcelain. See CHINA CLAY.

KARACHI was the capital of PAKISTAN; over one million people live there. It is an important airport, and the chief seaport of Pakistan. The new capital is Islamabad. See also INDIA.

KEATS, John, was born in 1795. Although he died when he was only twenty-six (in 1821), he is one of the great English poets. Two of his poems which boys and girls can enjoy are *To a Nightingale* and *To Autumn*. Here is the first verse of a more difficult poem (*La Belle Dame Sans Merci*)—notice the lovely "tune" it has:

> *"O what can ail thee, Knight-at-arms,*
> *Alone and palely loitering?*
> *The sedge has wither'd from the lake*
> *And no birds sing."*

KENYA is a republic within the British Commonwealth. Nairobi is the capital and over 500,000 people live there. Most of the people are Africans. They grow maize and millet for food, and many of them keep cattle.

European settlers still occupy a part of the Kenya highlands, where the soil is good for farming. Wheat, maize, tea, and coffee are some of the crops grown here, and cedar from the forests is an important export, for the manufacture of pencils. From the coastal region comes cotton, copra, sugar, and cashew nuts.

There are lots of wild animals in Kenya, including the lion, the African elephant, and the black rhinoceros.

KING, a ruler of a state or country called a "kingdom." In Britain the King or Queen rules according to the advice of Parliament, and cannot make laws as kings used to do. The Sovereign is acclaimed as the rightful ruler at his Coronation, and wears a Crown on State occasions like the opening of Parliament. See also HOUSE OF COMMONS; HOUSE OF LORDS; POLITICS.

KINGFISHER, a bird found in most parts of the world. It is usually noted for its brilliantly-coloured plumage. Often seen in Britain, the kingfisher makes its nest in a hole in the bank of a stream or river, where it is sure to find plenty of fish. Its vivid blue and chestnut plumage makes a bright splash of colour as it dives into the water for its prey.

Some of the tropical kingfishers live on insects and earthworms, and the kingfisher of AUSTRALIA (the kookaburra) lives on insects, lizards and frogs. Unlike other members of the family, it does not always live near water. See colour frontispiece.

KINGSLEY, Charles, born in 1819, was an English writer who became famous for his children's books. He was Professor of Modern History at Cambridge, and wrote historical novels as well. *Westward Ho!* and *Hereward the Wake* are two very exciting stories. *The Water Babies*, for younger children, tells the story of Tom, a little boy who worked for Mr. Grimes, the chimney-sweep. One day he ran away, and was changed by the fairies into a water-baby. Then all his adventures began; he met some strange people, like Mrs. Bedonebyasyoudid and Mrs. Doasyouwouldbedoneby, but you must read the story if you want to know what happened. Although Kingsley died in 1875, his stories are still loved as much as ever.

KIPLING, Rudyard, a famous English writer, was born in India in 1865. He wrote many exciting stories and poems with India as the background. His books include *Kim, Soldiers Three, Plain Tales from the Hills.* His children's books include stories about animals, like *The Jungle Book* and *The Second Jungle Book*, which tell the story of Mowgli, who was brought up by wolves, and made friends with Baloo the bear and the other jungle animals. He also wrote a famous school story, *Stalky & Co.* Of his poems, *If* is probably the best-known. Kipling died in 1936.

KIWI, a flightless bird, found in NEW ZEALAND. It has a very long beak which it drives into the ground to dig out worms. The Maori chiefs formerly used the feathers of the kiwi for their cloaks, and so many of the birds have been killed that the government has had to make laws to protect them. See also BIRDS.

KNITTING, a way of making a material or garment using only one thread. The thread, which is usually of wool, is made into a chain of loops by means of two knitting-needles. A tube of knitted material, such as a sock, may be made without seams by using four needles. Knitted material is made in factories by power-driven machines called knitting-frames.

Here are some simple knitting instructions. You could begin by making a scarf for Teddy.

Casting-on means making the first row of loops on the knitting-needles. The picture on page 171 shows you two ways of doing this. The *thumb method* gives a firm, even edge. Leave a length of wool long enough for the number of stitches you want to make, and make a slip-knot on the needle (1). Pull the loose end of wool gently until the loop fits the needle, but make sure it is not too tight. Then hold the needle in your right hand, and keep the ball of wool to your right. Take the loose end of wool in your left hand. Loop it over your thumb (2) and push the needle through the loop from front to back (3). Bring the wool from the ball round the point of the needle (4) and pull this loop through the loop on your thumb. Slip your thumb out, and pull the loose

Charles Kingsley wrote about little Tom.

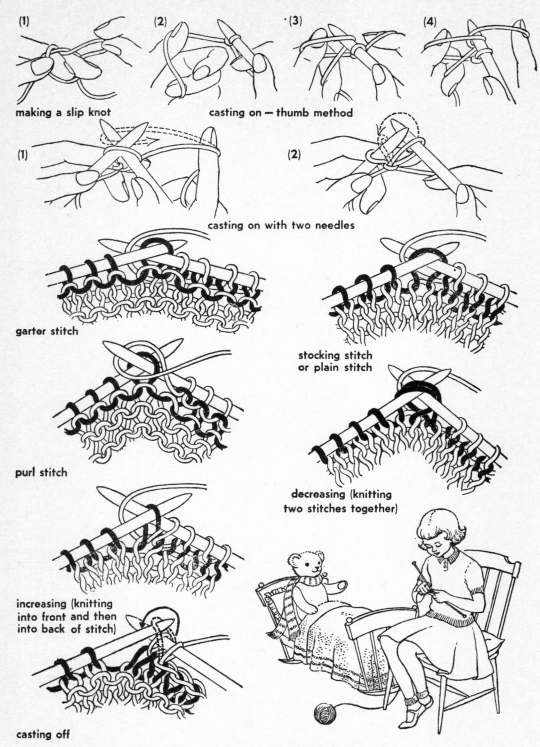

(1) **(2)** **·(3)** **(4)**

making a slip knot   casting on — thumb method

(1) **(2)**

casting on with two needles

garter stitch

stocking stitch
or plain stitch

purl stitch

decreasing (knitting
two stitches together)

increasing (knitting
into front and then
into back of stitch)

casting off

You can follow any pattern once you know the simple knitting stitches.

end of wool gently until the stitch on the needle fits firmly. Repeat until you have as many stitches as you need.

Casting-on two needles: make a slip-knot on the left-hand needle, push the point of the right-hand needle through the front half of this loop, from front to back (1). The right-hand needle should slide under the left-hand needle. Bring the wool from the ball round the point of the right-hand needle and draw it up between the two needles. With the point of the right-hand needle pull the wool through the loop. Slip the new loop on to the left-hand needle (2). Then slip the right-hand needle under the front of the last loop on the left-hand needle. Bring the wool round the point, between the two needles, and draw into a new loop. Repeat until you have as many stitches as you need.

Many different kinds of stitches can be used to make different patterns. *Garter stitch* is the pattern made by rows of plain knitting. *Stocking stitch* is the pattern made by knitting one row plain, one row purl.

Plain knit stitch. When you have cast-on the number of stitches you need, hold the needle with the stitches on it in your left hand. Push the right-hand needle into the front half of the first loop from front to back. Bring the wool round the point of the right-hand needle and pull the new loop on to the right-hand needle. Then slip the old loop off the left-hand needle. Repeat until you reach the end of the row. The wool is kept at the back of the work in plain knitting.

Purl stitch. When you have cast-on the number of stitches you need, hold the needle with the stitches on it in your left hand. The wool is kept to the front of the work in purl knitting. Bring the wool over the right-hand needle, and push the needle into the front half of the first loop from the back to the front. Bring the wool between the two needles and round under the point of the right-hand needle, and pull the new loop on to the right-

hand needle. Then slip the old loop off the left-hand needle. Repeat to the end of the row.

Casting-off is the way of removing the stitches from the needle when the knitting is completed, and finishing them off so that they do not come undone. Here are two ways of doing this.

Single cast-off. Knit or purl the first two stitches. Then use the left-hand needle to pick up the first stitch on the right-hand needle. Lift the first stitch over the second stitch, and slide it off the right-hand needle. Now knit or purl the next stitch on the left-hand needle and again lift the first stitch on the right-hand needle over the second stitch, to slide it off the needle. Continue in this way until you reach the end of the row. Pull the end of the wool through the last stitch.

Double cast-off. Push the right-hand needle through the first two stitches on the left-hand needle. Bring the wool round the point of the right-hand needle and pull through as you do in knit-stitch, but slip this new loop back on to the left-hand needle. Repeat, until you reach the end of the row. Pull the end of the wool through the last stitch.

If you are making a jumper for Teddy, you will have to shape the neck and arm-holes. When your knitting pattern tells you to increase or decrease, this is how to do it.

Increasing. Do this in plain knit stitch. First knit a stitch in the usual way but do not slip the old loop off the left-hand needle. Now pass the point of the right-hand needle into the back half of the same loop as before and knit another stitch in the usual way. Slip the old loop off the needle. You now have two stitches in place of one.

Decreasing. Push the point of the right-hand needle into the first two stitches on the left-hand needle and simply count them as one stitch. Either knit or purl them in the usual way, slipping both the old loops off the needle at the end. You now have one loop in place of two.

172

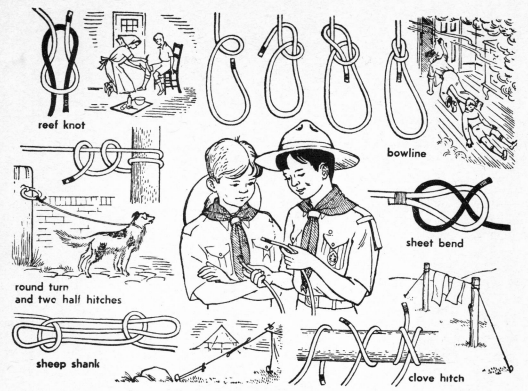

reef knot

bowline

round turn
and two half hitches

sheet bend

sheep shank

clove hitch

Many different kinds of knots can be made for various purposes.

KNOTS. This word has two meanings: it is a fastening used to tie up or to join string or ropes; it is also the measure of speed of a ship.

The picture above shows some kinds of knots used for different purposes. A *reef knot* joins ropes of the same thickness. It can be used, too, in emergency first-aid. A *bowline* makes a loop that will not slip. A *round turn and two half-hitches* secures a rope to a ring. A *single sheet bend* secures a rope to a ring or to a thicker rope. A *sheepshank* takes up the slack when a rope is fixed at both ends. A *clove-hitch* ties a rope to a rail or post.

In the days of sailing-ships, when sailors wanted to know how fast a ship was travelling they had a reel of rope, marked with knots every $50\frac{2}{3}$ feet, and a log of wood tied to the end. They dropped the log over the stern of the ship and counted how many knots reeled out in half a minute. This gave the number of "knots" the ship was making.

Half a minute is $\frac{1}{120}$ of an hour. $50\frac{2}{3}$ feet is $\frac{1}{120}$ of a nautical mile (that is, of 6,080 feet). So the number of knots which are pulled out in half a minute gives the number of nautical miles per hour that the ship is sailing.

The Log Book gets its name from this primitive way of measuring the speed of a ship. See LOG; NAVIGATION.

KRAKATOA, one of the East Indian islands, between Java and Sumatra (see INDONESIA). In 1883 a volcanic explosion blew a cubic mile of it into the air. The bang was heard in Sri Lanka, two thousand miles away, and the dust from the explosion got into the upper atmosphere and circulated round the earth for about two years. This dust made beautiful red and golden sunsets in many countries. See LIGHT.

L

LABORATORY, a room or building, specially equipped for scientific EXPERIMENTS in PHYSICS, or CHEMISTRY, or BIOLOGY.

LABOUR, the name of a political party in Britain which has a policy broadly based on SOCIALISM. See also CONSERVATIVE; COMMUNISM; POLITICS.

LAKE. There are several kinds of lake. Land may settle down and the hollow may fill up with rain water (for example, Lake Victoria, in Africa). Or a rift valley may have happened when the earth was cooling—it occurs when a narrow block of land sinks as if supports had given way beneath it—and the sunken place gets partly filled with rain water (for example, Lake Tanganyika and Lake Malawi in Africa). The exit of a river may be blocked, and the valley fill up with the river water: this often happens when, in a colder age, a GLACIER has made the valley and left its mass of stones and soil at the foot (called a "moraine"). The lakes of the LAKE DISTRICT in the north-west of England were formed in this way. See VALLEYS.

LAKE DISTRICT, a district in north-west England famous for its beautiful lakes and mountains. Although it is the wettest part of England, many people spend holidays there in order to enjoy the scenery. There are few good roads, and the best way to see the district is to walk. The farmers keep sheep on the fells.

LAKE DWELLINGS are primitive houses built on wooden stakes or on little artificial islands in a lake. Pre-historic remains of these have been found in Switzerland and elsewhere, and this type of house is still found in Borneo and other East Indian islands. See HOUSES.

LAND AND SEA BREEZES. Cold air is heavy and descends or flows downwards. Warm air is light (because it has expanded with the HEAT) and rises or flows upwards. Along the sea-coast when the hot sun shines on land and sea alike, the land gets

During the day there is a cool sea breeze, at night a cold land breeze.

174

hotter than the sea, the air above the land rises upwards, and air from the sea flows in to fill the gap. When it does so, we feel the breeze. At night the land quickly loses its heat, but the sea loses heat more slowly. Hence the warm air rises from the sea, and cold air from the land flows towards the sea. These daily movements of the air are called land and sea breezes. See also EXPANSION.

LARIAT, a cowboy's rope, made of fibre or braided rawhide. It is from 30 to 100 feet long, with a slip-noose at one end, and is used to catch runaway or stray animals. (In earlier days, the term "lariat" was used by some cowboys to mean a fibre rope, but to others it meant a short rope with a noose at one end which was used to tether animals while grazing.)

If the cowboy is on horseback, he carries the rope on the right side of the saddle. When he is ready to lasso the animal he holds the coil with his left hand and whirls the noose round above his head until it spins into a large loop. Then he throws the loop over the horns or head of the animal. The slightest pull draws the noose tight.

If the cowboy is not on horseback he does not spin the rope above his head, and he is more likely to catch the animal by throwing the lariat in its path to catch its feet, and trip it up. See also LASSO; RODEO.

LARVA, the first stage in an insect's life. The creature that hatches from the egg is called the larva. (The plural is larvae). Grubs, caterpillars, and maggots are all larvae. The term larva is also used of the corresponding stage of many other creatures. See INSECT.

LASSO. The meaning of this word has changed from its original sense. Nowadays it is another name for a cowboy's rope, or LARIAT, but originally it was used as a verb. Cowboys used to lasso an animal with a lariat. See also RODEO.

LATITUDE. The EQUATOR is an imaginary line which divides the earth into two hemispheres. We could draw another line like this halfway between the equator and the North or South Pole, and then still others slicing the globe sideways, so to speak, at regular intervals. These are lines of latitude. They are drawn on most maps. The one halfway between the

There are many ways of throwing a lariat.

equator and North Pole is referred to as "latitude 45 degrees North." See also GLOBE; LONGITUDE; NORTH; NORTH STAR.

LAVA, rock which has flowed in a molten state from a VOLCANO. The GIANT'S CAUSEWAY is part of a sheet of lava. Sometimes lava solidifies in the core of a volcano. It is very hard rock and is not worn away quickly by rain. The island called Ailsa Craig in the Firth of Clyde is the remains of a core of lava, and so are Arthur's Seat in Edinburgh, and the Bass Rock in the Firth of Forth.

LAW. The laws of a country are made by the government. They are the rules which help us all to live together in peace and harmony. If we are thought to have broken any of the rules we are taken to a court of law, tried and, if found guilty, given the punishment attached to the offence. See also BARRISTER; EVIDENCE; JUDGE; JURY; POLICE.

LEAD is a heavy METAL which is fairly soft. Lead pipes can be bent to fit round corners easily, and strips of lead were often used with slates to make roofs waterproof. An ALLOY made of two parts lead and one part tin is called solder. It melts very easily.

LEAF. Plants build up food from sunlight and the carbon-dioxide gas, CO_2, in the air by *photosynthesis* (see PLANTS). This takes place in the green leaves of plants. The leaves are arranged to get as much light as possible, and breathing-pores (stomata) on the under-surface of each leaf take in oxygen and carbon-dioxide and water. They also get rid of the water that the plant does not need. See also DECIDUOUS TREES; EVERGREENS.

LEAP YEAR. There are nearly $365\frac{1}{4}$ days in a year. The most convenient way to deal with the quarter-day is to have 365 days in most years and 366 days in every fourth year, or leap year. This extra day is added to February, which usually has twenty-eight days. In a leap year it has twenty-nine days.

LEATHER is made from the skins of horses, cows, sheep, goats and other animals. It is very skilled work to make leather which is soft and durable. The skins are first soaked in water, the hair is loosened by soaking in lime-water and removed by scraping, and then the skins are tanned by soaking them in a solution of tannic acid. This is obtained from the bark of the oak tree and other sources. Chromium salts are now used a great deal in tanning, as the process is quicker.

LEBANON is a small country on the eastern shore of the Mediterranean Sea. Beirut is the capital. "The mountains of Lebanon" and "the cedars of Lebanon" are often mentioned in the Bible. These lovely cedars with their fan-like dark branches and evergreen leaves are now grown in many parts, but the forests of Lebanon have almost disappeared.

LEG. A human leg consists of two parts, the shank and the thigh. The thigh is the upper part of the leg, and it contains a large bone which meets the body at the hip-joint. The other end of the thigh is joined to the shank at the knee, which is protected by a small bone called the knee-cap. The shank contains two bones, the front one being called the shin; the other is hidden beneath the muscles of the calf. The shank ends at the ankle, where the foot is attached to the leg. See FIBULA.

LEMON, one of the citrus fruits, the others including the orange, lime, grape-fruit and citron. Lemon-juice contains a large amount of citric acid. The low-growing lemon-tree, which is probably a native of India or China, was long ago introduced into Europe and successfully cultivated in Spain and Sicily. It was later introduced into the United States of America where it grows in California.

LENS. This name is given to a part of the eye which bends the light-rays so that they fall on the retina (see EYE). Artificial lenses, usually of glass, have many uses, but the purpose is always the same—to change the direction of the light-rays. A BURNING-GLASS, or magnifying-glass, is a typical lens. Various kinds of

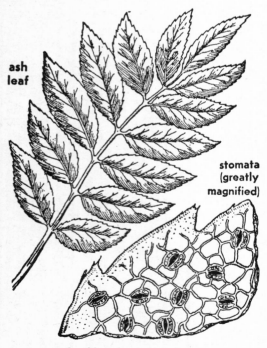

ash leaf

stomata (greatly magnified)

A leaf has breathing-pores.

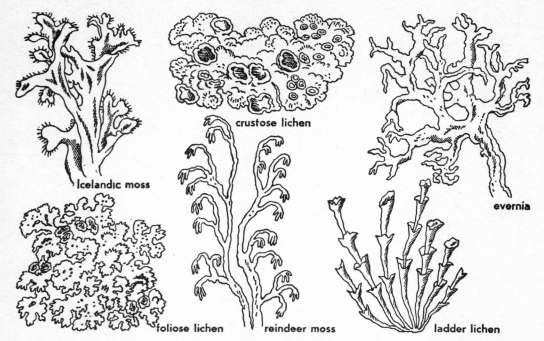

Icelandic moss

crustose lichen

evernia

foliose lichen

reindeer moss

ladder lichen

A fungus and an alga together form a lichen. Some of them are beautifully coloured.

lenses are used in cameras, and in MICRO-SCOPES and TELESCOPES.

Some people need glasses with special lenses because the lenses in their eyes are not strong enough. Some need *convex* lenses, which bend the light-rays so that they meet at one point. This is called the focal point. Others need glasses with *concave* lenses (that is, thinner in the middle than at the edges), because the lenses in their eyes are too strong already. A concave lens bends the rays outward, away from the focal point.

LEOPARD, one of the big CAT family, which is found in Africa, India, China and elsewhere. It is also called the panther in the Old World. The leopard is not quite as big as the tiger, but the natives fear it even more because it can climb trees, and they have to watch the trees as well as the ground when leopards are about.

The leopard varies in colour from pale yellow to black, marked with black spots very close together. It hunts at night for antelope, baboons, wild pig and other prey.

LIBERAL PARTY. See POLITICS.

LICHEN, a low form of plant-life in which two quite different kinds of plants have combined to help each other. One kind is a FUNGUS which extracts part of the plant-food from the wood, bark or stone on which it grows. The other kind is an alga, a plant which contains chlorophyll; the cells of the alga are entangled in the threads of the fungus. The lichen has no leaves, but the cells of the alga supply carbohydrates by *photosynthesis*, just as leaf-bearing plants do. (See LEAF.)

Many lichens look like grey-green papery scales, but others resemble long, tangled masses of hair hanging from the branches of trees. At one time brilliant dyes were obtained from them, but today they are most valuable in the Arctic regions, where they form food for the REINDEER. See also PLANTS.

LIFE-BELT, a belt made of cork or other light material which will float in water, and so prevent the person wearing it from sinking and drowning. Life-belts

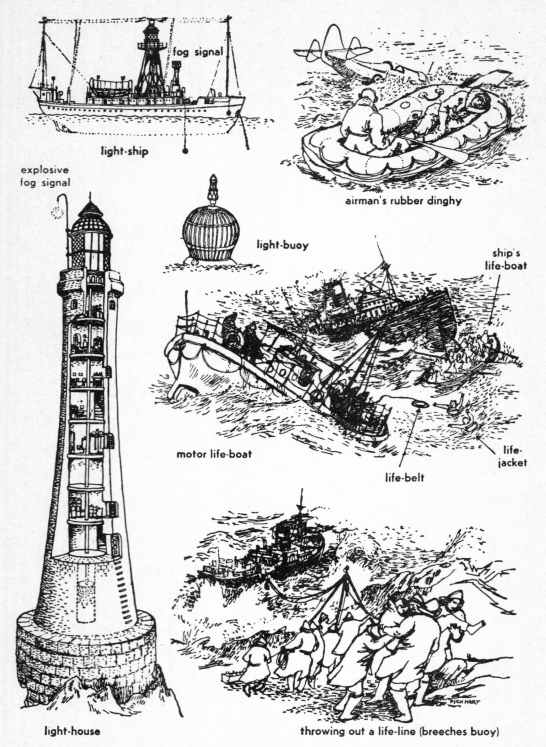

fog signal

light-ship

explosive
fog signal

airman's rubber dinghy

light-buoy

ship's
life-boat

motor life-boat

life-belt

life-
jacket

light-house

throwing out a life-line (breeches buoy)

Light-houses give warning of danger; when men get shipwrecked they must be rescued.

in the form of large rings, painted white, are often seen on piers and the railings of ships. These are ready to be thrown into the sea to help anybody who falls overboard. Some life-belts are made of rubber and have to be blown up like balloons or swimming "wings."

LIFE-BOAT. Ships must carry life-boats in case the ship sinks. There are other life-boats around the coast which go out to rescue sailors in danger. They are very strong, with buoyancy chambers round the sides and special arrangements for getting rid of any water that gets into the boat in rough weather. All British vessels are now motor-boats with engines in waterproof casings.

LIFE-CYCLE, the series of stages through which a living creature passes from its own birth to the birth of its offspring, which then repeat the story. The life-cycle of a MOTH begins with the egg and passes through the stages of caterpillar and chrysalis to the fully-grown moth, which then lays more eggs. See also BUTTERFLY; FROG; INSECT.

LIGHT. Sunlight contains rays of many kinds. The human eye can see only some of them. There are short rays which give violet light, and long rays which give red light, with blue, green, yellow and orange in between in that order. There are still shorter waves, called ULTRA-VIOLET LIGHT, and there are longer rays called INFRA-RED RAYS. These can not be seen by the human eye. Heat-rays and radio rays are longer still.

The shorter the rays the more easily are they stopped by particles of dust in the atmosphere. In a town like London the ultra-violet waves hardly get through at all. A great many of the short violet and blue waves are scattered by the dust in the upper air, and it is this which makes the sky blue. When there is moisture about, the greens and yellows are also scattered, and when there is FOG only the long red rays get through, and so the sun looks red. Motorists do not, of course, use

a red headlamp in fog because it would look like the rear lamp of another car, but they can use the next longest wavelength, the orange colour. The carbon ARC LIGHTS give a very bright violet light, but it would be of no use in light-houses, for a little fog would make it quite invisible.

All these waves travel at the same speed, 186,000 miles per second. See also PRISM; RAINBOW; REFLECTION; REFRACTION; SPECTRUM; WAVE; and the colour page facing page 161.

LIGHT-BUOYS. These are used to mark dangerous waters so that ships will avoid rocks or sand-banks. See also BUOY; LIGHT-HOUSE; LIGHT-SHIP; NAVIGATION.

LIGHT-HOUSE. In dark and stormy weather it is very difficult for sailors at sea to be sure the ship is keeping to the course that has been marked on the chart (see NAVIGATION), so lights are placed at dangerous parts of the coast-line to guide them. A light-house is a high tower with a powerful light at the top; a special LENS sends out strong beams of light in a series of flashes. These flashes are controlled by a clockwork device. Sailors know which light-house they are near by the kind of flash it gives, and from the chart they know whether the ship is in danger of running-aground on a sand-bank, or of being broken up on the rocks. In foggy weather, warning signals are also sent out by a fog-horn. See also BUOY; LIGHT-BUOYS; LIGHT-SHIP; NAVIGATION.

LIGHTNING is the flash of light caused by a huge spark of electricity jumping from one cloud to another, or from a cloud to earth. If this forked lightning is a long way off you may only see its reflection in the sky. This reflection is called sheet-lightning.

It is because LIGHT travels faster than SOUND that we see the lightning first, and hear the THUNDER some time later.

LIGHT-SHIP, a special kind of ship, fitted with a powerful light and fog-signals; it sends warning signals to ships which are

Abraham Lincoln was head of the party that wanted to free the slaves.

wonderful speech after the Battle of Gettysburg later the same year. His speech was very short, but it went down in history. It ended with these words:

"We here highly resolve that . . . this nation under God shall have a new birth of freedom, and that government of the people, by the people, for the people, shall not perish from the earth."

The war ended in April, 1865. Five days later, on 14 April, President Lincoln was shot as he sat in a box at the theatre. He died the following day.

getting into dangerous waters. See also BUOY; LIGHT-BUOYS; LIGHT-HOUSE; NAVIGATION.

LINCOLN, Abraham, was born in 1809. His parents were very poor, and he had little schooling, but he taught himself a great deal. He was made President of the UNITED STATES OF AMERICA in 1860.

Since the eighteenth century, negro slaves from West Africa had been shipped to North and SOUTH AMERICA to work as servants or as labourers on the tobacco and cotton plantations. By the time that Lincoln came to power, SLAVERY had been abolished in the northern states but not in the south. Lincoln wanted to do away with it in all the states but he knew there might be CIVIL WAR if he tried to end it completely at that time. However, the North and the South disagreed over many things besides slavery, and war broke out in 1861.

Lincoln proclaimed the freedom of the slaves in January, 1863, and made a

LION, a huge CAT, which lives in Africa and parts of Asia. The male, when fully-grown, measures about nine feet from nose to end of tail. The lioness is smaller than the male. Some lions have big, full manes, but not all. The lion is often called the King of Beasts, because of its great strength, and tremendous roar. It usually hunts for food at night, and is so powerful that it can kill even big animals like the buffalo, or the ox. The lion is rather lazy, however, and finds it is less trouble to catch antelopes and zebras. See also CARNIVORES, and the picture of cats on page 51.

LISTER, Joseph, Lord, born in 1827, was the English surgeon who discovered how to keep germs out of wounds by the use of ANTISEPTICS. He insisted on absolutely clean hands, clean towels and dressings, and the sterilization of instruments. He also used a carbolic spray to sterilize the part of the body on which he was operating. Lister died in 1912.

LIVERPOOL, an important seaport on the River Mersey. It supplies the great cotton manufacturing towns of Lancashire with raw cotton from overseas, and much of the wheat and meat for all England comes to this port.

LIVINGSTONE, David, born in 1813, went as a missionary and explorer to Africa, which was then known as the "Dark Continent." He was a doctor, and he made friends with the natives, healed the sick, and did everything he could to help them. He worked for a time around Lake Nyasa and Lake Tanganyika and made many important discoveries (see VICTORIA FALLS). He also explored the sources of the Nile, the Zambesi and the Congo. Livingstone died in Africa in 1873, but his body was brought to England and buried in Westminster Abbey.

LIZARDS belong to the group of REPTILES. They are found in most parts of the world, except the polar regions, but the biggest and the most brightly-coloured lizards are most numerous in the tropical countries.

The common lizard and the sand lizard are only a few inches long. These, with the slow-worm (or blindworm), are well-known in Britain. The monitors are the largest lizards, sometimes reaching a length of seven feet.

Some lizards can shed their tails and grow new ones. This is very useful when they are trying to escape from an enemy. See also BRONTOSAURUS; CHAMELEON.

chameleon

gecko

moloch

frilled lizard

slow-worm

MW

All these creatures are different kinds of lizard.

LOBSTER, a large CRUSTACEAN which lives in the shallow seas, sheltering in crevices in the rocks and coming out to feed mainly at night. When alive it is dark blue or nearly black, marked with red or orange on the under surface. It turns red on being cooked. The two large CLAWS are slightly different in size, the larger being armed with blunt knobs for crushing. When it is alarmed, a lobster swims backwards with powerful strokes of the tail.

LOCK. A lock is a short stretch of a CANAL sealed off by huge water-tight gates, one at each end. It is used to raise or lower boats from one level of water to another, and so get them past waterfalls and other such dangers.

When a boat is going to a lower level it sails into the space between the two gates. Then both gates are shut, and the water between them is allowed to flow away into the lower canal until the boat comes down to that level. Then the front gate is opened, and the boat sails through.

When a boat is going to a higher level, the gates are shut and the water is let in from the higher level until the boat rises to the new level. Then the front gate is opened and the boat sails through.

LOCOMOTIVE. An engine on wheels which pulls coaches or wagons along special rails. It may be driven by oil, electricity, or steam. The Stockton and Darlington railway was the first to provide a public passenger-service, and George Stephenson's steam-driven locomotive *Active* (later named *Locomotion*) was designed for the opening run in 1825. Four years later Stephenson designed the *Rocket* for the Liverpool and Manchester railway. See also BOILER; ENGINE; RAILWAYS; STEAM-ENGINE; STEPHENSON and colour plate facing page 257.

LOCUST, a member of the group of INSECTS. Like the GRASSHOPPER, it has hind legs which are specially developed for leaping. Sometimes a swarm of locusts takes wing, and flies great distances. When they land, they may strip an entire area bare of crops. See also INVERTEBRATES.

LOG, NAUTICAL. This is a way of measuring the speed of a ship (see KNOTS). Modern logs are special instruments which work in much the same way as the speedometer works on a car or a bicycle. The log is fixed to the stern of a ship and tows a small propeller through the water. The rate at which the propeller rotates is shown on the dial of the log. See also NAVIGATION.

LOGARITHMS. These are special numbers calculated from ordinary numbers and listed beside them in long tables. One of their chief uses is to provide a short

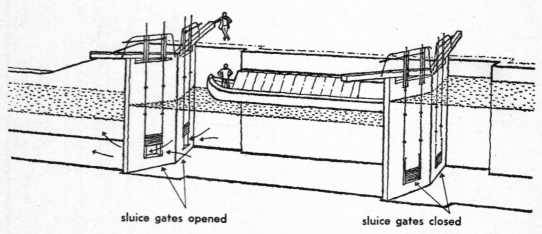

sluice gates opened   sluice gates closed

A lock is a device by which a boat can go from one level of water to another.

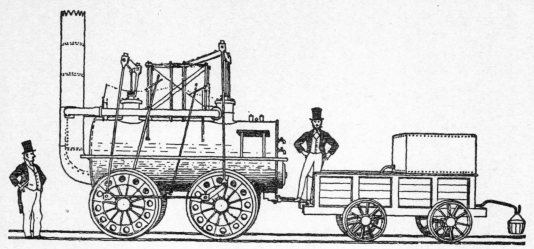

Stephenson designed this steam locomotive for the Stockton-Darlington railway.

method of multiplying very large numbers together, and doing other kinds of difficult sums. To multiply two large numbers you find their logarithms in the tables and then just *add* these together. The result is another logarithm, and the ordinary number beside this in the tables is the answer to your multiplication sum.

LONDON, the largest city in the world, is the capital of Britain and of the BRITISH COMMONWEALTH OF NATIONS. The ancient City and the County of London with surrounding suburbs form the Greater London area, and over seven million people live here.

London is the home of the British PARLIAMENT, which meets at Westminster. It is a great industrial area, and an important centre of banking and of commerce. It is also one of the greatest seaports in the world. Ships from many distant lands sail up the river Thames, bringing cargoes of ivory, spices, tea, tobacco, grain, meat, and other goods.

London has been a famous and important town for so long that it has a wonderful history. It attracts many visitors from other countries, and air-routes to and from all parts of the world operate from London Airport. See also BUCKINGHAM PALACE; ENGLAND and map facing page 33.

LONGITUDE. Lines are drawn on MAPS of the earth's surface, or on a GLOBE, to help us to find any place in the world. Lines drawn parallel with the EQUATOR are called lines of LATITUDE. Lines drawn to pass through the North and South Poles are called meridians or lines of longitude. The line of longitude which passes through Greenwich is very important, because we describe a place as being so many degrees east or west of it. For example, if someone is trying to find New York on a map, you can say that it is 74 degrees west of Greenwich; San Francisco is $122\frac{1}{2}$ degrees west, Calcutta is 88 degrees east, and so on.

LOVEBIRDS. See BUDGERIGARS.

LUNGS, the organs of breathing or RESPIRATION. They are spongy bags lying in the chest, and are connected to the windpipe by the bronchial tubes. Each lung contains many small air-spaces, and the circulation of air through these in breathing enables the BLOOD to take up oxygen and give out carbon dioxide.

LYNX, a member of the CAT family, found in Canada, Europe and Asia.

LYRE-BIRD, a beautiful bird found in AUSTRALIA. The male has a wonderful tail which looks like a MUSICAL INSTRUMENT called the lyre. The bird is a clever mimic.

M

MACADAM, a road-surfacing material, named after John McAdam, a Scottish road surveyor who invented a completely new way of making roads. Instead of laying a foundation of heavy stone, he used a thin layer of broken stones and rolled them down to make a flat surface. This gave a solid level road from which rain water quickly drained away. These "macadam" roads were less expensive to lay, and they lasted longer. McAdam lived from 1756 to 1836.

MADRID, the capital of SPAIN. It is in the centre of the country and has a population of about three million.

MAGELLAN, Ferdinand, a Portuguese sailor who discovered the Strait of Magellan in the south of South America. His ship sailed through it, across the Pacific Ocean, and round the world and home again. Unfortunately, Magellan himself was killed by natives in the Philippine Islands (1521). This was the first ship to sail round the world. See also EXPLORATION.

MAGNA CARTA. See JOHN.

MAGNIFYING GLASS, a glass which makes things look bigger than they really are. The LENS in a magnifying glass is convex—that is, it is thicker in the centre than it is at the edges. See also BURNING GLASS; CONVEX.

MAIZE, or Indian corn, is a GRAIN which grows in large cobs, and is as important a food as wheat. It was first brought to Europe by Columbus. Very large crops are grown in North America, and production is increasing in Brazil, the Argentine, and Russia. See also GRASSES.

MALAWI. See NYASALAND.

MALAY PENINSULA, a long, narrow peninsula of south-east Asia, stretching from Burma to the island of Sumatra, in INDONESIA. See also MALAYSIA.

MALAYSIA, part of the BRITISH COMMONWEALTH OF NATIONS. It is made up of several separate states: the former Federated Malay States, Sabah (Br. N. Borneo), and Sarawak. Great quantities of rubber, palm oil, and tin are exported as well as tin, iron ore, and bauxite.

MAMMALS, animals which feed their young with milk from the mother's body. Human beings, apes, monkeys, horses, elephants, whales, seals, walrus, kangaroos and bats are all mammals. This way of feeding the young developed late in the history of the world. No FOSSILS of mammals are found except in the newer rocks.

MAMMOTH, a great hairy elephant with very long curved tusks, which was hunted by primitive man. Remains of many of these are found in Siberia and elsewhere.

MANCHESTER, a city and inland port of Lancashire, England. It is the chief trading centre of the world for cotton goods made in Lancashire. The Manchester Ship Canal, which connects the city with the sea, is $35\frac{1}{2}$ miles long.

MANUSCRIPTS. Before the invention of PRINTING in the 15th century all books had to be written by hand. The Latin word *manuscript* means "written by hand." Specimens of Roman manuscripts were found in Herculaneum, under the lava which buried the city. Greek manuscripts, written about 300 B.C., were found in Egypt, where the dry desert conditions preserved them. Manuscripts on papyrus, written by Egyptians before 2,000 B.C., and sometimes illustrated, have also been found. See also CAXTON; MIDDLE AGES.

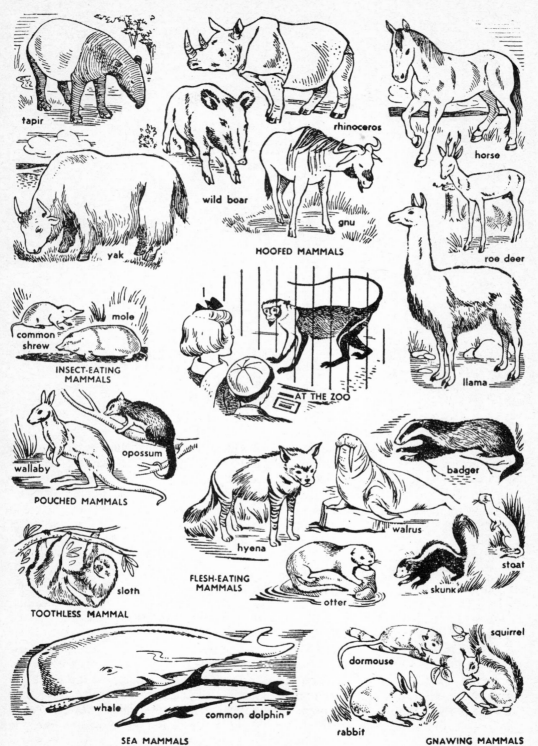

tapir

rhinoceros

horse

wild boar

gnu

yak

HOOFED MAMMALS

roe deer

common shrew

mole

INSECT-EATING MAMMALS

AT THE ZOO

llama

wallaby

opossum

POUCHED MAMMALS

badger

hyena

walrus

sloth

FLESH-EATING MAMMALS

otter

skunk

stoat

TOOTHLESS MAMMAL

dormouse

squirrel

whale

common dolphin

rabbit

SEA MAMMALS

GNAWING MAMMALS

Mammals are the highest order of animals with backbones.

By means of maps we can tell where we are.

MAPS. The best way to represent the earth's surface is on a large GLOBE, but a globe is not very convenient to carry about, so we also make maps on paper. There are many different kinds of map. Some show the shape of a country, and its physical features, that is, rivers, mountains, forest land and so on. Others show political divisons, or rainfall, or population. Sometimes CONTOUR LINES are drawn on a map to show heights.

All maps are drawn to a SCALE. If a large map is drawn of a small area then one inch on this map may represent a mile on the ground. If a small map is drawn of a very large area, then one inch on this map may represent several hundred miles. The scale is always shown on the map.

Sailors use maps as well, as an aid to NAVIGATION, and these maps are called CHARTS. See also LATITUDE; LONGITUDE.

MARCONI, Guglielmo, was born in Italy in 1874. He became famous as a scientist and an inventor, and was the first to discover a really satisfactory way of sending messages by wireless. Although he did not invent RADIO he was the first to use aerials. Marconi died in 1937.

MARCO POLO was born in Venice in 1254. He was only a boy of seventeen when he left Venice to begin his travels. His father and his uncle had been to China, and when they went again they took young Marco with them. It was a terrible journey to go overland to China in those days—over the high Pamir Mountains and through the Gobi Desert—but they all got there safely and were well received by Kublai Khan, the ruler. Marco was a great favourite and made many interesting journeys from China. He also learned a great deal from the advanced civilization which existed in China at that time. After about twenty-four years the three explorers returned to Venice. The wonderful stories they told were not believed at first, but gradually people found they were true. It was Marco who dictated the book about their travels, and copies are still in libraries. He died in 1323.

MARS, the name of the Roman God of War. The words "March" (the month) and "martial" come from "Mars."

MARS, the name given to one of the planets, probably because part of its surface has a reddish tinge. In order of distance from the sun the first four planets are Mercury (nearest the sun), Venus, Earth, Mars.

MARY I, Queen of England from 1553 to 1558, was the daughter of HENRY VIII and Catherine of Aragon. Henry VIII had defied the Pope and made England a Protestant country, but Mary restored the Roman Catholic religion and married the Roman Catholic king, Philip II of Spain. During the last three years of her reign more than three hundred Protestant martyrs were burnt at the stake, including bishops Cranmer, Ridley and Latimer. For these deeds she became known as "Bloody Mary." During her reign, too, England suffered the loss of CALAIS—

Mary Queen of Scots.

her last foothold in France. See also EDWARD III; HUNDRED YEARS' WAR.

MARY II. See WILLIAM III.

MARY QUEEN OF SCOTS was the daughter of James V of Scotland. He died very shortly after she was born in 1542, so she became Queen of Scots while only an infant. When Mary was five years old, she was sent to live with relatives in France until she was old enough to marry the Dauphin of France in 1558. He became King in 1559, but died the next year.

Mary returned to Scotland in 1561. Four years later she married her cousin, Lord Darnley. They were not happy together, and Darnley became jealous of Mary's secretary, Rizzio, because he thought that Rizzio had too much influence over the Queen. Mary was a Roman Catholic, and the Protestants feared that she would restore this religion, which had been suppressed in Scotland in 1560, before her return from France. Darnley joined forces against the Queen, and Rizzio was murdered in the Palace of Holyroodhouse in March, 1566. Darnley later declared that he was not guilty of the plot against the secretary.

In 1567 Darnley was murdered at Kirk O' Field, and Lord Bothwell was named

Cranmer met a martyr's death.

187

as his murderer. When, only a few months later, the Queen was married to Bothwell, there was a general rebellion by the Scottish nobles, and Mary had to agree to give up the throne to her baby son (he was born in 1566). See also ELIZABETH I; JAMES I.

MATHEMATICS. There are different branches of mathematics which help us to solve problems dealing with numbers and quantities.

Arithmetic is a way of dealing with known quantities. In its simplest form it began by counting on the fingers. Addition, SUBTRACTION, MULTIPLICATION and DIVISION all come under the heading of arithmetic.

Algebra is a way of dealing with quantities by using letters instead of numbers.

Geometry deals with lines, ANGLES, and circles and their relationship.

Trigonometry means the measurement of triangles. It is very useful for working out problems in SURVEYING.

Before 2000 B.C. the Egyptians knew that a triangle with sides of 3, 4, and 5 units had a right-angle, and they used this knowledge for dividing out the fields. Both the Egyptians and the Babylonians used geometry and arithmetic in their study of the stars.

The Greeks also knew how to calculate the circumference and the area of a circle from the diameter, and about 200 B.C. ERATOSTHENES calculated the size of the earth fairly accurately.

Nowadays scientists can measure the distance of the sun, moon and stars, and the speeds at which they are moving. They can predict the tides, and the eclipses of the sun and moon for years ahead. It is knowledge of mathematics which enables them to do these things. See also AREA; MENSURATION.

MECCA, a city in Saudi Arabia, the birthplace of MOHAMMED. He founded the religion of Islam and his followers are called MOSLEMS or Muslims. Thousands of pilgrims visit Mecca every year. See map on pages 20 to 21.

MEDICINE. From the earliest times men have tried to prevent illness or to cure illness, first by superstitious belief in witch-doctors and then by science. Hippocrates, who lived in Greece about 400 B.C., is called the "Father of Medicine" because he not only treated many sick people and made them well, but he studied cause and effect, as scientists do now, and gradually built up a sound knowledge of how doctors should study and work. Most of this Greek knowledge was lost after the fall of Rome, but gradually discovered again after about a thousand years.

MEDITERRANEAN, the large inland sea which divides Europe from Africa. It joins the Atlantic Ocean through the narrow Straits of Gibraltar and so the ocean tides do not affect it very much. Spain, France, Italy, Greece and other countries have lovely seaside towns on the Mediterranean, and because the Sahara Desert weather conditions move north over this sea in the summer (see CLIMATE) one can be sure of brilliant sunshine during all the summer months. See map on page 99.

MELBOURNE, one of the two largest towns in AUSTRALIA; over three million people live in the city and its suburbs. It is the capital of the State of Victoria. Much Australian wool is exported from this port, and leather is manufactured.

MELODRAMA is a play that is full of thrilling incidents. The actors exaggerate every emotion and action in order to excite the audience. The villain is always very wicked, the hero is always handsome and kind, the heroine is always sweet and good. Although all kinds of impossible adventures take place everything usually ends happily.

MELON. This large, juicy fruit is related to the cucumber, and can be grown easily in hot countries. The original kind came from Asia and is known as the musk melon. Other varieties are the canteloupe and honeydew, and the large water-melon which has been known to weigh as much as forty-five pounds!

MELTING POINT is the temperature at which a solid becomes a liquid. The melting point of ice is one of the important points on a thermometer. On the Fahrenheit thermometer it is marked 32 degrees, on the Centigrade thermometer it is marked 0 degrees.

MENDELISM. Mendel was a monk who carried out remarkable experiments on heredity in plants. Like many other great discoverers he died a disappointed man. He published his wonderful discoveries in 1866, but it was 1900 before scientists began to understand the importance of his work. Briefly, Mendel discovered that certain characteristics are much more likely to be inherited than others, and in many cases he could predict accurately the results of crossing certain plants.

MENDELSSOHN, Felix, born in 1809, was a famous German musician. His music to *A Midsummer Night's Dream* is fairy-like, and his *Songs without Words* are still very popular. He died in 1847.

MENSURATION deals with the measurement of lengths, AREAS and volumes. Here are six interesting relationships:

The circumference of a circle is $3\frac{1}{7}$ times as long as the diameter, or $2 \times 3\frac{1}{7}$ times the radius. We sometimes write this as $c = 2\pi r$. (π stands for $3\frac{1}{7}$ and is pronounced *pie*.)

The area of a circle is $3\frac{1}{7}$ times as great as the square on the radius.

The area of a rectangle is its length × its breadth.

The area of a triangle is *half* the area of the rectangle on the same base.

The area of the surface of a cylinder (without ends) is its height × its circumference.

The area of each end is πr^2. The circumference $= 2\pi r$. Make a paper cylinder and then open it out as a flat sheet. We now get a rectangle. One side equals the circumference of the cylinder, the other side equals the length of the cylinder. So as the area is its height × its circumference, the area of the curved surface $= 2\pi r \times l$.

The area of a sphere is exactly the same as the area of a cylinder (without ends) which fits round it and is the same height.

Archimedes discovered this relationship and was so pleased with the discovery that he asked that this diagram should be engraved on his tombstone, and it was.

MESOPOTAMIA. See IRAQ.

MESSINA, Strait of, a channel from two to twelve miles wide that separates southern Italy from Sicily. In ancient times sailors feared sailing through the strait because of the dangerous rocks and strong currents. See SCYLLA and CHARYBDIS.

METALLURGY, the study of METALS. The metallurgist knows which ORES are most valuable, how to extract the pure metal from the ore (for example, iron from iron oxide, copper from copper sulphide), and how to get the little bits of pure gold out of the rocks. He knows how to make iron which will stand great pressure, or is very tough, or very hard, and he knows how to make ALLOYS of all kinds.

METALS. Gold, silver, copper, tin, lead and zinc are metals, and including ALLOYS there are about eighty-six more. All metals (except alloys, like BRASS), are ELEMENTS, which means they cannot be broken down into anything simpler.

METAMORPHOSIS. This is the change of form through which some creatures pass during growth. See BUTTERFLY; FROG; INSECT.

METAPHOR. If we say: "Tommy is a tortoise," we mean he is very slow. If we say: "Daddy can be quite a volcano" we mean he can "blow up" occasionally. Such remarks are called *metaphors*. If we say: "He is as slow as a tortoise," or "He blows up like a volcano" or "She is pretty as a daisy"—these are called *similes*.

METEOR. Many small objects revolve round the sun besides the planets. Some-

People of Mexico.

metre is divided or multiplied thus:

10 millimetres = 1 centimetre
10 centimetres = 1 decimetre
10 decimetres = 1 metre
10 metres = 1 decametre
10 decametres = 1 hectometre
10 hectometres = 1 kilometre

In measurement of length, the *metre* is the standard. This is 39·37 inches.

1 kilometre is about $\frac{5}{8}$ of an English mile.

If you go shopping in France, you might buy a litre of wine. This is a measure of volume, and is about $1\frac{3}{4}$ pints. If you buy a pound of butter, this is a measure of weight. 1 kilogram is about 2 lb., so you would order half a kilo.

MEXICO, a republic in North America. It is hot, because it is near the equator, but a high ridge of mountains goes through it, and there are volcanic peaks on which there is snow all the year round, so that almost anything could be grown here. Maize is the most important crop, but sugar-cane, rice, cotton, and wheat are cultivated also. Its forests give us mahogany. It has still great quantities of silver, and much gold, lead and zinc. And it has enormous quantities of petroleum. The River Rio Grande del Norte divides most of Mexico from the United States. There are over 48 million people in the country; they are of Spanish, American-Indian, or mixed descent and about ninety per cent speak Spanish.

Mexico City is the capital, and the chief ports are Tampico and Vera Cruz.

MICA, the name of a group of rock-forming minerals. Mica splits into thin transparent sheets, and is a very good insulator of electricity. Because of its resistance to very high temperatures and its transparency, it is used for windows of lanterns and furnaces; it can also be used in a variety of ways in powdered form.

MICHELANGELO, born in 1475, was a very great Italian artist, poet and sculptor. He was told by Pope Julius II to paint pictures on the ceiling of the Sistine Chapel in Rome. Michelangelo did

times one of these comes close to the earth and is attracted to it. It flies towards the earth, meets the atmosphere first, and the friction with the air makes it white hot, or vaporizes it altogether. Occasionally a large piece hits the surface of the earth. These objects are called meteors; if they reach the surface of the earth they are known as meteorites.

METEOROLOGY means the study of the atmosphere and its effect on weather and CLIMATE. The air around the earth is heated strongly at the equator and this sets up winds which bring rain to certain places, and drought to others. Meteorologists study all the things which influence climate, and they forecast the kind of weather we are likely to get. It is very difficult to forecast the weather in Britain because the country is in the track of circular eddies of air (see CYCLONE), which come across the Atlantic, and we are never sure that one type of eddy will not break up and be replaced by another different one.

METRIC SYSTEM, a system of measurement introduced in France in 1791. It is particularly useful for scientific calculations because it is worked out in units which are multiples of 10. The not want to do this because he was much happier carving figures out of stone. But he obeyed the Pope and produced some of his best paintings, even though he had to lie on his back on a special platform to paint on the ceiling. He also designed the dome of St. Peter's Cathedral, and made a famous statue of David. He died in 1564.

MICROPHONE, an electrical instrument with a disk, which shakes when sound waves hit it. The louder the sound, the more the disk shakes. The shaking disk presses on charcoal grains packed behind it, so changing an electric current passing through. The changing current can be sent along a wire or through the air to a receiver. Microphones are used a great deal in broadcasting.

MICROSCOPE. By a combination of magnifying glasses small objects can be made to appear a hundred, or even a thousand times bigger than they really are. One can see, for example, the living creatures swimming about in a drop of pond water. Doctors, biologists, chemists, geologists, and other scientists all use microscopes in their work.

MIDDLE AGES, the period of one thousand years between the break-up of the Roman Empire and the Renaissance, or revival of learning (roughly A.D. 500 to A.D. 1500).

The first half of this period is sometimes known as the DARK AGES because learning played very little part in the lives of the people. The monks worked very hard, looking after the sick and the poor. They also tried to keep knowledge alive by their teaching, and by copying the writings of the Greeks and Romans on parchment. Some of them produced beautiful MANU-SCRIPTS illustrated in wonderful colours and decorated in gold-leaf.

The friars added their efforts to those of the monks. Like the monks, they took vows of religion, but instead of living in monasteries they travelled about, preaching as they went. Their teaching spread through Europe and Asia.

Many monasteries and churches were built in Europe; at first they were mostly in the Romanesque style of ARCHITECTURE, but later on new ideas were put into practice and builders used a more elaborate design which became known as the Gothic style. The same highly-decorated style was brought into use in sculpture, too, and craftsmen made wonderful carvings in stone and wood.

Music was another popular form of art, and minstrels used to wander from one castle to another, to entertain the nobles. They sang merry songs, and ballads, and helped to preserve the stories of courageous deeds.

Courage was greatly admired, and in the Middle Ages a knight was expected to defend the weak and helpless, to fight, and if necessary, to die, for the Christian faith. Many knights went off to the CRUSADES.

Two famous orders of knighthood were founded at this time. Ever since Jerusalem became the centre of Christian pilgrimage

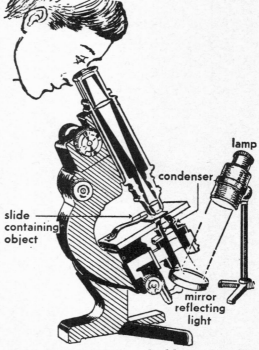

slide containing object

condenser

lamp

mirror reflecting light

A microscope is very valuable to scientists.

191

Musicians and jesters entertained the nobles

Monks cared for the sick and the poor

Ladies were skilful weavers

Glass-blowing was a delicate art

How they lived in the Middle Ages.

there had been an hospice or HOSPITAL there. The Knights of the Order of the Hospital of St. John of Jerusalem banded together to nurse the sick and to care for the poor. The Knights Templars were warrior monks who protected the pilgrims to the Holy Land. See also CAXTON; CHAUCER; FAIR; FEUDAL SYSTEM.

MIGRATION. Many animals set out on long journeys at certain times of the year. Some, like the EEL and the SALMON, return to their breeding-grounds, others leave cold climates where it is difficult to find food, to spend the winter in warmer lands. Birds which come to Britain in the summer include the cuckoo and the swallow; they travel from North Africa and leave Britain in the autumn. Winter visitors, like the fieldfare, travel to Britain from their breeding-places farther north.

In North America, the caribou leave their feeding-grounds in the north and travel southward. In Scandinavia hordes of lemmings migrate from the mountains to lower ground. Butterflies and moths also migrate.

MILAN, a great industrial city in Italy. Silk, chemicals and machinery are some of the things made here. Milan is famous for its wonderful Gothic cathedral of white marble, and for its Opera House, La Scala.

MILTON, John, born in 1608, was one of the great English poets. He had a profound knowledge of the classical languages and literature, and of books of all kinds. He was a courageous writer, and championed Cromwell's cause so boldly that at the Restoration he was lucky to escape imprisonment or death. His most famous poems are *Paradise Lost* and *Paradise Regained*. He died in 1674.

MIMICRY. Some creatures when attacked are very fierce while others are nasty to the taste. Both kinds tend to get left alone by possible enemies. There are other creatures that are similar in appearance to the dangerous or the bad-tasting ones so that they get mistaken for them although they may not be at all dangerous and may be quite good to eat. Hence, they, too, are likely to escape their enemies.

This business of one creature looking like another and so deriving some benefit from it is called mimicry. The hornet, for example, is an insect with a fierce sting which few birds would care to eat, and the hornet clearwing moth is a harmless animal which survives because it looks like the dangerous hornet.

MINING means getting minerals out of the ground. We mine coal, salt, iron ore, lead ore, gold, diamonds, and so on.

MIRAGE. If a stick is put into water, say at 45 degrees, it appears to be bent upwards. The denser water changes the direction of the LIGHT waves. In the hot desert the air near the sand gets very hot, and expands, and so becomes less dense than the air above it. This sometimes has the effect of making distant trees look near at hand. In the Arctic icefield the air near the ice becomes very cold and dense, and the rays of light are distorted so that sometimes a ship at some distance away is seen as an image in the sky, but upside down. A false image of this kind is called a *mirage*. See also REFRACTION.

MIRROR, a highly polished surface made to reflect rays of LIGHT without getting them mixed, and so to reflect a view of an object. An ordinary mirror, or looking-glass, is a piece of plate glass on the back of which a thin film of silver has been deposited. Mirrors are sometimes made of brightly polished metals such as silver, nickel and stainless steel. See also REFRACTION.

MISSISSIPPI, the biggest river in North America. It gives its name to one of the American states. With its tributary, the MISSOURI, it is over four thousand miles long, and a great, broad river which brings down much mud.

MISSOURI, River. Rising in the Rocky Mountains, in the UNITED STATES, the Missouri flows for nearly three thousand miles before it joins the MISSISSIPPI near St. Louis. It is the Mississippi's longest tributary, and together they make the longest river in the world (over four thousand miles).

MISTLETOE. Some plants live as PARASITES on other living plants. Mistletoe is only partly a parasite. It is an evergreen shrub which has leaves but no roots, so it attaches itself to other plants, such as the apple tree and the poplar, by suckers which penetrate the bark. In this way the mistletoe can feed on the tree by taking in the water and salts it needs and make its own food by *photosynthesis* (see PLANTS). In the winter it produces pearly white berries in the forks of stems and is used for Christmas decoration.

MODELLING can be done with plasticine, clay, wood, stone and other substances. School children often begin with soaked newspaper and paste.

MOHAMMED, a prophet of Arabia, lived from 570 to 632. He founded the religion of Islam ("Submitting" oneself to God) which teaches, "There is but one God and Mohammed is his Apostle." Those who practise this religion are called MOSLEMS or Muslims.

The religion spread to North Africa and to India. In Palestine, in the eleventh century, the Moslems and the Turks hindered Christian pilgrims visiting the Holy Land, and this led to the wars of the Cross, or the CRUSADES. See also MECCA.

MOLE, a little animal, about six inches long, which burrows underground in search of worms. Mounds are made by the soil it digs out. It has powerful, short forelegs for shovelling out the soil, and tiny eyes, which are protected by the fur on its body.

MOLLUSC, a member of the group of animals which includes oysters, scallops, cockles, mussels, limpets, winkles, whelks, snails and slugs. One branch of the molluscs covers the octopuses, cuttle-fish, squids and nautilus. See BIVALVES; INVERTEBRATES; MUSSEL; SHELLS.

MONASTERY, a building in which MONKS live. At the time of the REFORMATION the monasteries were closed in England and in northern Europe, and in the nineteenth century the monks were turned out from France and other countries. See also ABBEY; MIDDLE AGES.

MONEY. Primitive people used to exchange things, for example, cows for cloth, or clay pots for arrows, but it was soon found convenient to have something by which to measure the value of articles. In some places people used to ask: "How many cows is it worth?" But cows are awkward things to use as money, and soon many people were using gold instead. Gold is easily kept, everybody wants it, it does not rust or go bad in any way, and it is easily hammered out and divided into pieces. For many years most countries had gold and silver coins as money. Nowadays paper notes are more often used. Paper money has no value in itself, but the government and the banks arrange that goods can be exchanged for it.

MONGOOSE, a little animal, about the size of a large rat, which lives in Egypt and India. It is kept as a pet in India because it attacks and kills snakes.

MONK, a man who lives in a MONASTERY and gives his life to religion and the service of mankind. The monks kept religion and education alive during the Dark Ages. See also MIDDLE AGES.

MONKEYS, those mammals which, with the APES, are most like man. They are called Primates. They are found in tropical and sub-tropical countries. Monkeys of the Old World usually run on all fours, and have long tails; they can store food in their cheek-pouches. The best-known are the guenons of Africa, the mangabeys and the macaques. The chacma of south Africa, and the mandrill of west Africa

The mongoose is an expert snake-killer.

mandrill

chacma baboon

rhesus monkey

gibbon

brown capuchin

marmoset

orang-utan

chimpanzee

gorilla

M.W

Monkeys and apes belong to the highest class of mammals.

195

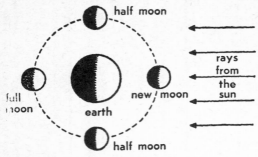

half moon

rays
from
the
sun

full
moon

earth

new moon

half moon

Phases of the moon.

are both members of the group of BABOONS. The baboons are noted for their vivid colouring. Although they are good climbers they prefer to live on open ground.

The monkeys of the New World are smaller, and do not have cheek-pouches. They live in dense jungle, and can hang by their tails. The capuchins of South America make amusing pets; so do the pretty little marmosets. Other well-known monkeys include the howler monkeys and the woolly monkeys. The lemurs are often included in this order.

The apes are tailless. They include the GORILLA, the orang-utan, the CHIMPANZEE and the gibbon.

MONSOON, a seasonal wind usually accompanied by torrential rains. The most important monsoon is that in INDIA and south-eastern Asia. The great high plateau of Tibet gets very cold in winter, and the cold, heavy air slides down the slopes and pushes air across India and China. In the summer the land gets hotter than the sea, and the hot air expands and rises. Air is now drawn in from the sea over India and China. This air is filled with moisture, and when it rises over mountains it expands, cools and drops some of its moisture as rain.

In Northern Australia, around the Gulf of Carpentaria, there is a similar monsoon. As Australia is on the southern side of the equator and gets its summer when India gets its winter, these two monsoons blow in the same way at the same time. The summer monsoon is blowing inland in Australia just as the air is blowing out to sea in India, and when the cold air from the land in Australia is blowing out to sea, air is blowing in from the sea over India and south-eastern Asia. See HEAT; LAND AND SEA BREEZES.

MOON, the body which goes round the earth, in the same way as the earth goes round the sun. The moon is about $\frac{1}{50}$ the size of the earth. If its path was in the same plane as the path of the earth round the sun, we should get an ECLIPSE of the sun once a month and an eclipse of the moon once a month. The path of the moon is tilted a little to the earth's path, so we only get eclipses occasionally. The picture above shows why we sometimes see a full moon, a half moon, or other parts of it.

The moon turns on its axis once a month and goes round the earth once a month, so we always see the same side of the moon. If the earth did this the length of a day would be exactly the same as the length of a year. It is the moon pulling on the waters of the earth which is the cause of the TIDES in the sea.

MORE, Sir Thomas, was born in England in 1478. He became famous as a writer and as a statesman. His most popular work is *Utopia*, which he wrote originally in Latin. It was published in 1516, but was not translated into English until much later. The book is about the ideal form of government and way of living.

Sir Thomas More became Lord Chancellor in succession to Cardinal WOLSEY, but he disagreed with HENRY VIII when the King quarrelled with the Pope, and resigned in 1532. Two years later Parliament passed the Act of Supremacy which made the Church of England independent of Rome. More would not recognize Henry as the Head of the Church, so he was arrested and charged with treason and sent to the Tower. He was brought to trial, and beheaded in 1535.

MOROCCO, the country around the Great Atlas Mountains in North Africa. Rabat is the capital, and Casablanca is the largest city and an important port. North of the mountains it is a fertile country, where grain and Mediterranean fruits are grown (olives and citrus fruits are the chief products), but south of the mountains it is rather like the Sahara Desert.

Morocco leather is a beautiful leather made from the skins of goats.

MORRIS, William, lived from 1834 to 1896. He loved beautiful things, and wanted to encourage other people to appreciate beauty as well; he was a distinguished poet and painter, and counted Rossetti and Burne-Jones among his friends. With them, he founded in 1861 a firm of decorators and manufacturers which produced lovely fabrics and wallpapers, and furniture. Their designs brought about a great change in public taste.

In 1890 Morris founded the Kelmscott Press; he designed the type, and some finely printed and decorated books were published. Some were reprints of English classics, and some were Morris' own works.

His poetry includes the *Life and Death of Jason* (first published in 1867), *The Earthly Paradise* (1868-1870) and a verse translation of the *Odyssey* (1887). His later work included romantic prose such as *News from Nowhere*, which had socialism as its theme.

MORSE, a method of sending messages by telegraphy. Various combinations of dots and dashes are used to represent letters of the alphabet and numbers. An American, Samuel Morse, invented this system. He lived from 1791 to 1872. The code he used has been adapted for transmission by cable as well as radio, and

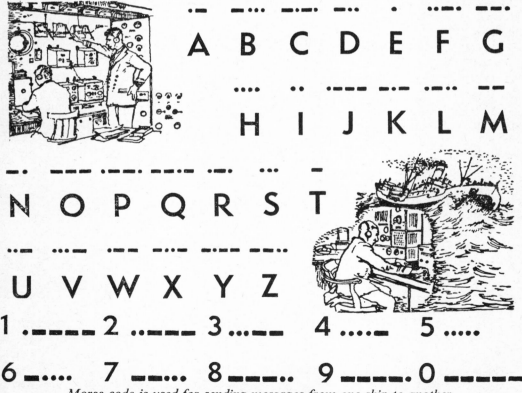

Morse code is used for sending messages from one ship to another.

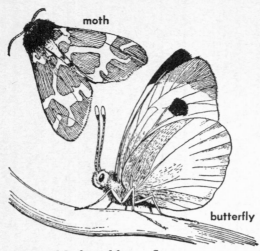

moth

butterfly

Moth and butterfly at rest.

an International Code is used in Europe. See also TELEGRAPHY.

MOSCOW is the capital of Soviet Russia and of the U.S.S.R. The Russian State began in the forest around Moscow and spread gradually over large parts of Europe and Asia. Russia now has over 130 million people.

MOSES, the lawgiver who led the Israelites from bondage in Egypt to Palestine, which was called the Promised Land. See ISRAEL.

MOSLEMS (Muslims) are the followers of the Islamic religion founded by MOHAMMED. They worship one God, saying prayers five times a day, and fasting for one special month in the year. The place of worship is called a mosque, and the sacred book of Islam is called the Koran. It is the aim of every Moslem to make a pilgrimage to MECCA, birthplace of the prophet.

MOSQUITO, a gnat, or small fly, which punctures the skin and draws blood. There are many kinds of mosquito, and one in particular, the *anopheles*, is a serious danger in some countries for it spreads the germs that cause malaria.

MOSS, a simple little plant which usually grows in damp places. Mosses have stems, leaves and hair-like roots, but these do not take in water like those of flowering plants. Mosses multiply by spores instead of seeds.

MOTH, an insect which belongs to the same group as the butterfly. It usually flies about in the evening or at night. Its wings are flat when it is resting, while the wings of the butterfly are usually upright, and another difference is that the moth does not have knobbed ANTENNAE.

MOTOR-CAR, a road vehicle containing an engine which provides the power to drive it along. Most motor-cars are driven by petrol engines, but there are also electric cars. The engine is usually built in the front, and is protected by the bonnet, but cars with their engines at the back are also made.

MOUNT EVEREST. See EVEREST.

MOUSE, a small RODENT. The true mice, such as the house-mouse, the harvest-mouse, and the long-tailed field-mouse, have large ears and eyes. VOLES have small ears and small eyes.

MOUTH, the opening through which food and air is taken into a body. In human beings and most animals it is in the lower part of the face, and is closed by the lips. It contains the teeth and TONGUE, and its roof is known as the PALATE. All these parts of the mouth are used in speaking clearly, as well as in eating. Any narrow opening through which things may pass may be called a mouth, and so we speak of the mouth of a bottle, river, cave, cannon, and so on. See also TASTE.

MOZART, Wolfgang Amadeus, born in 1756, was one of the great musicians. He was composing music when he was five years of age, and was taken on tour as a performer on the harpsichord when he was six. He wrote over six hundred important compositions which delight audiences in every generation. Mozart died in 1791, at thirty-five years of age.

MULTIPLICATION is a quick method of adding any number of like quantities together, such as 3 fours, or 150 centuries.

The sign used in ARITHMETIC for multiplication is ×, and when we read, for example, 6 × 9 we say "six *multiplied by nine*," or "six *times* nine." Our multiplication tables tell us that the answer is 54, but the inventors of the tables found that out by *adding* six nines (or nine sixes) together.

MUSCLE, the part of the body which deals with movement. It has the power of contraction when it gets a signal from a nerve, and it is the contraction of the bundle of muscle fibres called the BICEPS which lifts the forearm. But the complexity of the mechanism is amazing. Before the biceps muscle contracts it has to telephone to the triceps muscle to tell it to relax quickly, for that muscle acts in the opposite way to the biceps. And if you are lowering something carefully your biceps muscle does not just relax and let the object fall on the floor, it allows the muscle fibres to stretch out slowly.

The muscles which narrow and widen the pupil of the EYE, and the muscles which keep the heart and digestion going, work away quietly themselves whatever we are doing. See BRAIN; HAND; SPINE.

MUSHROOM, a kind of FUNGUS which grows wild in open fields in all parts of Europe. It is also cultivated, being sown in beds of manure in the form of spawn. This is a tangle of white, threadlike branches, which sends up the mushrooms as its fruit. The spores which may give rise to new spawn and new mushrooms are carried on the pinkish-brown gills on the under-side of the "umbrella."

MUSIC. When one speaks there is usually a *tune* as well as words. We know from the *tune* of the voice how the person feels towards us. Musicians can express all human feelings in their music: joy, sorrow, anger, fear, reverence, and so on. There are martial tunes to please our moods of aggression, lullabies to please us when we are tired, dance tunes, sorrowful tunes, and so on. In symphonies, concertos, oratorios, and other big works, a great many human emotions are expressed. And, of course, people who enjoy music soon like to compare one composer with another, and one performer with another. Bach, Handel, Haydn, Mozart, Beethoven, Schubert, Brahms, are some of the most famous composers.

MUSICAL INSTRUMENTS are often arranged in groups according to the way they are played, and the sounds they produce. Thus in an ORCHESTRA there are groups of PERCUSSION, BRASS, woodwind and string instruments.

As well as listening to the work of famous composers, played by skilled musicians, people have always enjoyed making music for themselves; this has been true since the earliest times when the chief instrument of music was the human voice, and early man expressed his joy or sorrow in native chants.

Some instruments are associated with certain countries, or with a certain period in history. The clicking of *castanets*, for example, and the caressing notes of a Spanish *guitar* conjure up a picture of Spanish dancers. The skirl of the Highland pipe, or *bagpipe*, sets feet dancing to a Scottish reel or recalls moments in history when soldiers have marched into battle to the stirring notes. The *lute* was a favourite instrument in England at the Court of Elizabeth I, when madrigals were sung in her honour. In its various forms, the *harp* was popular with the ancient Greeks and Romans, the Welsh bards were famous for their playing of this instrument, and it is known also as the national symbol of Ireland. See also BANJO; REED INSTRUMENTS; VIOLIN; WIND INSTRUMENTS.

MUSSEL, the name of a MOLLUSC which has a pair of hinged shells to protect its body (see BIVALVES). Some species, including the edible mussel, live in the sea; others are freshwater mussels. They have a long foot from which strong, hair-like threads can be put out to anchor them to rocks or stones.

N

NAIL, a short piece of specially hardened wire sharpened to a point at one end and flattened to a head at the other, like a pin. Some nails are made from round lengths of metal and others from oval lengths of metal. A third kind of nail is the "cut" nail, and this is stamped out of a flat sheet of metal.

NAILS (of animals) show us how the body adapts itself to what is required of it. In horses, cows and sheep the hard nail becomes the hoof, covering and protecting the end of the foot. In the cat the nail is a claw, used for catching prey and climbing trees. Our nails, at the ends of our fingers, are very useful for gripping very small objects but, if we needed them for digging or scratching, they would soon grow much stronger again as they were in early man.

NANSEN, Fridjtof, born in 1861, was a famous Norwegian explorer and a diplomat. In his ship the *Fram* he set out in 1895 in an attempt to reach the North Pole, but although he got nearer to it than any one who had tried before him, he was not successful. As a statesman he assisted in the separation of Norway from Sweden in 1905, and became the first Norwegian Ambassador to London in 1906. Nansen died in 1930. See also EXPLORATION; POLAR EXPLORATION.

NAPOLEON BONAPARTE, born in the island of Corsica in 1769, was a very clever soldier who became Emperor of France after the French Revolution. He built up a splendid army and conquered many of the surrounding countries. He was also a very able statesman, but like most dictators he was ambitious and aggressive and attempted too much. He invaded Russia and reached Moscow, but the Russians set fire to the city before he entered it (1812), and he and his army had to find their way back to France through the bitter Russian winter. Only one in ten of his soldiers returned. Before this he had intended to invade Britain, but NELSON defeated the French fleet at the Battle of TRAFALGAR (1805). In 1815 his army was defeated by Wellington at the Battle of WATERLOO, in Belgium, and Napoleon was sent to the island of ST. HELENA for the rest of his life. He died in 1821.

NATIONAL ANTHEM, a song which becomes the National song and is sung on important occasions. "God Save the Queen" is the British National Anthem, and the "Marseillaise" is the French. A national anthem soon becomes associated with the glory and the sufferings of a country, reminding us of its great men and women.

NATIONAL HEALTH SERVICE is paid for by taxes, partial charges, and weekly NHS contributions. The latter are collected with the National Insurance contribution in a single weekly stamp from everyone in Britain who earns money regularly. The money is used to keep hospitals going and to pay the doctors and

Napoleon Bonaparte.

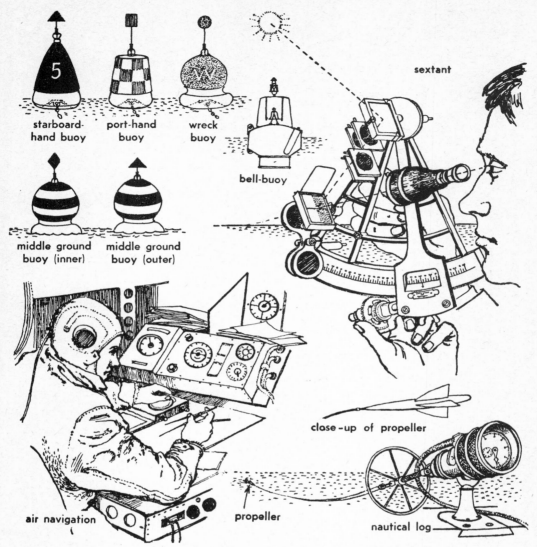

starboard-hand buoy

port-hand buoy

wreck buoy

bell-buoy

middle ground buoy (inner)

middle ground buoy (outer)

sextant

air navigation

close-up of propeller

propeller

nautical log

There are many aids to navigation for the sailor and the airman.

nurses for taking care of sick people. It also enables everybody to have a doctor or go to hospital when they are ill without having to pay any more money, and to get medicines, spectacles, false teeth, and other such things very cheaply.

NAVIGATION. Sailors must know where they are on the ocean and in which direction they should sail in order to reach their destination. This work is called navigation. The navigator can plot the position of the ship on a CHART. The position is known roughly because the captain can tell its speed by means of the LOG, and its direction by means of the COMPASS. He makes allowance, of course, for ocean currents and winds. Sailors can also find their LATITUDE by using a SEXTANT, and LONGITUDE by using a CHRONOMETER, and from these two readings they can tell whether they are keeping on their course.

Aeroplanes need navigators too, of course. They use the same methods as the

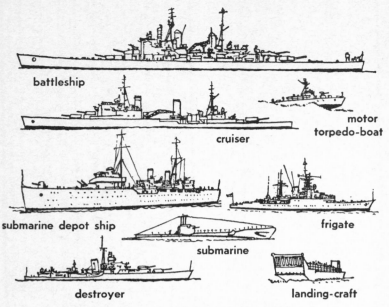

A navy has many kinds of special ships.

battleship

motor torpedo-boat

cruiser

submarine depot ship

frigate

submarine

destroyer

landing-craft

sailors do. Nowadays sea and air navigators are helped by radio beams from fixed stations whose positions are known, and also by RADAR devices which enable them to see through fog and darkness. See also BUOY.

NAVY. The navy of a country is made up of ships specially built and manned for warfare. The British Navy has saved Britain from invasion on several occasions (see ARMADA, NAPOLEON, WORLD WAR). A modern navy has AIRCRAFT-CARRIERS, BATTLESHIPS, cruisers, DESTROYERS, SUBMARINES, and other ships. See also CONVOY.

NAZARETH is the small town in Galilee where JESUS lived with His parents.

NECTAR, the sugar solution that is secreted in flowers, from which bees make honey. In their search for nectar insects fly from flower to flower and in this way the pollen is carried from one plant to another. See FERTILIZATION; FLOWER.

NEEDLES, The, a group of three rocks, like tall pillars, west of the Isle of Wight in the English Channel. They are marked by a light-house.

NEGROES are natives of the area between the Sahara and the equator, in Africa. Their dark skins protect them against the strong sun. Many have curly hair, thick lips and broad, flat noses. After the discovery of America large numbers were taken by force from the Slave Coast and other parts of Africa, packed into the holds of ships and sent to be sold as slaves in America and in the West Indies. Slavery was abolished in the British Empire after the Act of Emancipation of 1833 and in America after the American Civil War. Negroes still live in America, and there are now about twenty-two million of them there.

NELSON, Horatio, born in 1758, joined the Navy when he was only twelve years old. He became one of Britain's greatest admirals. He was skilful, bold and fearless in leading his fleet into action. He lost an eye in one battle, an arm in another, and was killed in the hour of his greatest triumph—at TRAFALGAR in 1805.

NELSON'S COLUMN is a monument to the famous admiral in Trafalgar Square, London. Copied from a Corinthian column of the Temple of Mars at Rome, it forms the pedestal for the statue of Nelson, and is about 170 feet high.

NEOLITHIC. For half a million years early men used chipped flints and wooden spears to help them to kill wild animals for food. This was known as the Old STONE AGE. A few thousand years before the Egyptian civilization began, men had learned to polish the flints and put handles on them to use as axes. They had also learned to make wooden BOWS, wooden arrows with flint tips, and simple boats, and they had learned to grow corn and keep animals for food. This later age is known as the New Stone Age, or the Neolithic Age. Civilization began soon after this in Egypt, Babylon and Phoenicia, and spread to Greece and Rome.

NEON is a gas which is present in small quantities in the air. Neon lights are made by putting a little neon gas in a long glass tube and passing an electric current through the gas.

NEPAL is an independent State between INDIA and Tibet. It lies on the southern slopes of the HIMALAYAS and the highest peak, Mount EVEREST, is within its borders. Rice, millet, oil-seeds and tobacco are grown in the fertile valleys and cattle and timber are other important exports. The Gurkhas, famous as fierce warriors, come from Nepal.

NEPTUNE is a planet farther from the SUN than the EARTH. The earth takes one year to go round the sun; Neptune takes 165 years. It was discovered in an interesting way: the farthest planet we knew about before 1846 was Uranus and the astronomers found that it seemed to get slightly out of its proper path at times. Two mathematicians thought it must be pulled out of its path by another planet, so they calculated where the other planet would be, told the astronomers to turn their telescopes on this place and, sure enough, they found the new planet, and called it Neptune. See also MARS; SATURN; SOLAR SYSTEM.

NERVOUS SYSTEM. In a simple creature such as a SPONGE all the cells are very much alike. If you put a live sponge through a mincer you would just divide it into a lot of little sponges which could go on living as if nothing had happened. But in the higher animals all the cells have a special task to perform. Some are sensory cells, whose job it is to watch for heat, cold, pressure, tastes, or smells, and so on. Some are muscle cells, whose job it is to move the animal, and some are nerve-cells, which carry messages. The nervous system is the mass of nerve-cells coming from the BRAIN and through the spinal cord (see SPINE). It includes the nerve-cells which function in all parts of the body. The brain and spinal cord form a great and complicated telephone exchange for the use of the whole body. For example, if you accidentally put your hand on a hot pipe, the sensory cells in your hand feel the dangerous heat and at once transmit a warning message to the spinal cord, which transmits the message to the muscles of the arm, which hurriedly pull the hand away. These cells all do their work even when we are asleep. See also REFLEX ACTION; SENSES.

Nelson was killed at the moment of victory.

203

NEST, a shelter or resting-place made by birds in which to lay their eggs and hatch and rear their young ones. The name may be used for any snug resting-place, and especially one used by young animals. Turtles and crocodiles make nests in the sand. Sticklebacks build under-water nests in the stream. In fact, the story of the stickleback is rather amusing.

First, the male makes the nest with water weeds, and binds them together with slime from his own body. Then he goes off to find his mate. She may be unwilling to go into the nest, in which case he pushes and prods her until she does, and stays on guard until she has laid her eggs. But she is not allowed to stay after that. He drives her out, and goes off to find a second, and sometimes a third, mate until he is satisfied that there are enough eggs in the nest. Then he seals it up and waits for the young to hatch. When they are ready to come out he opens the nest at the top but he still watches over the young

until they can face life in the pond on their own. (See also STICKLEBACK.)

The nesting habits of some birds are sometimes very strange. The hornbill, like the stickleback, does not trust his mate. The nest is made in a hole in a tree, and as soon as the eggs are laid the male seals up the entrance to the hole leaving only a small opening through which he can feed the imprisoned female. The weaver finches weave strands of grass into a pouch-shaped nest, and the TAILOR-BIRD sews leaves together to make a hanging pocket.

NET. Sometimes you may see a label showing a *weight* followed by "net," such as "2 lb. net." This means that the packet contains two pounds of the substance in it, the weight of the packet itself not being counted.

NETS, Fishing, are made of cords which are knotted to form a mesh. There are many different kinds. For example, fish such as the HERRING are caught in drift nets, while fish such as the halibut are caught in trawls. See FISH.

The stickleback drives his mate into the nest.

Netball is a popular game.

NETBALL, a ball-game played on a hard court, marked in an oblong of 100 feet long and 50 feet wide. There are two teams of seven players each. These are the goalkeeper, centre, defending centre, attacking centre, defence, attack and shooter. The object of the game is to throw the ball (it is rather like a football) into the opponents' goal, which is a circular net, open at both ends, supported at the top of a pole 10 feet high. The ball must not be carried, but is thrown from one member of a team to another.

NETHERLANDS, The (Holland), the name of a small country between Belgium and Germany. AMSTERDAM is the capital. The Parliament buildings and the Palace are at The Hague. A quarter of the land is below sea level, but the Dutch have built dykes to keep the sea out. They grow crops and bulbs and feed cattle on the land. The Dutch are good sailors and shipbuilding is an important industry. See also DYKE, ZUIDER ZEE.

NEWFOUNDLAND is an island in the Atlantic, off the east coast of CANADA. With Labrador, on the mainland, it forms a province of Canada. It is the nearest place across the Atlantic for aeroplanes flying from Britain. The seas are shallow and great quantities of fish are caught by fishermen from Britain and other countries, as well as by the local fishermen. There is also plenty of TIMBER, and water power to grind it into pulp for making paper.

NEW SOUTH WALES, one of the States in AUSTRALIA. There are fields of wheat, great areas of grass which feed sheep and cattle, and valuable minerals in the mountains. Nearly all Australia's coal comes from here. The capital is Sydney.

NEWSPAPER. The chief task of a newspaper is to tell its readers of important or interesting events as soon after they happen as possible. Reporters are sent to the scene of each event to find out the facts and write down the news. They may then telegraph their accounts of what has happened to the newspaper office, where a News Editor reads them. He picks out the most interesting items and has them set up in type for the printing machines. About midnight every night the machines start printing the next morning's papers, and each may print, cut, fold, count and tie into bundles more than 30,000 papers per hour! The bundles are then rushed to the railway stations and sent to all parts of the country so that they are ready for delivery at breakfast-time.

The Netherlands, another name for Holland.

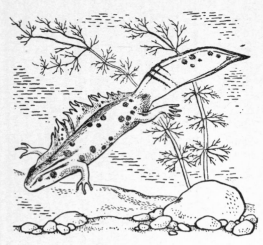

Male crested newt.

NEWT. There are many species of this AMPHIBIAN in Europe and northern Asia, and they are commonly found in ponds and ditches in Britain. The three British varieties are the smooth, the palmate and the crested newt. They lay their eggs singly under the leaves of water plants. Their food consists of flies, slugs, worms and small pond creatures. See also FROG; TOAD.

NEWTON, Sir Isaac, born in 1642, was one of the greatest of mathematicians. He stated the law of gravity, discovered why a PRISM breaks up sunlight into

Sir Isaac Newton.

colours, and invented the reflecting telescope. He died in 1727. See GRAVITY; LIGHT.

NEW YORK is the name of a State and of a city in America. The city is one of the largest in the world, with a population of over eleven and a half million people. It is an important seaport, and many of the Atlantic liners call there. The city is built on solid rock and the buildings can be made so high that they are called skyscrapers.

NEW ZEALAND consists of two large islands and some smaller ones. The country is part of the BRITISH COMMONWEALTH OF NATIONS and is almost exactly opposite Britain. If you had a globe to represent the earth and held it between two fingers with one finger on Britain, the other would be almost on New Zealand. It has excellent grassy plains called the Canterbury Plains, from which come Canterbury lamb, wool and dairy produce. The capital is Wellington. There are still many Maoris there, the people who were there before the white man arrived.

NIAGARA is a river in NORTH AMERICA which flows from Lake Erie into Lake Ontario. Its valley gets narrow and steep, and the whole wide river then falls down about 160 feet, to make the famous Niagara Falls. The power of the falling water is used to make electricity.

NICKEL is a metal like silver which is useful for many purposes. It can be used to give a bright surface to cutlery, bicycle handlebars, and so on. It can be mixed with brass to give a silver-like alloy (German silver), and it can be mixed with steel to give nickel steel, which is much stronger than ordinary steel for many purposes.

NIGER, a great river in West Africa. It rises in central Guinea, near Sierra Leone, and flows away north towards the Mediterranean, into which it used to flow. Now, however, it turns round near Timbuktu and flows south into the Gulf of Guinea. See the map on page 7.

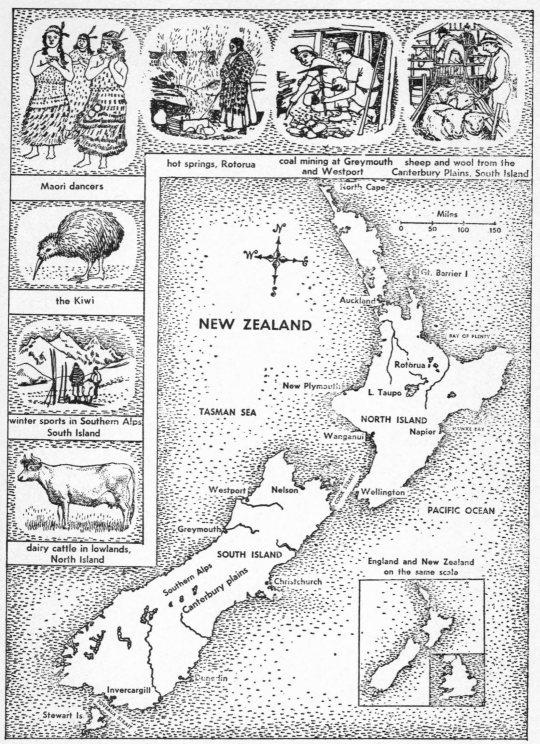

Maori dancers

the Kiwi

winter sports in Southern Alps
South Island

dairy cattle in lowlands,
North Island

hot springs, Rotorua

coal mining at Greymouth
and Westport

sheep and wool from the
Canterbury Plains, South Island

Miles
0   50   100   150

North Cape

Gt. Barrier I

Auckland

NEW ZEALAND

BAY OF PLENTY

Rotorua

New Plymouth

L. Taupo

TASMAN SEA

NORTH ISLAND

Napier

HAWKE BAY

Wanganui

Westport   Nelson

Wellington

PACIFIC OCEAN

Greymouth

SOUTH ISLAND

England and New Zealand
on the same scale

Southern Alps

Canterbury plains

Christchurch

Dunedin

Invercargill

Stewart Is.

New Zealand and some of the things found there.

207

NIGERIA is the country around the lower NIGER. It is a member of the BRITISH COMMONWEALTH OF NATIONS in West Africa, with a population of over sixty-six millions. From the equatorial part we get palm-oil, palm kernels and cocoa. In the higher, more northerly parts,

Scene in Nigeria.

cattle, sheep and goats are reared, cotton and groundnuts are produced, and tin is mined. Lagos is the capital. Up to 1850 it was the centre of the African slave trade. See NEGROES; SLAVERY.

NIGHTINGALE, a bird famous for its sweet singing; it visits the south of England in the summer. It is smaller than a thrush and sings most beautifully at night.

NIGHTINGALE, Florence, was born in 1820. When quite young, Florence Nightingale was very interested in nursing people, and in those days that was unusual for girls of well-to-do families. When she heard how the British soldiers wounded in the CRIMEAN WAR were being neglected, she organized a team of nurses, and with her strong and forceful personality persuaded the War Office to let her go to help. Some of the army doctors and other officers did not want women interfering with their work and put difficulties in her way, but she fought through all opposition, opened up a wonderful hospital, and made such a success of nursing the sick and wounded soldiers that she became famous all over the world. The British public subscribed £50,000 for her and she used the money to found an institution for training nurses. She died in 1910.

NILE, a great river in Africa. Its water comes from the equatorial rains which fill Lake Victoria, and flows across the Sahara Desert to the Mediterranean, a distance of over four thousand miles. If it were not for its tributary, the Blue Nile, which comes from ETHIOPIA, the water would all have dried up before it reached the Mediterranean. The Blue Nile begins to flood in June, and by September the main river has risen about twenty-five feet and flooded the Egyptian fields. The mud left behind is fertile soil on which crops of wheat, maize, cotton, rice and sugar cane are grown—sometimes three crops in a year. DAMS have been built across the Nile to store up its water. See EGYPT.

NINEVEH was the ancient capital of the ASSYRIAN Empire. It stood opposite where Mosul now stands, on the River Tigris. The remains of Sennacherib's palace in Nineveh have been discovered. The city was destroyed about 600 B.C.

Nineveh is mentioned in the Bible (Genesis, chapter 10, verse 11). It was to Nineveh that Jonah was sent in the Bible story of Jonah and the great fish.

NITROGEN. About four-fifths of the air is nitrogen gas. Plants must have nitrogen. Beans and peas can take some from the air, but most plants can absorb it only as nitrogen compounds from the soil. See also OXYGEN.

NOAH. The Bible tells the story of an ancient flood which was said to have destroyed all mankind except Noah and his family. They saved themselves and many animals by building a huge ark which sailed safely on the waters until the floods had gone down.

NOMADS, tribes of people who have no settled home, but live in tents or similar dwellings and move about with their livestock wherever there is pasture. Nomadic people live chiefly in North Africa and Central Asia.

NORMAN ARCHITECTURE. The Romans built round arches for doors and windows, and the Normans, when they came to Britain in 1066, introduced the round style of arch. That is why this type of building is called Norman architecture. See also ARCHITECTURE.

NORTH. The Earth spins on its axis once every day, and if we picture it as an orange with a knitting-needle stuck through it for an axis (or axle), the two ends of the knitting-needle which stick out would show the positions of the two "poles" of the Earth. Though there are no actual poles there, these two places on the Earth's surface are known as the North and South Poles. The one in the same half of the world as Britain is called the North Pole, and a star which happens to be almost exactly over it is called the NORTH STAR or POLE STAR. There is no star directly over the South Pole. The word North is used to mean "in the direction of the North Pole or of the Pole Star," or just facing in that direction. It also means that half of the world which has the North Pole at its centre, and especially the regions closely surrounding the North Pole.

NORTH AMERICA is that part of the continent which contains CANADA, MEXICO and the UNITED STATES. The high Rocky Mountains run along the west coast, and the smaller Appalachian Mountains run near the east coast, and there are great plains in between. The river MISSISSIPPI which, with its tributary the MISSOURI, forms the longest river system in the world is in North America.

The British and French settlers began on the east coast, which is nearest Europe, and gradually spread over the whole country, leaving less and less space for the Red Indians whose home it was. Later the

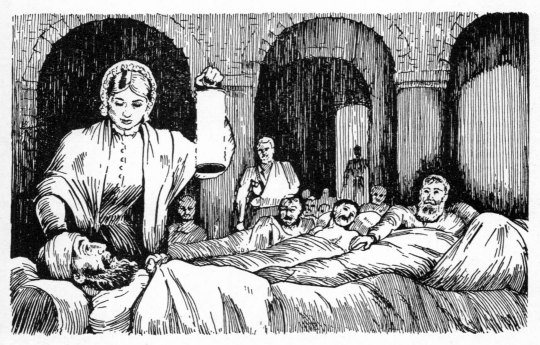

Florence Nightingale nurses the soldiers wounded in the Crimean War.

governments of the United States and of Canada kept special areas for them to live in. These are called Indian Reservations.

NORTHERN IRELAND consists of the north-east part of IRELAND. It forms part of the United Kingdom of Great Britain and Northern Ireland. Cattle are reared and oats, potatoes and flax are grown. Belfast, the capital, is important for its linen industry, and for its shipyards, which are supplied with steel and coal shipped from Scotland.

NORTHERN LIGHTS, the luminous glow sometimes seen in the sky of northern lands at night. Also known as the *aurora borealis*, it may appear as a great arc of light, or in long, darting beams, and is often brightly coloured. Similar lights known as the *aurora Australis* are sometimes seen in the southern half of the world.

NORTH POLE. See NORTH and POLAR EXPLORATION.

NORTH SEA, the sea between Britain and the continent of Europe. It is not a deep sea, and there are shallow banks, like the Dogger Bank, where fish are plentiful.

NORTH STAR. See POLE STAR.

NORWAY, a country in the north-west of Europe. It is larger than Britain, but is mountainous and cold, and the population is only almost four million. Most of the people live around Oslo, the capital, or around the fiords, where there is fertile land and good fishing. There are great forests of good timber. This is exported, or made into pulp for paper.

NOSE, the organ through which we breathe air into our lungs. It warms the air and keeps out the dust in the air. When you smell something (such as food or a rose) what happens is that tiny particles from the thing you are smelling are touching the nerve endings in your nose and the message they send to your brain is the smell.

NOTATION, MUSICAL. It is convenient to write down notes for singing and playing, as well as words for speaking.

The notes are written on five parallel lines, called a stave, higher notes being written above lower notes. To know where you are, you must know the exact note on one particular line of the stave, for that will give the relative positions of all the other notes. This is shown by a sign called a clef put at the beginning of the stave—

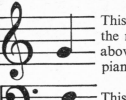

This is the treble clef; the note shown is the G above middle C on the piano.

This is the bass clef; the note shown is the F below middle C on the piano.

In piano music both clefs are used, one for each hand. The note middle C, which falls between the two staves, is written in a short (ledger) line.

NOUN, a word used as the name of a person or thing, such as John, table, victory, team, tadpole.

NUMBER, when you count: "One, two, three, four . . ." you are naming the cardinal numbers, and these are used to show a total quantity of items present. Thus, you may have *three* potatoes on your plate, and *four* fingers on each hand. But numbers are also used to show the order of things, as when you say you came *fourth* in your class, or that you live in the *tenth* house past the church. The words: "First, second, third, fourth . . ." are therefore called the ordinal numbers.

NUNS, women who wish to devote themselves to a religious life of prayer and worship by retiring from the world into a CONVENT.

NYASA, now Malawi, is a lake in one of the rift VALLEYS in Africa. This extends from Lake Malawi to Lake Albert.

NYASALAND, former British Protectorate in Central Africa. Now an independent republic and renamed Malawi. Still a member of British Commonwealth. Farming is the chief occupation.

O

OAK, one of the most valuable trees. British ships were built of oak before the days of iron and steel ships. The oak tree grows in many countries, generally in temperate regions. Its seed is the ACORN.

OASIS, a fertile place in a desert. Even in the Sahara Desert rain falls occasionally and the water sinks through the sand until it is stopped by a layer of rock. It then flows to the lowest level (which may be in the heart of the desert) and forms a spring or pool. Vegetation soon grows there, of course.

OBOE, a woodwind MUSICAL INSTRUMENT with a double reed in the mouthpiece. See also ORCHESTRA; REED INSTRUMENTS.

OBSERVATORY. From earliest times men have studied the movements of the sun and other heavenly bodies. Before 1600 Tycho Brahe, a Danish astronomer, had made wonderfully exact observations from a building fitted with telescopes and other instruments. A building of this kind is called an observatory. A famous observatory was founded at Greenwich by CHARLES II to find out facts about the positions of the sun and stars as a help to sailors.

OCEAN CURRENTS. The regular winds blowing over the ocean tend to move the water in definite directions. The Gulf Stream is one current which flows from the Gulf of Mexico across the Atlantic Ocean towards Northern Europe. The movements of the earth and the different temperatures of the oceans also cause currents.

The Sargasso Sea in the North Atlantic has a mass of seaweed which collects in the centre of the currents. This is where the eels come to breed. The Gulf Stream brings warmer water to Britain. In the Pacific Ocean the Kuro Siwo Current brings warmer water to parts of the west coast of North America.

OCTOPUS. The octopus has eight arms, lined with suckers to enable it to catch and hold its prey. The big ones live in deep water in warm countries. The sperm whale is not afraid of them, however. The remains of large octopuses are sometimes found in the stomach of this whale.

ODYSSEUS was the hero of a long story poem by HOMER called the *Odyssey*. When the siege of Troy ended, Odysseus set out to return to his home on the island of Ithaca. On the way he had a number of adventures. He was wrecked on the coast of Africa. He managed to escape from the one-eyed giant, Cyclops. He came to the island of Circe, an enchantress, who turned all his companions into pigs. When they were made human

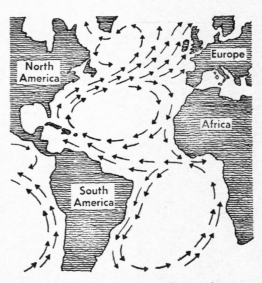

Ocean currents of the Atlantic Ocean.

again, he sailed to another island and was delayed there for seven years. At last, after wandering for ten years, he reached his home and found his wife, Penelope, still waiting for his return.

The Romans gave the Greek heroes and gods Roman names, and the Latin name for Odysseus is Ulysses.

OILS. When petroleum, an oil found under the ground, is distilled, the lightest oil, petrol, boils off first, then the paraffin oil, then the heavy oils used for lubrication, and a petroleum jelly is left. Oils are also obtained from palm trees, ground nuts, coconuts, olives, and other sources. Whale oil is used for making margarine and for other purposes.

OLD TESTAMENT. About three-quarters of the Bible is a history of the Jewish people and is known as the Old Testament. One of the earliest books to be written down was that of Amos, the first of the prophets, and this was written about 750 B.C. There are thirty-nine books in the Old Testament, beginning with Genesis. Much of the wisdom of the early civilizations is in these books, and the wisest men of all ages and in many countries have studied them for guidance.

OLIVE, an evergreen tree which grows in Italy, France, Spain, Greece, Turkey, and other countries around the Mediterranean Sea. The fruit is in the form of dark green berries, like small plums, from which olive oil is squeezed out.

The olive is often mentioned in literature. In the story of Noah and the Flood it was an olive leaf which the dove brought back. Greek and Roman athletes competed for an olive wreath, and "to hold out the olive branch" means to offer peace and friendship.

OLYMPIC GAMES, originally a national festival of the GREEKS, held every fourth year. The festival included sports such as running, wrestling, and throwing the discus, and there were also horse races and chariot races. The Olympic Games were revived in 1896 and are now an international competition held every four years, in a different country each time.

OMNIBUS, a Latin word which means "for all." The name was applied to carriages in which anyone could ride for a small payment. The shortened form "bus" is now generally used.

OPERA. Music can express all emotions, and in the late sixteenth century composers began to set dramatic stories to music calling them operas. The Italians, who sing a lot and enjoy singing, produced many good operas, some of which are performed today—Verdi's *Il Trovatore*, for example. Wagner, a German, wrote most elaborate operas with wonderfully complicated orchestration. He could represent a ship in a storm at sea (in *The Flying Dutchman*), or galloping horses (in *The Valkyrie*) in a most vivid way, and many people are not only interested and excited by such music, but enjoy trying to understand how Wagner produced these wonderful effects.

OPTIMISM is a hopeful view of life. Pessimism is a despondent view of life. Someone said: "The optimist's glass is always half full, the pessimist's is always half empty." That expresses the difference very well. Whether one is an optimist or a pessimist depends largely on the way one was brought up in the early years of life.

ORANG-UTAN. See APE.

ORANGE, a favourite fruit, grown in Spain and other countries with a Mediterranean type of climate, such as South Africa and California. Growers can now produce delicious oranges, large, juicy, sweet, and almost without seeds.

ORCHESTRA. The modern symphony orchestra consists of the following instruments: Violins, violas, 'cellos and double basses; flutes, oboes, clarinets and bassoons; trumpets, horns, trombones and tubas; drums, cymbals, triangle; and sometimes a few other instruments. This great and complicated orchestra has been gradually developed from simple orchestras; but Haydn and Mozart were writing

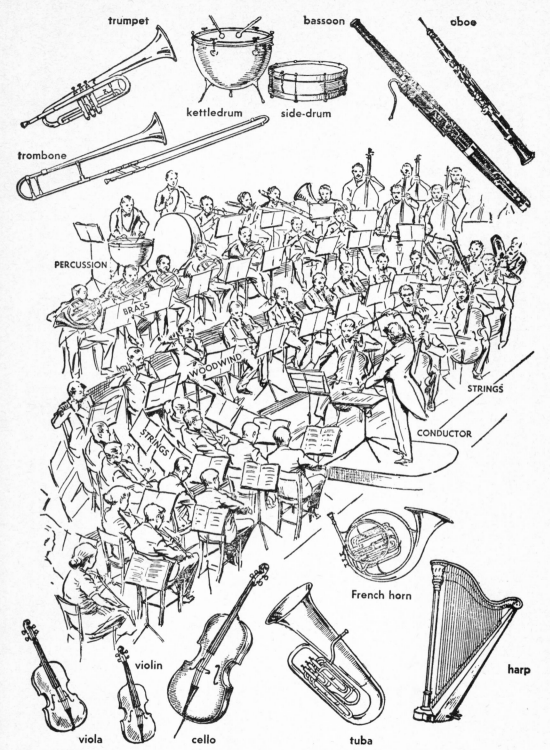

Some of the instruments used in an orchestra and how the players may be arranged.

their music about 1780 for orchestras of this kind, although there were not so many players.

ORDNANCE SURVEY. When the government army entered Scotland in 1745 to suppress the Jacobite rebellion, they got into difficulties because they had no maps of the country. Because of this, first Scotland, and then England, was surveyed, and reliable maps made. Surveyors first measure a distance accurately on a level piece of ground. This is the base. Then by measuring the angle to, say, a church spire, from each end of the base, a triangle can be drawn to SCALE on paper and the position of the church can be marked accurately on this.

In the picture BC is the base, drawn to a scale of 1 inch = 1 mile. CBA is the angle to the church spire (45 degrees) from the left end of the base. BCA is the angle (60 degrees) from the other end of the base. Where the two lines meet is the position of the church spire (A). When all objects have been plotted from this base, another side of the triangle, AC, forms a new base from which to work, and so on.

Thus the whole area is surveyed. See also MAPS; SURVEYING; THEODOLITE.

ORE. Gold is found as a metal, but iron is always found in combination with oxygen or other elements. If pure iron were formed on the earth it would soon turn to rust, and it is from rust, or iron oxide, that most of our iron is made.

Similarly lead, zinc and other metals have to be separated from other elements, usually by smelting. Iron oxide in the ground is called iron ore. Lead sulphide in the ground, a compound of lead and sulphur, from which we get lead, is called lead ore.

ORGAN, a musical instrument which produces sounds by air being blown through a number of pipes of various lengths. The longer the pipe, the deeper is the note. Modern organs can produce a great variety of notes.

OSTRICH, the largest bird. It lives in the Kalahari Desert and in Arabia and elsewhere. Ostriches have very small wings and cannot fly, but they have long and powerful legs with which they can outrun a horse or kill a man. The female lays ten

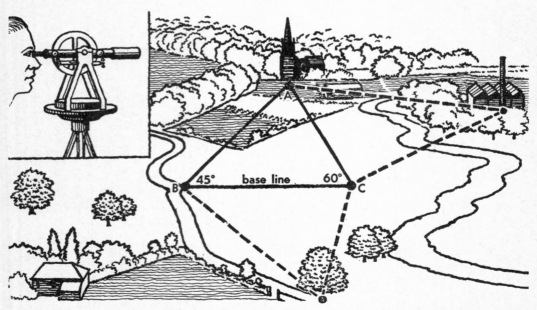

45°   base line   60°

B   C

Surveyors making an ordnance map can use a theodolite (inset) to measure angles.

214

The ostrich cannot fly.

or twelve eggs, each weighing about three pounds. The hen sits on these by day, the cock taking his turn at night. There are ostrich farms in South Africa where ostriches are kept for producing feathers for feather dusters.

OTTAWA, the capital city of CANADA, situated in Ontario on the Ottawa River, which flows into the St. Lawrence at Montreal. At Ottawa is the Canadian Parliament House, the Supreme Court, the National Museum, and other important buildings. There are two cathedrals and a university, while the industries include paper-making, flour-milling and the manufacture of machinery.

OTTER, a MAMMAL which lives around rivers and feeds on fish. It has webbed toes and a flattened tail. The common otter is found in Europe and northern Asia; the Sea Otter is to be seen around the islands of the North Pacific.

OWL, a BIRD OF PREY which hunts mainly at night. Both its eyes look forwards, and each is surrounded by a circular disk of radiating feathers, giving the well-known owl-face. There are two hundred different kinds of owls in the world, ranging from the pigmy owlet, about six inches long, to the great eagle-owl, which is as large as a buzzard.

OXFORD is the county town of Oxfordshire, and stands where the River Cherwell joins the River Thames. The city became important because of its ancient university. Some of the colleges of the university were founded over seven hundred years ago. The colleges have so many tall towers that a famous poet called Oxford the "city of dreaming spires."

OXYGEN is a gas which forms one-fifth of the air and is essential to life. Airmen flying to high altitudes carry cylinders of oxygen with them, and these are also carried sometimes by divers, firemen, mountaineers and others; for if the body is short of oxygen for even a few minutes it cannot live. When a substance burns it is combining with oxygen and giving out heat in the process. See also NITROGEN.

OYSTER, the most valuable shell-fish. Oysters are found in great numbers in the seas around the United States, but in England they have now to be cultivated in special beds in the sea. Whitstable, at the mouth of the Thames, has many famous oyster beds.

The oysters from which pearls are obtained are of a different type, growing in warm waters, as, for example, in the seas off JAPAN.

Barn or Screech Owl.

215

P

PACIFIC OCEAN. There are two great oceans on the earth, the Atlantic and the Pacific. The Pacific is the larger, and covers a quarter of the surface of the globe. This is more than all the continents cover. New Zealand, the East Indies, the Philippines and Japan are some of the many islands formed by half-submerged mountain ridges. Hawaii, or the Sandwich Islands, in the middle of the Pacific, were raised up by volcanic action. The oceans are about two miles deep, but here and there are mountain peaks five miles high, and ocean deeps five miles down. One place, off the Philippine Islands, is six and a half miles deep. See the maps on pages 20–21 and 166.

PAINTING. Primitive man used to paint animals in black, red and yellow colours on the walls of his caves. The picture on page 52 gives you some idea of this. In the Egyptian and Mesopotamian civilizations many colours were used for painting pictures, and some lovely paintings on walls still exist which were painted in Crete about 2,000 B.C.

In a gallery of painting you may see beautiful pictures painted by Botticelli, Leonardo da Vinci, MICHELANGELO, Titian and other famous Italians who lived in the fifteenth and sixteenth centuries, there may be pictures by RUBENS, VAN DYCK, and Frans Hals, who lived in the sixteenth and seventeenth centuries, and by Rembrandt, who lived from 1606 to 1669. Portraits by Rembrandt are particularly lovely. There may be pictures by the painters El Greco and VELASQUEZ, who lived in Spain about 1600. The English painters, REYNOLDS, Gainsborough, CONSTABLE and Turner, may be represented, and there may be pictures by Cézanne,

who lived in France, and VAN GOGH, who lived in Holland. These artists lived in the eighteenth and nineteenth centuries. See also page 217, and the entry on ART.

PAKISTAN, a part of India in the days when India was governed by Britain. When in 1947 India became a self-governing country the people of the western and eastern parts decided to govern themselves because they are MOSLEMS, while most Indians are HINDUS. The new country was divided into two parts, separated from each other by northern India. The eastern section seceded from the government in 1972 as the Republic of Bangladesh. Wheat and rice are grown, and cotton and jute are also important crops. The capital of Pakistan is Islamabad. See page 156.

PALAEOLITHIC AGE (Old STONE AGE) refers to the time when men had only learned to use chipped flints and wooden spears and to make fires. They must have lived in this way for hundreds of thousands of years before they discovered how to polish the flints, to use them as axes, or hammers, and to make arrows with flint tips and shoot them from bows. When men advanced to this New Stone Age or NEOLITHIC AGE, they soon progressed towards civilization.

PALATE, the roof of the MOUTH. The front part is supported by bone and is called the "hard" palate. The back part contains no bone and is called the "soft" palate. See also TASTE; TONGUE.

PALESTINE, formerly the name of a country in south-west Asia, at the eastern end of the Mediterranean. In 1948 Palestine was divided into two parts, one part forming the new Jewish republic of ISRAEL, the other part becoming part of the

Leonardo Da Vinci

Rembrandt

Velasquez

Van Dyck

Constable

Van Gogh

Cézanne

Gainsborough

These drawings are based on self-portraits of some very famous painters.

217

Arab kingdom of JORDAN. Oranges, grape-fruit and other fruits are important exports. Haifa, Jaffa and Tel Aviv are the chief ports. See also JERUSALEM.

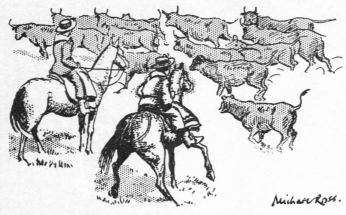

Cattle are raised on the Argentine pampas.

PALMS, very valuable trees which grow in tropical countries. We get coco-nuts from one kind of palm, dates from another, sago from a third, and oil from others. Wax and other valuable substances are also obtained.

PAMPAS, the temperate grasslands in southern BRAZIL and the ARGENTINE. They feed enormous numbers of cattle; and great quantities of wheat are raised in favourable areas.

PANAMA CANAL, a CANAL which allows ships to sail through central America. It is fifty miles long, over forty feet deep and rises by means of locks eighty feet above sea level. It is broad enough at places to allow two ocean liners to pass each other. Ships sailing from the Atlantic to the Pacific can shorten their journey very much by sailing through this canal.

Giant Panda.

PANDA, a name given to outwardly different animals. The smaller pandas are almost cat-like and live in the trees in northern India. The larger Giant Panda looks much like a bear, and lives in China and Tibet.

PAPER. The Chinese were very probably the inventors of this material, early in the Christian era. Later, Arab traders intro-duced it to Europe. It is made from chemically treated pulp fibres from various plants and also from rags and wood-pulp.

PARABLE. A parable is a story which illustrates the point that the speaker is trying to make. Jesus often used such stories to make His hearers quickly see the differ-ence between right conduct and wrong. Especially through par-ables like "The Good Samaritan" or "The Prodigal Son" did He preach His message of love and forgiveness.

PARABOLA. The reflecting mirrors of searchlights and motor lamps are parabolic, be-cause this shape throws a parallel beam from a point of light near the reflector. See also CONIC SECTION.

Parachute.

PARACHUTE, the umbrella-like struc-ture which enables a man to descend safely from a height. It was probably Leonardo da Vinci who first worked out the idea. Nowadays, whole regiments of soldiers jump out of aeroplanes to capture a piece of country, or get behind the enemy's lines. Food, ammunition, motor bicycles and even guns are dropped by the same means.

PARAKEET, a name given to any PARROT with a long tail. BUDGERIGARS, or

218

lovebirds, for example, are sometimes spoken of as parakeets.

PARASITES, animals or plants which live on or in other animals and plants, feeding on them while they are alive. A plant parasite usually lacks the green colour of ordinary plants. Animal parasites are divided into two groups. There are those which live outside the body, such as fleas and lice, living on the skin and sucking blood, and there are those which live inside the body, such as tapeworms, spending their lives in the intestines of another animal, absorbing its food. See also FUNGUS; PLANTS.

PARCHMENT, writing material made from the skin of sheep or goats, and used before PAPER was invented. It is still used sometimes for important documents.

PARIS is the capital of FRANCE. It is a beautifully planned city, with many lovely buildings, palaces, and public monuments. It is situated in a fertile river valley, at the centre of the French railway system. Paris is a large city with a population of two and a half millions, and, like LONDON, is full of historical interest.

PARLIAMENT. See HOUSE OF LORDS; HOUSE OF COMMONS.

PARROTS, beautifully coloured birds which can be trained to talk. There are various kinds, called PARAKEETS, cockatoos, and BUDGERIGARS or love birds. The grey parrots live in West Africa. Others live in the warmer parts of America, Australia, New Zealand and elsewhere.

PARTRIDGE, a greyish-brown game bird, plumper and somewhat bigger than a pigeon and found throughout Europe and in Great Britain. Partridges live in families or coveys of from five to twenty birds, continuing to do so long after the young are able to fly. They nest on the ground and their eggs (between ten and twenty) are fawn in colour.

PASTEUR, Louis, born in 1822, was a famous French scientist who first discovered the importance of germs. Disease among the silkworms was ruining the silk industry in France. Pasteur discovered the cause and how to cure it. He discovered the cause of anthrax, and how to prevent the disease spreading. He discovered why milk and beer go sour. Pasteur died in 1895. See also LISTER.

PEACOCK, a bird like a very big pheasant. The male has beautiful tail feathers which it can spread out like a great fan. The wild peacock lives among the trees in India and south-east Asia.

PEARL. When a piece of grit or a PARASITE gets inside the OYSTER's shell, the oyster oozes a liquid around this foreign body, and the liquid solidifies into a pearl. This process goes on and the small pearl gradually becomes a large one.

Some years ago, Japanese merchants had a remarkable number of good pearls for sale. People wondered where they came from. Then it was found that the Japanese were collecting oysters, putting a bit of hard pearl in each, dropping the oysters back in the water and waiting for the pearls to grow. Pearls are still obtained in this way.

Parrots can repeat words.

PELICAN, a bird which, like the CORMORANT, lives on fish. It has a large beak, and the bottom half of the beak has loose skin which acts as a bag, in which the bird can keep fish for a future meal.

PENDULUM. If a weight is swung from a piece of string thirty-nine inches long, the weight will take one second to swing each way. The longer the string, the longer the time taken to complete the swing; the shorter the string, the shorter the time taken to complete the swing.

The pendulum of a clock which has to keep accurate time is made so that its length does not alter with hot or cold weather. See also TIME.

PENGUINS live in great numbers in the southern hemisphere. They are all excellent swimmers and feed on fish, but they cannot fly. The largest penguins, called Emperor Penguins, of the ANTARCTIC, stand three feet high.

PENICILLIN comes from a mould and destroys many GERMS which are harmful to human beings yet does not harm human tissue itself. See FUNGUS.

PENINSULAR WARS (1808–1814) were fought in Spain and Portugal. Napoleon had told these countries not to trade with Britain, and because they did

The pelican lives on fish.

not obey this order at once he sent an army to take control of them. Britain sent an army to help Spain and Portugal. After many successes and retreats, the British army drove the French troops back to their own country. WELLINGTON became the British commander when Sir John Moore was killed at Corunna.

PEPYS, Samuel, born in 1633, kept a diary from 1660 to 1669. It was written in shorthand, and when it was deciphered in 1822 people realized at once what an important document it was. Pepys's accounts of the Great PLAGUE of London (1665) and of the FIRE OF LONDON (1666), both of which he actually saw, are wonderfully interesting. Pepys held important Government posts, doing much to rebuild the Navy. He met the King and many well known people of his time, and describes them exactly as he thought of them. He was very frank in all he said. Pepys died in 1703. See also CHARLES II.

PERCUSSION INSTRUMENTS are MUSICAL INSTRUMENTS that are played by striking—drums, cymbals, tambourines, triangles, tubular bells and others. The three drums called the tympani are tuned to give different notes and are important instruments in symphonies. See also ORCHESTRA.

Penguins are birds that cannot fly.

15th century—Edward IV

early 16th century—
Henry VIII

late 16th century—Elizabeth I

early 17th century—
Cromwell

late 17th century—
Charles II

early 18th century—
George II

late 18th century—
George III

early 19th century—
George IV

late 19th century—Victoria

early 20th century—
Edward VII

Some period costumes taken from different ages of history.

the producer directs a rehearsal

scene shifters at work

actors wait in the wings   a scene from "Peter Pan"

electricians and prompter

wardrobe mistress

an actor makes up

A play is a story acted on the stage—there are many people involved besides the actors.

PERENNIAL, any plant which lives for several years, especially those which are not trees or shrubs. Perennial plants usually "die down" before winter, and send up new stems each spring, but some keep a few of their old leaves until the new ones begin to appear. Examples of perennials are the primrose, peony, snapdragon and iris.

PERIOD COSTUME, a style of dress typical of a period in history. A historical play is called a costume-piece when the actors are dressed in the fashion of the time in which the story is set. Through the centuries people have had many different ideas about dress, and you can see some of the styles they liked in the colour plate facing page 224.

The Greeks and Romans wore tunics, usually made of woollen material, which fell into graceful folds. The Normans had tunics and loose cloaks; sometimes they added bands of embroidery. By the thirteenth century, clothes were more closely-fitted to the body, but remained simple in design. In the fourteenth century patterns in the form of heraldic badges decorated the dress; the fifteenth and sixteenth centuries were much more splendid, when rich velvets, gold thread embroidery, and jewels were used. In strong contrast to the severity of the Puritan dress in the early seventeenth century, laces, ribbons, pleats and muffs brightened the later Restoration period in England. The crinoline and the bustle were two more elegant fashions, following in the eighteenth and nineteenth centuries. See also DOLLS; HATS.

PERSIA (IRAN) is a country in ASIA, between the Persian Gulf and Afghanistan. Much of it is a sandy desert, but with the help of IRRIGATION, crops are grown in places. Sheep and goats are kept, and the inhabitants make the valuable Persian rugs from the wool. Oil is the chief wealth, however. It is found in great quantities in the south-west of the country. See map on pages 20–21.

PERSIAN GULF separates Iran from Arabia. The rivers Euphrates and Tigris

Perspective is an effect brought about by distance.

flow into it. There are valuable pearl fisheries in the Gulf.

The Persian Gulf flows into the Indian Ocean through the Gulf of Oman.

PERSPECTIVE. The farther away objects are, the smaller they appear to the eye or camera. We may be in doubt whether we are looking at a bird or an aeroplane, and when we look at two parallel lines (for example, railway lines) the distance between them seems to get less the further they stretch from us until they seem actually to join at the point where they disappear.

Photography is a popular hobby. It becomes even more interesting if you

In drawing pictures artists usually allow for perspective, tending to show the world as our eyes see it rather than as our minds know it.

PERSPIRATION, or sweat, is oozed out by the sweat GLANDS in the skin. The body gets rid of some waste products by this means, and the process also helps to regulate the temperature of the body.

PERTH. Two towns have this name, one on the River Tay in Scotland, and one on the south-west coast of Australia.

PERU, a country in SOUTH AMERICA which lies on each side of the Andes Mountains, near the Equator. The coastal strip gets no rain, but water is got fairly easily from the many mountain streams. Sugar, cotton, maize and rice are grown. Cattle and sheep are reared on the mountain slopes, and valuable minerals and oil are found. The population is over thirteen million and the capital and largest town is Lima.

PETER, one of the twelve disciples of Jesus. He was a fisherman named Simon when Jesus found him and renamed him Peter.

PETROLEUM is the natural OIL from which petrol, paraffin, lubricating oil and petroleum jelly are obtained. Petroleum is found in the United States, Soviet Russia, Venezuela, Rumania, Persia, Canada, Australia and other countries, and is obtained by BORING wells.

PHARISEES were an ancient order of religious teachers amongst the Jewish people. Because they kept strictly to the laws and ceremonies of the Church but sometimes behaved selfishly, their religion often seemed insincere.

PHEASANT, a game-bird introduced into Britain by the Romans. The cock pheasant is brilliantly coloured and has a tail about two feet long. The hen pheasant is dull brown, speckled with black. Pheasants roost in trees but feed on the

Drying negatives

Making contact prints

Drying prints

Glazing prints

Mounting prints

...evelop your negatives yourself, and from them make your own prints.

ground, eating grain, insects, berries and roots. The nest is a hollow in the ground, and from ten to fourteen eggs are laid in it.

PHOENICIANS lived at the eastern end of the Mediterranean Sea, on the strip of land between the coast and the Mountains of Lebanon. They were wonderful sailors, and brought corn and linen from Egypt; ivory, ebony and cotton fabrics from India; spices from Arabia; and tin from Cornwall. They must have had good ships and have known a good deal about navigation to make these voyages. They also knew how to make glassware, and beautiful purple dye from shellfish, and they were good miners and builders. Altogether they became a wealthy and civilized people. They were not a warlike people, however, and the Assyrians, Babylonians and Persians successively took control of their country. The Phoenicians also founded the city of Carthage in North Africa, which for a time was a serious rival to mighty Rome.

PHOTOGRAPHY. If you are in a dark room and a pinhole is bored in one of the window shutters, a bright picture of what is outside can be seen on a white surface held up near the pinhole. The camera, too, has a tiny hole fitted with a LENS and controlled by a shutter which opens when you take a picture. In the back of the camera is a flat surface—a glass plate or a FILM which has been specially prepared with chemicals that are sensitive to light. This surface is affected by the various strengths of light thrown on to the film so when the film is developed with other chemicals an image appears on it. This developed film is called the negative, and from it you can then make prints, called photographs.

PHOTOSYNTHESIS. See PLANTS.

PHYSICS is the science which studies force, motion, light, heat, electricity, sound, and other natural happenings.

223

Astronomy and chemistry were once branches of physics, but they have become so important that they are now regarded as separate sciences. Faraday and Lord Kelvin were great English physicists. RADAR and the use of ATOMIC ENERGY are two recent discoveries of the physicists.

PHYSIOLOGY is the study of the working of the body.

PIANO. This musical instrument has developed from such simple instruments as the harp which are played by plucking strings or wires of different pitch. Inside the piano are many taut wires, the long ones giving low notes, and the short ones giving high notes. They are not plucked but are struck by little hammers, each made to work by playing the appropriate key on the keyboard. On each wire is a little pad of felt. Before the hammer strikes the wire, the pad moves off the string, and the hammer, after it strikes, also moves away a little, so that the wire continues to vibrate and give a note so long as the finger holds down the key. All the other strings are damped by their pads. If, however, the right pedal is pressed down, all the pads come off the

strings

hammer

damper

action

pedals

The strings of a pianoforte are made to vibrate by the action of little hammers.

wires, and if a note is struck it will continue to go on sounding even after the finger has left the key. Chords can thus go on sounding while other notes are sounded against them. Pianists use this "sustaining pedal," as it is called, to sustain harmony, even in soft passages. It is not in any sense a "loud pedal" as some bad pianists think. It must be released to damp all strings before a new chord is played, or the effect is just a muddle of sounds. The left pedal is depressed to get softer sounds, and can be called a "soft pedal." This pedal moves the hammers nearer the strings, so that they do not get up so much speed when struck, or it moves the hammers a little to the side, so that only one of the two or three strings for each note is struck by the hammer. The piano was originally called the pianoforte. "Pianoforte" means "soft and loud," but the piano can not only be played softly and loudly, it can give a different quality to notes of the same loudness, depending on how the sustaining pedal is used. Beethoven and Brahms were both very good pianists.

PICCOLO, a small flute. It is half the length of the flute and so plays an octave higher. See ORCHESTRA.

PIG, a cloven-hoofed animal with a heavy body, short legs, and a powerful snout for digging out roots. Its natural food consists of roots and such fruit as acorns and beech-nuts. Wild pigs live in the forests, but they were all killed off in Britain during the seventeenth century. The male, or boar, has powerful tusks for defence against enemies. Pigs were domesticated and kept for food in Europe nearly 3,500 years ago, and probably much earlier in China.

PIGEON, one of the strongest fliers among birds. It can fly at the rate of about forty miles per hour and is still used occasionally to carry messages, or for racing against other pigeons.

PIG IRON. Iron ore, coke and limestone are heated together in the BLAST FURNACE until molten iron is formed at the bottom of the furnace. This is run out into moulds and allowed to cool, so as to form blocks of crude iron, called pig iron. This can be melted again and made into iron objects.

PIGMENTATION is the colouring in the body tissue, and in the hair. The SKIN consists of a number of layers; the dermis is the deeper layer and the epidermis is the outer layer. The deepest layers of the epidermis are made up of cells which contain black granules of pigment (melanin). These get more concentrated when the skin gets a lot of sun. That is why people who live in a hot climate have darker skins than the people who live in cooler lands. Their hair, too, tends to be black.

See also RACES OF MANKIND.

PIKE, a fairly large fish found in the rivers of Europe and America. It lives on other river fish and seems to fear none of them.

PILE-DWELLINGS. In the later STONE AGE, men sometimes built HOUSES on piles over a lake, or a quiet sea shore, so that wild animals or enemies could not attack them suddenly. The remains of such houses have been found in Switzerland and elsewhere, and we know when they were built by the flint arrow heads and other remains which are found in the houses. In New Guinea houses of this kind are still being built.

Domestic pig.

225

The Pilgrim Fathers sailed from Plymouth.

PILGRIM FATHERS, a group of about a hundred men and women who in 1620 left England in a ship called the *Mayflower*, and sailed to America to live there. JAMES I, King of Great Britain, would not allow the Puritans to worship in their own way, and these brave Puritans sailed to the New World which Columbus had discovered to get freedom to worship as they pleased. They and their descendants had a very difficult time, but out of their efforts came a great new nation, later the United States.

PINE, a tree which grows straight up like a mast. It produces its seeds in cones. There are great forests of pine trees in Russia, Sweden, Germany and other countries.

PINEAPPLE, a delicious fruit grown in the tropics. The hard outside is cut off and the tough core bored out, and the fruit is cut into slices or cubes and served with the juice. Much of it is sent abroad in tins.

PIRATES were seamen who used to attack ships and steal their cargoes. This was often done in the olden days. There used to be pirates in the Norwegian fiords, in the Grecian archipelago, the Caribbean Sea and similar places where it was easy to hide. One seldom hears of a pirate ship nowadays. It would soon be chased and caught by a warship.

PISTON, the round, flat plate inside a cylinder which moves with the pressure of steam in a STEAM ENGINE, or the pressure of gases in a motor engine. The piston moves the piston rod and that turns the wheels. See also ENGINE.

PLAGUE, a very infectious disease which kills many people. We read in the Bible about plagues in Egypt, and in the fourteenth century a plague, which the people called the Black Death, killed millions of people in Europe. The Great Plague of London killed seventy thousand people in 1665. Samuel PEPYS wrote an account of it in his diary.

PLANTS. Like animals, plants can breathe, grow and reproduce themselves; some plants, such as the Volvox and seaweeds, can even move about. The biggest difference between plants and animals is in their feeding. Animals must have plants to feed upon, but plants do not need animals.

Every living thing is made up of cells. Sometimes there is only one cell, sometimes there are millions of cells. Plants have in addition a green substance called *chlorophyll*, which absorbs the sun's rays to release energy. This process is called *photosynthesis*. It helps plants to obtain the substances they need. Water and air supply carbon (from carbon dioxide), hydrogen and oxygen, which together make *carbohydrates*. Nitrogen and mineral salts are obtained from the air and from the soil.

The only plants which do not get their food in this way are those which have no chlorophyll, such as MUSHROOMS and toadstools. They often live as PARASITES on other plants. See ANNUALS; BIENNIAL; FUNGUS; PERENNIAL; ROOT.

PLASTICS is the name given to new materials which chemists have made by various methods. We can have plastic watch-glasses or lenses or windscreens, which do not break easily. Telephones and nylon stockings are made from **other**

kinds of plastic material. Chemists can make plastics of any colour, which can be moulded when hot into any shape, and when cool may be hard, like bone, or soft, like cellophane, or drawn into thread like a spider's web.

PLATEAU, a plain which has been raised high above sea level. The plateau of Tibet is an enormous area, over twelve thousand feet high, but it is not level. The plateau of Antrim is a great sheet of lava which welled up from the inside of the earth and covered the hills (see GIANT'S CAUSEWAY). Scotland was once a plateau about four thousand feet high, but rivers have gradually carved it into valleys and have carried much of the soil into the sea. The hardest rock remains at the tops of the mountains, and some of them are still over four thousand feet high. Ben Nevis is the highest mountain peak in the British Isles.

PLATING is the process of covering a cheap metal, like brass, with a film of more valuable metal, like gold or silver. Silver-plated spoons look like silver spoons and are much cheaper. Cans made of thin sheet steel would soon rust if they were not plated with tin.

PLATINUM is a very expensive metal, heavier than either lead or gold. It is not affected by any ordinary acid, and for this reason is very useful to the chemist.

PLATO was one of the greatest of the Greek philosophers. He lived from 428 to 347 B.C. He was a disciple of SOCRATES and his books are still studied by educated people in all countries.

PLAY. A play as we know it today is a story acted on the stage in a theatre. At first plays were about the people in the Bible and helped to tell the Bible stories as part of the Church services. Later they were presented at street corners on wheeled platforms on special occasions, and later still special buildings were built for dramatic purposes. By this time plays were being written about historical people and soon afterwards they were written about imaginary people. During SHAKE-

These pirates have made their victims walk the plank, then buried the stolen treasure.

227

SPEARE'S lifetime the DRAMA grew up; there were many kinds of plays—historical plays about great people of the past, tragedies about the wicked and the unfortunate, and comedies about people with very human failings that make us smile. There were moralizing plays to make us better, and farces in which everything gets funnier and more mixed-up than we can ever hope to find it in real life. In modern times plays got less poetic and more realistic so that we seem to be looking into the lives of the people whose story we observe.

The modern pantomime is a different kind of play, which developed from the acting of a story in dumb show to the telling of a story in words and music. Among plays for children, two of the most popular fairy tales are *Cinderella* and *Peter Pan*. Sir James Barrie wrote the play of *Peter Pan* first, and the story of the play was published in book form as *Peter Pan and Wendy* a few years later.

PLIMSOLL, Samuel, was born in 1824. He was called "the Sailors' Friend," because he worked hard as a member of Parliament to prevent ships going to sea overloaded. Overloaded ships are likely to sink in a storm and drown all the sailors. As a result of his efforts a law was passed that every ship must have a loading line painted on the side. The ship must not be loaded so that it sinks so much in the water that this line disappears from view. It is called the Plimsoll line. Samuel Plimsoll died in 1898.

PLOUGH is used for turning over the land so that fresh soil comes to the surface for the next crop to grow on. The importance of ploughing the land has been known since the earliest times. The Ancient Egyptians used the plough.

POETRY. All language is rhythmical, but poetry is more rhythmical than prose. It is thought expressed in words that dance rather than walk, words that seek to move your imagination and touch your heart. Here is a simple poem that does this:

"Four ducks on a pond,
A grass-bank beyond,
A blue sky of spring,
White clouds on the wing.
What a little thing
To remember for years—
To remember with tears."

The poet tries to make you see what he saw, and feel about it what he felt. This is a lyrical poem. Poets can also tell stories in verse and when they do so we call their work narrative poetry. See also RHYTHM.

POLAND is a country of eastern Europe. Owing to wars, its boundaries have been changed many times. Most of the country consists of a low plain. On this land the farmers grow rye and potatoes, and keep pigs. The capital is Warsaw. See the map on page 99.

POLAR EXPLORATION. The attempt to reach the North and South Poles and to make maps of the land around them is called Polar Exploration. The North Pole was first reached by the American, Peary, in 1909, and the South Pole by the Norwegian, Amundsen, in 1911, followed a month later by Captain Scott. Other men to explore the vast sheets of ice which cover the poles include Byrd, Nansen, Shackleton and Wilkins. See EXPLORATION.

POLE STAR, a star which is visible in the northern half of the sky, and is almost exactly overhead at the North Pole. It is known also as the North Star. It is a very useful star for navigators in the northern hemisphere, for the angle it makes with the horizon (its elevation) gives the LATITUDE. If the North Star is overhead, that is, at elevation 90 degrees, one is at latitude 90 degrees, that is, at the North Pole. If the North Star is on the horizon, that is, at elevation 0 degrees, one is at latitude 0 degrees, at the Equator.

POLICE, the body of people responsible for maintaining law and order. In England, policemen are sometimes nicknamed "Bobbies" after Sir Robert Peel who founded the London Police Force. New Scotland Yard is the headquarters of

watchman
late 16th century

Bow Street runner
late 18th century

a Charlie
17th to 19th century

a Peeler
early 19th century

on the beat

Scotland Yard

mounted police

traffic control

river police

radio cars

protection

smash and grab alarm

women police

D.H. Ralphs.

The police force is an organization to keep order and enforce the law.

229

the London Metropolitan Police. They patrol the streets, test the doors of shops to see that thieves have not broken in, direct the traffic and help to keep people safe.

Political speaker in Hyde Park, London.

POLITICS. Every country needs a government to find solutions for the big problems that arise in the course of our living together as a people in a world full of other peoples! Politics is everything that has to do with making a government and with creating the policies (and the rival policies) towards the main problems of the day. Political parties exist to reflect the rival beliefs and aims within a nation.

In Great Britain there are three main political parties—Conservative, Liberal and Labour. Every five years the people have to elect a new Parliament to govern them. The country is divided into areas, called constituencies, and at an ELECTION the people who live in each area must send one man or woman to represent them in Parliament. They choose their members by voting for them, and most of the new members belong to one or other of these three political parties. The party which gets most members elected forms a Government, and the less successful parties together form the Opposition. The leader of the Government party usually becomes Prime Minister. He at once chooses the best of his supporters to be put in charge of the big departments of State, such as the Treasury, Home Office, Foreign Office, Ministry of Education and Board of Trade. These men are called Ministers, and the chief among them form the Cabinet, a sort of committee led by the Prime Minister. The Cabinet Ministers are the "managers" who run the country according to the political ideas of the Government party. The job of the Houses of Parliament is to make new laws when necessary and discuss broad issues of the day. See also BALLOT; HOUSE OF COMMONS; HOUSE OF LORDS.

POMPEII, an ancient Roman city situated on the Bay of Náples. Behind it stands the volcano Vesuvius, which erupted in A.D. 79 and buried the entire city to a depth of twenty feet in boiling mud and ashes. About two thousand people were killed, but more than a thousand years passed before anybody attempted to dig out the ashes and examine the ruins. Today, the remains of the houses, shops, temples and theatres bring something of the distant past to our modern gaze.

Ruins of Pompeii.

PONTOON, a boat or floating tank used to support a heavy weight. Pontoons are used to lift wrecks off the bottom of the sea, and to raise and lower piers with the flow and ebb of the tide. A pontoon bridge is a row of boats placed side by side across a river to support a light wooden roadway.

POPE, Alexander, born in 1688, was the leading English poet in the eighteenth century. He wrote poems with lines rhyming in pairs, called couplets. While most poets write about things they like, Pope enjoyed writing about the things he didn't like, and wrote many a stinging remark which was unkind but probably deserved. He died in 1744.

POPE, The, title given to the Bishop of Rome, as Head of the Roman Catholic Church. He rules over the Vatican City, a papal state in Rome.

PORCUPINE, an animal found in most of the warmer parts of the world, and known for its armour of long sharp spines. The European porcupine is about two feet long and has black and white hair. Its quills or spines are decorated with black and white rings. The animal uses them as spears by running backwards at an enemy. Porcupines do great damage to gardens, where they eat roots and vegetables.

Porcupine.

PORPOISES, dolphins, narwhals, pilot whales and killer whales form the family of "toothed-whales." The common porpoise is black with white on the belly. It feeds on such fish as herring, whiting and sole. Usually no more than six feet long, porpoises live in "schools" which sometimes come close inshore to feed. See WHALE.

PORTUGAL is a small country on the extreme west of Europe, bordering on the Atlantic Ocean. It is a little bigger than Ireland, and its population is about the same as that of London. The capital city is Lisbon, on the River Tagus, while Oporto, on the River Douro, exports port wine. Although nearly half the country is waste land, Portugal is mainly a farming country, producing wines, fruits of all

Scene in Portugal.

kinds and timber. Fishing is an important industry, and SARDINES are packed in tins for export. Portugal was once a great sea-power, her famous sailors including Bartholomew Diaz (who first sailed round the Cape of Good Hope in 1488) and Vasco da Gama. Portuguese sailors discovered Brazil about 1500, and for three hundred years Brazil was a Portuguese colony. Today, Portugal's largest colonies are Angola and Mozambique, both in Africa. See the map of Africa on page 7 and the map of Europe on page 99.

POTTERY. Hollow articles such as pots, dishes and vases are called pottery when they are made of baked clay. They may be made shiny and watertight by melting a thin layer of a glass-like substance over them, as in cups and saucers, or they may be left rough and unglazed as in flower-pots. Another name for coarse pottery is earthenware, but the best

231

This shows you what type looks like and how words are printed.

and finest kinds are known as china or porcelain. (Dresden, in Germany, is famous for the manufacture of porcelain figures.) Round-shaped articles like vases are made on a potter's wheel, which is one of the oldest machines known. A lump of wet clay is put in the centre of the wheel, which is then spun round while the potter shapes it to the form required. See also CHINA CLAY; KAOLIN.

POULTRY. Domestic fowls and farmyard birds, including ducks, geese and turkeys, are called poultry. Well-known breeds of FOWLS include Orpingtons, Plymouth Rocks, Rhode Island Reds, Wyandottes, Leghorns and Dorkings. Bantam fowls are dwarf forms bred from the larger varieties and are not a separate species of fowl.

PRAIRIE, a level, grassy stretch of land in North America, where herds of BISON used to roam. Farmers now grow wheat on great areas of the prairie. The fields are so large and flat and treeless that the farmers can use big machines for ploughing, sowing, and harvesting. Much of Britain's bread is made from wheat grown on the Canadian prairies.

PRAYER is a request made by a person of low rank to one of higher rank, or by any person to God. The Lord's Prayer is a model prayer given by Jesus Christ to His disciples.

PRAYER BOOK, a book containing examples of prayers for people who find it difficult to make their requests known to God. The Church of England *Book of Common Prayer* contains all the prayers said regularly during the Church services, in the order in which they are used, as well as giving instruction in the other parts of the services. It includes the marriage, burial, and Holy Communion services, and contains the Church Calendar.

PRETORIA, the administrative capital of the SOUTH AFRICAN REPUBLIC, and also capital of the province of Transvaal, in which it is situated. It stands on the railway about a thousand miles north-east of Cape Town and thirty-five miles from Johannesburg, in a gold-mining area. In addition to the Government and Parliament Buildings, Pretoria contains the Transvaal University College and many other fine buildings.

PRIEST. The word "priest," or "presbyter," means "elder," and refers to an official of a church who conducts the services. A priest is a minister of religion, a clergyman.

PRINTING is done by means of types, which are small blocks of metal with raised letters standing up on their ends. Types bearing the right letters are set together to make words, and a roller smeared with printing-ink is passed over them. A sheet of paper is now pressed on to the inked type, and comes off with the words printed on it. Any number of copies can be made if the type is freshly inked each time.

Printing from hand-carved wooden types was invented in Germany by Gutenberg about 1440, but today we use metal types made by pouring molten metal into hollow moulds. In Linotype the moulds of the letters are first set until a whole line of words has been put together, and then molten metal is poured in to make the entire line of type in a single piece of metal. In Monotype the letters are cast separately. These methods allow the moulds to be used again and save the printer having to stock huge quantities of ready-made letters.

Printing by pressing sheets of paper on to a tray of type is called "flat-bed" printing, but in printing newspapers the type is made into a solid curved plate which is fixed round a roller. The paper passes between this roller and another one, which keeps it pressed tight against the type, like a sheet going through a mangle or wringer. This is called "rotary" printing, and the paper is printed first on one side and then on the other. See NEWSPAPER.

PRISM. This is the shape taken by any regular solid with flat sides and flat parallel ends. A box of building bricks is full of prisms. A new flat-sided pencil (before being cut) is a prism. So, too, is a plank.

A prism with ends like triangles is a triangular prism. Such a prism made of glass has the power of splitting up white light into the colours of the rainbow—red, orange, yellow, green, blue and violet. See SPECTRUM.

PROPELLER. A propeller is a screw working at the stern of a ship or behind the main plane of an aeroplane so as to *push* the craft forward. An air-screw which *pulls* an aeroplane from the front is properly called a tractor screw, but the word propeller is now usually used for this too.

PROPHET, a person who is thought to be able to see into the future and to foretell what will happen. In the Bible, a prophet is a person especially chosen by God to declare His will and judgements. The major or most important prophets are Isaiah, Jeremiah, Ezekiel and Daniel. The twelve others are called the minor prophets.

PROSE is the ordinary form of what we say or write every day. It is the common form of expression. When we write a letter to a friend we write prose. The stories we read are written in prose.

PSEUDONYM, a name used by a writer instead of his real name. Mark TWAIN is the pseudonym of Samuel Clemens. Lewis CARROLL is the pseudonym of Charles Lutwidge Dodgson.

PUMP, a device for forcing fluids to move from one place to another. Water-pumps are used to raise water from deep wells, and air-pumps are used to force air into bicycle tyres, or to force it out of a container in order to create a vacuum.

PUNCH AND JUDY, a PUPPET play in which Punch is the hero and gets the better of all his enemies. He has a hooked nose, a hunched back and a squeaky voice. Judy is his wife, and other characters include dog Toby and a crocodile. The play is performed by glove puppets worked by someone hidden in a canvas framework which can be set up easily at the seaside or at a fair.

PUPA. See CHRYSALIS.

PUPPETS. One kind of puppet is a small doll with a hollow head and arms which can be used as a kind of glove. You put your hand inside the puppet with your forefinger in the head, your thumb in one arm and your second finger in the other. You now move your fingers and make the doll wag its head, bend its body, and wave its arms. You can act little plays with several puppets if you get a friend to help you. You can make it more realistic if you build a small stage like the one used in Punch and Judy shows. Another type of puppet is suspended on strings and is worked from above the stage.

The puppets shown here all have a head made from a tennis ball:

Make a hole in the ball (with a penknife) big enough for your finger. Wind a paper strip ($1\frac{1}{2}$ in. wide) round your finger to make a roll and put an elastic band or some transparent sticky tape round to hold it firm. Push this paper roll into the hole in the ball (it must fit tightly).

Before doing the face scrub the ball with soap and water, otherwise your paint may not stay on. Paint the face and add such details as ears, hair and hat.

The puppets have a cloth body which hides the hand of the operator. This garment is gathered round neck and sleeves and should not be too tight for your hand to move comfortably. A piece of plastic-covered wire is threaded through the hem of the body; so that you can slip your hand inside the puppet quickly during a performance. The wire has a loop by which the puppet can be hung upside down; this is a good way of storing the actors.

Impy has a cork nose fastened to the ball with a pin, and two spiral wire feelers which are pushed into holes made with a bradawl or knitting needle. Painted cork, or wood beads, at the end of each feeler give them the necessary weight to nod when the puppet moves.

The ears can be made from coloured

IMPY

basic garment
9 in. long and
approximately
6 in. wide

CLOWN

It is easy to make these glove puppets, an

felt ears

tennis ball

paper roll for finger

wire loop for hanging

RABBIT

you can have a lot of fun putting on a show to entertain your friends.

paper stuck to the head with transparent sticky tape.

Impy can be painted whatever colour you imagine him, and please make him look impudent and perky.

Invent your own clothes for him, based on the simple shape shown in the diagram. Try coloured paper streamers stuck to his arms and chest.

The Clown's face is painted direct on to the white tennis ball. He has big flappy paper ears and a fringe of raffia hair.

The hat is cut from half a circle of paper which is folded over to make a cone shape with the straight edges pinned together. The hat is stuck to the head at the back.

Lace collar and cuffs are made from paper doilies. Sew the body from chequered gingham and decorate with large woollen pom-poms or buttons.

Use felt or old gloves to make enormous hands and stuff them with cotton-wool.

Rabbit can be white or spotted, with long pink felt ears. Two layers of felt stitched together along the edges will make them stiff. (Strong paper can be used instead.)

Whiskers made from broom bristles are stuck on the face and a tail made from fur or wool can be sewn on to the back.

PYGMIES are small people who live in the dense tropical forests of Central Africa. They are about four feet six inches or less in height. They have dark skins, black curly hair, and wear very few clothes. Most of them are very shy, and some have never seen a white man. Their huts are made of the branches and leaves of trees. For food they gather fruits, roots, and other things, and they kill large animals with poisoned arrows.

Pyramids of ancient Egypt.

PYRAMID, a large stone building of the shape shown in the picture. Most of the pyramids were built as tombs for the kings of Egypt. The best known is the Great Pyramid at Giza, near Cairo. It was built nearly five thousand years ago, and is higher than St. Paul's Cathedral.

PYRENEES, a range of mountains which separate France from Spain. The slopes are steeper on the French than on the Spanish side, and water power from some of the mountain streams has been used to make electricity.

PYTHON, a large SNAKE related to the BOA CONSTRICTOR. Like the boa it is not poisonous, but kills its prey by coiling round the body of its victim and crushing it to death. Pythons are found in Africa, Asia and Australia. All pythons are large, but the largest lives in Malaya and grows to a length of thirty feet.

Pygmies live in the Congo.

Q

QUAKERS are members of a religious body, founded in the seventeenth century, and properly known as "The Society of Friends." They were called Quakers because an English preacher, George Fox, spoke of "quaking at the word of the Lord."

William Penn, the son of a famous admiral, became an active member of the Society. He was given a grant of land in North America in 1681 and founded the Quaker colony of Pennsylvania. Penn lived from 1644 to 1718.

Quakers believe that it is wrong to settle quarrels by war or fighting, and have long been famed for their unselfish way of living. They try to model their lives on the teaching of Jesus Christ.

QUARRYING is obtaining rocks or heavy minerals from places where they occur near the surface of the ground. A quarry driven into the side of a hill produces a cliff from which the rock may be detached by blasting with explosives.

QUART, a measure of volume equal to a quarter of a gallon.

QUARTER, a fourth part. If you divide anything or any quantity into four equal parts, each part is called a quarter. Thus, a gill is a quarter of a pint, and 4 oz. is a quarter of 1 lb. (16 oz.).

QUARTER-DECK. On the old wooden battleships, like Nelson's *Victory*, this was the stretch of deck between the small, raised poop deck in the stern and the main-mast. In a modern warship it is the part of the after-deck set apart for the officers.

QUARTZ. Rock-crystal or quartz is a natural crystal of silica, the substance of which most sand-grains consist. Quartz is extremely hard, usually colourless, and transparent like glass. Stained by other minerals it forms amethyst (purple) or cairngorm (yellow).

QUEBEC, an eastern province of CANADA. The majority of the population is of French extraction. Quebec is also the name of the capital of the province; it is an important port.

QUEEN, the title given to a woman who is head of a monarchy, as in the Netherlands. The wife of a KING is the Queen Consort.

QUEENSBERRY, John Sholto Douglas, 8th Marquess of, a famous patron of boxing who drew up a set of laws for fair fighting, known as the Queensberry rules. They are still applied to all contests in Great Britain. He lived from 1844 to 1900.

QUEENSLAND, the second largest of the six states of AUSTRALIA, in the north-east part of the country. More than half of Queensland lies in the tropics, and the weather is hot, especially in the north. On the farms there are large numbers of sheep and cattle. Much of the water for these animals comes from artesian wells.

QUICKSILVER. This is the old name for the metal mercury, which has such a low melting-point that it is liquid at ordinary temperatures. It is silvery in colour and is used in thermometers.

QUIXOTE, Don, the fictitious hero of a story by Cervantes, a Spanish writer of the seventeenth century. Don Quixote imagines that he is a famous knight and that he must go in search of adventure. He rides on an old horse, wears rusty armour, and takes with him a faithful old servant, Sancho Panza. He imagines that he is fighting his enemies when he charges a flock of sheep and he attacks windmills thinking them to be giants.

R

RABBIT, a wild animal which spread from south-west Europe in Roman times and is now found all over Europe except in the extreme north and east. It was introduced into Britain at the time of the Conquest, and has since been taken to many other parts of the world. Three pairs taken to Australia in the eighteenth century multiplied so rapidly that the country was soon overrun and the rabbit became Australia's worst pest. A female rabbit, or "doe," has on an average ten to eleven young a year.

RACES OF MANKIND. The three basic racial groupings are Caucasoid, Negroid and Mongoloid. They are not distinguishable by skin pigmentation (colour) alone, but involve differences in texture of hair, conformation of cranium, nose, mouth and eyes and numerous other minor anatomical details. Caucasoid peoples include not only the races of Europe and "white" America, but a large proportion of Indians and Arabs. The Negroids are almost exclusively African in origin; but the Mongoloid races embrace the Chinese and Asiatic Mongols, and all the races of American Indians and Eskimos. There is no scientific evidence to suggest that one race is inherently superior, mentally or physically, to any other.

RADAR is a method of detecting distant objects when you cannot see them, and it does this by sending out an invisible beam of radio waves. If these strike any object they are reflected back again, and detected by a special radio receiver which shows them as spots of light on a screen. Thus radar is a way of seeing in the dark or through fog; it is used by the captains of ships to detect icebergs, and approaching aeroplanes are detected by radar.

RADIATION. This really means shining, or sending out rays like the sun, but it includes all kinds of rays besides the ones we can see. In addition to the LIGHT rays there are the invisible X-rays, ultra-violet rays, and infra-red rays. All these rays travel in the form of waves, like ripples travelling across a pond, and the differences between them are due entirely to the differences in the lengths of their waves. The X-rays are shortest, and the longest waves in this kind of radiation are radio waves. The radiation from radium and other radio-active substances includes streams of small particles which are shot out like bullets. See also RADIO-ACTIVITY.

RADIO. This is a way of sending messages by means of long-wave radiations called radio WAVES, which will pass through most ordinary objects. See RADIATION. They are produced by electricity, and can be made to vary in strength according to the vibrations of a voice or musical instrument, or any other sound. These waves travel at an enormous speed, and are picked up by receiving aerials and other metal objects. A radio receiver responds to the slight variations in the strength of the waves received, and thus produces in its loud-speaker an exact copy of the voice, musical instrument or other sound which caused them.

RADIO-ACTIVITY. The atoms of some of the rarer elements are in a state of breaking up, changing slowly into other elements. They do this entirely on their own account, and at the same time send out various kinds of rays. The most common rays include the "alpha-rays," which are streams of electrified atoms of the gas helium; "beta-rays," which are streams of electrons; and "gamma-rays," which are very similar to X-rays only of shorter wave-length. See RADIUM.

RADIO-TELESCOPE, a special kind of telescope, consisting of a large metal bowl which picks up radio waves coming from the stars. It can also be used as a RADAR transmitter and receiver for detecting distant stars or space satellites.

RADIUM, a rare, silvery-white metal which tarnishes rapidly in contact with the air and is very radio-active. It was discovered by Pierre and Marie Curie. The radiations consist of alpha, beta and gamma rays, and they destroy living tissues, causing severe burns. They have been used by doctors to destroy unhealthy parts of the body which cannot easily be got at. See RADIO-ACTIVITY.

RADIUS. This word has two meanings. First, it is the distance from the centre of a circle to its circumference. Second, it is the name of one of the bones in your fore-arm.

RAILWAYS. The first railways, like the first buses, were horse-drawn, a notable line being the Grand Surrey Iron Railway which ran from Wandsworth, London, to Croydon and Merstham, in Surrey, about 1800. The first public steam railway ran from Stockton to Darlington, in Durham, in 1825, and this was followed by the rapid building of railways in other countries. Most of Europe and America had railways by 1850, and today there are about three-quarters of a million miles of railways in the world—enough to reach the moon three times. See also LOCO-MOTIVE, and colour plate facing page 257.

RAIN. The clouds consist of an immense number of tiny droplets of water. Some of these droplets join up to form bigger drops, which are so heavy that they fall to the earth as rain. Sometimes they come down gently in quite small drops, and we call this drizzle. The heaviest rainfall comes from the huge, dark THUNDER clouds. If the fall is very heavy indeed, we call it a cloudburst.

RAINBOW, the coloured bow that we see in the sky when the sun shines on falling rain. It is caused by the white LIGHT from the sun being reflected and split up into its colours by the water drops. These colours are red, orange, yellow, green, blue, and violet. The red is on the outside edge of the bow, and the violet on the inside. Sometimes a second bow is formed, with the colours in the reverse order. See the colour plate facing page 161.

RAINFALL, the depth of rain that would collect on the ground during a certain period, if none were allowed to escape. It is usually measured either in inches or in millimetres. An instrument called a rain gauge is used for measuring the rainfall.

RAISIN. This is the name now given to certain kinds of grapes which are dried in the sun or by heat and stored. Raisins contain a high proportion of sugar and have a flavour quite unlike that of the grape from which they are obtained.

RALEIGH, Sir Walter, a famous sailor and courtier who lived in the reign of ELIZABETH I, from 1552 to 1618. It is now quite certain that he did not introduce either tobacco or the potato into Europe, though the stories say that he did. He never went to Virginia, though he sent an expedition

Sir Walter Raleigh.

239

there, and his visits to South America were made long after the potato was in use in Europe. The potatoes he grew in Ireland he seems to have obtained from a London herbalist. In 1595 he made his first voyage to Guiana to explore the River Orinoco. He hoped to discover the city of El Dorado, whose streets were said to be paved with gold, but though he found no gold he wrote a book describing his adventures. He also wrote a *History of the World* and many other books and poems. He was executed at Westminster in 1618, after an unfair trial on a charge of treason.

RANGOON, the capital and chief seaport of Burma, standing near one of the mouths of the great Irrawaddy River. In the north of the city is a large pagoda, the most sacred building of the Burmese people. This pagoda is higher than St. Paul's Cathedral, and the roof is covered with pure gold and precious stones.

RAT, a small, gnawing animal belonging to the same group as the VOLE, MOUSE, RABBIT and SQUIRREL. There are only two

Rat.

kinds of rat in Britain, the black rat (found only in a few seaports) and the larger brown rat, or common rat. A very large brown rat may measure a foot in length and have a tail of eleven inches, but there are no special kinds of "sewer" rats, as some people believe. See also RODENT.

RATCHET AND PAWL, a device to allow a wheel to turn in one direction only. The ratchet is a wheel with notches cut in its rim, and the pawl is a piece of metal arranged so that one end rests on the rim of the ratchet. When the ratchet is turned in one direction the notches slip past the end of the pawl, making the "click-

Ratchet and Pawl.

click" heard when clockwork is wound up. But the ratchet cannot be turned in the opposite direction because then the pawl catches in a notch and prevents further movement. The pawl is often held against the ratchet by means of a SPRING.

RATIO AND PROPORTION. This is a way of showing how much bigger one thing is than another. If one box is twice as big as another, their sizes are said to be in the *ratio* of two to one, and this is written neatly $2 : 1$. The ratio $2 : 1$ is exactly the same as

Rattlesnake.

(say) the ratio $8 : 4$, or, as we may write it in symbols, $2 : 1 : : 8 : 4$. This expression is called a *proportion*, and it is read, "Two is to one as eight is to four."

RATTLESNAKE, a large American snake, slow in movement and having at the end of the tail a series of horny rings known as the rattle. If disturbed, the snake shakes its tail to make a low rattling noise, but the purpose of this is not known. Rattlesnakes have large fangs (poison-teeth) and can inject a heavy dose of poison into their victims. In the northern United States they sleep through the winter coiled up together in hundreds.

RAY, ELECTRIC, a fish related to the SHARK, but with a flattened body like its other relative, the common skate. The flat form of the fish is caused by the large fins, which are joined to the head and run along the sides of the body. There is a slender tail. On the under-surface of the electric ray large areas of muscle beneath the skin have been converted into electric cells, capable of giving a severe shock.

RECEIPT, a written statement acknowledging that a payment for something has been made, and given by the recipient to the person who has paid. This person can then produce the receipt if asked to pay again. Receipts are often written at the foot of the bill which is being paid.

RECORDER, a musical instrument which is something like a flute or musical pipe. It is played by blowing through the whistle mouth-piece and moving the fingers on the nine little holes.

RECTANGLE, a four-sided figure in which all the angles are right-angles. The sides opposite each other must be equal. A rectangle in which *all four* sides are equal is called a *square*.

RED CROSS, the emblem of the great service founded in 1864 to help the sick and wounded in war, and known as the Red Cross Society. The Red Cross did wonderful work in the two WORLD WARS, and now there are branches in all parts of the world.

RED INDIANS. See INDIANS, AMERICAN.

RED LEAD or "minium," is a red oxide of lead. It is formed by the combination of lead with oxygen and corresponds to the rust of IRON. It is used for sealing joints in gas-pipes, and in making paints for painting over metal to prevent it going rusty.

RED SEA, a narrow inland sea, separating the shores of Saudi Arabia and north-east Africa. It was connected with the Mediterranean on the north, through the Gulf of Suez and the SUEZ CANAL, and with the Arabian Sea on the south. Coral reefs make navigation difficult.

REDUCTION. In chemistry, reduction means taking oxygen away from substances which contain it, and it is therefore the opposite of oxidization, which means adding oxygen to things which have not got it. Good examples of reduction are found in the extraction of some metals from their ORES. These ores are oxides, or combinations of their metals with oxygen, and they are smelted by heating them with coke. This joins with the oxygen to make carbon dioxide, a gas which immediately escapes, and the pure metal remains. See also BLAST FURNACE.

REED INSTRUMENTS. These are MUSICAL INSTRUMENTS in which the sound is made by the vibration of a thin tongue or "reed" of metal, wood or cane. In a mouth-organ you can usually see the small brass reeds quite easily. The principal reed instruments used in ORCHESTRAS are the OBOE, clarinet, bassoon and cor anglais.

REFLECTION. We see things by the rays of LIGHT which come back from them to our eyes. The light rays start from the sun, a fire or a lamp, and then "light up" the objects we are looking at. When they strike the objects they bounce off in all directions, and those which happen to reach our eyes enable us to see the objects. Their "bounce" or change of direction is called "reflection." When they bounce off a smooth, polished surface like that of a mirror, they are not scattered in all directions. They simply turn about and travel off in proper order in a new direction. If they now enter your eye you get a view of the lamp they started from, not of the mirror.

REFLEX ACTION. This is an automatic action of the kind you make when a sudden loud noise startles you, or when you are pricked by a pin. You jump back, or perhaps spin round, without stopping to think about it. If you burn your finger with a match you pull it away quickly; if something moves towards your eye you blink. These are all reflex actions, and they happen much too quickly for you to think about what you are doing. In each case, a sensation travels along a nerve to the spinal cord, which automatically sends back a message telling your muscles to do whatever is necessary without delay. See also BRAIN; NERVOUS SYSTEM; SPINE.

REFORM ACTS, the Acts which have reformed the British Parliament and given more people the right to vote at a general election. In 1832 the middle class were given the right; in 1867 town workers were added. Five years later the Ballot Act made voting secret. After 1884 most men

John Knox, religious reformer.

could vote, and women won the right, after a great and long agitation, in 1918.

REFORMATION. During the MIDDLE AGES there was only one Church, or form of Christian worship, in western Europe, and the Pope was at its head. Gradually the Church lost its great power and, in the sixteenth century, began to split into national Churches. In these the language of the people took the place of Latin, and there were many other changes. At a great meeting in Germany some reformers led by Martin Luther protested against a decision of the Church of Rome, so they became known as Protestants. Luther translated the Bible into German.

HENRY VIII condemned Luther's teaching, and the Pope rewarded the English King with the title *Fidei Defensor* (Defender of the Faith). Henry later denied the authority of the Pope and the Church of England was established, but the title still appears on British coins.

Other leaders of the Reformation were Jean Calvin, a Frenchman, and John Knox, a Scottish reformer. Knox lived in the reign of MARY I, during which many Protestants were persecuted. The form of worship with the Pope at its head is now called the Roman Catholic Church.

REFRACTION. This name is given to the bending of rays of LIGHT when they enter or leave a transparent substance like water or glass. It is refraction which causes a stick thrust into a pond to appear bent, and which causes objects seen through uneven window-glass to have queer shapes. The LENSES used in telescopes and microscopes are made to refract the light so as to give magnified views of the things seen through them.

REGIMENT, the unit of an army which is commanded by a Colonel or Lieutenant-Colonel. It is divided into battalions, and these in turn are divided into companies.

REGULATOR. In STEAM ENGINES, this is the valve which lets steam pass into the cylinders. It can be opened or closed slowly, letting in more or less steam, and so it regulates the rate at which the engine works.

REINDEER, an animal of the DEER family living in the Arctic regions of Europe and Asia, and also North America, where it is known as the caribou. Both bucks (males) and does (females) carry antlers, which are shed or cast off every year. As a protection against cold, the small ears and the muzzles are covered with soft hair. The body is covered with a woolly under-fur. The hoofs are broad and spreading, giving a firm hold even on icy ground. Reindeer feed on grass and leaves, and on a LICHEN known as reindeer moss, from which they remove the snow with their hoofs.

RENAISSANCE, the great revival of art, music, poetry and drama, combined with a new spirit of adventure, which spread from Italy to the western countries of Europe, from the fourteenth to the sixteenth century. A new interest in learning stirred men's minds, and the great writings of the ancient Greeks were translated and studied. The New World was discovered, the telescope was invented to discover new worlds in the skies, and, in Elizabethan England SHAKESPEARE towered over other poets and dramatists, while Bull, Gibbons, Byrd and many others led the world of music.

REPRODUCTION. Animals and plants produce offspring by means of special cells. There are male cells and female cells. The female cell is called an ovum or egg; in animals the male cell is called the sperm, and in plants the pollen. When the male cell of a plant unites with the female cell, a seed is formed.

Many of the simple forms of life reproduce by growing large and then splitting into two, one big one thus becoming two small ones, which then start growing big on their own account (see AMOEBA). Some plants grow swellings or "buds" on various parts of their bodies, and the buds then break off and lead separate lives. Many plants are able to reproduce in this way, whether they also produce seeds or not. See FERTILIZATION.

REPTILES, land animals in which the body is protected by a layer of scales. They are said to be "cold-blooded" because their blood takes on the temperature of their surroundings. When this temperature falls, the reptile becomes sleepy. That is one reason why the reptiles, which include SNAKES, LIZARDS, TURTLES, TORTOISES and CROCODILES, are not found in cold

Retriever.

countries, but are most numerous in the warmth of the tropics.

REPUBLIC, a State in which the people choose their own head, instead of having a Sovereign who comes to the throne by right of birth. The United States of America is a republic, ruled by a President elected by the people.

RESERVOIR, a large tank usually built of brick and lined with cement, used to store water for the use of a town or village. There are two kinds of reservoir, open and covered. The open reservoir holds the water before it has been filtered and made fit for drinking; the covered reservoir holds the purified water, and is roofed over to keep the water clean. Reservoirs are often built high up, so that the water will flow naturally from them down the pipes to the houses.

RESPIRATION, or breathing, is necessary to keep the body supplied with oxygen. The LUNGS, like a pair of bellows, take in air and then blow it out again. While the air is in them, the lungs extract the oxygen from it and the blood carries the oxygen to all parts of the body. The blood carries back waste products from the body to the lungs and these are sent out from the body in the form of stale gas when the lungs breathe out again.

RETRIEVER, a breed of dog used for retrieving, or fetching, game that has just been shot. Retrievers are medium-sized dogs, and there are two principal varieties. One is black with a flat, wavy coat; the

M.W.
Reindeer.

243

The fall of the Bastille signalled the beginning of the French Revolution.

other is black or liver-coloured, with a short curly coat. In addition, there are the Labrador and golden retrievers.

REVOLUTION. This word means "turning round," and is used in history to describe any violent or sudden change in the way of life. In the seventeenth and eighteenth centuries new methods of farming were known as the "Agricultural Revolution"; changes in manufacture were called "the Industrial Revolution." Some revolutions, when governments are overturned, are sometimes very violent. Such was the French Revolution which began in 1789 with the storming of the Bastille, the prison fortress in the heart of Paris.

In 1792 France was proclaimed a republic, and the following year the King, Louis XVI, was executed. His queen, Marie Antoinette, was put to death by the guillotine nine months later. NAPOLEON BONAPARTE rose to power, and later proclaimed himself Emperor of the new French Empire in 1804.

REYNOLDS, Sir Joshua, a famous English portrait painter who lived in the eighteenth century. He not only painted the portraits of most of the famous men and women of his day but he also wrote about painting and taught other people how to paint. He invited other painters to join together in a group which formed the Royal Academy. Reynolds was its first President. He lived from 1723 to 1792.

RHINE, a river which rises in Switzerland, flows through western Germany, and enters the North Sea from Holland. "Father Rhine," as the Germans call it, is the busiest river in Europe. On it long trains of barges carry coal, minerals, and grain, and many important cities stand on its banks. Along the beautiful Rhine Gorge are the ruins of many medieval castles. See the map on page 124.

RHINOCEROS, a large, hoofed animal, with a bulky body and short legs, a tough, almost hairless hide, and a large head with small eyes and ears. Rhinoceros horn consists of matted hair.

There are several species of rhinoceros; those of Africa have two horns set on the snout, while the Indian rhino has only one. The rhinoceros of Sumatra, a much smaller animal, carries two horns.

RHODES, Cecil John, a famous statesman, was born in England in 1853. He joined his brother in South Africa in 1870, and made a lot of money from the newly-discovered diamond-fields at Kimberley. He was Prime Minister of Cape Province from 1890 to 1896. Then he settled in Rhodesia. Rhodes worked hard to promote British influence throughout the world. His ambition was to see a federation of South Africa under British rule, but this did not come about until eight years after his death in 1902. By his wish, most of his wealth was used to provide scholarships at the University of Oxford for British, German and American students.

RHODESIA AND NYASALAND, FEDERATION OF, British territory in Central Africa consisting of Nyasaland, Northern and Southern Rhodesia, producing copper and tobacco. In 1964 the Federation was dissolved: Northern Rhodesia as Zambia, and Nyasaland as Malawi, became independent republics. Zambia and Malawi are both members of the Commonwealth. Rhodesia declared her own independence in 1965.

RHUBARB belongs to the same family as the common wild plants dock and sorrel. The cultivated rhubarb came originally from the colder parts of Asia. It grows from a thick fleshy root, and the stalks owe their sharp taste to salts of oxalic acid. The leaves are poisonous.

RHYME. Words are said to rhyme when their final syllables sound alike. To make a perfect rhyme the vowel sound in each word must be the same to the end of the word and the letters at the beginning must be different, as in "cat" and "mat."

RHYTHM. Movements which are repeated over and over again make a rhythm as in dancing, swimming or running. A heavy stress on notes at regular intervals gives us rhythm in music. In the same way the stress of the voice on certain words and syllables when we speak makes rhythm. This is very noticeable in all poetry and makes it pleasant to read aloud.

Merrily| merrily| shall I live| now

Under the | blossom that| hangs on the

bough.

RIB, any one of a number of small, curved bones forming a framework to protect the internal organs of the chest. At one end each rib is joined loosely to the backbone, and at the other most of them are joined to the breastbone. Human beings have twelve pairs of ribs, including five pairs of "false" ribs, which are so-called because they do not join with the

breastbone. The last two pairs of these have free ends and are called "floating" ribs. See also SKELETON.

RICE, the chief food of millions of people living in Asia. Rice is the seed of a grass of which there are more than a thousand varieties. China, Japan, Burma, Thailand, Java, and Southern India are the principal rice-producing countries, but it is also grown in Egypt, northern Italy and the southern states of the United States.

RICHARD I, Richard the Lion-Heart, King of England from 1189 to 1199. He fought against Saladin in the Third CRUSADE. Captured by his enemies while on the way home, he was found by the minstrel Blondel and had to be ransomed. Richard held many lands in France, which the French king wished to gain for himself, and he had hardly returned to England when he had to take an army to France. There he was killed by an arrow, and his brother John became king.

RICHARD II, King of England from 1377 to 1399. He came to the throne at

Richard the Lion-Heart.

245

the age of ten, and the country was governed by his uncles. In 1381 the people of Kent refused to pay their taxes and rebelled. Led by Wat Tyler they marched to London, where the young King met them and promised to help them. He never kept his promise, though when he was older he showed himself a wise ruler. Then he quarrelled with the barons, and while he was away in Ireland his cousin Henry claimed the throne. Richard was taken prisoner and forced to give up the crown, and a year later he died in Pontefract Castle, in Yorkshire.

RICHARD III, Richard "Crookback," became King of England in 1483, when he imprisoned the boy King, EDWARD V, and his brother in the Tower, where they are said to have been murdered. He was a cruel and ruthless king, and in 1485 he was killed fighting his rebellious barons at the battle of Bosworth.

RIFLE, a gun which causes the bullet to spin round when it is fired, and so gives better aim. It does this by having a corkscrew-like groove cut in the inside of the barrel.

RIO DE JANEIRO, the chief seaport of BRAZIL, and one of the largest cities of SOUTH AMERICA. The city has one of the finest and most beautiful harbours in the world. Around the city are mountains covered with forests. One peak, the Sugar Loaf, rises from the waters of the harbour to a height of over a thousand feet.

RIVERS, large streams which flow into the sea, or sometimes into a lake or another river. The spot where a river rises, or begins, is known as its source, and the path it follows is its course. It enters the sea or lake by its mouth.

RIVET. A rivet is a fastener used to join two or more things together; when fixed it resembles a nail with a head at each end. Before fixing, a rivet has only one head, but after being pushed through the hole prepared for it the second head is formed by hammering it. Large rivets,

such as are used to fasten steel plates together, are made red-hot before being fixed, so that when they cool and contract they make a very firm joint.

RIVIERA, the narrow strip of land lying between the mountains and the sea on the Gulf of Genoa. It is partly in France, partly in Italy. Facing the sun, and protected from cold northerly winds by the mountains, the Riviera has a mild winter. Here the famous holiday resorts, Cannes, Nice, and Monte Carlo have grown up. The district is noted for flowers and fruits.

ROADS. The Romans built very fine roads two thousand years ago, and as their chief use was to enable their foot-soldiers, cavalry and chariots to move quickly over long distances, they were made as smooth and straight as possible. Modern roads have to carry very much heavier vehicles and are often made of concrete instead of stone. They may also be made of granite chippings with tar, or asphalt, or even with wooden blocks. Where the traffic is busiest there may be two parallel roads, one for vehicles going in one direction and the other for those going the opposite way. In some places special tracks are added for the use of cyclists, while most roads have footpaths at their sides for pedestrians. Long main roads seldom have names, but in Great Britain they have all been numbered according to their importance. Thus, the Great North Road is A1, and the road from London to Brighton is A23. An "arterial" road is simply a main road which receives traffic from several smaller roads, and a "by-pass" road is one especially built to carry long-distance traffic round a town instead of through it. Special motorways are for fast traffic only. See MACADAM; ROAD SIGNS; ROMAN ROADS.

ROAD SIGNS. These are the warning signs placed beside roads to tell the drivers of cars and other vehicles what to look out for on the stretch of road ahead. They may include an order to "Stop" or

Robin Hood and his merry men baited the Sheriff of Nottingham.

announce a speed limit, or give any other warnings for the safety of everybody who is using the road.

ROBIN, a member of the thrush family and a favourite because of its sweet song and fearless manner. Robins have the habit of searching for insects where the ground has been disturbed by the feet of large animals. The robin sitting on the gardener's spade is treating him as just another large animal disturbing the earth. The robin is noted for selecting strange nesting sites, such as a broken kettle or teapot, or an old hat thrown away in the hedge.

ROBIN HOOD is the hero of many legends which date from the fourteenth century. He was said to be the leader of a merry band of outlaws who lived in Sherwood Forest when Richard I was King of England. They hunted the King's deer, and had many adventures, especially when the Sheriff of Nottingham tried to catch them. Traditionally, they robbed rich travellers in order to help the poor.

Robin's companions included Maid Marian, Friar Tuck, Little John, who was really very big, and a little man called Much. No one could rival Robin with the longbow, and one story tells that he rescued one of his men who was about to be hanged by shooting an arrow through the rope.

ROBINSON CRUSOE, the hero of a story by Daniel DEFOE.

ROB ROY, a Scottish outlaw at the time of the Jacobite rebellion of 1715, the purpose of which was to put James Edward, the "Old Pretender" on the British throne. His adventures are told in *Rob Roy*, a novel by Sir Walter SCOTT.

ROCKS. The solid materials of which the surface of the earth is made are called rocks, except when they happen to be ground to a powder like sand. But even sand, gravel and clay are considered to be rocks by geologists. See also IGNEOUS ROCKS.

ROCKETS move by the recoil from their own exhaust-gas. When you fire a

the golden hamster eats nuts, berries and grain

the hamster keeps itself very clean

a hutch in an out-house, free from draughts and direct sunlight

food is carried in cheek pouches and hoarded

a nest made of hay and wood-wool

The golden hamster is a rodent which makes an interesting pet.

pistol or gun, it gives a backward "kick" just as the bullet leaves the muzzle—this is the recoil. As long as a rocket spurts out gas and smoke and flame from its tail, there is a similar recoil pushing it along in the other direction. Ordinary sky-rockets burn gunpowder, but elaborate rockets are now made which burn liquid fuel and travel to tremendous heights at speeds of several thousand miles an hour.

ROCKY MOUNTAINS, the system of mountain ranges in western NORTH AMERICA which forms the backbone of the continent. It stretches over two thousand miles from Alaska to New Mexico. Many of the mountains are over ten thousand feet in height.

In the Canadian Rockies there is lovely scenery, with snow-covered peaks, glaciers, and mountain lakes.

RODENT, a member of the largest group of animals in the class of MAMMALS. Rodents are gnawing animals such as the RAT, MOUSE, SQUIRREL, PORCUPINE, VOLE and BEAVER. Their front teeth continue to grow as the animal would otherwise wear them out with its gnawing. Some of these animals make fascinating pets, like the dormouse and the golden hamster.

In its wild state the hamster is a great menace to crops, for it will make many raids at harvest-time, filling its cheek-pouches with grain and hurrying with it to its underground hiding-place. It builds an elaborate burrow with several rooms, one in which to live and the others to serve as store-rooms for its winter food supply. See also GUINEA-PIG.

RODEO, a round-up of the cattle on an American ranch. It is often made the occasion of an exhibition of the cowboys' skill in lassoing, breaking-in wild horses, riding steers (young oxen), and similar feats. Any such exhibition may be called a rodeo (pronounced ro-*day*-o). See also LARIAT; LASSO.

ROMAN BRITAIN. By the first century B.C. the Romans had conquered the lands all round the Mediterranean, and wanted to add Britain to their Empire.

248

Roman armies under Julius CAESAR invaded Britain in 55 and 54 B.C., but it was not until A.D. 43 that the conquest began. Then, for four hundred years Britain was ruled by the Romans. They built towns, made ROADS, improved agriculture, and protected the country against the Picts in the north and the Anglo-Saxon pirates from the North Sea. In 410 the Roman soldiers left Britain in order to defend Rome against the tribes attacking it.

ROMAN NUMERALS. On some clocks we can still see the numerals used by the Romans. People first of all counted on their fingers. I stands for 1 because it looks like one finger. II looks like two fingers and III like three fingers. V looks like a handful of fingers, five. IV means one less than five, four. (On clocks today four is shown as IIII, but that is not a real Roman numeral.) VI means one more than five, six. X looks like two handsful of fingers, ten. Other numbers are L for 50, C for 100, D for 500, CM for 900 and M for 1000. 1957 would be written as MCMLVII in Roman numerals.

ROMAN ROADS. In all the lands they conquered, the Romans built strong, straight ROADS to connect their towns and camps. In Britain, London was connected with the north by Ermine Street, now called the Great North Road. Watling Street went from London, through the Midlands, to Wroxeter and Chester, and these were connected by crossroads, such as Fosse Way. Other main roads joined London and Bath, London and Exeter, London and Dover.

ROME, the capital of Italy, and the country's largest city, standing on the River Tiber. For centuries Rome was the capital of the Roman Empire. For even longer it was the centre of all western Christianity and is still today the centre of the Roman Catholic Church. One of the most famous of the ancient buildings of Rome is the Colosseum, or Coliseum, where gladiators fought, and races and other shows were held. There is a picture of it on page 15.

ROOK, a bird belonging to the crow family. It is very common in Britain. Its plumage is blue-black, and it has a white patch, bare of feathers, at the base of its beak. Unlike most crows, rooks nest in communities. They eat quantities of grain, and are a nuisance to farmers because of the raids they make on the crops.

ROOSEVELT, Franklin Delano, born in 1882, was President of the United States from 1933 to 1945, when he died. The Japanese attack on Pearl Harbour in 1941 brought America into the Second WORLD WAR, and Roosevelt proved himself a strong leader and wise statesman.

There are many exciting events in a rodeo.

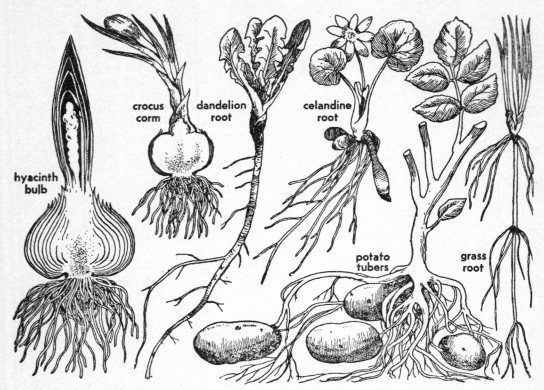

hyacinth bulb

crocus corm

dandelion root

celandine root

potato tubers

grass root

Roots grow downward away from the light. They provide the plant with water and salts.

ROOT, the part of a PLANT which is underground. Its purpose is to extract water and minerals from the soil, and sometimes to store food for the plant's future use. The food may be stored in a special swelling called a "tuber," as in the potato, or in a thickened "tap-root," as in the carrot. See also BULBS; CORM.

ROPE and ROPE-MAKING. Rope is a name used for any thick string or cord made by twisting together a number of smaller strands. At one time this was done by hand in a "rope-walk," but it is now done by machines. Fine ropes may be made of cotton, linen, manilla or hemp, and coarse ropes of jute, sisal or coconut fibre ("coir"). Very strong ropes are made of steel wires twisted round a hemp core.

ROSES, WARS OF THE. In 1399 Henry, Duke of Lancaster, seized the throne of England from his cousin· RICHARD II, and became HENRY IV, the first of the Lancastrian kings. Other nobles thought they might do the same, but it was not until the reign of HENRY VI that rebellion became serious. Opposition to an unpopular king soon became a struggle for the throne between the House of York, whose badge was a white rose, and the House of Lancaster, which later adopted a red rose for its emblem. Though the Yorkists gained the crown, the struggle continued until both roses were united in the House of Tudor. See HENRY VII.

ROTATION OF CROPS, a method of FARMING by which the same field is not required to produce the same crop two seasons running. A crop takes nourishment from the soil, and this needs replacing before the same crop can be grown satisfactorily again. By choosing the right crops and growing them in the right order (or "rotation"), a farmer may return to the same crop every four or five years.

One system of rotation is: wheat, potatoes, barley, clover—and then wheat again.

ROUNDERS, an outdoor game played by two teams of nine players with a small, hard ball and a round bat. The bowler tosses the ball to the batsman, who hits it and then runs from base to base round a diamond-shaped area. He may be "out" by being caught (as in cricket), or by being touched with the ball by a fielder while between two bases. In a casual game of rounders where a soft ball is used, the ball may be thrown at the striker by a fielder. Other differences are that there may be any number of players and more than four bases.

RUBBER is prepared from the juice of a tropical tree, which grows wild in BRAZIL but is chiefly cultivated in MALAYA. Cuts are made in the bark of the tree and the milky juice, called "latex," oozes out and is collected in cups. The latex is then treated chemically, when it sets hard to form "crêpe" rubber or "elastic." Mixed with a little sulphur it forms "India" rubber, and heated with more sulphur it becomes "vulcanized" into the rubber of hot-water bottles and rubber balls. With lamp-black added it becomes rubber for tyres, and it can be further hardened to form "vulcanite" and "ebonite," from which small solid articles are made.

RUBENS, Peter Paul, a Flemish painter who lived from 1577 to 1640. He lived for a long time in Antwerp, and visited Italy, painting many great pictures. Some of these are to be seen in public picture galleries, and are especially notable for their rich colour and their human figures.

RUGBY, a game of FOOTBALL played by two teams of fifteen players each, though a variation of this (called Rugby League football) has only thirteen players a side. The ball is not round like an ordinary football, but oval, and the players are allowed to handle it. It was first played at Rugby School about 1840. Rugby School is an old public school in the market-town of Rugby, in Warwickshire, England.

RUMANIA, a country of south-east Europe which has very hot summers and very cold winters. The name is often spelled Romania, for in the days of the Roman Empire it was inhabited by Roman colonists. Most of the people are peasant farmers, who grow maize and wheat, and there are also oilfields. The capital is Bucharest.

RUSSIA. The modern name for this country is the Union of Soviet Socialist Republics, or the U.S.S.R. It covers nearly half of Europe, and more than one-third of Asia. In the north it extends into the cold bare lands within the Arctic Circle. In the south the summers are so hot that cotton can be grown. There are sixteen republics in the Union, and the capital of the whole country is Moscow. See map on pages 20 to 21.

RUST, a red oxide of iron formed when iron or steel is attacked by the oxygen of the air. This happens only when there is moisture present, so that knives and other articles of iron or steel should always be kept dry.

RYE, the hardiest of the cereals or GRAINS. It is able to survive the severest weather and grows successfully even in poor soils. Rye is widely cultivated in eastern Europe.

Rounders, a popular outdoor game.

251

S

SAFE, a very strong steel box or cupboard with a lock which cannot be easily forced open. Some safes have locks which cannot be opened at all until a dial has been set to show a special number called the "combination," which is known only to the owner.

SAFETY LAMP, a lamp that can be used in coal mines without fear of setting fire to the gas and causing an explosion. Electric torches are now used, but in the first safety-lamps the flame of an oil lamp was surrounded by wire gauze, which prevented gases burning inside it from setting fire to those outside. See DAVY.

SAFETY-VALVE, a device fitted to a BOILER to allow the steam to escape if there is too much for safety. It is really just a hole closed by a lid or stopper, which is kept down by a spring or heavy weight. When the steam pressure becomes very great the stopper begins to open and lets steam escape which might otherwise burst the boiler.

SAHARA, a vast, sandy desert in North Africa, stretching from the Atlantic shore in the west to the Nile valley in the east. There are a few oases where travellers may find water, and caravan routes running from oasis to oasis enable the Sahara to be crossed on camel-back. There is also a motor route from Morocco to Timbuktu. The Sahara is by no means an entirely flat area. There are mountains in the central part which rise to several thousand feet.

SAIL, a large surface of paper, canvas or other light material intended to catch the wind and make it do work. The sails of a sailing-ship cause the wind to blow the ship along; the sails of a wind pump cause the wind to turn wheels which pump up water from the ground. See also YACHT.

SAINT BERNARD, a famous pass over the ALPS. There is a hospice, or MONASTERY, at the top of the pass, and once upon a time the monks who live there used St. Bernard dogs to help them find travellers lost in the snow.

SAINT GOTTHARD, an important pass over the ALPS which connects Switzerland with northern Italy. The railway from Lucerne to Milan runs through the TUNNEL beneath the pass. The tunnel is nine and a quarter miles long.

SAINT HELENA is an island in the South Atlantic Ocean belonging to Great Britain. Although it is in the tropics, the island has a pleasant climate, being cooled by the south-

In the Hoggar Mountains of the Sahara.

Zulu warrior

Algerian dancers

Portuguese girl

Greek shepherd

Sudanese boy

Tyrolean woodman

people of Central America

Chinese women

woman of Senegal

farmer of Yugoslavia

woman of India

Japanese woman

Spanish dancers

Some national costumes.

Scene at a railway station as the train comes in.

east trade wind and an ocean current. NAPOLEON was banished to St. Helena in 1815, and died there in 1821.

SAINT JOHN, one of the disciples of JESUS. It is not certain whether one of the GOSPELS and *The Epistles of Saint John* were written by this disciple or by someone of the same name.

SAINT LAWRENCE, a river of NORTH AMERICA which empties into the Gulf of Saint Lawrence, which itself empties into the Atlantic Ocean. With the Great Lakes, which supply it with water, the St. Lawrence is one of the most important river systems in the world, providing a waterway extending about halfway across the continent. It is frozen for about five months each year, and it has several waterfalls, which are got round by locks; these locks and the deep-water channel in the river make up the St. Lawrence Seaway.

SAINT LUKE. There are four accounts of the life of JESUS (see GOSPELS). St. Luke wrote one of them some years after Jesus died. He was a friend of SAINT PAUL, and went with him on some of his travels. *The Acts of the Apostles*, which describes these journeys, was also written by St. Luke. See also APOSTLES; BIBLE.

SAINT MARK was the first to write his account of the life of JESUS. He founded the Christian Church at Alexandria. See also APOSTLES; BIBLE; GOSPELS.

SAINT MATTHEW, the writer of one of the four GOSPELS. It was written about the same time as the Gospel of SAINT LUKE, that is, about A.D. 70, and a little later than that of SAINT MARK. It contains the Sermon on the Mount (Chapter 5), and the Lord's Prayer (Chapter 6). See also APOSTLES; BIBLE.

SAINT PAUL. Saul, an educated Hebrew of Tarsus, a town in Asia Minor, was known also by the Latin name of Paulus. A student of the ancient law, he persecuted the early Christians, until he saw JESUS CHRIST in a vision. Afterwards Paul became one of the most zealous of the founders of the Christian Church. See also APOSTLES; BIBLE; GOSPELS.

SAINT PAUL'S CATHEDRAL. When St. Paul's was burnt down in the Great Fire of London in 1666 Christopher WREN built the new St. Paul's, which is one of the finest buildings in England. It has a wonderful dome which can be seen from many parts of London. During the Second WORLD WAR St. Paul's was damaged in the heavy bombing raids on London in April, 1941. Many historic buildings were hit.

St. Paul's Cathedral.

SALMON, a large, fresh water FISH which spends most of its life in the sea, but comes up the rivers to breed. It is remarkable for its ability to leap up small waterfalls and get over dams in order to lay its eggs in the sandy beds of upland streams. When the young salmon hatch out they are called alevin, then fry, parr and smolt, in that order. When they are about two years old they swim down the rivers to the sea. If they return within a year they are called grilse. Most, however, do not return to the river of their birth until they are fully-grown salmon, about three or four years old. After spawning in the rivers many die but a few get back to the sea. Salmon are plentiful in many rivers of Scandinavia, Britain and America.

SALMON-TROUT, a sea-going trout, belonging to the salmon family but distinct from it.

SALT. The chief mineral dissolved in sea-water is called salt, but it is known to chemists as *sodium chloride* because it consists of the metal sodium combined with the gas chlorine. Similar combinations of other metals with other gases or non-metals are also called salts by chemists, for example, Epsom salts, which is *magnesium sulphate*.

253

Samson had the strength of a giant.

SALVAGE means saving, and it is used of shipwrecks and deserted ships, and of their cargoes, which are called flotsam if found floating about but jetsam if thrown out of a ship and washed up on the beach. A large part of salvage work is done by divers. The word salvage is also used of saved materials like old paper, rags, bones and scrap metal, which can be treated and used again in new products.

SAMSON was a hero of the OLD TESTAMENT, famous for his great strength. After slaying a thousand of his enemies with the jawbone of an ass, as is told in the *Book of Judges*, Samson was betrayed into their hands by the woman he loved, Delilah. After they had blinded him they brought him to a great feast, to mock him. Seizing two pillars of the house Samson pulled the building down, destroying himself and his enemies.

SAND is rock that has been broken down into very small particles. These particles, or grains, are too small to be called gravel, and too large to be called silt, or clay. A hard, glassy mineral called quartz is found in most kinds of sand, and in SANDSTONE.

SANDSTONE is rock that consists of grains of SAND cemented together by another substance. The type of sandstone depends on the nature of this binding material. Quartz is the commonest mineral in sandstone, as it is in sand.

SANDSTORM, a storm in which a large quantity of SAND is blown by a strong wind. It is commonest in such dry regions of the earth as the SAHARA. Sand gets into the eyes, ears, nose, and mouth, and sometimes it is impossible to see more than a few feet. The CAMEL, however, is adapted to desert conditions; its eyes are heavily-lidded, and it is able to close its nostrils against the storm.

SANITATION, the means of keeping places used by people or animals healthily clean. It includes the laying of drains and the collection of rubbish from dust-bins.

SAP, the juice of a PLANT. The sap consists chiefly of water absorbed by the roots. It contains minerals dissolved in it and carries them to every part of the plant through fine tubes. In the leaves it gathers sugar which it carries back to the roots. See also LEAF.

SARACENS were the Mohammedan peoples against whom the Crusaders fought.

SARDINE, a small, tasty fish, rich in oil. Large shoals are found off the coast of SARDINIA. The fish are often preserved in oil and packed in tins for export. France and PORTUGAL have important sardine industries.

SARDINIA, an island in the Mediterranean Sea belonging to Italy. It is mountainous, and has not much fertile soil. Many sheep and goats are kept there. See also SARDINE.

SATIRE. When a writer wants to make fun of people and the foolish things they do he writes a satire either in prose or in verse. His aim is to make people better by ridiculing their faults and follies.

SATURN is a planet which is about seven hundred and fifty times as large as

Saw-fish.

the earth; it is the sixth planet in order of distance from the sun. The most remarkable thing about Saturn when you see it through a TELESCOPE is the system of rings around it. These rings probably consist of a mass of small particles of solid matter. See also SOLAR SYSTEM.

SAUL was the first king to reign over Israel. The story of how he became KING and how DAVID was chosen to succeed him, is told in the *Books of Samuel* in the OLD TESTAMENT.

SAVANNA, a region in the tropics which is covered with long, coarse grass, and scattered trees, and is sometimes known as tropical grassland. It borders the equatorial forest, and has a wet season and a dry season. There are large areas of savanna in AFRICA, where such animals as the giraffe, elephant and lion are to be found.

SAW-FISH, a large fish related to the SHARK. Projecting from its upper jaw is a long bony "beak" bearing two rows of sharp-pointed teeth. A saw-fish may be twenty feet long and have a saw six feet long. It is not to be confused with the SWORD-FISH.

SAXONS were peoples from North Germany who were amongst the invaders who crossed the North Sea to settle in Britain in the sixth century. Others were called Angles. Essex, Wessex, Middlesex, and Sussex were originally the lands of the East, West, Middle, and South Saxons.

SCALE. The scale of a MAP, drawing or model is its size as compared with that of the country or object it represents. It is generally shown by a small diagram like a ladder, the distance apart of the rungs giving the size at which inches, feet or miles are represented. The word "scale" comes from the Latin for ladder.

SCANDINAVIA, the three countries of north-west Europe now known as NORWAY, SWEDEN, and DENMARK. Their peoples are closely related, and their languages are similar. Norway and Denmark were the home of the VIKINGS, who were famous as sea raiders. One of them, Leif Ericsson, sailed from Greenland to North America about the year A.D. 1000.

SCHUBERT, Franz, was a famous composer. He was born in Vienna in 1797. He was the son of a school-teacher and was a teacher himself for a time.

Sardines are exported from Portugal.

255

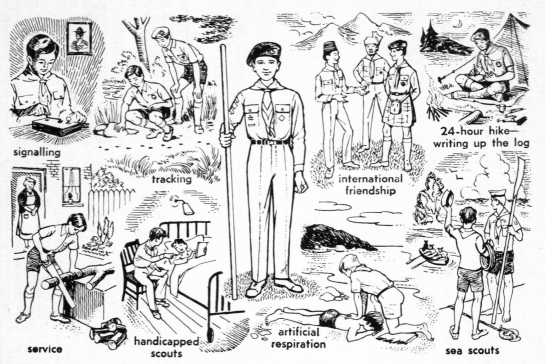

Through outdoor activities Boy Scouts learn to look after themselves and other people.

signalling

tracking

international friendship

24-hour hike— writing up the log

service

handicapped scouts

artificial respiration

sea scouts

Schubert composed all kinds of music including sonatas, symphonies and music for string quartets, but he is remembered chiefly for his songs, of which he wrote over six hundred. Schubert died in 1828 when he was only thirty-one.

SCHUMANN, Robert Alexander, born in 1810, was a German composer who became very well known for his pieces for the piano, and for his songs. He was also a teacher at the German town of Leipzig. In 1839 Schumann married Clara Wieck, who became a noted pianist and made his music very popular. He died in 1856.

SCOTLAND is that part of Great Britain which lies north of England, and includes the Orkneys and Shetlands, the Hebrides, and other islands. It can be divided into three regions. The Highlands contain lochs, or lakes, as well as mountains, and have much beautiful scenery; the Central Lowlands are the region of large towns and industries; the Southern Uplands are the region of hills and sheep farms. Edinburgh is the capital, with a population of over half a million.

SCOTLAND YARD. See POLICE.

SCOTT, Sir Walter, was a famous poet and novelist who wrote about Scotland, where he was born in 1771. He was very interested in the legends and ballads of the Scottish Border and travelled about to hear old people recite ballads that had never been written down. He knew a great deal of the history of Scotland and England and he delved into this for the themes and the background of his novels. The nineteenth-century reader revelled in these stories of times long past and Scott became very popular. Among his best novels are *Ivanhoe*, *Rob Roy* and *Guy Mannering*. Scott died in 1832.

SCOUTING is "spying out the land," especially when done by chosen scouts ahead of an advancing army. (BUFFALO BILL was a scout at one time.) Scouts are skilled in all kinds of tracking. The Boy Scout movement, founded by Lord Robert

Baden-Powell in 1908, teaches discipline and self-reliance, and members are trained in following trails by observing signs, and also in woodcraft, signalling, pioneering, camping, map-reading and other activities. Their motto is, "Be Prepared."

Boys from eight to eleven years old can join the CUB SCOUTS, from eleven to fifteen they can join the Boy Scouts, from fifteen to eighteen they become Senior Scouts, and from eighteen upwards they are called Rover Scouts. There are also Sea Scouts and Air Scouts.

The Scout movement is world-wide, and a great camp, or Jamboree, is held every four years; it is attended by scouts from all over the world, and a different country is the meeting-place each time. See also BROWNIES; GIRL GUIDES.

SCULPTURE. This is the ART of carving a figure out of some hard substance like stone or wood or ivory. Such carved figures have been made from earliest times in many different countries. The GREEKS made some wonderful statues out of marble, probably the finest sculpture in the world.

SCYLLA AND CHARYBDIS. Charybdis was an eddy or whirlpool in the Straits of Messina, between Italy and Sicily. In trying to avoid it, mariners often went too near a rock called Scylla and some were wrecked on that. So that when we are between two difficulties we sometimes say that we are between Scylla and Charybdis.

SEAL, a sea-animal found in all the cooler seas, but especially in the Arctic and Antarctic oceans. Their limbs are in the form of paddles or flippers, the hind-limbs of the true seals being directed backwards to lie either side of a very short tail. The shores of Great Britain are visited by Common and Atlantic seals, and, very rarely, a few walrus. See also MAMMALS; WALRUS.

SEA LION, a relative of the SEAL; unlike the true seal it has external ears, and it can turn its hind flippers forward

to move about on land, although it is very slow and awkward.

SEARCH-LIGHT, a powerful beam of light used to search the sky at night-time for enemy aeroplanes. The light from an electric arc is reflected into a long, narrow beam by means of a curved mirror.

SEA-SICKNESS is a feeling of sickness caused by the pitching and rolling of a ship. It seems to be due to a disturbance of the nerves of the stomach, but is also due partly to the upsetting of the sense of balance by the surging of fluids in the ears. Deep and regular breathing helps to prevent it, as do certain soothing drugs.

SEASONS, those periods of the year which clearly differ from one another in climate. They are largely due to the varying angles at which any part of the earth receives the sun's rays during its journey round the sun. The difference between summer and winter is thus greatest near to the poles. In temperate regions the year is divided into four seasons, spring, summer, autumn, and winter. In some tropical regions, however, where it is always hot, the seasons depend chiefly on rainfall, and the year is divided into a wet season and a dry season.

Seal with baby.

SEA-WATER is salty because various chemical salts are dissolved in it. The quantity of salts differs in different parts of the ocean, but on the average 1,000 ounces of sea-water contain about 35 ounces of salts. Of these 35 ounces, about 27 ounces consist of sodium chloride, or common SALT.

SEAWEED, a simple form of plant-life found growing in the sea. Many kinds of seaweed are known, and some, such as laver, are eaten. The largest plant in existence is the seaweed known as the giant laminaria, which grows to a length of several hundred yards.

SECRETARY BIRD, an African BIRD OF PREY. Its plumage is grey and white, and the curious tuft of feathers at the back of the head, looking like a quill pen tucked behind the ear, gives it its nickname. Although it is powerful in flight, it likes to stay on the ground, and if chased, will run rather than fly. Its very long legs give it a good turn of speed.

SECRETION means something extracted or set apart. In the bodies of animals there are special organs or GLANDS for secretion, and these extract particular substances (often from the BLOOD) and deliver them to the places where they are needed. For example, the kidneys secrete urine, the liver secretes bile, and the thyroid gland secretes a substance which controls growth. There are many other glands, large and small, doing similar work throughout the body.

SEDIMENTARY ROCKS. These are rocks formed from sediments and other deposits in the sea. SAND gets compressed, and sometimes cemented, into SANDSTONE, and mud into clay or shale.

SEEDS AND FRUITS. A seed consists of a tough coat enclosing the germ of the future PLANT, together with a store of food to give the young plant a start. A fruit is that part of a plant containing the seeds. A nut, for example, is simply a fruit with a woody coat, while a strawberry is a soft, juicy fruit having embedded in it a number of very tiny gritty seeds which you can feel with your tongue.

SEISMOGRAPH. This is an instrument for recording earthquakes. It consists chiefly of a heavy weight delicately balanced on a lever. When the earth trembles and shakes the pivot of the lever, the weight is so heavy it remains where it is and so the lever moves. Its other end bears a special kind of pen (a stylo) which records the earth-movements on a roll of paper.

SENEGAL, independent state in West Africa, south of the Senegal river. Saint Louis is the capital, Dakar is the largest town, and an important port and naval base. Maize and rice are grown, and groundnuts and gum are the chief exports.

SENSES. There are five chief senses: sight, hearing, TASTE, SMELL and TOUCH. They tell us all we know of the outside world, and may act either independently or together. Smell and taste, for example, are closely linked, and if the sense of smell is lost, the sense of taste is largely lost, too. The sense of touch is distributed over the whole surface of the body, but is more marked in some places, such as the finger-tips. See also REFLEX ACTION.

SEPIA is a rich brown colour made from a pigment obtained from the cuttle-fish. It is used often by itself to paint pictures in one colour.

SERIES, a set of things arranged in order, or happening in order. Thus, a set of cigarette cards form a series, and so do the common numbers 1, 2, 3, 4, 5, 6 . . . and so on.

SEVEN WONDERS OF THE ANCIENT WORLD. These were: the Hanging Gardens of Babylon, built in a vast square of terraces, perhaps by Nebuchadnezzar; the Pyramids of Egypt, now five thousand years old; the Tomb of King Mausolus, built in 353 B.C. at Halicarnassus on the Aegean shore; the Colossus of Rhodes, an enormous figure which once bestrode the entrance to the harbour and was destroyed by an earthquake in 224 B.C.; the Temple of Diana at Ephesus, which took 220 years to build; the Statue of Jupiter on Olympus, by Phidias, made of ivory and draped in gold; the Pharos of Alexandria, a tower five hundred and twenty feet high, with a fire on top to guide ships into the harbour.

SEVEN YEARS' WAR, a war between

Great Britain, Prussia and Hanover on one side, and France, Austria, Russia, Sweden, Saxony and Spain on the other. It lasted from 1756 till 1763, and one of its results was that France lost Canada to Britain. (Quebec was taken by General Wolfe in 1759, but he was killed in the battle on the Heights of Abraham.)

SEVERN, the longest river in Great Britain. It rises on Plynlimmon, a mountain in Central Wales, and enters the sea by the Bristol Channel. A tidal wave several feet high, known as the Severn bore, sometimes travels many miles up the river from the estuary. This occurs when a very high tide meets the river current, and causes a wall of water to run upstream.

SEWING MACHINE, a machine for sewing together pieces of cloth or leather, and other materials. It was invented by an American, Elias Howe, in 1846. In the sewing machine a needle pushes a loop of thread through the material, and a shuttle or bobbin then runs a second thread through the loop, which is pulled tight as the needle returns into position to repeat the process.

SEXTANT, an instrument for finding the exact angle that the sun or other heavenly body makes with the horizon. It is used chiefly by sailors, who can calculate their LATITUDE from such observations. See also NAVIGATION.

SHACKLETON, Sir Ernest Henry, famous British explorer, was born in Ireland in 1874. With Scott, he tried to reach the South Pole in 1901. A few years later he led another expedition which succeeded in getting within 97 miles of the Pole. Shackleton was knighted on his return in 1909. His last voyage was made in the *Quest.* He set sail in September, 1921, but was taken ill and died in the New Year. He was buried on South Georgia Island. See also POLAR EXPLORATION.

SHAFTESBURY, Earl of, Anthony Ashley Cooper, known as Lord Ashley before he became the seventh Earl of

Shaftesbury in 1851, roused PARLIAMENT to pass laws to help the women and children who had to work long hours in factories. He helped to stop children from being sent up chimneys to clean them. He founded training ships and a Refuge for the poor. His whole life was devoted to helping those in need. He lived from 1801 to 1885.

SHAKESPEARE, William, was born at Stratford-on-Avon, and baptised in Stratford church in 1564. He married Anne Hathaway, and they had three children—Susanna, and the twins Hamnet and Judith. Shakespeare went to London to seek his fortune and joined a company of players at one of the theatres outside the boundaries of the city. He earned his living by acting small parts, by rewriting old plays, and then by writing plays himself. These plays were very successful and Shakespeare was able to buy a fine house in Stratford-on-Avon, and later to retire there.

His plays are written in verse and are not always very easy to understand, but he created a multitude of wonderful characters and told many delightful stories,

William Shakespeare.

as in *A Midsummer Night's Dream,*
Twelfth Night and *As You Like It.*
These are all comedies. He also wrote
historical plays like *Henry V* and *Richard II,*
and tragedies such as *Hamlet, Othello* and
Macbeth. Although Shakespeare died in
1616, actors still perform his plays today
and lots of people want to see them. See
also DRAMA; PLAYS.

SHANNON, the longest river in the
BRITISH ISLES, and the chief river in
IRELAND. It flows across the Central
Plain, and in many places spreads out to
form lakes. Near to the mouth, however,
it flows more swiftly, and its power has
been used to generate electricity.

SHARK. The skeleton of a shark,
unlike that of all ordinary FISH, is made of
gristle instead of bone. Its body is long
and the skin is covered with tiny tooth-
like scales which make it rough to the
touch. The largest kind is the whale shark,
which may measure forty feet in length,
but the man-eating shark of the tropics
is often thirty feet long.

SHAW, George Bernard, was born in
Ireland in 1856 and came to London in
1876. He wrote reviews of plays and
concerts and after writing a few unsuccessful novels, began his long series of
highly successful plays. He was a gay
satirist full of new ideas and eager to tilt
at traditions and conventions which he
believed to be outworn. All his plays,
therefore, though amusing in themselves,
set out to startle people into thinking

*Native diver defending himself in the sea
against a shark.*

afresh about their beliefs and values.
Most of his plays are comedies, but the
most famous of all is his single tragedy,
St. Joan. The Prefaces to his plays are
almost as interesting as the plays themselves. He died in 1950.

SHEEP. There are about a dozen
different kinds of wild sheep. Most of
them live in Europe and Asia, but the
bighorn or Rocky Mountain sheep belongs
to North America, and there is another
in North Africa. All sheep are cloven-
hoofed and feed on grass. It is not known
from which wild species the wool-bearing
farm sheep is descended.

SHEFFIELD is a city in the West
Riding of Yorkshire, England, which has
become world-famous for the manufacture of steel and cutlery. IRON was
smelted there from local ore in the time of
William the Conqueror, and by the fourteenth century Sheffield was well-known

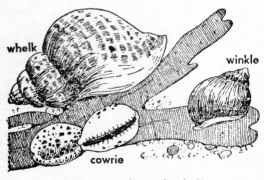

whelk

winkle

cowrie

Molluscs with single shells.

for its cutlery. One of the chief reasons for the importance of Sheffield steel has been the skill of its workpeople.

SHELLEY, Percy Bysshe, an English poet, was born in 1792. He had many misfortunes in his life and went to Italy to live. Here he wrote most of his best poetry. He loved to describe the bright and lovely scenery round him and liked the motion of clouds and winds. He wrote poems called *Ode to the West Wind, The Cloud* and *To a Skylark*. Shelley was fond of sailing, and one day in 1822 his small boat turned over in a sudden storm in the Mediterranean Sea and he was drowned.

SHELLS are developed on the outside of the bodies of animals which have no bones, in order to give them firmness and to protect them. Most of the shell-bearing animals are MOLLUSCS, and while some of these have two shells opening on a hinge, like cockles, mussels, scallops, and oysters, others have only one shell, like winkles, cowries, whelks and land-snails. The shells of all these creatures are made of carbonate of lime. See also BIVALVES; INVERTEBRATES; TORTOISE.

SHERIDAN, Richard Brinsley, was born in Dublin in 1751. As a young man he settled in London, and made his name as a dramatist; he later became a member of Parliament and held the post of Under Secretary for Foreign Affairs, but his fame rests on his theatrical interests and his plays are still performed today.

His play, *The Rivals*, was produced in 1775. The following year Sheridan became manager of the Theatre Royal, Drury Lane, where his comedy, *The School for Scandal*, was first presented in 1777. He died in 1816.

SHETLAND PONY, a small, hardy and stocky breed of horse which originated in the bleak Shetland Islands. It has a long, rough coat, and a long mane and tail. Shetland ponies, which are rarely more than three feet high, were once much used in coal mines, and they were also popular as mounts for children wanting a "pony ride."

SHIPBUILDING is carried on chiefly in the mouths of narrow rivers, where there is deep water and shelter from the ocean waves. The hull of a ship is built on a

The Shetland pony is the smallest breed of horse, but it is very strong.

log

raft

dug-out canoe

galleon

Chinese junk

barque (about 1840)

paddle-steamer (with sail)

paddle-steamer (without sail)

modern passenger liner

Ships have developed from a simple floating log to the great liners of today.

slope and when completed has to be launched by allowing it to slide down a wooden runway into the water. The engines and other equipment are generally added after the ship has been launched.

SHIPS. When man first ventured on the water he sat astride a floating tree. Then he learnt to hollow out a tree and make a proper canoe. To this he added sails and as his boats got bigger and bigger he was able to make longer and longer journeys, even across the seas and oceans. When steam engines were added to ships to drive them along, wood was found to be too weak to withstand the pounding of the machinery, so ships were made of iron and, later, steel. Today, the biggest ships of all, the liners, are just like huge hotels, with thousands of passengers living in private rooms, eating in lofty restaurants, and enjoying themselves in the cinema, swimming bath or ballroom. See also NAVY.

SHORTHAND is a way of writing as quickly as people speak. There are several systems in use. In ordinary writing many letters are used which are not really needed, and shorthand avoids the waste of time this causes. The word "dough," for example, contains five letters, yet it really has only two sounds in it. One kind of shorthand provides a single mark for the "d" sound ∣ and another for the "o" sound − and the whole word, ∣−, takes a fraction of a second to write instead of about two seconds.

SHRIMP. Like its close relative, the prawn, the shrimp is a CRUSTACEAN. It lives in the sandy pools on the shore, or in the shallow waters at the edge of low tide, where you can catch it with a net. A shrimp has a pair of "rabbit ears" in front of its head, whereas the slightly larger prawn can be recognized by its long, saw-edged horn.

SIAM. See THAILAND.

SIBERIA is a vast region of northern Asia, within the Union of Soviet Socialist Republics. It stretches from the Arctic Ocean to Mongolia, and much of it is covered with forests. The summer is quite warm, even in the north; but the winter, which lasts about six months, is the coldest on earth. The Trans-Siberian Railway, the longest railway in the world, crosses Siberia. The journey from Moscow to Vladivostock takes about ten days.

SIGNALLING is sending messages by signs instead of words. The signs may stand for letters, as in the MORSE code and semaphore alphabets, or they may stand for whole words or sentences, as in railway signals, road signs and the flags and buoys used in NAVIGATION.

SILK is the fine web spun by the caterpillars of some moths in making their cocoons. The caterpillars, or silkworms, are usually fed on mulberry leaves, and when they have spun their cocoons these are put into hot water so that the gum that binds the silk threads together is softened, and the ends of the silk float free. The ends are then pulled and the cocoons unwind, the fine silk threads being rewound on to wooden frames. Several delicate threads are twisted together to make one thicker, stronger thread. Finally, the silk is washed thoroughly to remove all the gum, and can be woven into material. See also CHRYSALIS; SPIDER.

Signalling by semaphore.

263

Ski-ing is an exciting winter sport.

SILVER is a brilliant, white metal which takes a very high polish. It is rather rare and, like gold, is one of the "precious metals." Pure silver is softer than copper, and is the best known conductor of both heat and electricity.

SINGAPORE is an island at the southern end of the MALAY PENINSULA and part of the BRITISH COMMONWEALTH OF NATIONS. It has a good harbour, and is one of the world's greatest seaports. Over three-quarters of the people are Chinese. They control most of the city's trade and outnumber the Malays by about four to one.

SINGING is the making of musical sounds with the voice. The lowest singing is called bass; then come baritone and tenor for men's voices. Higher still are alto and treble, which describe most children's voices. Contralto, mezzo-soprano and (highest of all) soprano are the women's voices. A person who sings alone is said to sing solo, though he (or she) may be accompanied by a piano or other instrument. Two or more persons may sing together in harmony, and this is called part-singing. If there are more than four such singers they are usually called a choir and their singing is known as choral singing.

SIPHON, a bent pipe or tube arranged so as to empty a pond or tank of water (or other liquid) by the pressure of the air. The pipe is first filled with water. Then the upper end of the pipe is kept under the water in the tank, and the other end of the pipe is passed over the edge of the tank and down to a lower level outside. So long as the pipe's outer end is lower than the level of the water in the tank, it will continue to empty the tank.

The word siphon is also used of a bottle of mineral-water with a spout and tap instead of a cork. The bottle contains gas under pressure to force the water out when the tap is opened.

SIREN, an instrument which makes a loud, wailing noise which can often be heard for a distance of several miles. Sirens are used on LIGHT-HOUSES and LIGHT-SHIPS to warn shipping in foggy weather, and in factories to call the people to work.

The sirens in the ancient Greek story were sea-nymphs, who sang so sweetly that they lured sailors on to the rocks.

SKELETON, the bony framework that supports the body. The skeleton of an INVERTEBRATE, if it has one, is usually outside its body. Thus, snails and oysters are enclosed in hard shells, and beetles and other insects in horny cases or tubes. The VERTEBRATES, on the other hand, have an internal skeleton of bone, which acts as a support for the muscles. Some vertebrates, like the TORTOISE, have an outer skeleton as well.

SKI-ING is a winter sport in which you travel at speed on skis, across snow-covered slopes. It includes racing and jumping. Skis are a kind of snow-shoe made of long, narrow slats of wood, which are strapped to the feet.

SKIN is the covering of the bodies of VERTEBRATES. It may be soft or tough, smooth or covered with hair, feathers or scales. All skins consist of a number of different layers, the outer layer being horny to withstand wear and tear. This layer is always being shed and replaced by a fresh layer of horny tissue supplied from the live skin beneath.

SKULL, the bony case enclosing the BRAIN and supporting the eyes, ears and nose of VERTEBRATES. The lower jaw is hinged to its under side.

SLATE is a greenish- or purplish-grey ROCK which splits easily into very thin slabs, which are then used for covering roofs. It is quarried in Wales, Cumberland and other places.

SLAVE TRADE, the selling of African NEGROES to the planters of the tropical lands of North America, the West Indies, and other regions, to work as slaves for their white masters. Slavery was abolished in British territories by the Emancipation Act of 1833, and in the United States in 1865, two years after LINCOLN's proclamation freeing the slaves. Nine per cent of the population of the United States are descended from the Negroes.

SLEEP enables the body to recover from tiredness resulting from poisons and to renew its stores of energy. During sleep we become unconscious and lose the power to feel or think. The working of the body is also slowed up. Breathing and the rate of the heart-beat become much slower.

SLEEPING SICKNESS is a disease common among the natives of West Africa, in which they feel drowsy and tremble a great deal. It may last for several years, but usually ends in death. It is caused by a very tiny creature which gets into the blood by the bite of an African fly.

SLIDE RULE, a device which resembles a ruler, but having a groove cut in it in which a second ruler slides. The two rulers are so marked that they can be set to give the answers to difficult calculations. In other forms of slide rule the rulers are triangular or circular in shape, and the sliding part may be a small metal frame which grips the ruler loosely.

SLOTH. There are two species of sloth living in the forests of Central and South America. They live up in the trees, feeding on the flowers and leaves and moving very slowly. They are difficult to see because the hairs of their bodies are grooved, and the grooves are filled with

The sloth hangs upside down.

microscopic green plants which make them the same colour as the foliage. Their toes are completely enclosed in skin, and bear long hook-like claws by which they hang upside-down from the branches.

SMELL, one of the primary SENSES. The organ of smell is the nose, where a special nerve from the BRAIN ends in a membrane situated high up inside. Very tiny particles taken into the nose by the air settle on this membrane, causing a message to be carried by the nerve to the brain. When it arrives we say we "smell" something.

SMUGGLING. To make sure that our manufacturers can sell their goods at a fair price, it is sometimes necessary to prevent certain foreign goods from being sold too cheaply. This is done by making anybody who brings the foreign goods into the country pay a tax called a customs duty. Smuggling is getting such goods into the country secretly, so as to avoid paying the tax. Goods on which duty has to be paid include tobacco, silk, jewellery, perfume, wines and brandy.

SNAIL, a low form of animal life found on land and in water. Snails are protected by a single, coiled shell, which they carry on their backs. The sea-snails include the whelk and the winkle. See also MOLLUSCS; SHELLS.

SNAKE, a kind of REPTILE with a long, worm-like body and no visible limbs. The skeleton of a snake contains many ribs, and its skin is covered with horny scales. The two top front teeth, or fangs, of some snakes are connected with a small bag of poison, and the bite of such snakes may be very dangerous. The COBRA and ADDER are examples. Other snakes, like the huge PYTHON, kill their prey by crushing it. Most snakes have a forked tongue, which they flicker in and out, but this is harmless.

SNOW is made up of ice crystals which sometimes fall to the ground singly, and sometimes joined together as flakes. The crystals are regular in design. They are formed when the TEMPERATURE of the air at cloud level is below freezing point. The water vapour in the air thus changes to ice crystals. Snow forms at different heights all over the earth. Even at the equator, mountains over about seventeen thousand feet are always covered with snow.

SOAP is made by boiling together in a large vat an oil or fat and an alkali like potash or soda. Olive-oil and coconut-oil are often used, but some soaps contain

Smuggling was at its height in the eighteenth century.

whale-oil, mutton-fat or fish-oil. When the boiling is finished, SALT is thrown into the vat, and this causes the soap to form a sort of scum floating in a liquid called the "spent lye." The spent lye is drawn off and glycerine is extracted from it. The soap is removed to iron frames, allowed to set hard, dried, and cut into slabs and bars or pressed into cakes.

SOCIAL INSECTS. ANTS, wasps and BEES live in organized societies like the inhabitants of human cities, and, with the white ants or termites, are known as the social insects. In each case the head of the society or colony is the queen; her only duty is to lay eggs to replenish the numbers of the colony. The rest, apart from a few males, are workers (undeveloped females), and share the duties of looking after the nest or hive. In some ant societies there are (in addition to the workers) a soldier caste, whose main duty is the defence of the nest.

SOCIALISM, a political theory of public ownership. Socialists believe that the industries which provide the wealth of a nation, such as coal-mining, and services such as transport, should be controlled by officials who are responsible to Parliament, and not by private owners. They also believe that the State should be responsible for the health, education and general welfare of its people. See also POLITICS.

SOCRATES was a very wise man who lived in Athens from 469 B.C. to 399 B.C. He talked to all kinds of people in the streets and in the market-place, asking them questions and leading them to discuss how men should live and act. In this way he taught people a good deal by making them think for themselves. Socrates wrote nothing himself but much of his teaching was written down by PLATO, who was one of his followers.

SODIUM, is a silvery-white metal which is very quickly tarnished by exposure to the air. It is so soft that it can be cut with a knife, and it reacts very violently with water to form caustic soda.

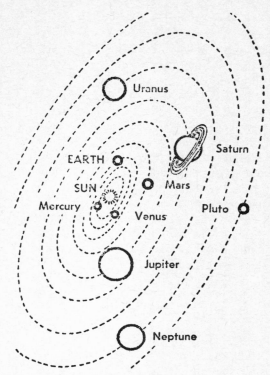

Planets travel round the sun.

It is obtained from common SALT, which is sodium chloride.

SOIL consists partly of fragments of rock of all sizes produced by the action of the weather on the larger rocks, and partly of a black substance called "humus" produced by the decay of dead plants. Soils have different qualities according to the kinds of rocks from which they are formed. The three chief kinds are clay, SAND and lime. A mixture of sand and clay is called loam, and one of lime and clay marl. The soil varies in depth from a few inches to several feet.

SOLAR SYSTEM is the name given to the sun and its family of planets and comets which revolve round it. The planets, in the order in which they occur as you travel outwards from the Sun, are Mercury, Venus, Earth, Mars, Jupiter, Saturn, Uranus, Neptune and Pluto. More than a thousand very small bodies called "asteroids" revolve round the sun between the orbits of Mars and Jupiter, and there are several hundred comets of all sizes revolving in long, oval-shaped orbits and trailing tails of gas behind them.

SOLICITOR, a lawyer whose work includes the transfer of property from one owner to another, and the drawing up of agreements and contracts. A solicitor may also arrange for a BARRISTER to appear in a court of LAW on behalf of his client.

SOLOMON was the third king of Israel, famous for his wisdom and for the great wealth which the wars of his father David had brought to the kingdom. He built a great TEMPLE at JERUSALEM and an even greater palace.

SOLUTION. A solution is a very thorough mixing up of a solid or gas with a liquid, the solid or gas becoming absorbed in the liquid. When dissolving, "going into solution," the particles of the solid (or gas) become separated and shuffled up with the particles of the liquid, and they cannot be separated again except by freezing or evaporating the liquid. The most common liquid used in making solutions is water, but substances which will not dissolve in water will sometimes form solutions in alcohol, benzene and other liquids.

SONNET. This is a short poem which has fourteen lines and a carefully worked-out rhyming scheme. The Elizabethan poets got the idea from the Italians, and since then many great English poets have written sonnets, including Shakespeare, Milton and Wordsworth.

SOOT is a powdery deposit of carbon found in chimneys.

SOPRANO. This is the highest singing voice in women and boys.

SOUND is the sensation you have when vibrations of the air reach your ears. The vibrations (which no eye can see) usually travel through the air, and are in the form of "push-and-pull" waves. The particles of the air between the object making the sound and your ear are jolted to and fro

like the wagons of a goods train which is being shunted. The wave travels through the air at about 720 miles per hour, and may be anything from ¾ of an inch to 77 feet long. The wavelength of the note called "middle C" is about 4½ feet, and about 256 such waves enter your ear every second while you are hearing it. The squeak of a bat is a sound-wave about ¾ of an inch long, some 20,000 being produced every second; this is the highest sound which human ears can hear. Sound-waves shorter than this are called "ultra-sonic" waves.

SOUNDING means finding the depth of water underneath a ship. This can be discovered by an echo-sounding machine fitted into the hull of a ship. A sound-wave is sent out and its echo from the bottom of the sea is picked up by a microphone. The depth of the ocean bed is calculated from the length of time that has passed between the sending out of the sound-wave and the receipt of the echo, and the result is shown on the dial of a recording machine in the wheelhouse.

SOUTH AFRICA is a REPUBLIC and no longer part of the BRITISH COMMONWEALTH OF NATIONS. It consists of four provinces. These are the Cape of Good Hope (Cape Province), Natal, Orange Free State, and Transvaal.

Pretoria is the administrative capital, and the Republic's Parliament meets in Cape Town. Durban, Port Elizabeth and Cape Town are important ports.

Lesotho and Swaziland, in southern Africa, and Botswana, in the south-west, are former British High Commission territories. All are now independent states within the Commonwealth.

In the Transvaal is the richest gold-producing area in the world, a district sixty miles long known as the Witwatersrand. Johannesburg, largest city in S. Africa, stands here. S. Africa also produces wool and diamonds. There are about four Africans and coloured people to every person of European descent and of recent years

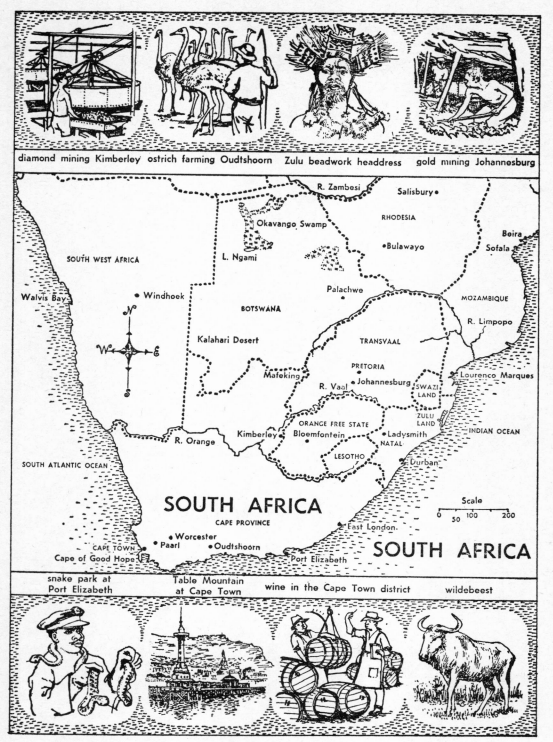

diamond mining Kimberley ostrich farming Oudtshoorn Zulu beadwork headdress gold mining Johannesburg

R. Zambesi
Salisbury•

RHODESIA

Okavango Swamp

•Bulawayo

Beira

Sofala

SOUTH WEST AFRICA
L. Ngami

Walvis Bay

•Windhoek

Palachwe

MOZAMBIQUE

BOTSWANA

R. Limpopo

Kalahari Desert

TRANSVAAL

PRETORIA
•Johannesburg

Lourenco Marques•

Mafeking•

R. Vaal

SWAZI
LAND

ZULU
LAND

INDIAN OCEAN

Kimberley• Bloemfontein•

ORANGE FREE STATE

•Ladysmith

R. Orange

NATAL

SOUTH ATLANTIC OCEAN

LESOTHO

•Durban

Scale
0   50   100   200

SOUTH AFRICA

CAPE PROVINCE

East London.

SOUTH AFRICA

•Worcester
Paarl•   •Oudtshoorn

CAPE TOWN
Cape of Good Hope

Port Elizabeth

snake park at
Port Elizabeth   Table Mountain
at Cape Town   wine in the Cape Town district   wildebeest

South Africa, and some of the things found there.

269

gathering coffee beans in Colombia and Brazil

nitrate crushing in Chile

Panama Canal

Cotopaxi in Ecuador

petroleum in Venezuela

Maté tea in Paraguay

alpaca in Peru

SOUTH AMERICA

South America and some of the things found there.

there has been great friction between black and white. See also RHODES; RHODESIA; SOUTH-WEST AFRICA.

SOUTH-WEST AFRICA, formerly German territory, is under the trusteeship of the United Nations. Windhoek is the capital. Exports include diamonds and copper.

SOUTH AMERICA, the southern part of the continent of America, forming a huge triangle three thousand miles in breadth and about four thousand five hundred miles in length. The southernmost point is Cape Horn. The great mountain chain of the ANDES extends along the western side of South America, and from it flows the river AMAZON eastwards through the forests of BRAZIL to the Atlantic Ocean. From Brazil, the largest country, coffee is exported, and from the ARGENTINE in the south, beef. Other countries are Bolivia, Colombia, CHILE, Ecuador, Paraguay, PERU, URUGUAY and VENEZUELA. On the north-east coast Guiana is divided into three parts, Guyana, Surinam and French Guiana. The chief languages spoken on the continent of South America are Spanish and Portuguese.

SPACE SATELLITE, a round casing full of scientific instruments which is carried up by rocket into outer space. Once released from the rocket, it travels through space, sending out radio messages so long as its batteries last.

SPAIN is the larger of the two countries in south-west Europe which form the Iberian peninsula, the other being PORTUGAL. Most of the interior consists of a plateau called the Meseta, where the summers are very hot and dry. Great quantities of oranges and olives are grown, and exported. MADRID is the capital.

SPARK, ELECTRIC, occurs when ELECTRICITY forces its way through something which does not readily conduct electricity. For example, when electricity forces its way through the air, enough energy is spent to make a little of the air white-hot,

and this is what we call an electric spark. The heat causes the air to expand suddenly and this gives rise to a crackling noise. LIGHTNING is simply a very big electric spark. See also THUNDER.

SPARKING PLUG, a device for making an electric spark inside the cylinders of petrol ENGINES, so as to explode the mixture of petrol and air supplied by the carburettor, thus forcing down the piston to turn the wheels. The electricity comes from a magneto or an ignition coil.

SPARTA was a city state of ancient Greece whose men were famous as soldiers.

SPECIFIC GRAVITY, the weight of a substance compared with the weight of an equal volume of water. Thus, the specific gravity of BRASS is 8, which means that brass is 8 times as heavy as water.

SPECTACLES are thin glass lenses mounted so that they can be worn in front of the eyes to correct defects in the sight. People suffering from "long sight" need to wear glasses with convex lenses; those with "short sight" need glasses with concave lenses. These alter the focus of light-rays on the retina of the eye. (See EYE; LENS.)

SPECTRUM. This name is given to the set of colours of which white LIGHT consists, and which may be seen in any RAINBOW. They are violet, blue, green, yellow, orange and red. When sunlight falls on to a cut-glass stopper, or a glass PRISM, the light is broken up into its separate colours, which may be seen as a small, vivid patch on a piece of white paper, if it is held in a suitable position. See the colour plate facing page 161.

SPEED seems to be the keynote of the modern age, but perhaps man has always tried to get about quicker and so save time for other things. Many men and women have achieved fame through their efforts to create new speed records in the air, on the water, and on land. Their success has been due to their courage and their skill, and to the ability of the designers and

Men have shown endurance and daring in their attempts to set up speed records on

engineers who invented and built the machines capable of giving the performance required of them.

The Wright Brothers built the first AEROPLANE and the historic flight in 1903 lasted for less than a minute. Yet from this beginning it took less than fifty years to develop jet aircraft that can travel faster than sound. Famous pilots include Bert Hinkler, Amy Johnson, Amelia Earhart, Charles Lindbergh, John Derry.

Sir Malcolm Campbell set up speed records both on land, with his racing car, and on the water with his famous speedboat *Bluebird*. His son, Donald, pushed the water speed record to 276·33 miles per hour on December 31, 1964. He also set a land speed record for wheel-driven cars: 403·135 m.p.h. in a gas-turbine engined car in July 1964. He improved on the water speed-record in his last, fatal run in *Bluebird* K7 on January 4, 1967. The unofficial speed was 328 m.p.h. The highest speed ever achieved on land is 650 m.p.h. It was achieved by Gary Gabelich at Bonneville Salt Flats, Utah, U.S.A., on October 23, 1970, during his 627·287 m.p.h. run in *The Blue Flame*.

Motor-cycle racing, on a speedway track or on a public road, is a competitive sport. Mike Hailwood of Great Britain and Giacomo Agostini of Italy are two motor-cycle champions whose names are known throughout the racing world.

Men also strive for speed without the help of machines in competitive athletics. In 1954 Roger Bannister became the first man in the world to run a mile in under four minutes. His time was 3 minutes 59·4 seconds. This record has since been beaten by many others.

SPEEDOMETER, a simple device for measuring the speed at which a wheel is turning or a vehicle is travelling. Most speedometers make use of the fact that when a weight is swung round in a circle on the end of a string, the faster it moves the farther it flies away from the centre of the circle.

SPHERE, a solid body whose outline appears to be a perfect circle from every point of view. It is the shape of a perfectly round ball.

SPHINX, the figure of a creature with the body of a lion and the head of a human being. The most famous is the Great Sphinx at Giza, near Cairo, which is carved in rock. It is 189 feet long, and represents the Sun god.

SPIDERS differ from INSECTS in having eight legs, and a body divided into two parts instead of three. Spiders have no

land, on the water and in the air.

antennae or feelers. All spiders can spin SILK, but they cannot all make webs or snares. The wolf-spiders hunt their prey instead of waiting for it to walk into a trap, but they spin silk to make cocoons for the eggs.

SPINAL CORD. See SPINE.

SPINE. This is also known as the spinal column or backbone. It consists of a long chain of small bones called vertebrae, separated by thin cushions of gristle (see CARTILAGE) and bound together by ligaments. The spine is the main support of the bodies of VERTEBRATES. It also contains and protects the main nerve-cord, the spinal cord, which runs from the brain to the hind-end of the body. See also BRAIN; NERVOUS SYSTEM; SKELETON.

SPONGE, one of the lowest forms of animal life. It is made up of millions of living cells with a framework, or skeleton, of horny or limy material. Some sponges take very beautiful shapes such as the glass sponge and the Venus Flower-basket. They live by drawing water in through fine pores on the surface of the body, extracting food and oxygen from it, and then driving the water out through large holes or vents. See also INVERTEBRATES.

SPONTANEOUS COMBUSTION occurs when something catches fire with-out being lit. For example, a damp hay-stack may begin to ferment inside and grow warm. If left alone it may become so hot that it bursts into fire by itself.

SPORTS are amusements involving physical skill, usually in the form of contests. There are six classes of sports: (1) outdoor team-games, such as CRICKET, FOOTBALL and HOCKEY; (2) athletic sports, like running, jumping and throwing the javelin; (3) individual contests, as in boxing, FENCING and wrestling; (4) water sports, like SWIMMING, rowing, yachting, diving and water-polo; (5) winter sports, such as skating, SKI-ING and TOBOGGANING; and (6) country pursuits, such as hunting, shooting and fishing.

SPRAIN, an injury to a joint caused by over-stretching the ligaments which bind it. The cure for a sprain is to apply hot and cold water alternately. At one time resting the joint was recommended, but now many people advise that it should continue to be used so that it does not get stiff.

SPRING, in nature, a natural outflow of water from the ground, often at the foot of a hill or cliff. It is generally caused by a layer of dense rock which prevents the rainwater that falls on the hill from soaking away. The spring-water flows away as a stream, and several such streams may combine to form a river. Sometimes natural hot water springs arise in volcanic areas. See GEYSERS.

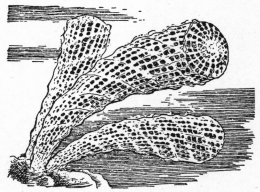

Venus Flower-basket sponge.

Squirrels build nests in high trees.

SQUIRREL, a member of the RODENT family, found in America, Europe and Northern and Central Asia. The red squirrel is the only species native to Britain but it is becoming rare. It is different from the American red squirrel although similar in colour. The grey squirrel is found in far greater numbers, and is very unpopular because it is so destructive to crops. Chipmunks and marmots also belong to the squirrel family, although they are ground dwellers and construct elaborate burrows.

STAGE. See PLAY; THEATRE.

STAINLESS STEEL is an ALLOY, or mixture, of steel with a small amount of chromium. Such steel does not easily rust.

STALACTITE, a deposit of limestone resembling an icicle and hanging from the roof of a cave. Stalactites are usually white in colour, and grow slowly in length as water containing limestone drips from them. See also STALAGMITE.

STALAGMITE, a deposit similar to a STALACTITE, but occurring on the floor of a cave. Stalagmites grow slowly upwards as water containing limestone drips on to them.

STANDARD TIME. Because the earth turns on its axis, no two places have the same time unless one is exactly north or south of the other. Thus, when it is noon in London it is afternoon at all places east of London and morning at all places west. The world has now been divided into a number of regions or zones, in each of which all clocks are set to the same time. This is called the "Standard Time" of their zone. The difference between the times of two zones next to each other is usually one hour, and most of the zones differ from Greenwich time by an exact number of hours. See also LONGITUDE; SUNDIAL; TIME.

STAR. The true stars are vast bodies of the same kind as the sun, though some of them are much larger and others much smaller than the sun. They are globes of intensely hot gases, chiefly hydrogen, and their light is produced by atomic energy changes going on inside them. The nearest stars are about 300,000 times as far away as the sun.

STARFISH. This is one of the Echinoderms, or spiny-skinned animals, which include the sea-urchin, brittle-star, seacucumber and sea-lily. All of them have their parts arranged in sets of fives. The common starfish has a central body with five arms pointing outwards from it like

Stalactites and stalagmites.

the rays of a star. It moves about by means of several hundreds of tube-feet, which are short movable projections on the under surfaces of the arms. See also INVERTEBRATES.

STATUE, a carving, made usually of stone or wood to represent some person. Sometimes statues are made larger than life-size to stand as an ornament in a park or public place.

STEAM is the vapour or gas given off when water boils. Like most other gases it is quite invisible. In the cool air it condenses into minute droplets of water, and these form the puffs which are visible an inch or two from the spout of a kettle of boiling water. The true steam remains invisible for a short distance from the spout. The puffs you can see have ceased to be steam.

STEAM ENGINE. When a quantity of water is boiled it turns into a much larger volume of STEAM. In trying to find room for itself, this steam pushes out in all directions with considerable force, and it can be made to work an ENGINE. There are two principal kinds of steam engine. In the first, the steam is made to push a piston to and fro inside a cylinder, and a jointed rod connected to the piston is made to turn a wheel, just as your arm can turn a handle. In the other kind, the turbine, the steam is made to blow a sort of windmill round. This windmill is a drum fitted with hundreds of small metal blades, instead of four large sails. The drum is enclosed in a case which prevents the steam escaping until it has done its work. See also LOCOMOTIVE; STEPHENSON.

STEAM HAMMER. This is a very heavy hammer which is raised to a certain height by steam-power. The steam is then made to push the hammer down and it falls with great force on to the steel piece to be shaped. Steam hammers are used for forging very large metal parts.

STEEL is IRON to which a fixed amount of carbon has been added. This has the effect of hardening the metal. Some steel also contains traces of other metals, such as CHROMIUM and tungsten, which toughen it or give it other special qualities required by engineers.

STEERING GEAR, the arrangement of levers, ropes or wheels provided for the steering of ships, cars and other vehicles. In a large ship the steering gear includes a small engine, for no hand-worked gearing would be strong enough to move the heavy rudder.

STEPHEN, King of England from 1135 to 1154. He was a grandson of William the Conqueror, and was "a mild man and a good." But when the barons began fighting for power Stephen proved a weak and unwise ruler. He imprisoned the bishops, who might have helped him, and allowed the barons to build castles for themselves all over the country.

STEPHENSON, George. Best-known as the builder of the *Rocket* STEAM ENGINE, George Stephenson lived from 1781 to 1848. He was born at Newcastle, and as a young man minded the steam pumping-engines at the coal-mines. He became an engine-builder, and soon turned his attention to the building of LOCOMOTIVES. His first locomotive ran successfully in 1814, and he built the first public steam railway, which ran from Stockton to Darlington, in Durham.

STEVENSON, Robert Louis, a famous writer who was born in Scotland in 1850. He was never very strong and began to write exciting adventure stories when kept in bed through ill-health. His most famous story is *Treasure Island*. He also wrote *Kidnapped* and *Catriona* and *Dr. Jekyll and Mr. Hyde*. To improve his health he sailed to the South Seas and lived on the island of Samoa until his death in 1894. The natives there called him the *Tusitala*, or "story-teller."

STICKLEBACK, a small freshwater fish common all over the northern hemisphere. In the breeding season the male grows red on the throat, when he is known as a "red-throat." The three-spined stickleback is the most common, although there are ten- and fifteen-spined sticklebacks, the last living in salt-water. See also NESTS.

STOCK EXCHANGE, a building where stocks and shares are bought and sold. Only members of the Stock Exchange are allowed inside, so that ordinary people who want to buy or sell shares have to employ a stockbroker who is a member to do their business for them.

STOCKHOLM is the capital and largest city of SWEDEN. It stands beside a channel which joins a large lake to the sea, and is built on both shores and on several islands. There are so many waterways through the city that it has been called the "Venice of the North."

STOMACH, a bag-like organ which receives the food we swallow and begins to digest it, before passing it on to the INTESTINES. The stomach is situated in the centre of the upper part of the ABDOMEN, level with the lower RIBS. Its walls contain layers of muscle which enable it to knead the food it contains.

STONE AGE, the period in the history of any country before the use of metals was discovered. The chief material used for making tools and weapons was stone or flint.

The early part of the period is called the *Old Stone Age*. Men lived in caves and obtained food by hunting wild animals: they used the skins to clothe themselves. Their weapons were very roughly made, and were not polished. Later, these primitive people learned to make better weapons. They also learned how to grow food, and to weave material from wool and flax. Instead of wandering from place to place, they built huts, and villages began to grow up. This became known as the *New Stone Age*. See also CAVE.

STONEHENGE, a very ancient open-air temple in Wiltshire, England, constructed of huge stones roughly trimmed and standing on end, with more stones laid across their tops, the whole array

forming a double circle. This is arranged so that an entrance faces the rising sun on Midsummer Day. Stonehenge was built by New STONE AGE inhabitants of Britain about four thousand years ago, and was already an ancient ruin before the DRUIDS found it and used it in the Iron Age.

STORK, a long-legged, long-beaked bird related to the HERON and also to the sacred ibis of Egypt. The twenty species found in various parts of the world are mainly coloured white and black. They have large wings, rounded bodies and short tails. The white stork of Europe  builds its nests on chimney stacks, and migrates in large flocks to Africa for the winter. See also MIGRATION.

Stork.

STRING, a coarse THREAD made of twisted animal or vegetable fibres. A violin string may be made of silk, or of a tough, elastic tissue obtained from a sheep and miscalled "catgut."

STUDY, HOW TO. You must first of all learn to read with care and to remember what you read. Sit comfortably in a good light when you are reading, and, if you can, in a quiet room. Read about things that interest you and try to find out as much as possible about your favourite subjects. It is a good idea to make short notes in pencil in a small notebook. This will help you to remember useful facts. You should talk to your friends and parents about things you are studying. If you have a hobby such as stamp-collecting, spotting railway engine numbers or keeping rabbits you should find out as much as you can about it. Read books and sometimes read certain parts of a book several times. Talk about your hobby to friends who have the same hobby. By reading, talking and making notes you will learn more about the things you are interested in. You can also learn a great deal by going to museums and art galleries, and to those exhibitions which are specially prepared for children.

STURGEON, a fish that lives in the sea, but comes up the rivers of Europe, Asia and North America in order to breed or spawn. The mouth, which is without teeth, can be stretched out to suck in the small animals on which it feeds. In Britain sturgeon are "royal fish" by an ancient law. This means that any caught are the property of the Sovereign. Their eggs are eaten as caviare, renowned as a delicacy.

STYLE. This often means the way one writes. A good style in writing is clear and simple, and says just what you want to say.

SUBMARINE, a vessel which will travel under water and so avoid being seen by an enemy. A submarine is only slightly lighter than water, so that when water is allowed to flood special tanks provided for the purpose the vessel rapidly sinks. It is then controlled by horizontal rudders as well as the vertical one, and thus can be steered up and down as well as sideways. While under water the officer of a submarine is able to see where he is going by means of a periscope, a long tube which can be raised above the surface or lowered out of sight as required. Most submarines are driven by diesel engines when on the surface, but by electric motors when under the water.

SUBTRACTION. See ARITHMETIC.

SUDAN, the region of AFRICA which lies south of the Sahara and Egypt and stretches from the Atlantic Ocean to the Red Sea. Most of the people are Negroes, for Sudan means "the Land of the Blacks." The name is also applied to the country due south of Egypt. In this area cotton is the chief crop, and the capital is Khartoum.

SUEZ CANAL, a ship CANAL about one hundred miles long which joined the Mediterranean Sea to the Red Sea across the Isthmus of Suez. It was cut through the desert and a number of lakes. Vessels had to steam slowly through it to prevent their wash from damaging the banks, and the journey took about twelve hours. The Suez Canal was chiefly important because it shortened the sea journey from Europe to the East. It has been closed since the Six Day War in 1967.

SUGAR is a sweet-tasting substance produced by most plants from the carbon dioxide in the air. The green colouring-matter in a LEAF, with the help of sunlight, is able to make the carbon dioxide combine with water to form sugar. Sugar is found abundantly in the tropical sugar-cane, the Canadian maple-tree and the European sugar-beet. Beet-sugar is not different from cane sugar, but other kinds of sugar are found in milk and grapes, grape-sugar being known as glucose.

SUMMER TIME. The sun rises so early during the summer that it seems a waste of good light to remain in bed, so Summer Time was invented to encourage everybody to get up an hour earlier. When Summer Time starts we simply put our clocks forward an hour. Then when our clocks say eight o'clock we are really getting up at seven.

SUN, a fairly ordinary type of STAR. It is a globe of white-hot gases, the chief of which is hydrogen. The diameter of the sun is about 110 times that of the Earth, so that in volume the sun is equal to

A submarine travelling under the water.

277

more than one and a quarter million Earths! It appears small because it is about ninety-three million miles away. The sun's light and heat are produced by atomic energy changes inside the sun, where the temperature is greater than twenty million degrees. The temperature of the sun's surface is about six thousand degrees, and the *sunspots* are cooler patches caused by upward streams of gas. The EARTH and eight other planets revolve round the sun. See SOLAR SYSTEM.

SUNDIAL. One of the earliest methods of measuring time was by means of the sun's shadow. On a sundial the hours are marked on the surface, a thin rod is fixed to the dial, and casts a shadow on to the carved figures. Other ways of telling the time were by the use of a knotted rope, or a marked candle, which was set light to and allowed to burn away, or by sand trickling through an hour-glass. See also PENDULUM.

SURVEYING, the work of measuring up the land and making an accurate MAP of it. It is done by dividing the land into convenient triangles, and setting up observation posts at their angles. The sides of the triangles are measured by means of a metal chain of twenty-two links, eighty chains making one mile. The angles of the triangles are found by means of THEODO-LITES, which also measure angles of altitude.

SWALLOW. Like its relatives the house- and sand-martins, the swallow has long wings, a stream-lined body and a forked tail. It is a summer visitor to Britain, and migrates to Africa for the winter. It feeds on insects caught on the wing. See also MIGRATION.

SWAN. Except for the black swan of Australia, all swans are white or mainly white. They have large, rounded bodies. Their necks are very long, so that they can search the bottom of a river or lake

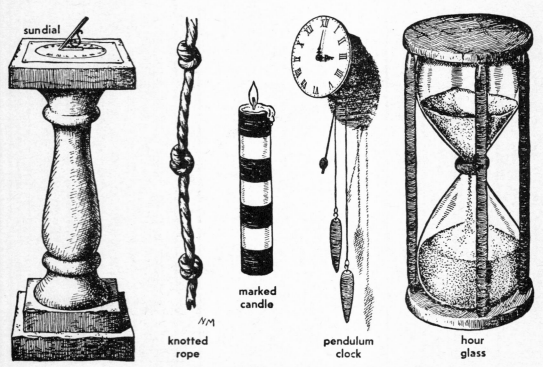

sundial

knotted rope

marked candle

pendulum clock

hour glass

There are many different ways of measuring time.

for food. They eat water-plants, insects and water-snails. A pair of swans mate for life. In the breeding season they make a large untidy nest in which the female lays eight eggs, while the male guards her. The mute swans of England are "royal birds," which means that only the monarch, or those holding a licence, may keep them.

Swan.

SWEDEN is one of the two countries of the Scandinavian peninsula, the other being Norway. The southern part is farming country, while the north is a land of forests. In the far north live the Lapps, with their herds of REINDEER. Sweden exports wood, wood-pulp, paper, and iron ore. STOCKHOLM is the capital.

SWIMMING, in either fresh or salt water, is both a "life-saving exercise" and a sport. There are many different strokes, or methods of swimming, from the simple breast-stroke to the crawl, a favourite in racing, and the backstroke, in which the swimmer floats on his back.

SWITCH. An electric switch is a device for breaking or joining up as required a wire carrying an electric current. When the switch is off the wire is actually broken and the current can no longer flow. When the switch is on the two ends of the wire are connected by a piece of metal, and the current flows again. The term switch is also used by railway engineers to mean what ordinary people call points. Such points are used where two railway tracks join, and enable a train to be switched from one track to the other. See the colour plate facing page 257.

SWITZERLAND is a small mountainous country in Central Europe, the southern half of which is occupied by the ALPS. The beauty of its mountains has helped to make Switzerland one of the playgrounds of Europe. Catering for holiday makers is an important industry, and another is the making of watches and clocks. Berne is the capital.

SWORD-FISH, a large fish in which the upper jaw is prolonged into a sharp-pointed sword. It does not bear teeth like that of the SAW-FISH. Found in the Atlantic Ocean, it may be fifteen feet in length and have a sword three feet long.

SYMBOL, something that is used to stand for something else. We may use a lion to stand for courage, or a lamb for meekness or a dove for peace. The lion, lamb and dove are used as symbols.

SYMPHONY, a musical work written to be played by the instruments of an orchestra and not just by a piano or violin. The symphony usually has four movements, a lively one to start with, a slow one, a merry one, and a quick stirring one to finish with.

SYNCOPATION. When the normal beat of a piece of music is suddenly changed so that the first note of each bar

Sword-fish.

does not take the beat, the music is said to be syncopated. It became very popular in dance music in the style of negro ragtime and jazz.

SYRINGE. The most important parts of a syringe are the short straight tube which forms its body and the plunger which fits inside it. If the open end of the tube is dipped beneath the surface of a liquid and then the plunger is pulled out, the tube is filled with the liquid by suction. It can be emptied again by pushing the plunger back, which forces the liquid out. A rubber bulb which can be squeezed is sometimes used instead of a plunger.

T

TADPOLE. The young of the FROG, TOAD, and NEWT live in water and breathe through gills. They are called tadpoles. They have a long tail bordered above and below by a delicate fin. Gradually, the lungs are developed and the gills are lost; the legs begin to grow, and the tail becomes smaller, until the tadpole has changed into its adult form and is ready to leave the pond to live on the land.

TAHITI is the largest and most important of the Society Islands, in the South Pacific Ocean. They belong to France. With its volcanic mountain peaks and its coconut palms, Tahiti is a beautiful island. The chief town and seaport is Papeete.

TAILOR-BIRD. There are many species of tailor-bird in southern Asia and the East Indian islands. They are small birds, green above, white below, and have long tails. Using its bill as a needle, and vegetable fibre as thread, the tailor-bird sews large leaves together, edge to edge, to make a hanging pocket in which the nest is built. See also NESTS.

TALLOW, grease made by melting down animal fat, especially that obtained from sheep. It was once used for making candles.

Tailor-bird.

TANGANYIKA, Lake, is a long, narrow, very deep lake in the southern part of central AFRICA. On its shores is the port of Ujiji, where the British explorer Stanley met DAVID LIVINGSTONE, for whom he was searching, with the famous words: "Dr. Livingstone, I presume?", in 1871. See also p. 310.

TANGENT, a straight line which just touches the edge of a circle, but does not cut into it, no matter how long it is. A railway line forms a tangent to a wheel resting on it.

TANK, a special kind of armoured car. It is completely protected with armour-plate, and travels on caterpillar TRACKS which are long enough to bridge a wide ditch. It is able to cross rough country,

Tank used in the Second World War.

climbing over fences and walls and crushing them by its weight. It is heavily armed with guns.

TAR. Coal tar is obtained by heating coal in a closed retort, so that it cannot burn. Coal-gas comes off with the tar, and the residue is coke. Coal tar is a thick sticky, black liquid from which hundreds of useful chemicals are prepared, including saccharine and the aniline dyes. Wood treated in the same way yields wood tar or creosote, used for preserving timber.

TASMANIA, one of the States of AUSTRALIA, is an island off the south-east coast of the continent. Over 100,000 people live in Hobart, the capital. Sheep-farming in the north and fruit-growing in the south provide wool and apples for export.

TASTE, one of the primary SENSES, by which we appreciate flavours. The organs of taste are special nerve-endings on the surface of the tongue and other parts of the MOUTH. When they are well-developed they are called taste-buds. Some groups of taste-buds are sensitive to bitter things, some to sweet things, and others to acid and salt flavours. In children, the whole mouth is lined with taste-buds, but many of these disappear as they grow up. See also PALATE.

TAXATION. It costs a lot of money to govern a country, to keep its navy, army and air force going, to maintain its social services and pay its officials; so as many people as possible must be made to give up some of their earnings to pay the bill. There are two chief kinds of taxation—taxes on goods and services and taxes on earnings. The tax on goods and services is called Value Added Tax. It is charged on the value of goods and services supplied, less the amount of tax paid by the supplier on the goods and services he has already received. The tax on earnings is called Income Tax and is charged according to how much money people receive every year.

TEA is made from the leaves of a small shrub which grows in tropical countries like India, China, and Sri Lanka. The leaves are picked and dried thoroughly. They are then covered with moist cloths and allowed to ferment. Then they are given a final drying.

TEAK, a tree which grows in the forests of south-east Asia. Its wood resists rotting in damp places, and it is therefore used for outdoor timber and in shipbuilding.

TEETH. There are three chief kinds of teeth in human beings—incisors or "front" teeth (which cut), canines or "eye" teeth (which tear), and molars or "back" teeth (which grind). They all consist of an inner pulp containing blood-vessels and nerves, surrounded by a thick layer of ivory or

dentine, and coated outside with a thin, hard enamel. Animals' teeth vary in shape according to their use, and range from the flat-crowned grinding molars of the grass-eaters to the sharp-pointed tearing teeth of the flesh-eating animals.

Alexander Graham Bell.

TELEGRAPHY. The electric telegraph enables you to send messages over long distances. A message is usually sent by means of a teleprinter, which is simply a typewriter joined by an electric cable to another typewriter far away. When the message is typed on the keyboard of one typewriter, the letters are printed on to a piece of paper fitted in the distant typewriter.

But for very long distances, the message can be put into MORSE code or a code consisting solely of holes punched into a strip of paper. Then the message is transmitted by machine at high speed along the electric cable to a distant machine, which prints the letters according to the code.

TELEPHONE. When you speak into a telephone the sound of your voice causes an electric current to vary in strength according to the vibrations you produce. At the receiving end this current causes a magnet to vary in strength in exactly the same way, and a thin disk of metal near the magnet vibrates so as to reproduce the sound of your voice. The telephone

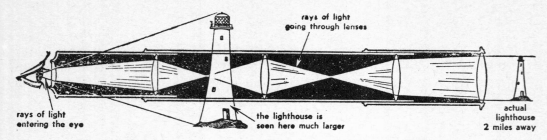

rays of light
going through lenses

actual
lighthouse
2 miles away

rays of light
entering the eye

the lighthouse is
seen here much larger

A telescope gives an enlarged view of a distant object.

was invented by the Scottish inventor, Alexander Graham Bell, in 1876. He lived from 1847 to 1922. See also EDISON.

TELESCOPE. In an ordinary telescope an image or small picture is formed by a low-power magnifying LENS called the *object-glass*, and this is enlarged by a high-power magnifying glass called the *eye-piece*. Such a telescope shows everything upside-down, but this does not matter if you are looking at the stars. If objects are required to be seen the right way up, extra lenses have to be added. In reflecting telescopes the object-glass is replaced by a magnifying mirror, which is more satisfactory for very large instruments. The world's largest telescope is on Mount Semirodriki in the Caucasus Mountains; its mirror is almost 20 feet across.

TELEVISION is possible because some substances are able to produce ELECTRICITY when LIGHT falls on them. In an ordinary camera, a picture is cast by a LENS on to the film, where it causes chemical changes, which are later made visible in the photograph. In a television camera, a picture is cast by a lens on to a plate. It causes electrical changes in the plate which are picked up very quickly by a cathode-ray moving from side to side in a zigzag fashion, and broadcast from an aerial. In the receiving set another cathode-ray moves over a screen in time with the ray sending the signals, and it makes the screen shine brightly or dimly according to the strength of the signals. It thus reproduces the picture, bit by bit, on the screen. But all the bits composing the picture flash into place at such a speed

that the whole picture is built up within a fraction of a second, and at any given moment your eyes seem to be seeing the complete picture.

TEMPERATURE. The temperature of a thing is its degree of heat or cold. This is measured by means of a THERMOMETER. When sick people are said to have a temperature it means that their blood is warmer than it should be. The normal, healthy temperature for a human being is 98½ degrees Fahrenheit. See also CHART.

TEMPLE, a sacred building, as at JERUSALEM, where the Israelites worshipped God. Solomon is said to have built the first temple. The GREEKS and Romans also built temples where they could worship their gods.

TENDON. This is a band of tough white tissue which fastens a muscle to a bone. Tendons are also called sinews.

TENNIS is a ball-game played on a hard court, or a grass court (when it is called Lawn Tennis). If only two players take part it is called "singles"; if four people play it is called "doubles." A doubles court is thirty-six feet wide and seventy-eight feet long. A singles court is not so wide, and is marked inside the limits of the doubles court. A line is drawn parallel with each side, and four feet six inches away from the outer edge, so the width of the singles court is twenty-seven feet. A net is stretched across the centre of the court, from a post at each end; this is three feet six inches high at the posts but is slackened so that it is only three feet high at the middle.

The aim of the players is to hit a ball

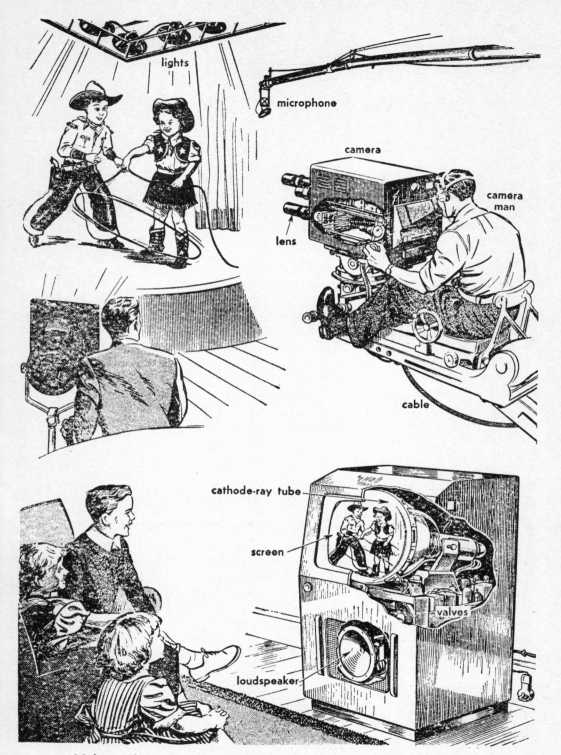

Making television pictures and receiving them on the television screen.

(made of hollow rubber covered with flannel) to and fro across the net. They use a special bat, called a racquet. This is a light oval frame of wood, across which are stretched strings of catgut, with a stout handle. If a player hits the ball into the net, or lets it bounce twice before hitting it (or misses the ball altogether!) that is a point to the other player.

The first point is counted as fifteen, the next as thirty, the third as forty. If a player wins four points in a row he wins the game. If the score is even, at forty-forty, it is called deuce, and a player has to gain two more points in succession to win.

TENNYSON, Alfred, Lord, was born in 1809. He was a famous English poet in the reign of Queen Victoria. Tennyson's best friend died when they were both young men and a long poem, *In Memoriam*, tells us the poet's feelings about his loss. He also wrote a number of story-poems about King Arthur and the Knights of the Round Table. Tennyson died in 1892.

TENOR. This is the high singing voice in a male choir.

TENTACLE, a name applied to a long, finger-like organ common in the lower forms of animal life, such as sea-anemones, coral polyps and jellyfish. Such tentacles are often armed with stinging-cells which kill their prey as they seize it. The arms of the octopus and cuttlefish are also called tentacles. These are fitted with suckers to enable them to grip their victims. See INVERTEBRATES.

TERMITES. See SOCIAL INSECTS.

TERRESTRIAL MAGNETISM. This is the magnetism of the earth, which causes compass-needles to point to the north and south poles. The magnetic north and south poles are not in quite the same places as the true north and south poles, and they change their positions slightly every year. Sailors and others who use a COMPASS have to allow for this. See also NORTH.

TERRIERS are a group of domestic DOGS of several breeds, originally used in hunting, trapping and shooting game. The word "terrier" is French for hole in the ground, suggesting an association with rabbit hunting. Some breeds, such as the fox terrier and bull terrier, are named after the animal which they are trained to tackle. Others, like the Skye terrier and the Yorkshire terrier, are named from their place of origin.

TESTING OF MATERIALS. Before it is safe to use wood, metal or other materials for building or engineering work, it is necessary to test them to see how strong they are. Samples are taken and these are bent or stretched or compressed until they break. The builders and engineers then know exactly how much weight it is safe to let them support.

THACKERAY, William Makepeace, was born in India in 1811, but went to school in England. He was very fond of drawing and writing and some of his work appeared in the magazine *Punch*. He wrote many novels including the famous *Vanity Fair*, which tells the story of Becky Sharp and gives a picture of English society at the time of the war against Napoleon. His other novels also show Thackeray's interest in history. He died in 1863.

THAILAND (Siam), is a country of south-east Asia. It is part of INDO-CHINA. There are rich rice-fields in the eastern plains, and coconut plantations. Rubber, tin, and teak are also produced. Bangkok is the capital and chief port.

THAMES, the most important river in Britain, for the country's capital and leading seaport, LONDON, stands on its banks. It rises in the Cotswold Hills, and enters the North Sea by a long estuary. Above London a great deal of rowing and boating takes place on the river. One of the chief events of the year is the Oxford and Cambridge boat race from Putney to Mortlake.

THEATRE, a place or building where performances of plays and other entertainments can be watched by a large number of people. The earliest Greek theatres were in the open air, and by 500 B.C. there was a theatre at Athens which had stone seats for thirty thousand people. See also DRAMA; PLAY.

THEODOLITE, a small telescope mounted on a stand so that the direction in which it points can be read from a compass, and the angle to which it is tilted can also be read. Theodolites are used in SURVEYING the land. See also ORDNANCE SURVEY.

THERMOMETER, an instrument for measuring the degree of heat. An ordinary thermometer is a glass tube partly filled with the liquid metal mercury, or QUICK-SILVER. When warmed the mercury expands and runs up the tube. The degree of heat, or TEMPERATURE, is given on a scale which shows how far up the tube the mercury has run. On ordinary thermometers the boiling-point of water is marked 212 degrees and the freezing-point 32 degrees. This is called the FAHRENHEIT scale, but scientists use the Centigrade scale, in which boiling-point is called 100 degrees and freezing-point 0 degrees or zero. Normal blood temperature is $98\frac{1}{2}$ degrees Fahrenheit.

THERMOSTAT, an instrument which controls a heating apparatus to keep a steady temperature. A thermostat makes use of the fact that metals expand when heated, and a metal strip is used which will break a connexion in a wire circuit as it expands, and make it again as it cools.

THIRTY YEARS' WAR, fought in Central Europe between 1618 and 1648 between the Protestant princes and the Roman Catholic princes. The religious question was soon forgotten, and it became a war for power. At the end, Germany was a crippled country.

THORAX, the upper part of the body. In man, the chest which contains the lungs and heart, is called the thorax. In insects, the thorax is the part between the waist and the neck.

THREAD. Ordinary thread is made of linen fibres twisted together, and it is much stronger than cotton. See STRING.

THUNDER is the noise made by LIGHTNING, which is an enormous electric spark. The heat produced by the spark causes the air to expand suddenly, or explode, and the thunder is the noise of the explosion followed by its echoes from clouds and the earth.

TIBER, the river of Central Italy on which Rome stands. It carries down so much sediment that its mouth has advanced two miles into the sea since Roman times.

TIBET is a country in Central Asia (now a special territory of Communist China). Lhasa is the capital. It is the highest country in the world, for it stands on a plateau over ten thousand feet above sea level. The YAK, which is very strong and hardy, is the chief beast of burden. Tibetans are very fond of China tea mixed with yak butter and salt. They are extremely religious people, about one-quarter of the men being Buddhist priests, or lamas. Their religious head is the Dalai Lama, now exiled in India.

TIDES are caused by the attraction of the moon and sun, for the water of the sea yields to the attraction more readily than the solid earth does, and becomes heaped up on the side of the earth facing the sun or moon. The pull of the moon is much stronger than the pull of the sun. When the sun and moon are in line so that they both pull in the same direction, we get extra high tides, or spring tides. When they are at right-angles so as to hinder each other, we get the lesser tides known as neap tides. A high tide occurs every twelve hours twenty-six minutes.

TIGER, one of the two largest members of the CAT family, the other being the lion. Tigers have yellow coats striped with black, and are found in most parts of Asia. They prey on deer, wild pigs and antelopes, killing them by breaking their necks. A "man-eater" is usually an old tiger too feeble to hunt the swifter animals, or a tigress seeking food for her cubs.

In Canada lumber-jacks cut down trees and float the timber down rivers to the saw-mills.

TIMBER is wood before it has been made into anything, and it may be a freshly felled tree or in the form of boards and planks of various sizes. Freshly felled trees in very large numbers are known as lumber, and in countries like Canada they are taken from the forests to the timber-merchants by floating them down the rivers. This work is done by the lumber-jacks.

TIME is measured by dividing the period the earth takes to turn once on its axis into 24 equal hours. Each hour is then divided into 60 minutes, and each minute into 60 seconds. A day is not exactly the time taken for the earth to turn on its axis, but the period from noonday to noonday. Because the earth travels round the sun as well as spinning on its axis, the ordinary day is about 4 minutes short of 24 hours. A week is a period of 7 days, but a month is not an exact number of days. A lunar month is the time from one new moon to the next, and it is equal to about 27 days $7\frac{3}{4}$ hours. For ordinary purposes we use the 12 artificial "calendar" months, the lengths of which vary from 28 days for February to 31 days. This rhyme will help you to remember the number of days in the month:

Thirty days hath September,
April, June, and November.
All the rest have thirty-one,
Excepting February alone,
Which has but twenty-eight days clear
And twenty-nine in each leap year.

A year is the time taken for the earth to travel once round the sun, and this is neither an exact number of days nor an exact number of lunar months. It is about $365\frac{1}{4}$ days, but we reckon it as 365 days. This means that every four years the odd quarters amount to one whole day lost. We then have what is called a leap year, because we restore the lost day by adding it on to February, giving that month 29 days. See also STANDARD TIME.

TIN is a silvery white METAL. An ALLOY of tin and lead beaten very thin makes tinfoil or "silver paper," but nowadays foils are made of aluminium and other metals as well as tin. Modern pewter is an ALLOY consisting mainly of tin, with some lead or copper.

TINPLATE. Ordinary tins are made of tinplate, which is a thin sheet of steel, coated with tin to prevent it from rusting.

TISSUE is a material or substance made up of cells and forming part of a living body. Thus, skin is a tissue, bone is a tissue and even blood is called a tissue by biologists.

Toad.

TOAD. The two species of toads in Britain are the common toad and the natterjack. The first has a warty skin and is brownish in colour; the natterjack has a smoother skin and is greenish, with a yellow stripe down the back. Toads are AMPHIBIANS, and lay their eggs in water in strings, not in clusters like frogs' eggs. See also TADPOLE.

TOBACCO is a plant grown chiefly for its use in smoking and in the manufacture of snuff. It also contains nicotine, a valuable insect poison. The leaves are prepared for smoking by fermenting and then drying them; snuff is made by grinding their central ribs to a fine powder. Tobacco is grown all over the world in sub-tropical countries, and it can even be grown in England.

TOBOGGANING, an outdoor SPORT in which a small sleigh or toboggan is ridden down slopes of hard snow. Speeds of seventy miles an hour are sometimes reached.

TOKYO is the capital and largest city of JAPAN. It has many beautiful parks and gardens, and ancient temples as well as tall modern buildings. The city has often suffered from earthquakes. In 1923 an earthquake and the resulting fires killed about 100,000 people and destroyed 370,000 homes.

TON, a weight equal to 2,240 pounds or 20 hundredweights. The "short" ton, which is used in the United States, is equal to 2,000 pounds, and the "metric" ton or "tonne" is 2,204·6 pounds.

TONGUE, a fleshy organ on the floor of the MOUTH in VERTEBRATES. It is used to taste with, and also to catch or take in food, and to raise water into the mouth. In man it is also an organ of speech. The tongues of birds are hard and horny; those of snakes are forked. The tongues of chameleons, frogs and toads are sticky and can be shot out to catch insects. See also SENSES.

TONIC SOL-FA NOTATION, a method of indicating musical notes that was introduced into the schools in the nineteenth century. The notes in the scale were given the names doh-ray-me-fah-soh-lah-te-doh, and doh could be struck on the piano anywhere as the keynote of a scale. See also Musical NOTATION.

Tobogganing is fun.

TONSILS, a pair of GLANDS guarding the entrance to the throat. Their purpose is not fully understood, but they probably help to protect the body from germs entering through the mouth. See also GERM.

TOOLS are devices which help you to make things. They include cutting tools such as chisels and saws, gripping tools such as pliers and pincers, and machine tools such as lathes and presses.

TORNADO, a violent storm in which winds of tremendous strength blow round and round a centre. As the storm moves along, trees are uprooted, buildings are destroyed, and often people are killed. There is usually heavy rain and thunder with the tornado. Such storms are frequent in the Mississippi basin of the United States.

TORPEDO, a cigar-shaped missile fired from warships or submarines, or dropped from aircraft. Once in the sea it travels under its own power, usually by a compressed-air engine driving two propellers. In its nose is a heavy charge of high explosive which blows up when it strikes its target.

TORTOISE, a REPTILE with the body enclosed in a bony box covered with a horny shell. The name tortoise is usually kept for those which live on land or in fresh water, the sea forms being known as TURTLES. The tortoises all belong to the warmer parts of the world. They move very slowly and live to a great age, though the only accurate record is for a tortoise which lived for just over 150 years.

TOUCAN, a bird of South America. Its plumage is usually brilliantly-coloured. The toucan is a small bird, but it has an enormous beak which gives it an unbalanced appearance. This also is vividly-coloured, varying with the species. It feeds chiefly on fruit, but will attack and devour smaller birds and their eggs.

TOUCH, one of the five main SENSES. The organs of touch are at the tips of fine nerves buried deep in the skin. They make us aware of anything coming into contact with the skin. See also REFLEX ACTION.

TOURNAMENT, a competition to find the best player at a game, such as chess or tennis. The players are divided into groups where they play against each other. The losers drop out, but the winners form new groups and play other winners, and so on until only one winner (or winning team) is left. Alternatively, each player may play every other player.

In the MIDDLE AGES a tournament was a friendly fight or "joust" between knights on horseback, performed before spectators. From this, any large naval or military spectacle or display of prowess has also come to be called a tournament. See also ARMOUR.

TOWER BRIDGE, the bridge which crosses the Thames just by the Tower of London. Its carriage-way opens to allow large ships to pass through, each half being raised like the hinged lid of a box. Above this is a footway, 142 feet above the river, but it is no longer used.

TOWER OF LONDON, an ancient fortress, palace, and prison, built to guard the river approach to London. The central keep, known as the White Tower, was built for William the Conqueror. The outer walls and towers were added by later kings. If one entered from the river,

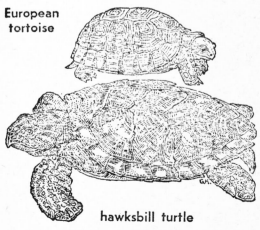

European tortoise

hawksbill turtle

Tortoise and turtle.

through Traitors' Gate, one would be following the steps of Sir Thomas More, Anne Boleyn, Lady Jane Grey, and many other unfortunates who were beheaded there. The Tudor monarchs used it as a royal residence, and the Warders of the Tower still wear Tudor costume.

TRACK, CATERPILLAR. This is a long, jointed band of metal plates that runs over two or more wheels. Caterpillar tracks are used instead of ordinary wheels in TANKS and in some kinds of TRACTOR.

TRACKS, RAILWAY. The first railway tracks were L-shaped girders, the upright part serving as a guide to keep the wheels from slipping off the rails. In modern tracks rolled steel bars are used, and instead of a guide, the wheels themselves are flanged on the inside to keep them on the rails. At first, square blocks of stone were used to support the rails at intervals, but these were soon replaced by wooden sleepers. Modern rails rest on metal "chairs" which are bolted to the sleepers. See the colour plate facing page 257.

TRACTOR, an engine designed to pull a heavy load. The word is used especially of a vehicle driven by a powerful petrol or diesel engine intended to pull a plough, harrow, or other farm implement. Such tractors are fitted with very large wheels and tyres to enable them to bridge the bumps and hollows of rough land, while some have caterpillar TRACKS.

TRADE UNION, a union of the workers in a particular trade, such as a union of railwaymen, or miners. When different trades combine it is called a Trades Union. By agreements with their employers, unions have in many ways improved conditions of work.

TRADE WINDS are steady winds which blow from the North-east and the South-east towards the equator. They are called "Trade Winds" because they have been used by sailing-ships trading between the coasts of Africa and India since the time of the Romans.

Yeoman Warder of the Tower of London.

TRAFALGAR was the great sea battle in which NELSON, in command of a British fleet, fought against NAPOLEON'S French and Spanish fleets, which were about to escort a French army to invade Britain. (Nelson's ship, the *Victory*, may still be seen at Portsmouth.) He sent out the famous signal: England expects that every man will do his duty. Nelson was killed in the battle, but he knew that the enemy was defeated and that his country was safe. The date was 1805. Trafalgar Day is still celebrated on 21 October.

TRAGEDY, a PLAY with an unhappy ending about some human disaster.

TRAIN FERRY, a vessel containing a long flat deck on which railway lines are laid, so that the carriages of a train may be run on board and transported across the water. A special dock is required with arrangements for linking up the track on the ship with the normal land track.

TRANSFUSION is the operation of transferring the blood of one person into the body of another. It can also be used for the operation of putting other fluids into different parts of the body if they are needed. Blood transfusion has saved the lives of many people who have lost too much of their own blood through injury.

289

TRANSPORT. This term covers all the ways by which people and goods can be carried from one place to another. The earliest methods were by pack-horse, camel or other animals, moving along narrow tracks, but as soon as rafts were invented heavy loads were often floated down rivers. There was also the sledge, which has been used for thousands of years for rapid transport across ice and snow. With the invention of the wheel came the wagon and all kinds of vehicle, and for many centuries these were pulled along by horses and oxen. To serve them proper ROADS had to be built, and from that time most of the world's land transport has been along roads. Meanwhile, the raft became the SHIP, propelled by wind or oars. When engines were invented they were soon adapted to drive both vehicles and ships, and it was not long before the aeroplane came to provide yet other forms of transport.

TREE, a woody perennial plant having a main stem or trunk, and many woody branches springing from it. Any self-supporting plant more than ten feet high is called a tree. See CONIFERS; DECIDUOUS TREES; EVERGREENS.

TREVITHICK, Richard, was a British engineer who invented a STEAM ENGINE. He made several LOCOMOTIVES, and in 1801 built the first steam road-carriage. He was born in Cornwall in 1771, and died in 1833.

TRIAL, an attempt to test or find out the capabilities of something, as when a new aeroplane is "tried out." The special meaning of trial is the attempt to find out the truth about a person accused of a crime. Such a person is taken to a court of justice to be tried. See EVIDENCE; LAW; JUDGE; JURY.

TRIANGLE, the shape formed by any three straight lines arranged to enclose a space. Every triangle has three angles and the sum of the angles equals two right-angles. See also ANGLE; GEOMETRY; MATHEMATICS; TRIGONOMETRY.

TRIBE, a group of people who claim to be descended from a common ancestor, speak the same language, and have the same simple form of government. The members of a tribe are loyal to their chief or leader and are usually firmly united in the face of their enemies.

TRIGONOMETRY, is the study of the relations between the sides and angles of TRIANGLES. It is used in SURVEYING for calculating the heights of mountains, and distances which cannot easily be measured. It enables astronomers to measure the distance away of the moon and other bodies, and is used in many branches of engineering.

TROMBONE, a brass instrument rather like a long TRUMPET. It has a sliding tube fitted inside another tube. The person blowing down the mouthpiece of the trombone can move the sliding tube to change the note, and so play a tune. See ORCHESTRA.

TROPICS, the region that lies between the Tropic of Cancer (latitude $23\frac{1}{2}$ degrees N.) and the Tropic of Capricorn (latitude $23\frac{1}{2}$ degrees S.). Within this region, the weather is always hot. It is sometimes known as the Torrid Zone.

TROUT, a fish which belongs to the same family as the SALMON. There are many species, of which the salmon-trout, the rainbow trout and the European brown trout are probably the best-known.

The salmon-trout spends much of its life at sea, but, like the salmon, returns to the rivers to spawn. The rainbow trout is a brilliantly-spotted fish, numerous in the streams of the Rocky Mountain region, and in other parts of the world. The European brown trout is common in the rivers of Britain, and provides excellent sport for the fisherman.

TROY was an ancient city on the North-west tip of ASIA MINOR, with a legendary history made famous by HOMER in the great epic poem called the *Iliad*. Most of this is concerned with a long war between the Greeks and the people of

packhorse

sledge

raft

ox cart

sailing ship

early aeroplane

early train

engine-driven ship (about 1890)

early motor-car

Many inventions have helped the development of the means of transport.

Troy, who were known as Trojans. During this Troy was besieged for ten years.

TRUMPET, a brass instrument which has many different shapes. It is played by blowing into the mouthpiece. Sometimes it is fitted with valves like small pistons, which you can press up and down with your fingers to make different notes and so play a tune. See ORCHESTRA.

TUNDRA, regions of marshland round the Arctic and Antarctic. These tracts of land are frozen in the winter and become swampy areas in the summer, and there is little vegetation. MOSS and LICHENS, however, flourish, and provide food for the REINDEER and caribou.

TUNNEL. The longest tunnels in the world are those used by London's underground trains, which run on more than 100 miles of underground track. Many railway tunnels have been driven through mountains, one of the longest being the Simplon Tunnel in the ALPS, which measures nearly 12½ miles. Other tunnels have been constructed under rivers, the largest under-water tunnel in the world being the Kanmon Tunnel between Shimonseki and Kyushu, Japan.

TURBINE, STEAM. See STEAM ENGINE.

TURKEY, a country at the eastern end of the Mediterranean. Turkey still has a small area in Europe, round Istanbul. Turkey is separated from ASIA by the Bosporus and the DARDANELLES.

Istanbul, the largest city of Turkey, and an important seaport, lies on the rail route across Europe to Asia. Formerly named Constantinople, and the capital of the Turkish Empire until 1923, it was founded in A.D. 330 by the Roman Emperor Constantine.

Most of Turkey, however, lies in ASIA, on the plateau of Anatolia. Ankara is the capital and Izmir (Smyrna) is the chief port. Sheep, cattle and goats are reared on the high plateau of the interior, and tobacco, figs, olives and vines are grown in the coastal areas of the BLACK SEA and the MEDITERRANEAN.

TURTLE. There is no real difference between the turtle and the TORTOISE, and the names are often given different meanings in different parts of the world. In general, the name turtle is kept for those living in the sea. The largest turtle, the leathery turtle or luth, may be seven feet long and weigh nearly half a ton. The green turtle and the Hawksbill turtle are well-known because we get turtle-soup from the former and real tortoiseshell from the latter.

TWAIN, Mark, an American writer whose real name was Samuel Clemens. He was born in 1835. His book *Tom Sawyer* tells an amusing tale of young scamps living on the banks of the MISSOURI. *Huckleberry Finn* gives a picture of the rough life on the MISSISSIPPI when Mark Twain himself was a boy. He died in 1910.

TYNDALE, William, English preacher and Protestant martyr, lived during the reign of HENRY VIII. Most of his life was spent abroad in exile, and his translation of the New Testament, from the original Greek into English, was published in Germany in 1525. This translation was forbidden in England. His work, however, was used as a basis for the Authorized Version of the BIBLE which was prepared in the reign of JAMES I and is still used. Tyndale was put to death in 1536.

TYPHOON, a severe tropical storm, in which winds may blow at 100 miles per hour in a circle measuring about 150 miles in diameter. The centre of the circle, which is calm, is called the "eye of the storm."

TYROL, a province in western Austria, a country of central Europe. It is famous for its mountain scenery, and many tourists go there each year. Innsbruck is the capital. The Brenner Pass connects Innsbruck with Bolzano, in Italy, and that part of the Tyrol south of the Pass was handed over to Italy after the First World War. Agriculture and mining are the chief industries.

U

ULSTER. See NORTHERN IRELAND.

ULTRA-VIOLET LIGHT, rays of the same kind as light-rays, except that their wave-length is just too short to enable them to be seen by human eyes, though they may be visible to certain insects. They can be detected by means of a screen coated with a sensitive material which absorbs them and sends out visible light in exchange. Sunlight at the earth's surface contains a very small quantity of ultra-violet rays, and these are beneficial to us, causing vitamin D to form in our skins. Ultra-violet rays are harmful in large quantities. See also LIGHT.

ULYSSES, the Roman name for tne Greek hero Odysseus, who fought in the Trojan War, and had many adventures on his way home to Ithaca. His story is told by the Greek poet HOMER.

UNIFORMS. When bows and arrows, spears, or swords were the chief weapons of attack, soldiers used to wear protective clothing made of leather, and later, of metal. After gunpowder and other explosives and heavy cannon were brought into use, the type of warfare changed. Soldiers could not move about quickly in heavy ARMOUR, so instead they were given uniforms made of cloth.

Cromwell's soldiers of the seventeenth century still wore breastplates and helmets as well. Their coats were of red material,

Colour Sergeant of the Grenadier Guards.

and this colour was worn by British soldiers up to the time of the Boer War. Then it was thought that khaki would be less noticeable on the field of battle. More colourful uniforms are still worn by British soldiers when they are marching in parades and so on, and breastplates are still worn by the HOUSEHOLD CAVALRY when they ride along in processions. (See also GUARDS.)

In modern warfare a soldier wears a special uniform called battledress.

Colour Sergeant of the Black Watch.

UNION JACK, the British National FLAG. It is made up of three separate crosses, representing England, Scotland and Ireland. The red cross parallel to the sides of the flag, with a white background, is England's flag of Saint George. After James VI of Scotland became JAMES I of England in 1603 the flag of Saint Andrew of Scotland, a white diagonal cross with a blue background, was added. Ireland was united with Great Britain in 1801, and Saint Patrick's cross, a red diagonal cross with a white background was added.

UNION OF SOUTH AFRICA. See SOUTH AFRICA.

UNION OF SOVIET SOCIALIST REPUBLICS. See RUSSIA.

UNITED KINGDOM. England, Scotland and Wales together form Great Britain: with NORTHERN IRELAND these countries form the United Kingdom. See also BRITISH ISLES.

UNITED NATIONS ORGANIZA-TION, or UNO, has as its members 131 states which have promised to help keep the world at peace, to defend countries against foreign attackers, to help poor countries to better themselves by trading with them, to settle disputes between other countries when asked to do so, and many other such praiseworthy objects. Its headquarters are in New York.

UNITED STATES OF AMERICA. This country consists of fifty separate states joined together under one government. It is by far the richest and has the largest population of any country on the continent of AMERICA. It produces more coal, petroleum, electricity, iron, copper, lead, and zinc than any other country in the world. Crops of maize, tobacco, and cotton are also the greatest in the world. Most of the people are descended from Europeans. There are also millions of NEGROES, the descendants of former slaves. The capital is Washington, in the District of Columbia.

UNIVERSE, the whole of space, and everything that is in it, is called the universe. It is believed to contain at least 50 million million million stars, and to be so vast that a ray of light would take 10,000 million years to travel across it at 700 million miles per hour. The earth is a comparatively tiny body which revolves round a star which we call the sun. See SOLAR SYSTEM; SUN.

UNIVERSITY, a place of learning of the highest kind. When students who attend know a subject very well, they can get a very high distinction which is called a degree. They may obtain degrees in many different subjects.

URUGUAY is the smallest country in SOUTH AMERICA. It lies along the mouth of the River Plate and forms an extension of the pampas of the ARGENTINE. Cattle and sheep rearing are the main occupations on these grasslands, and the chief exports are wool and meat. Montevideo is the chief port, and the capital of the republic.

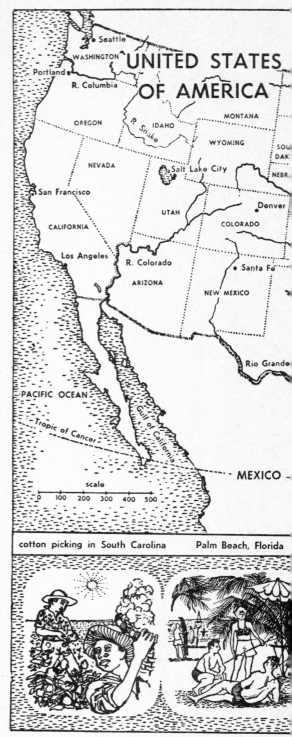

cotton picking in South Carolina   Palm Beach, Florida

Map of the United States of America,

294

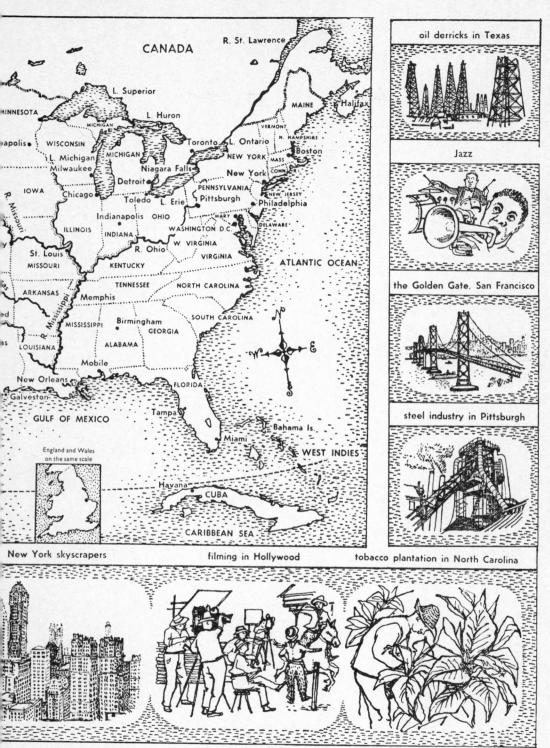

oil derricks in Texas

Jazz

the Golden Gate, San Francisco

steel industry in Pittsburgh

New York skyscrapers

filming in Hollywood

tobacco plantation in North Carolina

...howing the States, except for Alaska and Hawaii, and some things that are found there.

V

VACCINATION. This word comes from the LATIN *vacca*, a cow. At first, vaccination meant taking a fluid from a cow suffering from cow-pox and introducing it into the body of a human being, because it was found that a person thus treated would be unlikely to catch small-pox, a very dangerous and, at one time, common disease. The vaccine, as the prepared fluid is called, is inserted into a scratch in the skin. Vaccination has now come to be used for similar treatments for the prevention of other diseases.

VACUUM FLASK, a vessel, usually bottle-shaped, for keeping liquids warm or cool. The flask has double walls, the space between them being a vacuum, which means that even the air has been pumped out of it. This makes it very difficult for heat to get into, or escape from, the flask, and anything put into it stays at the same temperature for a very long time.

VALENCIA, a province of eastern Spain, and the name of the capital of the province. An historic city, it was once the capital of an independent kingdom established by the Moors, who came from Africa, and the Moors' way of building has been copied by later builders.

The climate is mild and dry, and oranges, lemons, grapes, dates and many other kinds of fruit are grown. There are many industries; exports include silk and cigars, leather goods, and wool and linen fabrics.

VALLEY. When rivers flow across the land they wash away a good deal of soil and presently make long, V-shaped channels for themselves. These are called valleys. In very cold countries glaciers, which are rivers of slowly moving ice, make similar but U-shaped valleys. Rivers which wind about sometimes make very wide valleys with flat bottoms called plains. Valleys with very steep sides are often called gorges.

VALVE, a tap or other device to control the flow of liquids or gases. In STEAM ENGINES valves admit the steam to the cylinders; in petrol engines they admit the petrol and air, and afterwards allow the exhaust gas to escape. The valve on top of a balloon lets some of the gas escape when the balloonist wishes to come down. A SAFETY-VALVE is one which opens by itself when the pressure against it becomes dangerously high.

VANDALS, a barbarian race who lived in Northern Germany, and invaded Europe about 170 A.D. They overran Spain and North Africa in the 5th century. In 455 they attacked and plundered Rome. As they did not understand or admire works of art they destroyed them, so that their name came to be used as a description of someone whose behaviour is rough and coarse. Between them, the barbarian races of the Goths, the Vandals and the Franks, destroyed the Roman Empire, and nearly ended Christianity, the religion of the Roman Empire.

VAN DYCK, Sir Anthony, famous Flemish painter, was born in Antwerp in 1599. He spent some years in Italy, where he painted scenes from the Bible as well as portraits of kings and queens. He came to England in 1632 as Court painter to CHARLES I, and he was made a knight in the same year. Some of his finest paintings are of King Charles and his Queen, and other famous people of the English Court. Van Dyck died in 1641.

VAN GOGH, Vincent, Dutch painter, was born in North Brabant in 1853. He was a schoolmaster for a little while, and then decided to become a minister in a church, and it was not until 1880 that he wanted to be a painter. In 1888 he went to live in Arles, in the south of France, and the French painter Paul Gauguin joined him there for a while. But Van Gogh began to suffer from mental strain and had to be looked after. He continued to paint, and the drawing on page 217 is based on a portrait of himself done by the artist after he had cut off his own ear in a fit of madness. He died in 1890.

VAPORIZATION is the changing of solids and liquids into gas. There are two chief kinds of vaporization, evaporation and sublimation. In evaporation a liquid changes into a gas, as when water becomes steam. In sublimation a solid becomes a gas without passing through the liquid state. All substances are vaporized at very high temperatures. The word vaporization is also used for the production of vapour by forcing a liquid through a fine spray, as happens in a carburettor.

VATICAN CITY, a tiny State inside the city of Rome, on the right bank of the river Tiber. It is ruled over by the POPE. It contains the Vatican Palace, and the famous cathedral of St. Peter's.

VEIN, one of the branching tubes carrying BLOOD back to the HEART. A vein is similar to an ARTERY but has thinner walls. It also has valves at intervals to prevent the blood flowing back the wrong way.

VELASQUEZ, Diego Rodriguez de Silva y, famous Spanish painter, was born at Seville in 1599. He became Court painter to Philip IV of Spain. He also painted scenes from the Bible and history, and landscapes. Velasquez died in 1660.

VENEZUELA, a country in SOUTH AMERICA, on the coast of the Caribbean Sea. It has rich oilfields, and is now second only to the United States in production. Some of the wells are sunk in the bed of Lake Maracaibo. The capital is Caracas, which has a wonderful mountain road and an electric railway to the port of La Guaira.

VENICE, a city and seaport of Italy. Venice is built on 118 islands in the Lagoon of Venice, a stretch of water at the head of the Adriatic Sea. Narrow canals separate the islands and take the place of streets. People travel by gondolas or motor-boats. The Grand Canal flows through the main part of the city, and it is spanned by the Rialto bridge, on which is built a double row of shops, with a wide footway between them. The bridge leads to the Rialto island, the chief centre of commerce.

Venice is famous for its many lovely buildings; amongst them are the Palace of the Doges, and the cathedral of St. Mark's, which attract many tourists.

VENTRILOQUISM. Human beings use their eyes to tell from which direction a sound is coming. A ventriloquist first speaks in his normal voice, using his lips, and the audience knows that it is he who is speaking. Then the ventriloquist speaks in a different voice while keeping his lips almost perfectly still. At the same time he makes the lips of a doll on his knee move and the audience has the impression that it is the doll which is speaking.

VENUS, the second planet in order of distance from the sun. It is the brightest of the planets, and the nearest to the earth, and is sometimes known as the Evening Star. Like the earth, it is surrounded by an atmosphere, which appears to have many clouds. See SOLAR SYSTEM.

VERB, a word that tells what is done or what exists. It is the doing-word in a sentence, for example: He *carried* the dog home. Poppies *grow* in that field.

VERNE, Jules, was a French novelist who wrote stories about the future and the wonderful inventions of science which were yet to come. His book *Twenty Thousand Leagues Under The Sea* foretold the submarine, and *A Journey Round The Moon* introduces the idea of travelling in space. His works were an early version of the exciting, scientific stories in boys' magazines of today. He lived from 1828 to 1905.

VERSAILLES is a town in Northern France, twelve miles from Paris, where Louis XIV built a great palace. In 1919, at the end of the First WORLD WAR, the Treaty of Versailles was signed here between the Allied Powers and Germany.

VERSE is a sequence of words having strongly marked rhythm and with rhymes occurring at regular intervals. It is written in lines which show clearly where the rhymes fall and which help you to express the swing of the rhythm when you read it aloud:

> *The friendly cow all red and white,*
> *I love with all my heart:*
> *She gives me cream with all her might,*
> *To eat with apple-tart.*
> R. L. Stevenson.

When verse is so good as to move you very much we call it POETRY.

VERTEBRA, any one of the small bones making up the spinal column or backbone. See SPINE.

VERTEBRATES are animals with backbones. This group includes fish, amphibians, reptiles, birds and mammals. See also INVERTEBRATES; SPINE.

VESUVIUS is a VOLCANO near the city of Naples in Italy. After being quiet for many centuries, Vesuvius erupted with a tremendous explosion in A.D. 79. One of the three towns destroyed by it was POMPEII. By digging away the LAVA, much has been discovered about life in the ancient town. Another violent eruption took place in 1631, and killed thousands of people. Since that year, the volcano has never been altogether quiet.

VETERINARY SCIENCE is the study and treatment of the diseases of animals, especially domestic and farm animals. It includes also first-aid to animals.

VIBRATION is a shaking or trembling, the same movement being repeated over and over again at equal intervals of time.

All waves are examples of vibrations, and sounds consist of vibrations in the air. A clock PENDULUM performs a very slow vibration. See SOUND; WAVE.

VICTORIA, Lake, is the largest lake in Africa, being more than three times the size of Wales. On its northern shore is the chief source of the River Nile. The equator runs across the lake at its northern end.

VICTORIA, Queen, of Great Britain and Ireland, was born in 1819. She succeeded WILLIAM IV in 1837, when she was eighteen, and reigned until 1901. Lord Melbourne was Prime Minister when Victoria came to the throne, and other great statesmen of her reign include Peel, Palmerston, Gladstone and Disraeli (who proclaimed her Empress of India in 1876). In 1840 the Queen married Prince ALBERT of Saxe-Coburg-Gotha, and they had five daughters and four sons. The eldest became EDWARD VII.

VICTORIA CROSS, an award for the greatest acts of bravery, founded by Queen VICTORIA in 1856 after the CRIMEAN WAR. On the cross are inscribed the words: "For Valour."

VICTORIA FALLS, a great waterfall on the River ZAMBESI, in AFRICA. As the river approaches the falls, it becomes about a mile in width. Then it tumbles into an almost vertical chasm, over three hundred feet deep. Spray from the falling water rises high above the falls. Before LIVINGSTONE discovered the Victoria Falls, natives had told him about the "Sounding Smoke," the "sound" being the roar of the falls, and the "smoke" the cloud of spray.

VIENNA is the capital and largest city of Austria, standing on the right bank of the River Danube. Before the First World War it was the capital of the great Austro-Hungarian Empire. After that war, when the empire was broken up, Vienna lost much of its importance.

VIKINGS were the Danes and Northmen, the "Sons of the Fiords," who sailed in their narrow ships to conquer and

Michael Ross

*The Vikings travelled **across** the seas in ships like this.*

plunder, a thousand years ago. Some reached Iceland, Greenland and even America, as yet unknown to Europeans. Others settled in France, in Italy, in Russia and in the British Isles. Alfred the Great defeated them but could not drive them away. For a time one of them, Canute, ruled England. The Normans, who conquered England in 1066, were descended from Vikings who had settled in France. The word Norman means North-man.

VINE. Any plant that requires support for its stem and climbs either by tendrils or by twining its stem around another plant is a CLIMBING PLANT. The vine is a climbing plant which bears grapes, but the name is now used also for the hop, and for other plants which creep or trail over the ground.

VINEGAR is an acid liquid which has many domestic uses besides its value in the preparation of food. It was first obtained from fermented wine, but is made also from apple juice, malt liquor, or wood alcohol. Sometimes flavouring is added, as in tarragon vinegar, and garlic vinegar.

VIOLA. This is the name of the alto VIOLIN. It is slightly larger than the ordinary violin, has four strings, and is played with a bow. Its notes sound lower that those of the violin. See ORCHESTRA.

VIOLIN. This is a wooden box of a special shape. It has four strings stretched over a small wooden bridge and fastened to four tuning pegs at the end of a long neck of wood. When a bow is drawn across a tight string a musical sound is made. Then if the player puts his finger on one end of the string, making the free part shorter, he can make a higher note. On the four strings he can play many notes. See ORCHESTRA.

VIOLONCELLO. See CELLO.

VIPER, a poisonous snake having its fangs attached to a movable bone so that they lie flat against the roof of the mouth when not in use. The many species of viper in the world include the ADDER, the Gaboon viper of Africa (which is five feet long and has fangs an inch long), and the RATTLESNAKE.

VITAMINS are chemical substances necessary in very small amounts for the healthy working of our bodies. Without vitamin A you would find it more difficult

Vole with its young.

to see in a dim light; without vitamin B you would suffer a disease called beri-beri; without vitamin C you would suffer from scurvy; without vitamin D you would get rickets. There are several other vitamins, but we are likely to get all we require if we eat ordinary meals sensibly cooked.

VOICE. The sound of the voice is produced by air being driven between the vocal chords. These are two membranes or thin lips stretched across the wind-pipe. When the air forces them apart their own muscles immediately bring them together again. This action is repeated so that the air comes through the mouth in a series of puffs. When these come rapidly enough they make a sound-vibration. See SOUND; WAVE.

VOLCANO, a mountain made of the cinders and ashes of rocks which have been thrown up from a deep hole leading into the interior of the earth. The rocks come up in a hot, molten state, and are often thrown high into the air. When cool, some of them form pumice-stone. The opening to the hole, which is at the top of the volcano, is called the crater. See VESUVIUS.

VOLE, a small gnawing animal, not unlike the rat and mouse. In Britain there are the water-vole, bank-vole, and many varieties of field-vole. They all live in holes in the ground.

VOLGA, the longest river in Europe, flowing through European RUSSIA into the Caspian Sea. Its length is 2,325 miles, and the Russians call it "Mother of all the rivers." Although it is frozen for three to·

five months in the year, the river is important chiefly as a trade route. Canals connect it with the Baltic Sea, White Sea, and Black Sea. It also has important fisheries.

VOLT, the measure of force of an electric current. It does not tell you how much electricity there is, but only how strongly it is forcing its way along.

VOLUME. This word really means *size*; not length merely, nor width, nor thickness, but all three multiplied together. For example, the volume of an oblong block of ice 11 in. long, 10 in. wide, and 10 in. thick is $11 \times 10 \times 10$ cubic inches, which is 1,100 cubic inches.

VULTURE, a large BIRD OF PREY related to the EAGLE and HAWK. Vultures have their heads and necks almost bare of feathers, and they have blunt claws. They feed on carrion (that is, the bodies of creatures which they have not killed themselves but have found already dead). The true vultures belong to Europe, Asia and Africa. The American vultures belong to a different family, and include the giant condor of the Andes, with a wing-span of nine feet. They are powerful in flight, and have very keen sight.

Giant condor of South America.

WAGNER, Richard, was a famous German musician. He composed many operas, some based on German myths and legends. He lived from 1813 to 1883. See also OPERA.

WALES, that part of Britain to the west of England, is largely mountainous. Many country people still speak Welsh. There is sheep farming in the mountains, and dairy-farming in the valleys. South Wales is the most important region. Here much coal is mined in the narrow valleys and there are great steelworks. Cardiff is the capital and chief seaport. Wales is famous for its scenery.

WALLACE, Alfred Russel, was a British naturalist who lived from 1823 to 1913. He formed a theory of evolution like DARWIN'S, but without knowing of Darwin's work, and showed how the animals in the islands round Australia are different from those in nearby islands belonging to Asia. The line dividing the islands is called "Wallace's Line."

WALLACE, Sir William, was the leader of the Scots who fought to prevent EDWARD I of England from conquering Scotland. He was born in 1274. After some early victories he was defeated at Falkirk, in 1298, but escaped to the hills. Six years later he was betrayed, sent to London, and executed in 1305, but his work was brought to a successful completion by Robert BRUCE.

WALRUS, a heavily-built creature of the Arctic Ocean, a relative of the SEAL. Walruses live in herds, feeding on shellfish. Both males and females have tusks, often nearly two feet long.

WATER is the most plentiful liquid on the earth's surface, and a most necessary substance to all forms of life. Water is practically colourless, tasteless and odourless, and has the power to dissolve many solids (such as salt). Water freezes to form ice, and boils to form steam. It consists

The walrus has long tusks.

chemically of the gases hydrogen and oxygen combined together in the proportion two parts hydrogen to one part oxygen. This is written as H_2O.

WATER-BIRDS. Many birds are thoroughly at home in the water. Some, like the DUCK and GOOSE, have webbed feet. The mallard and the teal are two handsome members of the same family; they are strong in flight as well as being excellent swimmers. The diver, otherwise known as the loon, is a magnificent swimmer, but is helpless on land. So is the little grebe, or dabchick. Unlike the diver, its feet are not fully webbed, but its fleshy toes serve as paddles.

WATER-COLOUR. See PAINTING.

WATERLOO. After nearly twenty years of war, NAPOLEON had been conquered, in 1814, and sent as a prisoner to

James Watt realized the power of steam

the island of Elba, when Europe heard with alarm that he had escaped! Forming a new French army, Napoleon once more challenged Europe. In 1815 he was met near Waterloo in Belgium by a British force under the Duke of WELLINGTON and a Prussian force under Blücher. Napoleon was defeated and sent to St. Helena, an island "a thousand miles from anywhere."

WATT, James, who lived from 1736 to 1819, was born at Greenock, near Glasgow. Until his time the only STEAM-ENGINES were the suction engines used to pump the water out of coal-mines. They were very wasteful, for at each stroke of the engine

Wellington was known as the "Iron Duke".

the cylinder had to be filled with hot steam, and then cooled with cold water so as to condense the steam. The cylinder then became a partial vacuum and sucked in the piston. But James Watt saw that it would be much better to let the steam blow the piston out by its own force, and so invented the high-pressure, hot-cylinder engine of the kind still used today. He is said to have first realized this power of steam while watching the lid of a kettle bob up and down as the water boiled.

WAVE. There are two kinds of waves: transverse or up-and-down waves, like those on the sea; and longitudinal or to-and-fro waves, like those which pass along the length of a goods train when the end wagon is struck by the shunting-engine. Light waves and radio waves are of the transverse kind, but SOUND waves are longitudinal.

WEIGHTS AND MEASURES. For many purposes it is necessary to know the exact quantity of a substance or material, and this can be given either as its weight or its size. In Britain, weights are reckoned in pounds or parts of a pound, a pound being the weight of a certain lump of platinum kept by the Board of Trade. Sizes may be given in either lengths or volumes, lengths being based on the yard, which is the exact distance between two gold studs let into a platinum bar kept by the Department of Trade. See VOLUME

WELDING is a method of joining metals by melting their surfaces together. To do this, very high temperatures are required, and these are usually obtained by burning the gas acetylene in a jet of pure oxygen. The temperature of the oxy-acetylene flame is about 3,000 degrees Centigrade. This will easily melt steel.

WELLINGTON, Arthur Wellesley, 1st Duke of, was a famous soldier and statesman. He lived from 1769 to 1852. After distinguished military service in India, he returned to Europe and fought in the great struggle against NAPOLEON. His victories in Portugal and Spain, for

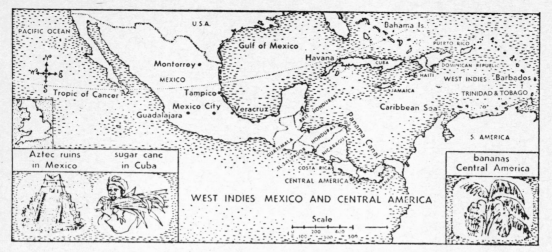

Sugar, spices and tropical fruits come from the West Indies.

which he was made first a Viscount then Duke of Wellington, played a great part in Napoleon's defeat. For the final victory at WATERLOO, Wellington was again responsible. Afterwards the "Iron Duke" played an important part in British politics and was Prime Minister from 1828 to 1830.

WEST INDIES, a large group of islands lying between the great land masses of North and South America. Nearly all of them are within the TROPICS. Violent hurricanes sometimes sweep over them and cause great destruction. Sugar cane is grown on almost all the islands, and arrowroot, nutmeg and mace are also important products.

WESTMINSTER ABBEY is a great ABBEY church built on the site of an ancient Saxon church. It was founded by Edward the Confessor. Since WILLIAM I most English monarchs have been crowned there. Much of it was rebuilt by HENRY III, and other parts have been added from time to time. Many of Britain's greatest men, soldiers, statesmen, poets, musicians, kings and princes, are buried in Westminster Abbey.

WHALE, a fish-shaped MAMMAL living in the sea. Its front limbs are flippers, and the tail bears horizontal flukes for swimming. The body is without hair except in the young, which have a few bristles on the snout, and it is protected by a thick layer of fat called blubber. Whales are of two kinds, whalebone whales and toothed whales. They are the largest of all animals,

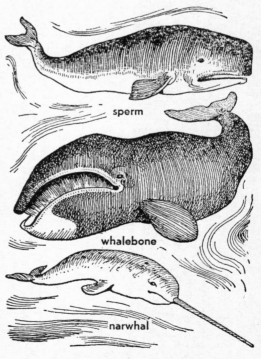

Three kinds of whale.

303

William the Conqueror defeated King Harold at the Battle of Hastings.

living or extinct, the blue whale of the Antarctic measuring up to 100 feet in length and weighing up to 120 tons.

WHALING. Whales are caught chiefly for their fat or blubber, but also for whalebone and for the wax-like substance ambergris used in making perfumes. Whale-liver-oil is also of value, and various meat preparations are made from the flesh. Whales are caught by means of harpoons, fired from special ships called whale-catchers. A modern harpoon is a heavy steel dart attached to a long cable. When it strikes the whale it explodes. The dead whale is towed back to the whale-factory ship, which is so shaped that the body of the whale can be hauled aboard and dealt with on the spot. Whaling is carried on chiefly in the ANTARCTIC Ocean from December to April. See also GREENLAND.

WHEAT is the name of a cultivated grass. When the seed is harvested we call it GRAIN. From grain we get the flour from which bread is made. See also GRASSES.

WHIRLWIND, a circular eddy in the atmosphere. When the air blows in a small circle it forms a sort of tube which is very nearly empty of air, just as when the water runs out of the bath in a circle it forms a tube or funnel of water. In the air, the empty tube sucks up dust and large objects and so becomes visible as a whirlwind. Over the sea it forms a waterspout.

WIGHT, ISLE OF, an island off the south coast of England, separated from the mainland by the waters of the Solent and Spithead. It has several holiday resorts, Cowes being a centre for yachting.

WILLIAM THE CONQUEROR. In 1066 William, Duke of Normandy, landed in England with a small army, and, after defeating Harold, the English King, near Hastings, marched on London. There he was crowned King. During the next six years there were many English rebellions, which he crushed with great cruelty, but after defeating HEREWARD THE WAKE he had no more trouble. The Normans built castles, and the English worked on the lands of their new overlords. By his strong rule William I helped to make England a united nation. He died in 1087.

WILLIAM II, nicknamed "Rufus" because of his red hair and ruddy complexion, was King of England from 1087 to 1100. He was a cruel and unjust ruler, and was killed by an arrow while hunting deer in the New Forest. "Rufus' Stone" stands near the spot where he fell.

WILLIAM III. William III was a grandson of CHARLES I, and his wife Mary II was a daughter of JAMES II. They were called to the throne of Great Britain and Ireland in 1688 as joint King and Queen. William III spent his life fighting the French in the Netherlands, and, though William rarely gained a victory, the French King, Louis XIV, was glad to accept terms of peace in the end. Mary II died in 1694, and William III in 1702.

WILLIAM IV. King of Great Britain and Ireland from 1830 to 1837, William IV was known as the "Sailor Prince" because of his interest in the navy. He was succeeded by Queen Victoria.

WIND is air moving over the surface of the earth. Winds are caused by the air becoming lighter in some places than in others. The light air rises, and the surrounding air blows in to take its place. This often happens when the air over a warm country becomes heated, for hot air is lighter than cold. See also LAND AND SEA BREEZES.

WIND INSTRUMENTS. These are MUSICAL INSTRUMENTS which produce a note when the player blows into them. Examples are trumpets, trombones, horns (made of brass), and flutes, bassoons, oboes and clarinets (made of wood). See also ORCHESTRA.

WINE is made from fermented grape-juice. The vineyards of France are famous for the fine quality of the grapes grown there, and the wine made from them. Wine is given the name of that part of the country in which the grapes are grown, so Burgundy is the red wine and white wine from that district; Bordeaux is another important wine-producing district. (In England the red wine of Bordeaux is often called claret.) A lighter wine is produced in Champagne. We get hock from the valley of the Rhine, and Moselle from the valley of the Moselle. These are suitable wines to accompany a good lunch or dinner. From Spain we get sherry which is exported from Jerez-de-la-Frontera. There are different kinds, from a fine, light sherry to drink before dinner to a heavier, sweeter quality, such as old brown, to have afterwards. Another after-dinner wine is port from Portugal. Other countries which produce wine for export include Australia and South Africa.

WITCHCRAFT. The ancient belief that supernatural powers can be invoked in the pursuit of personal gain. Traditionally witches were accused of trafficking with demons, that is, evil spirits, and were prosecuted by the Church. Many innocent people suffered terrible fates because they were accused of practising witchcraft. A few people still claim to be witches, but nobody takes them seriously any more.

WOLF, the largest member of the DOG family. Wolves are found throughout

The wolf is related to the domestic dog.

northern Asia and North America, but have become scarce in Europe, where they live in a few wild and mountainous districts only. Wolves often hunt in pairs, running down their prey. In winter they may gather in packs.

WOLSEY, Thomas, was Henry VIII's

305

chief adviser in the first part of his reign. He was born in 1471. He was made a Cardinal, a very high office in the Roman Catholic Church, by the Pope. When Henry quarrelled with the Pope, Wolsey fell from favour, and died at Leicester on his way to the Tower in 1530.

WOOD-CUTTING. To make a wood-cut the surface of a block of wood is carved away so that bits of the wood are left sticking up to form a picture. When the block of wood is inked over the ink sticks to the pieces forming a picture; when a piece of paper is pressed against the inked wood-cut the outlines of the picture will be put on to the paper. See also ENGRAVING; ETCHING.

WOOD-ENGRAVING, similar to a WOOD-CUT but the picture formed has white lines as well as black. See also ENGRAVING; ETCHING.

WOODPECKER, a woodland bird with short legs and strong claws for climbing. The tail feathers are spiked to assist the climb, and the beak is strong and chisel-shaped for digging into wood. The tongue is sticky for picking up insects.

WORDSWORTH, William, was born in the Lake District in Cumberland in 1770 and lived there most of his life. He died in 1850. He wrote poetry about birds and flowers, trees, lakes and mountains. Two of his most charming poems are *The Daffodils* and *To The Cuckoo*.

WORLD WAR, First, began on 4 August, 1914, and fighting continued until the Armistice of 11 November, 1918. It was fought by the forces of Germany, Austria, Hungary, Bulgaria and Turkey on the one side against the allied armies of Britain, France, Belgium, Russia, Japan and Serbia on the other. Italy joined the Allies in 1915, and America joined in 1917.

Most of the fighting was on land. Men fired from trenches dug in the ground. Battles raged in Belgium, France, Italy, the Balkans, Mesopotamia, East Africa and China. Some famous battles were fought at Mons, on the River Marne, at Loos, on the River Somme, at Ypres, at Verdun, at Passchendaele, and at Cambrai. Naval battles were fought off the Falkland Islands and off Jutland. Zeppelins dropped bombs on London and other cities. Millions of lives were lost, and millions of men were disabled. The war ended with the Treaty of Versailles in 1919.

WORLD WAR, Second, began on 1 September, 1939, with the German invasion of Poland. Great Britain and France had said they would go to the aid of Poland if that country were attacked. So began a second great war in which most countries of the world were to become involved, and in which fighting spread all over Europe, into Asia, North Africa, and the islands of the Pacific.

This time Italy was an ally of Germany, the Italian dictator, Mussolini, declaring war on Britain and France in 1940. In 1941 Germany declared war on Russia, and the Japanese attacked the American naval base at Pearl Harbour. Germany and Italy declared war against the United States, because Japan was helping them by attacking British lands in the Far East. After intensive battles on land, at sea, and in the air, Germany was invaded and surrendered in May, 1945, and Japan surrendered in September, 1945, after atom bombs had been dropped on two of her cities.

WORM. A large number of INVERTEBRATES having long, limbless bodies are included under the heading of "worms." The ringed worms include the earthworms, marine bristle worms and the leeches. Earthworms are important for the part they play in mixing and airing the soil.

WREN, Christopher. The Great Fire of 1666 destroyed a large part of London. Wren (born in 1632) was asked by the King, CHARLES II, to rebuild the city. He designed SAINT PAUL'S CATHEDRAL and fifty-two churches. He also designed some very fine buildings in Oxford and Cambridge. When he died in 1723 he was buried in St. Paul's Cathedral.

X

XANTHIPPE, the wife of SOCRATES; she had three sons, but none of them achieved fame. According to XENOPHON she had a quick temper, but there appears to be no real reason why she has become known as a nagging, shrewish woman.

XAVIER, St. Francis, was born in 1506 in Xavier in the north of Spain. While he was a student in Paris he became friendly with Ignatius of Loyola and helped him to form the Society of Jesus. In 1541 he went to India as a missionary and was very successful. In 1552 he set out on a journey to China, but he was taken ill with fever and died on the voyage.

XENOPHON, born at Athens about 430, lived until 354 B.C. He was a pupil and friend of SOCRATES, and was greatly influenced by him. Xenophon joined the army of Cyrus the Younger, who fought against his brother Artaxerxes II, King of Persia, in 401 B.C. Later, he fought with the Spartans against the soldiers of Thebes and Athens, and was banished from his native city. He lived for a while in Elis, near Olympia, and later settled in Corinth.

Xenophon is famous as a historian; his work includes the *Anabasis*, an account of the expedition of Cyrus; and the *Hellenica*, dealing with Greek history from 411 to 362 B.C. The *Memorabilia* is an account of the life and philosophy of Socrates.

XERXES I, son of Darius I, came to the throne of Persia and Media in 485 B.C. He continued his father's campaign of warfare against the Greeks. Setting out from Sardis in 480, he defeated the Greek fleet, and reached Thermopylae. Here a great battle was fought by Leonidas and his three hundred Spartan warriors, but the Persians broke through and plundered Athens. To the south, the Persian fleet assembled off the island of Salamis ready to strike the final blow. The Battle of Salamis was one of the most important events in Greek history, because it saved Greece from being under the orders of the Persians. The Persian fleet was destroyed and Xerxes was forced to return to Sardis. He left an army in Greece, but it was beaten in the Battle of Plataea in 479 B.C.

Xerxes was killed in 465 B.C. His son, Artaxerxes I, succeeded him and reigned from 465 to 425 B.C.

X-RAYS are rays of the same kind as LIGHT rays, only of much shorter wavelength. They are shorter even than ULTRA-VIOLET LIGHT, and cannot be seen with the human eye. They are produced when a cathode-ray strikes a positive metal plate, and have the power to pass through many substances which do not allow light to shine through them. Thus, they will pass through your shoe-leather and the flesh and blood of your foot, but not through the bones. They can be changed into visible light by means of a sensitive screen, and this enables you to see how your shoes fit. Doctors use X-rays to examine broken bones and other injuries inside people's bodies, and to find bullets, pins, or other such objects which have somehow got inside people.

XYLOPHONE, a MUSICAL INSTRUMENT which belongs to the group of PERCUSSION INSTRUMENTS. It is made of a series of wooden bars of different length, arranged in rows. Each bar sounds a different note when struck by small hammers. The modern xylophone is mounted on a framework, below which are suspended metal cylinders; they are tuned to each bar to help to make the notes ring out.

Y

YACHT, a small sailing ship used for pleasure-cruising or racing. Larger, engine-driven pleasure-ships are called steam-yachts or motor-yachts.

Racing yacht.

YAK, a type of strong, hardy wild cattle found on the wind-swept plateaux of TIBET and Central Asia. Standing five and a half feet high, the yak has long horns and a coat of very long, blackish-brown hair. The domesticated yak provides milk, meat, hides and hair (for tents), and is used for TRANSPORT also.

YANGTZE-KIANG, the longest and most important river in CHINA, is over 3,000 miles long; it rises in Tibet and drains and waters much of China. The river has many tributaries. It flows into the East China Sea near Shanghai. The Yangtze Gorges between Chungking and Ichang are famous for their beauty. Important commercial towns on the banks of the river include Chinkiang, Nanking, Hankow and Chungking.

YARMOUTH, Great, fishing port of Norfolk, England. It is the centre of the English herring-fishing industry. Herring are caught in drift-nets (see FISH); some are sold fresh, but many are preserved. Yarmouth is famous for "bloaters"; these are herring which are salted and partly dried over wood fires. Kippers are herring which have been split open, gutted, salted and well smoked.

YEAR, the length of time taken by the earth to travel once round the sun. This period is almost exactly $365\frac{1}{4}$ days, but for convenience we reckon the year to be 365 days in length. To make the reckoning more accurate, we add an extra day every fourth year. We call this fourth year a leap year. See also TIME.

YEATS, William Butler, Irish poet and playwright, was born in Dublin in 1865. He was one of the founders of the Irish Literary Theatre, which was established in Dublin in 1899 and later became famous as the Abbey Theatre. The principal figure of the nineteenth-century revival of Irish literature, Yeats became one of the first Senators of the Irish Free State in 1922. He died in 1939.

YELLOW-HAMMER, a bird belonging to the Bunting family. It is commonly found in hedges in Britain. The yellow-hammer has a yellow breast and brown plumage mottled with yellow on its head and back. It builds its nest close to the ground; the eggs are purplish-white, with dark brown-purple spots. Its call is said to sound like the phrase, "A little bit of bread and no cheese."

YELLOW SEA, an inlet of the Pacific Ocean, between Korea and north-east China. It flows into the East China Sea to the south.

YELLOWSTONE NATIONAL PARK, a public park in the United States of America, set aside by the Government as a home for wild birds and animals. It is a tract of forest land; most of it is in the State of Wyoming, part of it is in Montana and part in Idaho. There are many hot springs and GEYSERS, and the Grand Canyon of the Yellowstone is a magnificent deep gorge cut by a river and world-famous for the beautiful spectacle it presents. It forms a valley about 2,000 feet wide and over 1,000 feet deep.

YEOMEN OF THE GUARD, the Sovereign's oldest bodyguard, consisting of about a hundred old soldiers who rank as members of the Royal Household. They wear Tudor uniform, and are sometimes called "Beefeaters." At the opening of Parliament they search the vaults to see if another Guy Fawkes is hiding there!

YUGOSLAVIA, a country of south-east Europe, on the Adriatic Sea. It was formed in 1918 from Serbia and Montenegro and parts of the Austro-Hungarian Empire. It was renamed Yugoslavia and ruled by a king from 1929. In 1941 the country was invaded by the Germans, but after the war, in 1945, it was proclaimed a republic, under the dictatorship of Marshal Josip Broz, now known as Marshal Tito.

Belgrade is the capital, and other important towns are Zagreb, Sarajevo, and Skopje. The River Danube is the chief river. Most of the interior is mountainous, the Dinaric Alps of western Yugoslavia rising to a height of over 8,000 feet. There are lowlands in the north, and farming is the chief occupation.

YUKON is a territory in the extreme North-west of CANADA. Gold is mined on the Klondike river, and fur-bearing animals are trapped. Dawson City, near where the Yukon and the Klondike rivers join, became the capital in 1898, when the gold-rush was at its height.

Gold was discovered in the Yukon in 1896 and men rushed to make their fortunes.

Z

ZAGREB, the second largest city in YUGOSLAVIA, and an important centre of commerce and industry. Chemicals, textiles and machinery are made here. It is the capital of Croatia, a northern region of Yugoslavia.

ZAMBIA, name given to the former British territory of Northern Rhodesia when the Rhodesian Federation (see p. 245) was dissolved and Northern Rhodesia became in October 1964 an independent republic within the British Commonwealth.

ZAMBESI, a river of Central Africa, and the fourth longest on the continent. It rises in a marsh, and for part of its course forms the boundary between Zambia and Rhodesia. In spite of its rapids and waterfalls, the Africans use much of the river for travelling by canoe. The great Kariba Dam spans the Zambesi, turning part of it into a huge lake.

ZANZIBAR, a former British protectorate in East Africa, formed by the islands of Zanzibar and Pemba. It is also the name of the capital. Zanzibar and Tanganyika form an independent republic, Tanzania, within the British Commonwealth. Cloves and copra are exported.

ZEBRA. The zebras of Africa are close relatives of the horse and ass, from which they differ mainly in their striped coats. Once found in vast herds on the open plains, they are now much reduced in numbers. Some varieties, like the quagga, are now extinct, having been killed for their meat.

ZEBU, the Indian ox, is found also in East Africa and Madagascar. It differs from European cattle in having a great hump on the shoulders. The zebu is used to pull carts and ploughs.

ZEPPELIN, Count Ferdinand von, the German designer of a type of AIRSHIP to which he gave his name. He lived from 1838 to 1917. Zeppelins were used in air-raids in the First WORLD WAR.

ZINC, a soft, bluish-white metal much used for coating iron wire and corrugated iron sheets to prevent their rusting. Zinc is also used in the manufacture of dry batteries, and is an ingredient in brass (an ALLOY of copper and zinc). In the metal industry it is called spelter.

ZITHER, a stringed MUSICAL INSTRUMENT, very popular in the TYROL. It consists of a wooden box with strings stretched over the surface. The strings are plucked both with the fingers and with a plectrum attached to the thumb of the right hand.

ZODIAC, a belt of the sky, extending on each side of the earth's path round the sun. The paths of the sun, moon and planets lie within the Zodiac, which is divided into twelve equal parts, or signs, named after groups of stars called Constellations.

ZOOLOGY is the study of animals, and comes from the Greek *zoon* (pronounced *zo-on*) meaning animals. From the Greek word we also get our word, zoo. Zoology is pronounced: zo-*ol*-o-jee.

ZUIDER ZEE, now the Ijsselmeer, an inlet of the North Sea, on the north coast of the NETHERLANDS. It is over 80 miles long and over 40 miles wide. The Dutch are keeping out the water by building dykes, and draining and using the land for farming.

ZULU, a native tribe of South Africa. They are famous for their fighting qualities. Their territory became part of the province of Natal in 1897.

"What You Should Know" Supplements

The three sections which follow will enable you to brush up your Arithmetic and English, and to test your Intelligence.

ARITHMETIC

We are always counting. When we see people, we count their 2 arms, 2 legs, 2 eyes, 2 ears. We notice at once when one of them is missing.

We should never stop counting. When we see things in 2's, or 3's, or 4's, or 5's, or 6's, we should take notice. We can wonder at the little cells of the honey-bee, each with its 6 equal sides. How many sides has a 50p piece?

We can draw a triangle, with 3 sides and 3 angles; "tri" means three, so a triangle is a shape with 3 angles. A square has 4 sides and 4 angles. A pentagon has 5 sides and 5 angles; the name means five-sided. Hexagon means six-sided; the cells of the honey-bee are hexagons. Octagon means eight-sided; an octagon has 8 sides and 8 angles.

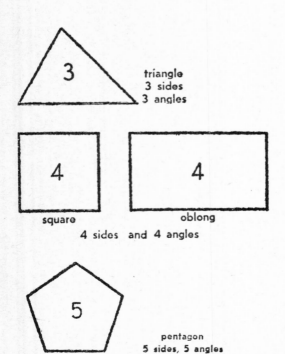

triangle
3 sides
3 angles

square
4 sides and 4 angles

oblong

pentagon
5 sides, 5 angles

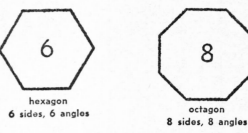

hexagon
6 sides, 6 angles

octagon
8 sides, 8 angles

WHAT NUMBERS REALLY MEAN

When we write a number we should be quite clear that the figure on the right stands for so many ones, or units. The figure before it stands for so many 10's, the figure before that for so many 100's, and the figure before that for so many 1,000's.

3,654 is really 3,000 + 600 + 50 + 4. 3,654 is a short way of writing that!

I. ADDING

We start with a pack of cards. Playing cards are pleasanter to handle, but squares of paper or cardboard, with numbers written on them, do very well. We want ten cards with the numbers 1 to 10. This is what we do:

1. We go through the cards and add up the numbers on them. The total should be 55. We shuffle the cards, or mix the papers, so as to have the numbers in a different order. Once more we add up the numbers and again the total should be 55. However we arrange the numbers, the total should be the same. The order of adding makes no difference to the total.

2. We put the cards in pairs, each pair to total 11. The pairs are:

10 + 1, 9 + 2, 8 + 3, 7 + 4, 6 + 5. That is five pairs, each 11. And five 11's is, of course, 55.

3. Let us set out three cards with the numbers in order, or in *sequence* as we say. Let us take: 7, 8 and 9.

312

We add them; the total is 24. And that, we notice, is three times the middle number. We try other sequences of three numbers 6–7–8, 5–6–7, and so on. The total is always three times the middle number.

The reason is not hard to find. If we take one from 9, and add it to 7, we change: 7–8–9 into 8–8–8.

And so with other sequences of three numbers.

4. If we take a sequence of seven numbers, say 2–3–4–5–6–7–8, the total is 35, and that is seven times the middle number, which is 5.

HOW TO CHECK YOUR ADDITION

How can we know if a sum is right? We can be almost certain that it is, if we work carefully, and check the answer in some way.

In adding, we start at the top, and add down. Then, as a check we start at the bottom, and add up.

Here is another kind of check which has points of interest:

267	267	628	1,071
385	385	39	1,230
419	419	563	2,301
628	1,071	1,230	
39			
563			
2,301			

At the left the six numbers are added. Then, the numbers are added in threes, and these two totals are added. The two answers agree.

If we want practice in adding, that is a useful way of setting ourselves exercises.

It provides good training and a check on our accuracy.

Test Yourself—1

1. (a) Write six consecutive numbers, 35, 36, 37, 38, 39, 40.
Add them in pairs, the first and last pair, second and fifth, third and fourth.

Try other sequences.
(b) Then try eight consecutive numbers.
2. (a) Write six numbers, one under another. Add them.
(b) Add them in 3's, and add the two totals.
(c) Add them in pairs, and add the three totals.
(d) Add five of the numbers, then add on the sixth.
3. Add all the numbers between 1 and 100 that end in 7.

(*Answers on page* 336)

II. SUBTRACTING

1. We make a copy of this rather odd dial. We put a finger on any number, say

3. Then we go round the dial like the hands of a clock, adding as we go:
3, 4, 11, 20, 22, 28, 36, 41, 45.
We start with another number, and go round again. The total is always 45.

2. Now we unwind. We start with 45, subtract 4, then 5, then 8, and so on until we reach 3. This is:
45, 41, 36, 28, 22, 20, 11, 4, 3, 0.
Those are the numbers we got before, but the other way round this time, and with the final 0 added as we take 3 from 3.

3. Let us start with 7, and go round twice:
7, 16, 18, 24, 32, 37, 41, 44, 45, 52, 61, 63, 69, 77, 82, 86, 89, 90.
Now we unwind twice, and so return to 0.

313

4. Let us look at these three sums:

(a)		(b)		(c)	
	326		326		139
−	187	−	139	+	187
	139		187		326

(a) is ordinary subtraction:

$$326 - 187 = 139$$

In (b) we subtract the remainder from 326, and so we get the first number we subtracted: $326 - 139 = 187$.

In (c) we add the two remainders, and so get back to the number we started with: $139 + 187 = 326$.

If we write A for the biggest number, B for the number we subtract, and C for the remainder:

$$A - B = C$$
$$A - C = B$$
$$B + C = A.$$

We can fill in any numbers we like for A and B, so long as A is bigger than B.

Suppose we make A = 750, and B = 289. Then:

$$C = A - B = 750 - 289 = 461.$$

Then $A - C = 750 - 461 = 289 = B$ and $B + C = 289 + 461 = 750 = A.$

That is a wonderful check on the accuracy of subtraction sums. When we have done the sum we add the two lower lines. The total should be the same as the top line.

Test Yourself—2

1. (a) Find $100 - 67$.
   (b) Subtract the answer from 100.
   (c) Add the two answers.
       Try other examples.
2. (a) Write 350. Subtract 67, then 67 from the answer, and so on. What is the last remainder?
   (b) Add the remainders in pairs, taking 350 as the first: first and last, second and fifth, and so on. What do you find?
   (c) How many 67's can be taken from 350? How many are left?
3. Write down four numbers, and add them. Subtract the first number from the total, then the second from your answer, then the third, then the fourth. What is left?
   Try other groups of numbers.
4. How many 76's in 600? Go on subtracting till you find out. What is left at the end?

(*Answers on page 336*)

III. MULTIPLYING

We simply have to know the tables, especially from the 2's to the 9's. These are the tables we need for ordinary multiplication.

1. Here is a neat way of setting out all these tables. We draw a 4½-inch square, divide the sides into half-inches, and join across.

In the top row of small squares we write the numbers 1 to 9. In the next row we write the even numbers, 2, 4, 6, up to 18. In the next line we write 3, and then continually add 3's, and write 3, 6, 9, up to 27, and so we proceed with 4's, 5's, 6's, 7's, 8's, 9's. The adjoining table shows what we should get: If we want to make sure of seven 8's we put a finger on the row beginning with 7; we run along this row to the column headed 8, and there we find 56, which is 7×8.

1	2	3	4	5	6	7	8	9
2	4	6	8	10	12	14	16	18
3	6	9	12	15	18	21	24	27
4	8	12	16	20	24	28	32	36
5	10	15	20	25	30	35	40	45
6	12	18	24	30	36	42	48	54
7	14	21	28	35	42	49	56	63
8	16	24	32	40	48	56	64	72
9	18	27	36	45	54	63	72	81

BEGINNING OUR SUMS

Let us look at these three multiplication sums:

```
   57        57        57
    8         6        48
  ───       ───     ─────
  456       342     2,280
    6         8       456
─────     ─────     ─────
2,736     2,736     2,736
```

In the first we multiply 57 × 8, and then the answer by 6. Altogether we have multiplied by six 8's, and that is 48.

In the second we multiply by 6 and then by 8. Again we have multiplied by 48.

In the last we multiply by 48 in the usual way. Whenever we have a multiplier that will *factorize* (that is, break down into smaller numbers which when multiplied together give the original large number) we have several ways of doing the sum. We can use them as checks on one another. Thus 36 = 12 × 3 = 9 × 4 = 6 × 6. We can multiply 12 by 3, or 9 by 4, or 6 by 6. We should always get the same result.

Now let us look at these two sums:

```
   47        28
   28        47
  ───     ─────
  940     1,120
  376       196
─────     ─────
1,316     1,316
```

It makes no difference to the product (or answer) whether we multiply 47 by 28 or 28 by 47:

$$47 × 28 = 28 × 47.$$

That is true of all multiplications.

Test Yourself—3

1. (a) Find the squares of numbers from 0 to 20. 0 × 0 = 0, 1 × 1 = 1, 2 × 2 = 4, 3 × 3 = 9, and so on, up to 20 × 20 = 400.
   (b) Take each square number from the one following it. There is something odd about the answers. What is it?
2. (a) Write 56 four times, one number under another. Add up.
   (b) Find 56 × 4.
   (c) Write the same number five times. Add up, and also multiply by 5.

3. (a) Write the table of 3's in a line 3, 6, 9, 12, up to 36.
   (b) Below write the table of 4's: 4, 8, 12, 16, up to 48.
   (c) Add the pairs of numbers. Which table do the answers give? Try other pairs of tables.
4. (a) Find 86 × 24.
   (b) Find 24 × 86.
   Try other pairs of numbers.
5. (a) 47 × 2. Multiply the answer by 12.
   (b) 47 × 3. Multiply the answer by 8.
   (c) 47 × 4. Multiply the answer by 6.
   (d) 47 × 24.
6. (a) 14 × 15 × 16.
   (b) 15 × 16 × 14.
   (c) 16 × 14 × 15.
7. Find 9,471 × 13.
8. Find 3,276 × 37.

(*Answers on page 336*)

IV. DIVIDING

1. When we divide, we sometimes split a number, or a quantity, into equal parts: halves, thirds, quarters (or fourths), fifths, sixths, and so on.

To get halves (2 equal parts) divide by 2,
   thirds (3 equal parts) divide by 3,
   fourths (4 equal parts) divide by 4,
   fifths (5 equal parts) divide by 5.
   sixths (6 equal parts) divide by 6.
And so we can go on.

2. Sometimes we want to find something rather different. We want to know how many 2's, how many 3's, how many 4's, and so on.

How many 2's? Divide by 2.
How many 3's? Divide by 3.
How many 4's? Divide by 4.
And so we can go on again.

3.　　　　　　　7)112
　　　　　　　　　16

We have found 112 ÷ 7. The answer is 16. We can read that answer in two ways:
   (a) A seventh of 112 is 16.
   (b) 112 contains 16 sevens (or 7 sixteens).

315

It is a useful practice to imitate division sums with a handful of beans, or counters, or large beads. That should help us to realize what the answer means.

We count out 24 beads. We put them out: 1 to the left, 1 to the right, and so on. We have divided the 24 beads into halves, and we find 12 in each half.

Once more we put out the beads, in 2's this time. And we find twelve 2's.

The division is the same for each method.

$$2)\overline{24 \text{ beads}}$$
$$12 \text{ beads}$$

We read the answer: half of 24 is 12, or 24 contains 12 twos.

We go on to arrange the beads in thirds; 8 in each third. Then we arrange them in 3's, and find 8 threes. We arrange them in quarters, and in 4's; in sixths and in 6's; in eighths and in 8's; in twelfths and in 12's.

We have chosen 24 beads to divide, because 24 divides exactly by so many numbers. If we had chosen 25 beads to divide, there would always be 1 over when we divide by 2, 3, 4, 6, 8, or 12.

What do we do about the remainder? It all depends on what kinds of things we are dividing. And also on what kind of answer we want.

REMAINDERS

1. When we are dividing beads all we can say is that there is 1 over, or 1 remainder. (Smashing the odd bead in two would merely destroy it.) The fact is that we cannot have an exact half of 25 beads. Nor can we divide 25 beads exactly into 2's.

2. If we were dividing 25 pounds of butter into halves, we could cut the last pound in two and put half of it with each 12 pounds. But if we are arranging 25 pounds of butter in parcels of 2 pounds, we should still be left with the odd pound over.

The two sums are as follows:

$$2)\overline{25 \text{ lb.}}$$
$$12\tfrac{1}{2} \text{ lb. (half of 25 lb.)}$$
$$2)\overline{25 \text{ lb.}}$$
$$12 \text{ parcels of 2 lb.} + 1 \text{ lb. over}$$

3. Lengths are not quite so awkward.

$$5)\overline{7 \text{ ft.}} \qquad\qquad 5)\overline{7 \text{ ft.}}$$
$$1 \text{ ft. 4 in.} + 4 \text{ in.R} \qquad 1 \text{ ft. } 4\tfrac{4}{5} \text{ in.}$$

The first of these sums would give us the answer to: What is a fifth of 7 ft. in whole inches? The second answer gives us a fifth of 7 ft. exactly.

ANOTHER WAY OF SEEING IT

1. There is another way of looking at division. We say it is the "inverse" of multiplication. That word means that it undoes what multiplication does.

$$12 \times 2 = 24 \text{ and } 24 \div 2 = 12$$
$$18 \times 3 = 54 \text{ and } 54 \div 3 = 18$$
$$14 \times 5 = 70 \text{ and } 70 \div 5 = 14$$

When we multiply and divide by the same number, we should always get back to the number we started with.

2. Let us look at a very awkward example, which is really very easy.

$$76\tfrac{19}{47} \times 13\tfrac{5}{19} \div 13\tfrac{5}{19}$$

If we were to work that out in parts, first multiplying by $13\tfrac{5}{19}$, and then dividing the answer by $13\tfrac{5}{19}$, it would indeed be awkward. *But*, we multiply and divide by the same number $(13\tfrac{5}{19})$, and so we get back to the number we started with. Without any working at all, we can say at once the answer is $76\tfrac{19}{47}$.

LONG DIVISION

Long division is not too easy, but it is not too difficult. If we have trouble with it we can give ourselves easy practice.

Let us try $5362 \div 20$:

$$
\begin{array}{r}
268 \\
20)\overline{5362} \\
40 \\
\overline{136} \\
120 \\
\overline{162} \\
160 \\
\overline{2\text{R.}}
\end{array}
$$

1. Division by 20 is no harder than division by 2. We say: 20's in 53. The same as 2's in 5. That is 2, so we write 2 over the 3. (Certainly not over the 5, because the number is 53, not 5.)

We subtract two 20's or 40. We bring down the 6. 20's in 136? The same as 2's in 13; that is 6. We write 6 in the answer, and subtract six 20's, or 120. Then 20's in 162? The same as 2's in 16; that is 8.

The answer is 268 + 2R. A twentieth part of 5,362 is 268, and 2 left over. There are 268 twenties in 5,362, and again there are 2 over.

2. Let us examine this long division sum carefully. It contains the little difficulty that sometimes makes long division seem hard.

$$\begin{array}{r} 306 \\ 29)\overline{8900} \\ 87 \\ \overline{200} \\ 174 \\ \overline{26}R. \end{array}$$

We begin with 29's in 89? 29 is nearly 30, so we say 3's in 8? That is 2 and 2 over. We have to be careful. It might be 3. And when we try 3, we find that it actually is 3. We subtract three 29's, which is 87. Then 29's in 20? The answer is 0, so 0 must go in the answer before we bring down the next figure. 29's in 200? 3's in 20? The answer is 6 and 2 over. To be on the safe side we try 7, but $29 \times 7 = 203$, and that is too many. So we put 6 in the answer, and subtract six 29's, which is 174.

3. We can read the answer to the sum given above: 8,900 contains 306 twenty-nines, with 26 over.

We can make the 26 over into another 29 by adding 3. So:
$$8,903 = 29 \times 307.$$
If we subtract 26 we get rid of the remainder.
$$8,900 - 26 = 8,874. \text{ So:}$$
$$8,874 = 29 \times 306.$$
We can always do that with the remainders in division sums.

Test Yourself—4

1. (a) $873 \div 9$.
   (b) What is a ninth of 873?
   (c) How many 9's in 873?
2. (a) $536 \div 8$.
   (b) What does the answer mean?
3. (a) Write 80. Go on subtracting 12's till you can subtract no more.
   (b) Find $80 \div 12$.
4. (a) 69×7.
   (b) Divide the answer by 7. Try other examples.
5. (a) $500 \div 8$.
   (b) Multiply the answer by 8. Add the remainder. Try other examples.
6. (a) $1,000 \div 7$.
   (b) Which is the nearest number below 1,000 that divides exactly by 7?
   (c) Which is the nearest number above 1,000 that divides exactly by 7?
7. (a) Write a number, say, 758. Divide by 20.
   (b) Multiply the answer by 20. Add in the remainder. Try other examples. Divide by 30, 40, 50, 60, 70, 80, 90.
8. (a) $360 \div 21$.
   (b) Multiply the answer by 21. Add on the remainder. Try also division by 31, 41, 51, 61, 71, 81, 91.

(Answers on page 337)

V. MEASURING LENGTHS

1. We measure short lengths in inches and eighths of an inch. The actual eighths are:

$\frac{1}{8}$, $\frac{2}{8}$ $(= \frac{1}{4})$, $\frac{3}{8}$, $\frac{4}{8}$ $(= \frac{1}{2})$, $\frac{5}{8}$, $\frac{6}{8}$ $(= \frac{3}{4})$, $\frac{7}{8}$.

A line $1\frac{3}{8}$ in. long is a little short of $1\frac{1}{2}$ inches. We might also say that $1\frac{3}{8}$ in. is a little more than $1\frac{1}{4}$ in. It is indeed half-way between $1\frac{1}{4}$ in. and $1\frac{1}{2}$ in.

Very often we measure in inches and tenths of an inch.

The heights of people and the lengths of rooms are measured in feet and inches.

The heights of mountains, and depths of the sea are measured in feet.

Ribbons and dress materials are measured in yards.

The distances between towns are given in miles.

2. A mile is the biggest of our ordinary units of length. We use it for such large measurements as the distance round the earth—nearly 25,000 miles, the distance of the moon—nearly a quarter million miles, and that is 10 times the distance round the earth. The sun is 93 million miles away.

EXAMPLES OF MEASUREMENT PROBLEMS

The practical problems we have in length are usually very simple:

1. How many lengths of 5 inches can we cut from 7 yards of ribbon?

We work in inches.

7 yards = 36 × 7 in. = 252 in.

The question now is: how many 5's in 252.

$$5)\overline{252}$$
$$\overline{50 + 2 \text{ over}}$$

The 2 over is of course 2 inches, because the 252 is inches. We can have 50 lengths of 5 inches, and there should be a small remnant 2 inches long. That is, if we have made all our 50 measurements with great care.

2. Sailors have their own measures of length. A fathom is 6 feet; this measure is used chiefly in giving the depths of the sea when soundings are taken.

"Full fathoms five thy father lies."
He was 30 feet down.

3. The height of Mount Everest used to be given as 29,002 feet. It is now said to be 29,028 feet. What is the latest height in miles?

We have to divide by 5,280:

```
              5 miles
    5,280)29,028 ft.
          26,400
          ───────
           2,628 ft.
```

The answer is 5 miles 2,628 feet. We may notice that
½ mile = 880 yards = 2,640 feet.

So we can say that Everest is practically 5½ miles high.

Test Yourself—5

1. (a) Change 7½ yards to inches.
   (b) How many 8-inch lengths can be cut from 7½ yards?
   (c) What length is left over?
2. How many yards in the following?:
   (a) ½ mile
   (b) ¼ mile
   (c) ¾ mile
   (d) ⅛ mile (or one furlong).
3. (a) From 1,760 subtract 340, again 340, and so on.
   (b) A race course is 340 yards long. How many laps to the mile?
   (c) How far in front of the starting post should the finishing post be?
4. The height of Mont Blanc is 15,781 feet. How much is that less than 3 miles?

(Answers on page 337)

VI. WEIGHT

1. At the grocer's or confectioner's we usually buy in pounds, halves, and quarters. And sometimes in ounces, halves, and quarters.

1 lb. = 16 oz. ½ lb. = 8 oz. ¼ lb. = 4 oz.
¾ lb. = 12 oz.

2. Large quantities of coal, cement, and other bulky materials are sold in tons and hundredweights (cwt.).

1 ton = 20 cwt.
1 cwt. = 112 lb.
so 1 ton = 2,240 lb.

A quarter is ¼ cwt. = 28 lb. or 2 stones.

SOME TYPICAL PROBLEMS

1. A manufacturer might want to know how many 1-oz. packets he can make up from 1 cwt.

```
    1 cwt. = 112 lb.
                  16
             ───────
               1,120
                 672
             ───────
               1,792 oz.
```

He could not be sure of getting exactly that number, because weighings are never quite exact. But he should get nearly that number.

2. A merchant might have a wagon of coal with a net weight of 8 tons 17 cwt. (The *net weight* is the weight of actual coal, without counting the weight of the wagon.) How many cwt. sacks does the coal fill?

```
Tons    cwt.
  8      17
 20
───
160
 17
───
177 cwt.
```

He should be able to fill 177 sacks.

3. Cartons are found to weigh 1 lb. $3\frac{1}{2}$ oz. (That is the *gross weight*—both carton and the material it contains.) What is the weight of a dozen cartons? And of a gross (12 dozen, or 144)?

```
 lb.   oz.
  1    3½
  12
 ───
 14    10   weight of 12
  12
 ───
175     8   weight of 144
```

The answer to the second question might be written as 1 cwt. 63 lb. 8 oz.

Test Yourself—6

1. How many pounds in the following? (*a*) A stone? (*b*) A quarter? (*c*) A hundredweight? (*d*) Half a hundredweight? (*e*) A ton?

2. (*a*) How many ounce packets could be made up out of $\frac{1}{2}$ cwt.? (*b*) How many 3-ounce packets?

3. A cubic foot of water weighs a thousand ounces. What is the weight in pounds?

(*Answers on page 337*)

VII. TIME

1. The only occasions when we want to add or subtract times are probably those when we want to find how long a train takes on a journey. The obvious way is to subtract the earlier time from the later. Thus:

Leaves 11.35 hours. Arrives 14.15 hours.

```
hours   minutes
 14      15
− 11     35
────
  2      40
```

The train takes 2 hours 40 minutes. In subtracting, take 35 from 60 ($= 25$) and then add the 15 ($= 40$).

2. It is useful to know the number of days in each month. So we remember:

"30 *days have September,*
April, June, and November,
All the rest have 31,
Excepting February alone,
Which has 28 *days clear*
And 29 *days each leap year.*"

3. A year is the time the earth takes to go round the sun. That is:

about $365\frac{1}{4}$ days.

The odd quarter, or near-quarter, is a great nuisance. We get over the awkwardness by having 365 days in a year, and saving up the odd quarters till they make a full day. Every four years we have to fit an extra day into the calendar. This extra day is added to February's 28, which thus becomes 29.

Years with the extra day are called leap years. To make it easy to remember, or find out, which are leap years it was arranged to have them in years which divide exactly by 4. We need not bother about hundreds in the date because all hundreds (and thousands) divide by 4.

1954: $54 \div 4 = 13 + 2R$. Not a leap year.
1956: $56 \div 4 = 14$ Leap year.
1958: $58 \div 4 = 14 + 2R$. Not a leap year.
1960: $60 \div 4 = 15$ Leap year.

1976, 1980, 1984, and so on, will be leap years.

Test Yourself—7

1. How many minutes in $3\frac{1}{2}$ hours?
2. How many hours in a week?
3. How many seconds in an hour?
4. How many seconds in a day?

5. Change 365 days to weeks.

6. Which of these years will be leap years? 1980, 1986, 1990, 1992, 1996, 1998.

7. How many days in each 3 months of the year: Jan.–Mar., April–June, July–Sept., Oct.–Dec.?

(Answers on page 337)

VIII. FACTORS

1. $6 = 2 \times 3$.

So 6 divides exactly by 2 and by 3. 2 and 3 are said to be factors of 6.

$18 \div 2 = 9$; $18 \div 3 = 6$; $18 \div 6 = 3$; $18 \div 9 = 2$.

18 divides exactly by 2, 3, 6, 9, so 2, 3, 6, 9 are all factors of 18.

24 divides exactly by 2, 3, 4, 6, 8, and 12. So all these numbers are factors of 24.

2. It is interesting to see that the factors can be arranged in pairs which multiply to give the number we began with.

$$2 \times 12 = 24$$
$$3 \times 8 = 24$$
$$4 \times 6 = 24$$

Let us look at the factors of 36.

$36 = 2 \times 18 = 3 \times 12 = 4 \times 9 = 6 \times 6$.

The factors are 2, 3, 4, 6, 9, 12, 18.

3. All even numbers have 2 for a factor. That is, indeed, what even numbers are.

Every third number has 3 for a factor. 3, 6, 9, 12, 15, 18, 21, . . .

Every fourth number has 4 for a factor. 4, 8, 12, 16, 20, 24, 28, . . .

Every fifth number has 5 for a factor. 5, 10, 15, 20, 25, 30, 35, . . .

And so on.

4. 2 and 3 do not divide exactly by any number except themselves. We cannot factorize them. We call them *prime numbers*. Other prime numbers are: 5, 7, 11, 13, 17, 19, 23.

Those are a few of the small prime numbers. There are many more.

Something to Do

We want a sheet of paper and a pencil. We write the numbers 1 to 10 in a line. We space them evenly. In the next line we write 11 to 20. And so on, till we reach 100.

This is what we get:

1	2	3	4	5	6	7	8	9	10
11	12	13	14	15	16	17	18	19	20
21	22	23	24	25	26	27	28	29	30
31	32	33	34	35	36	37	38	39	40
41	42	43	44	45	46	47	48	49	50
51	52	53	54	55	56	57	58	59	60
61	62	63	64	65	66	67	68	69	70
71	72	73	74	75	76	77	78	79	80
81	82	83	84	85	86	87	88	89	90
91	92	93	94	95	96	97	98	99	100

Now we come to the most interesting part. We can now find all the prime numbers up to 100. We cross off the numbers with factors, and the prime numbers are left.

We cross off all the even numbers, except 2, because these have the factor 2. That removes almost half the numbers.

We cross off every third number, except 3, because these have the factor 3. Half of them are already crossed off with the 2's. We need not bother about 4. $4 = 2 \times 2$, so all the 4's are crossed off with the 2's.

We cross off every fifth number, except 5. That is easy because they are all in one column. (The 10's are already crossed off.)

$6 = 2 \times 3$, *so the 6's went with the 2's.*

We cross off every seventh number, except 7.

$8 = 2 \times 2 \times 2$, $9 = 3 \times 3$, $10 = 2 \times 5$. *So the 8's, 9's, and 10's are already crossed off.*

The remaining numbers are ALL PRIME NUMBERS. They are: 2, 3, 5, 7, 11, 13, 17, 19, 23, 29, 31, 37, 41, 43, 47, 53, 59, 61, 67, 71, 73, 79, 83, 89, 97.

If you would like to know why we need not bother about any factor above 10, here is the reason. $100 = 10 \times 10$. If any number below 100 has a factor greater than 10 it must also have a factor less than 10. (If both factors were greater than 10, the product would be greater than 100.)

FINDING "COMMON FACTORS"

1. We sometimes want to find factors that are common to two or more numbers.

2, for example, is a common factor of all even numbers. 5 is a common factor of all numbers that end in 5 or 0.

2. Look at 24 and 36:

24 has the factors, 2, 3, 4, 6, 8, 12.

36 has the factors, 2, 3, 4, 6, 9, 12, 18.

So the common factors are 2, 3, 4, 6, and 12. 8, 9, and 18 are not common factors. The highest of the common factors is 12.

3. Look at 35, 70, 105.

35 has the factors 5 and 7.

70 has the factors 2, 5, 7, and 35.

105 has the factors, 3, 5, 7, and 35.

The common factors are 5 and 7.

We sometimes treat the number itself as if it were a factor. 35 is then a common factor of 35, 70, and 105. It divides exactly into all three.

4. We sometimes want to find a number into which several numbers will divide. The easy way is to multiply them:

3 and 5 both divide into $3 \times 5 = 15$.

7 and 9 both divide into $7 \times 9 = 63$.

5. (a) 2, 4, 8 all divide into $2 \times 4 \times 8 = 64$. That is true enough. But if we want a smaller number we may see that 2, 4, 8 all divide into 8. (b) 3, 6, 9 all divide into $3 \times 6 \times 9 = 162$. But we may notice that they also divide into 18. (c) 5 and 15 both divide into 15, which is much less than $5 \times 15 = 75$. (d) Let us start with 2, and go on doubling:

2, 4, 8, 16, 32, 64, 128, . . .

Whenever we stop, all the numbers divide exactly into the last one. $64 \div 2 = 32$; $64 \div 4 = 16$; $64 \div 8 = 8$; $64 \div 16 = 4$; $64 \div 32 = 2$.

(e) We get the same kind of result when we start with 3, and go on multiplying by 3:

3, 9, 27, 81, 243, 729, . . .

All those numbers divide exactly into 729.

Test Yourself—8

1. Which numbers are factors of 18?
2. Which numbers are factors of 30?
3. Which numbers are factors of 40? Arrange them in pairs which multiply to give 40.

4. How can we tell at a glance which numbers have 2 for a factor? Which have 5 for a factor?
5. Which numbers below 30 are prime?
6. Find the smallest number into which each of the following groups divide:

(a) 2, 4, 8, and 16.

(b) 6, 9, 18, and 36.

(c) 5 and 9.

(d) 2, 3, 6, and 9.

(e) 5, 10, 15, and 20.

(*Answers on page 337*)

IX. FRACTIONS

We cut an apple evenly in two. If the parts are equal then each is $\frac{1}{2}$, and the two $\frac{1}{2}$'s make the whole apple.

We sometimes talk about "the bigger half," but that is a little jest. If the two parts are really halves, they must be the same size.

Here are some shapes divided into halves:

When we cut a thing into 3 equal parts the parts are thirds:

For quarters, or fourths, we want 4 equal parts. It is easy to divide a square into quarters in various ways:

For fifths we want 5 equal parts. And so on. The number at the bottom of a fraction tells us how many equal parts. An eighth is $\frac{1}{8}$; 8 equal parts.

321

DENOMINATORS AND NUMERATORS

We call this number at the bottom of a fraction the "denominator." To "nominate" is to name, and "de" means down. So the denominator puts down the name of the fraction:

$\frac{1}{9}$; denominator 9; so $\frac{1}{9}$ is a ninth.

We can hardly help noticing that 3 thirds, 4 fourths, 5 fifths, 6 sixths, and so on, each make up the whole thing we divide. That is no more than to say that if we cut a thing into 12 equal parts, there are 12 of them. Of course.

Now let us cut a cake into thirds, and pull out one third.

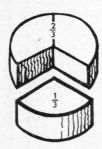

We now have $\frac{1}{3}$ and $\frac{2}{3}$. The 1 and 2 are called the "numerators," or numberers. They tell us how many thirds we take.

Here are shapes cut into fifths (denominator 5).

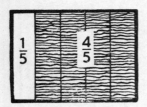 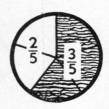

In the first we have shown $\frac{1}{5}$ and $\frac{4}{5}$. In the second we have shown $\frac{2}{5}$ and $\frac{3}{5}$. The numerators tell us how many fifths, what number of fifths.

We have seen fractions of shapes, let us look at fractions of numbers. Let us put out 12 counters, or beads, or beans. First we will divide them into thirds; 4 in each third.

We put 2 thirds together = 8.

$\frac{1}{3}$ of 12 = 4; $\frac{2}{3}$ of 12 = 8.

What is $\frac{2}{3}$ of 48? We begin by finding $\frac{1}{3}$; divide by 3.

48 ÷ 3 = 16; $\frac{1}{3}$ of 48 is 16.

So $\frac{2}{3}$ of 48 is 16 × 2 = 32.

What is $\frac{3}{5}$ of 60? We begin by finding $\frac{1}{5}$; divide by 5.

60 ÷ 5 = 12; $\frac{1}{5}$ of 60 is 12.

$\frac{3}{5}$ of 60 = 12 × 3 = 36.

$\frac{2}{5}$ of 60 = 12 × 2 = 24.

A STEP MORE DIFFICULT

Here is a pretty little trap for people who leap before they look:

$\frac{4}{9}$ of a number is 900. What is the whole number?

Ninths? Divide by 9. 900 ÷ 9 = 100. Easy!

Yes, but $\frac{4}{9}$ of 100 is not anything like 900. That won't do at all.

Suppose we had written, "4 ninths of a number is 900. What is 9 ninths?"

4 ninths is 900.

1 ninth is 900 ÷ 4 = 225.

9 ninths is 225 × 9 = 2,025.

We can check that answer by finding $\frac{4}{9}$ of 2,025.

$\frac{1}{9}$ of 2,025 = 2,025 ÷ 9 = 225.

$\frac{4}{9}$ of 2,025 = 225 × 4 = 900, as we were told.

BACK TO SHAPES

1. We draw a square. And really do draw a square. We divide it into halves, and then into quarters as shown in the following drawing:

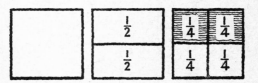

We see at once that $\frac{1}{2} = \frac{2}{4}$. We double the number of parts (the denominator), and at the same time we double the number we take (the numerator). So $\frac{1}{2}$ is the same fraction as $\frac{2}{4}$.

2. Now let us divide the square, with upright lines, into 3, 4, and 5 parts.

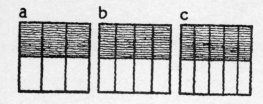

a   b   c

In *a* we see that $\frac{1}{2} = \frac{3}{6}$.

In *b* we see that $\frac{1}{2} = \frac{4}{8}$.

In *c* we see that $\frac{1}{2} = \frac{5}{10}$.

In each example we have multiplied top and bottom (numerator and denominator) by the same number, 3, or 4, or 5.

And, of course, we might have other numbers besides 3, 4, and 5. We might have 6, 7, 8, or any number we like. We can multiply the numerator and denominator of $\frac{1}{2}$ by any number we like, and we should still have a fraction equal to $\frac{1}{2}$.

3. Let's look carefully at these squares.

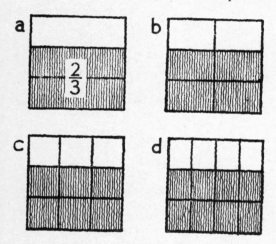

In *a* we have $\frac{2}{3}$ of the square shown.

In *b* we see that $\frac{2}{3} = \frac{4}{6}$.

In *c* we see that $\frac{2}{3} = \frac{6}{9}$.

In *d* we see that $\frac{2}{3} = \frac{8}{12}$.

We multiply both numerator and denominator by the same number, 2, 3, or 4, and we do not change the fraction.

Once more, it is easy to see that we might have other numbers, 5, 6, 7, or any number we like.

4. And we might have other fractions:

$\frac{3}{5} = \frac{6}{10} = \frac{9}{15} = \frac{12}{20}$

$\frac{5}{8} = \frac{10}{16} = \frac{15}{24} = \frac{20}{32}$ and so on.

5. Can we divide? Of course we can:

$\frac{4}{5} = \frac{12}{15}$ so $\frac{12}{15} = \frac{4}{5}$.

That is all there is to it. Division is the same as multiplication turned round the other way.

$\frac{1}{2} = \frac{7}{14}$ so $\frac{7}{14} = \frac{1}{2}$ and so on.

When we divide numerator and denominator by the same number we do not change the fraction:

$\frac{16}{48}$ is the same fraction as $\frac{8}{24}$ or $\frac{4}{12}$ or $\frac{2}{6}$ or $\frac{1}{3}$.

ADDITION OF FRACTIONS

1. We sometimes want to add fractions. We might want to add a third and a fifth. The trouble about adding them is that they are not the same kind of fraction. If they were both thirds or both fifths it would be easy.

$\frac{1}{5} + \frac{3}{5} = \frac{4}{5}$, with no trouble at all.

But thirds and fifths! And yet the answer is easy enough: we turn them into the same kind of fraction. $3 \times 5 = 15$, so we can turn both fractions into fifteenths:

$\frac{1}{3} = \frac{5}{15}$ and $\frac{1}{5} = \frac{3}{15}$.

$\frac{1}{3} + \frac{1}{5} = \frac{5}{15} + \frac{3}{15} = \frac{8}{15}$.

2. Let us look at another example:

$\frac{1}{2} + \frac{1}{4} + \frac{1}{8}$.

2, 4, and 8 all divide into 8, so we can turn each of the fractions into eighths:

$\frac{1}{2} = \frac{4}{8}, \frac{1}{4} = \frac{2}{8}$.

$\frac{1}{2} + \frac{1}{4} + \frac{1}{8} = \frac{4}{8} + \frac{2}{8} + \frac{1}{8} = \frac{7}{8}$.

3. $\frac{2}{3} + \frac{1}{4}$ is not much harder. We turn both into twelfths.

$\frac{2}{3} = \frac{8}{12}, \frac{1}{4} = \frac{3}{12}$.

$\frac{2}{3} + \frac{1}{4} = \frac{8}{12} + \frac{3}{12} = \frac{11}{12}$.

4. When we add whole numbers as well as fractions, we should remember that the whole numbers are more important than the fractions, even though they are much less bother. We add the whole numbers first.

$3\frac{1}{4} + 2\frac{1}{3} = 5\frac{3}{12} + \frac{4}{12} = 5\frac{7}{12}$.

IMPROPER FRACTIONS AND MIXED NUMBERS

1. What do we make of $\frac{8}{5}$? It is evidently more than 1, because 1 is only $\frac{5}{5}$. There is

evidently 1 whole, and $\frac{3}{5}$ as well.
$$\frac{8}{5} = 1\frac{3}{5}.$$

If we found $\frac{8}{5}$ for an answer it might very well be a correct answer, but $1\frac{3}{5}$ would usually be a better answer.

$\frac{17}{5} = 3\frac{2}{5}$ (5's in 17: 3 + 2R. 2 ÷ 5 = $\frac{2}{5}$).

$\frac{28}{3} = 9\frac{1}{3}$ (3's in 28: 9 + 1R. 1 ÷ 3 = $\frac{1}{3}$).

2. Now let us look at:
$$2\frac{3}{5} + 3\frac{1}{2} + \frac{7}{10}$$
(5, 2, 10, all divide into 10)
$$= 5\frac{6}{10} + \frac{5}{10} + \frac{7}{10}$$
$$= 5\frac{18}{10}$$
$$= 6\frac{8}{10}, \text{ or } 6\frac{4}{5}.$$

$5\frac{18}{10}$ is correct, but $6\frac{8}{10}$ is better, and $6\frac{4}{5}$ is better still.

3. Fractions in which the numerator is more than the denominator are sometimes called "improper" fractions. We can always change them into whole numbers and proper fractions. A whole number with a fraction is often called a "mixed number."

$\frac{20}{7} = 2\frac{6}{7}$. $\frac{20}{7}$ is an improper fraction. $2\frac{6}{7}$ is a mixed number.

4. A word in your ear! We can always read the bar in a fraction as if it meant "divided by."

$\frac{4}{5}$ is 4 ÷ 5, and 4 ÷ 5 is $\frac{4}{5}$.

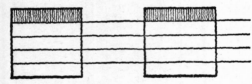

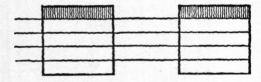

SUBTRACTION OF FRACTIONS

1. Subtraction is very much the same as addition. We want the fractions to be the same kind of fraction:
$$\frac{7}{8} - \frac{2}{3}.$$
8 and 3 both divide into 24.
$$\frac{1}{8} = \frac{3}{24}, \frac{7}{8} = \frac{21}{24};$$
$$\frac{1}{3} = \frac{8}{24}, \frac{2}{3} = \frac{16}{24}.$$
$$\frac{7}{8} - \frac{2}{3} = \frac{21}{24} - \frac{16}{24} = \frac{5}{24}.$$

2. There is sometimes a little awkwardness:

$3\frac{1}{3} - 1\frac{5}{8} = 2\frac{8}{24} - \frac{15}{24}$ (we subtract the whole number first).

We cannot take $\frac{15}{24}$ from $\frac{8}{24}$. But, we can change one of the 2 whole ones into $\frac{1}{24}$'s ($2 = 1\frac{24}{24}$).

So $2\frac{8}{24}$ becomes $1\frac{24+8}{24} = 1\frac{32}{24}$.

And now:
$$3\frac{1}{3} - 1\frac{5}{8} = 2\frac{8}{24} - \frac{15}{24}$$
$$= 1\frac{32}{24} - \frac{15}{24}$$
$$= 1\frac{17}{24}.$$

3. Let us look at another example:
$$7\frac{1}{4} - 3\frac{2}{5} = 4\frac{5}{20} - \frac{8}{20}$$
$$= 3\frac{25}{20} - \frac{8}{20}$$
$$= 3\frac{17}{20}.$$

MULTIPLYING FRACTIONS

1. Multiplying fractions is much easier than adding them.

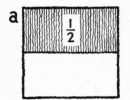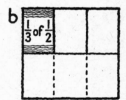

(a) shows $\frac{1}{2}$ of the square shaded.

(b) shows $\frac{1}{3}$ of $\frac{1}{2}$, and it is easy to see that that is $\frac{1}{6}$.

So $\frac{1}{2} \times \frac{1}{3} = \frac{1}{6}$.

For the denominator of the product we multiply the two denominators.

And we could have any other numbers in place of 2 and 3. Thus:

$\frac{1}{4} \times \frac{1}{3} = \frac{1}{12}$; $\frac{1}{5} \times \frac{1}{6} = \frac{1}{30}$, and so on.

2. (a) $\frac{1}{4} \times \frac{2}{3}$ is, of course, just twice $\frac{1}{4} \times \frac{1}{3}$.
$$\frac{1}{4} \times \frac{2}{3} = \frac{2}{12}, \text{ or } \frac{1}{6}.$$

(b) $\frac{3}{4} \times \frac{2}{3}$ is 3 times $\frac{1}{4} \times \frac{2}{3}$.
$$\frac{3}{4} \times \frac{2}{3} = \frac{6}{12}, \text{ or } \frac{1}{2}.$$

For the numerator of the product we multiply the two numerators.

And we could have other numerators. Thus:
$$\frac{5}{6} \times \frac{3}{4} = \frac{15}{24}, \text{ or } \frac{5}{8}.$$
$$\frac{7}{10} \times \frac{2}{3} = \frac{14}{30}, \text{ or } \frac{7}{15}.$$

3. $1\frac{2}{3} \times \frac{3}{10}$.

How do we manage that? The easy way is to turn $1\frac{2}{3}$ into thirds.

$$1\frac{2}{3} \times \frac{3}{10} = \frac{5}{3} \times \frac{3}{10}$$
$$= \frac{15}{30}, \text{ or } \frac{1}{2}.$$
$$2\frac{1}{4} \times 1\frac{1}{5} = \frac{9}{4} \times \frac{6}{5}$$
$$= \frac{54}{20}$$
$$= 2\frac{14}{20}, \text{ or } 2\frac{7}{10}.$$

4. Let us look at:

$$3\frac{1}{3} \times 1\frac{1}{5} \times 1\frac{1}{4} = \frac{10}{3} \times \frac{6}{5} \times \frac{5}{4}$$
$$= \frac{300}{60}$$
$$= \frac{30}{6} = 5.$$

We can make that rather easier if we divide before we multiply.

$$3\frac{1}{3} \times 1\frac{1}{5} \times \frac{5}{4} = \frac{10}{3} \times \frac{6}{5} \times \frac{5}{4}.$$

(We can divide top and bottom by 3, 5, 2, and 2 again. We cancel them, or cross them off, as we divide.)

$$\begin{array}{ccc} 5 & 2\ 1 & 1 \\ 10 & 6 & 5 \\ \overline{3} \times \overline{5} \times \overline{4} \\ 1 & 1 & 2\ 1 \end{array}$$

We are left with $5 \times 1 \times 1$ above, and $1 \times 1 \times 1$ below. There is no need to fill in the 1's, because multiplying and dividing by 1 makes no difference.

$$= 5.$$

DIVIDING FRACTIONS

1. Dividing is just as easy as multiplying. We turn the divisor upside down, and multiply:

$$\frac{3}{4} \div \frac{2}{3} = \frac{3}{4} \times \frac{3}{2}$$
$$= \frac{9}{8}, \text{ or } 1\frac{1}{8}.$$

2. We have been doing that, just that, all along. When we find a third of anything, we divide by 3. That is, to find $\frac{1}{3}$ or multiply by $\frac{1}{3}$, we divide by 3. We can write 3 as $\frac{3}{1}$. And $\frac{3}{1}$ upside down as $\frac{1}{3}$. Multiply by $\frac{1}{4}$; divide by 4. Multiply by $\frac{1}{5}$; divide by 5.

3. Notice that it is the divisor we turn upside down, because the divisor is the number we are working with.

Dividing by $\frac{2}{5}$ is the same as multiplying by $\frac{5}{2}$ or $2\frac{1}{2}$.

4. When we are dividing by a whole number and a fraction we begin by changing them into improper fractions.

Instead of $1\frac{2}{3}$ we use $\frac{5}{3}$.
Instead of $2\frac{1}{4}$ we use $\frac{9}{4}$. And so on.
Thus: $3\frac{1}{3} \div 1\frac{2}{3} = \frac{10}{3} \div \frac{5}{3}$
$$= \frac{10}{3} \times \frac{3}{5} \text{(cancel 5 and 3)}$$
$$= \frac{2}{1} \text{ or } 2.$$

Here are other examples:

(a) $2\frac{1}{4} \div \frac{3}{8} = \frac{9}{4} \div \frac{3}{8}$
$$= \frac{9}{4} \times \frac{8}{3} \text{ (cancel 4 and 3)}$$
$$= \frac{6}{1} \text{ or } 6.$$

(b) $5\frac{1}{3} \div \frac{1}{8} = \frac{16}{3} \div \frac{1}{8}$
$$= \frac{16}{3} \times \frac{8}{1}$$
$$= \frac{128}{3} \text{ or } 42\frac{2}{3}.$$

(c) $5\frac{1}{3} \div 8 = \frac{16}{3} \times \frac{1}{8} \text{ (cancel 8)}$
$$= \frac{2}{3}.$$

Incidentally we have found out: (a) $2\frac{1}{4}$ is 6 times $\frac{3}{8}$; (b) $5\frac{1}{3}$ is $42\frac{2}{3}$ times $\frac{1}{8}$; (c) $5\frac{1}{3}$ is $\frac{2}{3}$ of 8.

Test Yourself—9

1. Draw 4 small squares. Divide them into quarters in 4 different ways.
2. Draw a cake. Divide it evenly for 5 people. Shade $\frac{2}{5}$ of it.
3. (a) Find $\frac{1}{5}$ of 80. (b) $\frac{2}{5}$ of 80.
4. Find $\frac{4}{7}$ cwt. in pounds.
5. Divide an oblong to show that:
$$\frac{3}{4} = \frac{6}{8}.$$
6. Change these fractions by dividing top and bottom by the same number.
(a) $\frac{9}{18}$; (b) $\frac{15}{25}$; (c) $\frac{27}{36}$; (d) $\frac{56}{63}$; (e) $\frac{120}{150}$; (f) $\frac{125}{1000}$.
7. (a) $\frac{2}{3} + \frac{3}{4}$; (b) $\frac{4}{5} + \frac{1}{10}$; (c) $3\frac{1}{4} + 2\frac{1}{5}$; (d) $4\frac{2}{5} + \frac{5}{6}$; (e) $\frac{1}{3} + \frac{1}{9} + \frac{1}{27}$; (f) $\frac{1}{5} + \frac{3}{10} + \frac{7}{15}$.
8. (a) $\frac{3}{8} - \frac{1}{3}$; (b) $\frac{1}{7} - \frac{1}{8}$; (c) $\frac{1}{8} - \frac{1}{9}$; (d) $\frac{4}{5} - \frac{1}{6}$; (e) $4\frac{3}{4} - 2\frac{2}{5}$; (f) $5\frac{1}{3} - 2\frac{3}{4}$; (g) $7\frac{1}{8} - 3\frac{1}{2}$.
9. Draw 3 squares side by side. Divide them to show that:
$$\frac{3}{4} = 3 \div 4.$$

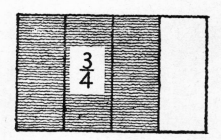

10. The oblong is shaded to show $\frac{3}{4}$. Draw a line to show that:
$$\tfrac{1}{2} \text{ of } \tfrac{3}{4} = \tfrac{3}{8}.$$
Cross-shade $\frac{1}{2}$ of $\frac{3}{4}$.

11. Draw and divide an oblong to show:
$$\tfrac{2}{3} \text{ of } \tfrac{2}{5} = \tfrac{4}{15}.$$

12. (a) $\frac{3}{5} \times \frac{3}{4}$; (b) $\frac{2}{3} \times \frac{3}{4}$; (c) $\frac{4}{9} \times \frac{3}{5}$; (d) $1\frac{2}{3} \times \frac{4}{5}$; (e) $1\frac{1}{4} \times \frac{2}{3} \times 4\frac{1}{2}$.

13. (a) $\frac{2}{3} \div \frac{5}{9}$; (b) $1\frac{1}{4} \div 3\frac{1}{2}$; (c) $1\frac{2}{3} \div 1\frac{1}{4}$; (d) $2\frac{2}{5} \div 1\frac{7}{8}$; (e) $3\frac{1}{3} \div \frac{5}{6}$.

(Answers on page 338)

X. "CONCRETE" FRACTIONS

There is a kind of fraction which is sometimes called a "concrete" fraction, because it comes in when we are dealing with materials. But it is a very poor name. The fraction is not a concrete material. It is a number.

1. These fractions come in when we ask such questions as:
What fraction of a pound is 12 ounces?
What fraction of an hour is 20 minutes?
What fraction of 5 feet is 18 inches?
What fraction of 120 men is 75 men?

2. In every case the answer is easy. We simply write down the one over the other:

$$\frac{12 \text{ ounces}}{1 \text{ pound}} \quad \frac{20 \text{ minutes}}{1 \text{ hour}} \quad \frac{18 \text{ inches}}{5 \text{ feet}} \quad \frac{75 \text{ men}}{120 \text{ men}}$$

A word in your ear: the quantity with "of" before it is the denominator.

3. The four answers given above are all correct. But they are not in good forms. We can improve them:

(a) $\dfrac{12 \text{ ounces}}{1 \text{ pound}} = \dfrac{12 \text{ ounces}}{16 \text{ ounces}} = \frac{3}{4}$.
12 ounces is $\frac{3}{4}$ of a pound.

(b) $\dfrac{20 \text{ minutes}}{1 \text{ hour}} = \dfrac{20 \text{ minutes}}{60 \text{ minutes}} = \frac{1}{3}$.
20 minutes is $\frac{1}{3}$ of an hour.

(c) $\dfrac{18 \text{ inches}}{5 \text{ feet}} = \dfrac{18 \text{ inches}}{60 \text{ inches}} = \frac{3}{10}$.
18 inches is $\frac{3}{10}$ of 5 feet.

(d) $\dfrac{75 \text{ men}}{120 \text{ men}} = \frac{15}{24} = \frac{5}{8}$.
75 men are $\frac{5}{8}$ of 120 men.

Test Yourself—10
1. What fraction of 360 is 54?
2. What fraction of 1,000 is 625?
3. What fraction of a pound is 14 oz.?
4. What fraction of 1 cwt. is 28 lb.?
5. What fraction of a day is 9 hours?
6. What fraction of a year is 73 days?

(Answers on page 339)

XI. AREA

1. We draw a square with sides one inch long. The space it covers on the paper is called a square inch. We usually call the space an area, because space can mean other things as well as area. The drawing has an area of one square inch.

2. There is an old catch question: how many inches make a square inch?

The answer you are expected to give is 4 inches. But that is quite wrong. 4 inches is certainly the distance round a one-inch square, but that is not the same as the space on the paper covered by the square.

Asking "how many inches in a square inch?" is like asking "how many oranges in a year?" Length and area are two different things. We measure short lengths in inches, and small areas in square inches.

3. We draw a one-inch square, and cut it out:

We cut the square in two across the middle, and put the two parts end to end.

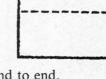

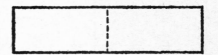

The oblong has exactly the same area as the square, but the shape is different, and the distance round is now 5 inches.

Let us now draw another one-inch square, cut it out, and cut it in four along the diagonals. We can arrange the four parts in various ways to form many different shapes, all with the same area of one square inch.

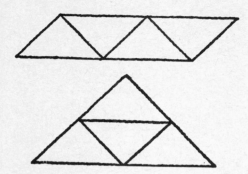

We should be quite certain that it is the space covered on the paper that is the area. Not the shape, and not the distance round.

4. We draw an oblong 3 inches by 4 inches. We divide the sides into inches, and join across. We have divided the oblong into one-inch squares, each with an area of one square inch.

We have 3 rows of 4 squares, so the area is:

$3 \times 4 = 12$ square inches.

5. And, of course, we might have any other numbers of inches in the sides of the oblong. We might have 3 inches and 5 inches.

3 rows of 5. $3 \times 5 = 15$. Area 15 square inches.

4 inches and 7 inches.

4 rows of 7. $4 \times 7 = 28$. Area 28 square inches.

And so on with other numbers of inches in the sides. Whatever the lengths of sides of an oblong, we multiply them to find the area of the oblong.

6. It is always true that:

length × length (or breadth) = area.

That is not quite the ordinary idea of multiplication, which is:

number × number = another number.

But the idea that length × length = area, works so well that we commonly use it.

We can say, or write:

5 in. × 9 in. = 45 sq. in.

45 sq. in. is the area of an oblong with sides of 5 in. and 9 in.

6 in. × 6 in. = 36 sq. in.

36 sq. in. is the area of a square with sides 6 in. long.

7. Here is a small drawing of a square with sides one foot long. The full-size

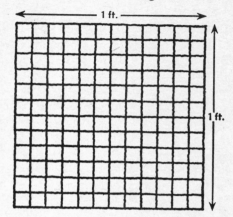

square covers an area which we call a square foot. And, just as with a square inch, it is the area that matters, not the shape, or the distance round.

We divide each side into 12 parts that represent inches, and join across. When we actually do this we soon begin to have a feeling of the large number of square inches.

12 rows of 12. $12 \times 12 = 144$. Area is 144 sq. in.

That is: 1 sq. ft. = 144 sq. in.

8. Here is a drawing which represents a yard square, with sides divided into feet.

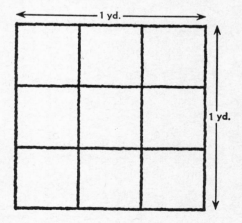

327

3 rows of 3. $3 \times 3 = 9$. Area is 9 sq. ft.
1 sq. yd. = 9 sq. ft.

9. 2 ft × 7 in. = ?

The answer is certainly an area. $2 \times 7 = 14$. So the area is 14 foot-inches. That is 14 times the area of an oblong 1 foot long and 1 inch wide.

We can get a more usual unit by having both lengths in inches:

2 ft. × 7 in. = 24 in. × 7 in. = 168 sq. in.

144 sq. in. = 1 sq. ft.

So 168 sq. in. = 1 sq. ft. 24 sq. in.

If we want the answer as a fraction of a square foot we have

$$24 \text{ sq. in.} = \tfrac{24}{144} \text{ sq. ft.}$$
$$= \tfrac{1}{6} \text{ sq. ft.}$$

The area is 168 sq. in. or $1\tfrac{1}{6}$ sq. ft.

Test Yourself—11

1. Draw an oblong 5 in. by 4 in. Divide it into inch-squares. What is its area?
2. Draw a 2-inch square, and divide it into inch-squares. Then rule off a $1\tfrac{1}{2}$-inch

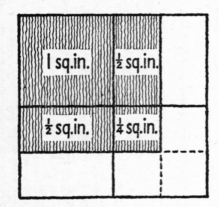

square and shade it. The area is in four parts: 1 sq. in. + $\tfrac{1}{2}$ sq. in. + $\tfrac{1}{2}$ sq. in. + $\tfrac{1}{4}$ sq. in.

$$= 2\tfrac{1}{4} \text{ sq. in.}$$
$$1\tfrac{1}{2} \text{ in.} \times 1\tfrac{1}{2} \text{ in.} = \tfrac{3}{2} \times \tfrac{3}{2} \text{ sq. in.}$$
$$= \tfrac{9}{4} \text{ sq. in.}$$
$$= 2\tfrac{1}{4} \text{ sq. in.}$$

3. What are the areas of the following oblongs?
   (a) 5 in. by 9 in.
   (b) 6 in. by $7\tfrac{1}{2}$ in.

(c) $2\tfrac{1}{2}$ in. by $3\tfrac{1}{2}$ in.
(d) 7 ft. by 18 ft.
(e) 3 ft. 6 in. by 8 ft.
(f) 9 yards by 24 yards.

4. A lawn is 58 feet long and 26 feet wide. What is its area?

5. Copy the drawing of a picture frame. Put in the measurements.
   (a) How long is the picture?
   (b) How wide is the picture?

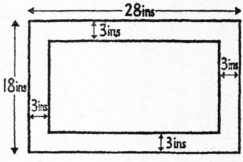

Question 5. Picture frame.

(c) What is the area of the picture?
(d) What is the total area of the frame?
(e) What is the area of the mount?

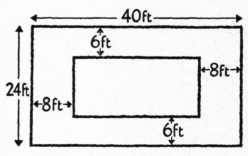

Question 6. Garden plan.

6. Copy the drawing of a garden with a grass plot in it.
   (a) How long is the grass plot? How wide?
   (b) What is its area?
   (c) What is the whole area of the garden?
   (d) What is the area between grass and walls?

7. A room is 28 ft. long, 18 ft. wide, and $9\tfrac{1}{2}$ ft. high.

(*a*) What is the area of the long walls?
(*b*) Of the short walls?
(*c*) What is the total wall area?
(*d*) What is the area of floor or ceiling?
(*Answers on page 339*)

XII. VOLUME

1. The volume of anything is the space it fills up.

A length has its length, and nothing else.

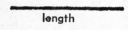

length

An area has both length and breadth.

area

A volume has length, breadth, and height.

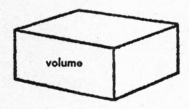

volume

It is easy to see that, with lines, oblongs, and cubes. It is equally true of other things.

The edge of a cube is length. The surfaces of the faces are areas. The whole of the cube, inside and outside, is a volume.

In a ball, or sphere, the diameter and radius are lines; so is the circumference. The curved surface is an area. The whole of the sphere is a volume.

2. Here an inch cube is represented. In

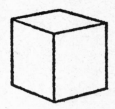

the real cube each edge is an inch long and each face is a square. The area of each face is a square inch, so the total area is 6 square inches.

The volume of the inch cube we call a *cubic inch*.

If we mould a cubic inch out of clay or plasticine, we can then press it into all kinds of shapes, without changing the volume. It is the size that makes the cubic inch, not the shape.

3. This drawing represents a solid called a *prism*. All the edges of every prism

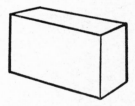

are straight lines. This particular prism is called an oblong prism because all its faces are oblong.

4. Suppose we have an oblong prism 4 in. long, 2 in. wide, and 3 in. high. We want to find its volume.

Let us draw the prism. There are three lines representing the length; the fourth is hidden. We divide each into quarters, and join across. Three lines represent the width; again the fourth is hidden. We divide the widths into halves and join across. Three lines represent the height; once more the fourth is hidden. We divide the heights into thirds, and join across. We thus divide the prism into cubic inches. How many are there?

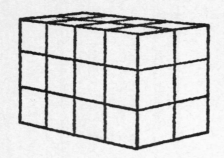

There are 3 layers of blocks. Each contains 2 rows of 4 blocks. 2 × 4 blocks in each layer.

2 × 4 in 3 layers.

The volume is 2 × 4 × 3 = 24 cu. in.

5. To find the volume of the prism we have multiplied length, breadth, and thickness. We have multiplied three lengths, and:

length × length × length = volume.

Of course, we could have any other lengths in place of 2 in., 3 in., and 4 in. Thus we might have 9 in. long, 5 in. wide, and 7 in. high. The volume is:

9 in. × 5 in. × 7 in. = 45 × 7 cu. in.
= 315 cu. in.

CUBES

1. This drawing represents a cube with sides one foot long. It has been divided into small cubes with sides one inch long.

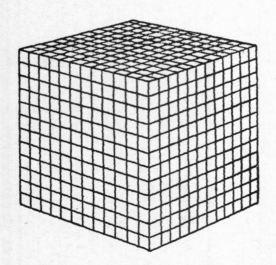

When we copy the drawing we should have a fairly big cube. Otherwise the divisions are very small. We soon begin to see that there must be a very large number of cubic inches.

There are 12 layers, and each layer contains 12 rows of 12. That is 12 × 12 = 144.

All 12 layers contain:
12 × 12 × 12 = 144 × 12 = 1,728.

In a cubic foot there are 1,728 cu. in.
1 cu. ft. = 12 in. × 12 in. × 12 in.
= 1,728 cu. in.

If we forget that number we can always find it again by means of 12 × 12 × 12, or 144 × 12.

2. The drawing which follows represents a cubic yard divided into cubic feet.

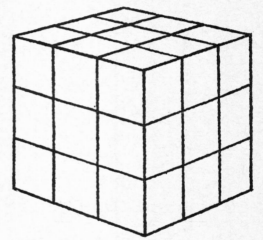

1 cu. yd. = 3 ft. × 3 ft. × 3 ft.
= 27 cu. ft.

3. Let us look at one or two examples.

(a) A room is 16 feet long, 14 feet wide, and 9 feet high. How much air-space does it hold?

The room is the shape of an oblong prism, so its volume is: length × width × height.

= 16 ft. × 14 ft. × 9 ft.
= 224 × 9 cu. ft.
= 2,016 cu. ft.

(b) A swimming bath is 50 yards long, and 20 yards wide. The water is 3 feet deep at one end, and 6 feet deep at the other end. How much water does it hold?

If the depth were evened it would be halfway between 3 ft. and 6 ft. That is 4½ ft.

So the volume is:

$$50 \text{ yd.} \times 20 \text{ yd.} \times 4\tfrac{1}{2} \text{ ft.}$$
$$= 150 \text{ ft.} \times 60 \text{ ft.} \times 4\tfrac{1}{2} \text{ ft.}$$
$$= 9,000 \times 4\tfrac{1}{2} \text{ cu. ft.}$$
$$= 40,500 \text{ cu. ft.}$$

MEASURING LIQUIDS

1. Instead of using a ruler or measuring-tape to measure liquids, we sometimes pour them into measuring vessels. These are made to hold exactly certain amounts. Milk bottles are made to hold a quart, or a pint, or half a pint, and sometimes a third of a pint. Other vessels are used to hold gallons.

We know, of course, that 2 pints make a quart, and 4 quarts make a gallon. So a pint is an eighth of a gallon.

2. When we are measuring quantities of water we usually want to know the volume in gallons. For small quantities there is no special difficulty. But large quantities, like the water in a swimming bath, often have to be measured in cubic feet.

We have an easy way of changing cubic feet into gallons.

$$1 \text{ cu. ft.} = 6\tfrac{1}{4} \text{ gallons.}$$

We need only multiply by 6¼.

The swimming bath held 40,500 cu. ft.:

$$= 40,500 \times 6\tfrac{1}{4} \text{ gallons}$$

$$\begin{array}{r} 40,500 \\ 6\tfrac{1}{4} \\ \hline 243,000 \\ 10,125 \\ \hline 253,125 \text{ gallons} \end{array}$$

Test Yourself—12

1. Copy this drawing of a cube.

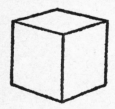

(a) How many faces has it?
(b) How many edges?
(c) If each edge is 1 inch, how long are all the edges?
(d) What is the total area?
(e) What is the volume?

2. Copy this drawing to represent a prism 5 in. long, 3 in. wide, and 4 in. high.

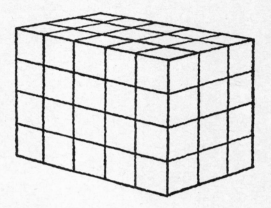

Divide it carefully into inch-cubes. What is the volume?

3. Find the volumes of the following oblong prisms:
   (a) 7 in. by 18 in. by 9 in.
   (b) 6½ in. by 12 in. by 15 in.
   (c) 1 ft. 8 in. by 2 ft. by 7 ft.

4. What is the volume of a tank 8 feet long, 7 feet wide, and 4 feet deep?
   (a) In cubic feet.
   (b) In gallons.

5. (a) Find $12 \times 12 \times 12$.
   (b) How many cubic inches in a cubic foot?

6. A block of wood has ends 2-feet sq. It is 9 feet long. What is its volume?

7. Find the volumes of cubes with edges:
   (a) 1 in. (b) 2 in. (c) 3 in. (d) 4 in.
   (e) 5 in.

8. (a) 1 cu. ft. = ? gallons.
   (b) A gallon of water weighs 10 lb. What does a cubic foot of water weigh?
   (c) How many ounces does a cubic foot of water weigh?

(Answers on page 339)

331

XIII. PERCENTAGES

1. We all know the word "cent," though we may not quite realize what it means. It comes from a word that means a hundred.

The American cent is so called because 100 of them make a dollar. A century is 100 years, or a 100 runs at cricket. *A Century of Inventions* is the name of an old book about 100 inventions.

2. We have at least three ways of expressing percentages. We use whichever happens to be most convenient.

5 per cent is 5 per 100, or 5 out of each 100, or $\frac{5}{100}$.

$6\frac{1}{2}$ per cent is $6\frac{1}{2}$ per 100, or $6\frac{1}{2}$ out of each 100, or $\frac{6\frac{1}{2}}{100}$.

The sign "%" means per cent.

(a) 10 per cent $= \frac{10}{100} = \frac{1}{10}$. To find 10 per cent of anything we merely divide by 10.

> 10 per cent of £150 = £15
> 10 per cent of 120 lb. = 12 lb.

(b) 5 per cent $= \frac{5}{100} = \frac{1}{20}$. To find 5 per cent we divide by 20.

5 per cent of £80 = £4.

5 per cent of 1 hour = 60 min ÷ 20
$$= 3 \text{ min.}$$

(c) $2\frac{1}{2}$ per cent $= \frac{2\frac{1}{2}}{100}$ (multiply top and bottom by 2).

$$= \frac{5}{200} = \frac{1}{40}.$$

$2\frac{1}{2}$ per cent of £360 = £360 ÷ 40 = £9.

$2\frac{1}{2}$ per cent of 1 ton = 20 cwt. ÷ 40
$$= \frac{1}{2} \text{ cwt.}$$

3. We ought to notice very carefully the difference between 50 per cent and $\frac{1}{2}$ per cent.

> 50 per cent $= \frac{50}{100} = \frac{1}{2}$.
> $\frac{1}{2}$ per cent $= \frac{\frac{1}{2}}{100} = \frac{1}{200}$.

When we want to make quite sure that people will not confuse 50 per cent and $\frac{1}{2}$ per cent, we often write the latter as "$\frac{1}{2}$ of one per cent."

> 50 per cent of £1,000 = £500.
> $\frac{1}{2}$ of 1 per cent of £1,000 = £5.

We should be disappointed if we were promised $\frac{1}{2}$ per cent of £1,000, and thought it meant 50 per cent!

Test Yourself—13

1. Look up in the dictionary the meanings of centenary, centenarian, centesimal, centigrade, centipede.
2. What is the meaning of 1 per cent?
3. (a) What is 1 per cent of £1,000? (b) What is 4 per cent of £1,000?
4. (a) $\frac{1}{3} \times 100 = $? (b) What is $\frac{1}{3}$ as a percentage? (c) What is $\frac{1}{4}$ as a percentage?
5. What is the meaning of "fifty-fifty"?
6. Change into fractions: (a) 50 per cent. (b) 25 per cent. (c) 75 per cent. (d) 100 per cent. (e) $12\frac{1}{2}$ per cent. (f) 15 per cent.

(Answers on page 339)

XIV. DECIMALS

1. Decimal comes from a word meaning ten. We call our way of counting a decimal system because it runs in tens. Before the units we have 10's, then 100's, then 1,000's. And:

> 1,000 = 10 hundreds.
> 100 = 10 tens.
> 10 = 10 units.

2. If we start at 1,000 we can go down in 10's:

> 1,000, 100, 10, 1.

What should the next figure stand for? Tenth of 1,000 = 100; tenth of 100 = 10; tenth of 10 = 1. And, of course, a tenth of $1 = \frac{1}{10}$. The figure after the units should stand for tenths.

3. We need some way of showing which is the units figure. When we are dealing with whole numbers, the units figure is always the last figure on the right, so there is no need to mark it. But when we add a figure meaning tenths, the units figure is no longer the last figure on the right.

We mark the units figure by putting a dot after it. In the number thirty-seven, 7 is the units figure. But if we alter it to 3·7, 3 is the units figure, the 7 stands for seven-tenths or $\frac{7}{10}$.

4. Some of the inches on a ruler are divided into tenths. We can use these inches to measure the lengths of short lines in inches and tenths. We find that a line is $2\frac{5}{10}$ inches long. We can conveniently write that as 2·5 inches.

5. The fractions are decimal fractions, and we often call them decimals, for short.

5·8 inches is the length of a line. We read that as "5 decimal 8" or "5 point 8." We know that the 5 stands for 5 inches. The 8 stands for 8 tenths of an inch, or $\frac{8}{10}$ inch.

5·8 is the same as $5\frac{8}{10}$, or $5\frac{4}{5}$.

6. Our currency is now "decimal currency," which makes the addition, subtraction, multiplication, and division of sums of money as straightforward as other calculations. Thus 100 pence = £1, and 683 pence = £6·83.

A gross of articles costing 80p each would cost:

$$
\begin{array}{r}
80p \\
\times 144 \\
\hline
8000 \\
3200 \\
320 \\
\hline
11520p \\
\end{array}
$$

11,520 pence = £115·20.

DECIMAL FRACTIONS

1. The great advantage of using decimal fractions is that we can add, subtract, multiply, and divide them with far less trouble than we usually have with ordinary fractions.

2. 1·7 in. + 14·2 in. + 29·6 in.

We set the lengths down, one under another. And we take care to have the dots (the decimal points) one under another. We do this so that we may have tens under tens, units under units, tenths under tenths.

$$
\begin{array}{rr}
1\cdot7 \text{ in.} & 17 \\
14\cdot2 \text{ in.} & 142 \\
29\cdot6 \text{ in.} & 296 \\
\hline
45\cdot5 \text{ in.} & 455 \\
\end{array}
$$

We add the lengths just as if they were whole numbers. The addition is exactly the same as for the sum on the right.

3. 14·6 in. − 7·9 in.

Again we set the numbers down with one decimal point under the other.

$$
\begin{array}{rr}
14\cdot6 \text{ in.} & 146 \\
7\cdot9 \text{ in.} & 79 \\
\hline
6\cdot7 \text{ in.} & 67 \\
\end{array}
$$

The subtraction is exactly the same as for the sum on the right.

4. 4·9 in. × 9.

$$
\begin{array}{rr}
4\cdot9 \text{ in.} & 49 \\
9 & 9 \\
\hline
44\cdot1 \text{ in.} & 441 \\
\end{array}
$$

We multiply 4·9 just as if it were a whole number. The working is the same as for the sum on the right.

5. 7·6 in. ÷ 8.

$$
\begin{array}{ll}
8)7\cdot6 \text{ in.} & 8)76 \\
\hline
\cdot9 \text{ in.} + \cdot4 \text{ in. R.} & 9 + 4R. \\
\end{array}
$$

The working of the division is exactly the same as for the sum on the right. We have to be careful about the remainder. It is not 4, but 4 tenths, so we write it ·4.

After the tenths we should have tenths of tenths.

$\frac{1}{10}$ of $\frac{1}{10}$, or $\frac{1}{10} \times \frac{1}{10} = \frac{1}{100}$.

So the second figure after the decimal point stands for hundredths.

14·67 stands for $14 + \frac{6}{10} + \frac{7}{100}$. And, of course, it is much neater to write it as a decimal.

Test Yourself—14

1. Draw a line 3·7 in. long. Continue it another 1·8 in. What is the total length? Then, but not till then, measure the whole length.
Try this with other lines.

2. Draw a line 5·3 in. long. From one end measure 1·8 in. How long is the other part? Then, but not till then, measure the other part.

3. What does the decimal point show? Where is it placed?

4. (a) 3·9 in. × 7.
   (b) 4·8 in. × 28.

(c) 5·6 ft. × 19.
(d) 4·6 yd. × 18.
5. (a) 5·4 in. ÷ 9.
(b) 16·1 in. ÷ 7.
(c) 1·5 in. ÷ 6.
(d) 12·8 in. ÷ 8.

(*Answers on page 339*)

XV. METRIC CONVERSIONS

Almost 90 per cent of the population of the world live in countries which use the metric system, in other words they do not measure distances in miles, or lengths in inches, or weights in pounds, as we in Great Britain have been doing for centuries, but use quite different units. Of course, this has made trade between countries needlessly difficult. A British company using quarter-inch diameter bolts, say, for manufacturing washing machines, could not order quantities from France, where the equivalent size bolt might be 6 millimetres, which is slightly smaller.

For many years attempts were made in Great Britain to scrap the old methods of weighing and measuring and to adopt the metric system. In 1965 the government agreed, and a programme was begun with the object of changing to the metric system gradually. It was hoped that by 1975 British industry would be using the metric system, which means, for instance, that carpenters would be buying planks of so many metres rather than feet, housewives would be buying potatoes in kilograms rather than pounds, and milk would be delivered in half-litres rather than pints.

Just as, in 1971, British people had to get used to buying and selling goods in new pence, and to stop thinking in terms of shillings and old pence, so gradually they will have to learn to use metric units rather than the present ones, which are called Imperial units. It is a good idea, then, to learn what the metric system is, and what the units of measurement are, and how to convert Imperial units into metric units and *vice versa*.

The metric system is a system of measurement in which the two most basic units are the metre, for measuring length, and the kilogram, measuring weight. The beauty of the metric system, which makes calculations easy, is that larger or smaller units than these are arrived at by multiplying or dividing these basic units by 10, 100, 1000, and so on. For instance, a kilometre is a thousand metres. It is obviously easy to change, or convert, kilometres into metres: all that is necessary is to add three noughts to the number. This is simple compared to changing miles into yards, which requires multiplying by 1760.

Just as "kilo" in front of "metre" means a thousand times, so a kilogram is a 1000 grams and a kilowatt, in electricity, is a 1000 watts. "Kilo" is a prefix, and other prefixes used in the metric system are as follows:

mega means a million times
kilo means a thousand times
hecto means a hundred times
deca means ten times
deci means a tenth part
centi means a hundredth part
milli means a thousandth part
micro means a millionth part.

In practice, it is convenient to use only the kilometre, metre, and millimetre. For instance, a measurement is more likely to be expressed as 100 millimetres than ten centimetres.

Thus:

$$1 \text{ kilometre}$$
$$= \quad 1,000 \text{ metres}$$
$$= 1,000,000 \text{ millimetres.}$$

Also, it is unnecessary to say that a length is 24 metres, 375 millimetres. It would be expressed as 24·375 metres. Notice that this length is also 2 decametres, 4 metres, 3 decimetres, 7 centimetres, and 5 millimetres, but clearly this is a much clumsier way of expressing it than 24·375 metres.

Similarly, in measuring weights, kilograms, and grams will be the units most often used, although an exception to the general rule mentioned above is met here, because 1,000 kilograms is not called a megagram, as we would expect, but a "tonne." A tonne is sometimes called a "metric ton" and is, in fact, very slightly less than a British ton.

CONVERSIONS

While both Imperial and metric units are used, it will sometimes be necessary to convert one unit into another, for instance a weight of 200 grams might be required in ounces. These conversions are made by multiplying, and the figure which one multiplies by is known as a "conversion factor." The important conversion factors are as follows:

Length
1 millimetre (mm.)	= 0·03937 inches or 0·04 inches approx.
1 metre (m.)	= 39·37 inches
1 kilometre (km.)	= 3,281 feet or 0·6214 miles (which is $\frac{5}{8}$ mile approx.)
1 inch	= 25·4 millimetres
1 foot	= 304·8 millimetres
1 yard	= 9,144 millimetres or 0·9144 metres
1 miles	= 1,609 metres approx.

Weight
1 gram (g.)	= 0·0353 ounces
1 kilogram (kg.)	= 2·2046 pounds
1 tonne (1,000 kg.)	= 2,204·6 pounds
1 ounce	= 28·35 grams approx.
1 pound	= 453·6 grams approx.
1 ton	= 1·016 tonnes approx. or 1,016 kilograms approx.

VOLUME

Liquid volume in the metric system is measured in litres. One litre is 1 cubic decimetre, or in the Imperial system 1·76 pints.

TEMPERATURE

Temperature in the metric system is measured in degrees Celsius, which are the same as degrees Centigrade, although the term Celsius is preferred.

The Celsius scale is based on the freezing point of water, which is 0°C, and the boiling point, which is 100°C. The equivalent temperatures in the Fahrenheit scale, which has been traditionally used in Great Britain, are 32°F and 212°F. To convert Celsius into Fahrenheit, one must multiply by $\frac{9}{5}$ and add 32.

Thus 70°C = 70 × $\frac{9}{5}$ + 32 degrees
Fahrenheit
= 158°F

To convert Fahrenheit into Celsius, one does the reverse:
deduct 32 and multiply by $\frac{5}{9}$.
Thus 98·4°F = (98·4 − 32) × $\frac{5}{9}$ degrees
Celsius
= 36·9°C

CONVERSION TABLES

Most people who need to convert regularly from the Imperial system to the metric system and *vice versa* use conversion tables. It is a good exercise which helps you to get used to metric measurements to make simple tables yourself. Imagine you had several varying lengths in feet and inches to convert into millimetres, and no printed tables were to hand. You could work out the millimetres in a foot, and in 1 inch to 11 inches. You would get a small table like this:

1 foot	=	304·8 mm.
1 inch	=	25·4 mm.
2 inches	=	50·8 mm.
3 inches	=	76·2 mm.

4 inches = 101·6 mm.
5 inches = 127·0 mm.
6 inches = 152·4 mm.
7 inches = 177·8 mm.
8 inches = 203·2 mm.
9 inches = 228·6 mm.
10 inches = 254·0 mm.
11 inches = 279·4 mm.

With this table, to convert 5 ft. 6 in. to millimetres, you multiply 304·8 by 5 and add 152·4, thus

$$304·8 \times 5 + 152·4$$
$$= 1,676·4 \text{ mm.}$$

Of course, printed tables are much fuller than this, and conversions can be looked up easily. The main problem is ensuring that the decimal point is in the right place.

Test Yourself—15

1. (a) Change 3 ft. 5 in. into millimetres
   (b) Change 20 miles into kilometres
2. (a) Change 15 metres into yards, feet, and inches
   (b) Change 800 millimetres into feet and inches
3. (a) Change 20 kilograms into pounds and ounces
   (b) Change 700 grams into ounces
4. (a) Change 2 lb. 2 oz. into kilograms
   (b) Change 4,200 kg. into tons
5. (a) Change 16 litres into pints
   (b) Change 6 pints into litres
6. (a) Change 40°C into °F
   (b) Change 180°F into °C

(*Answers on page 339*)

ANSWERS TO THE ARITHMETIC TESTS

Test 1

1. (a) 35 + 40 = 36 + 39 = 37 + 38 = 75.

   The pairs for all sequences of six numbers should give equal totals.

   (b) e.g., 54, 55, 56, 57, 58, 59, 60, 61. 54 + 61 = 55 + 60 = 56 + 59 = 57 + 58 = 115.

   Four pairs of equal totals for all sequences of eight numbers.

2. e.g. (a)

66
27
35
48
92
76
344

(b)

66	48
27	92
35	76
128	216
128	
216	
344	

(c)

66	35	92
27	48	76
93	83	168
93		
83		
168		
344		

(d)

66
27
35
48
92
268
76
344

3. 7 + 17 + 27 + 37 + 47 + 57 + 67 + 77 + 87 + 97 = 520.

Test 2

1. (a) 33.
   (b) 67.
   (c) 100.
2. (a) 350 − 67 = 283; 283 − 67 = 216; 216 − 67 = 149; 149 − 67 = 82; 82 − 67 = 15.
   (b) 350 + 15 = 283 + 82 = 216 + 149 = 365.

   Equal totals for the pairs.
   (c) Five 67's. Remainder 15.
3. e.g.

38	166	71
57	− 38	− 26
26	128	45
45	− 57	− 45
166	71	0

4. 600 − 76 = 524; 524 − 76 = 448; 448 − 76 = 372; 372 − 76 = 296; 296 − 76 = 220; 220 − 76 = 144; 144 − 76 = 68.

   Seven 76's. Remainder 68.

Test 3

1. (a) 0, 1, 4, 9, 16, 25, 36, 49, 64, 81, 100, 121, 144, 169, 196, 225, 256, 289, 324, 361, 400.
   (b) 1, 3, 5, 7, 9, 11, 13, 15, 17, 19, 21, 23, 25, 27, 29, 31, 33, 35, 37, 39.

   The sequence of odd numbers.

336

2. (a) 56
       56
       56
       56
      ───
      224
   (b) 56
        4
      ───
      224
   (c) The same total for each.
3. (a) 3, 6, 9, 12, 15, 18, 21, 24, 27, 30, 33, 36.
   (b) 4, 8, 12, 16, 20, 24, 28, 32, 36, 40, 44, 48.
   (c) 7, 14, 21, 28, 35, 42, 49, 56, 63, 70, 77, 84.
      The table of 7's.
4. (a)   86 (b)   24
        × 24   × 86
       ─────   ─────
        1,720   1,920
          344   144
       ─────   ─────
        2,064   2,064

5. (a)   47 (b)   47 (c)   47 (d)   47
         × 2   × 3   × 4   × 24
        ────   ────   ────   ────
          94   141   188   940
        × 12   × 8   × 6   188
        ────   ────   ────   ────
        1,128   1,128   1,128   1,128

6. (a)   14 (b)   15 (c)   16
         × 15   × 16   × 14
        ────   ────   ────
          140   150   160
           70   90   64
          210   240   224
         × 16   × 14   × 15
        ────   ────   ────
        2,100   2,400   2,240
        1,260   960   1,120
        ────   ────   ────
        3,360   3,360   3,360

7. 123, 123.
8. 121, 212.

Test 4

1. (a) 97. (b) 97. (c) 97.
2. (a) 67. (b) An eighth of 536. Or, the number of 8's in 536.
3. (a) 80, 68, 56, 44, 32, 20, 8.
   (b) 80 ÷ 12 = 6, and 8 remainder.
4. (a) 69 × 7 = 483. (b) 483 ÷ 7 = 69.
5. (a) 62 + 4 remainder.
   (b) 62 × 8 = 496; 496 + 4 = 500.

6. (a) 142 + 6 remainder.
   (b) 1,000 − 6 = 994.
   (c) 1,000 + 1 = 1,001.
7. (a) 758 ÷ 20 = 37 + 18 remainder.
   (b) 37 × 20 = 740; 740 + 18 = 758.
8. (a) 17 + 3 remainder.
   (b) 17 × 21 = 357; 357 + 3 = 360.

Test 5

1. (a) 270 in.
   (b) 33 lengths.
   (c) 6 in.
2. (a) 880 yd.
   (b) 440 yd.
   (c) 1,320 yd.
   (d) 220 yd.
3. (a) 1,760 − 340 = 1,420; 1,420 − 340 = 1,080; 1,080 − 340 = 740; 740 − 340 = 400; 400 − 340 = 60.
   (b) 5 laps.
   (c) 60 yd.
4. 15,840 − 15,781 = 59 ft.

Test 6

1. (a) 14 lb.   (d) 56 lb.
   (b) 28 lb.   (e) 2,240 lb.
   (c) 112 lb.
2. (a) 56 × 16 = 896 oz.
   (b) 298 packets, 2 oz. remainder.
3. 62½ lb.

Test 7

1. 210 min.
2. 168 hr.
3. 3,600 sec.
4. 86,400 sec.
5. 52 wk. 1 day.
6. 1980, 1992, 1996.
7. Jan.–Mar. 90 day (91 in leap year);
   Apl.–June 91 days;
   July–Sept. 92 days;
   Oct.–Dec. 92 days.

Test 8

1. 2, 3, 6, 9.
2. 2, 3, 5, 6, 10, 15.
3. 40 × 1 = 20 × 2 = 10 × 4 = 8 × 5.
4. Even numbers have 2 for a factor; end figure on the right must be 0, 2, 4, 6 or

8. Numbers ending in 5 or 0 divide by 5.

5. 2, 3, 5, 7, 11, 13, 17, 19, 23, 29.

6. (a) 16. (d) 18.
   (b) 36. (e) 60.
   (c) 45.

8. (a) $\frac{1}{24}$.
   (b) $\frac{1}{56}$.
   (c) $\frac{1}{72}$.
   (d) $\frac{19}{30}$.
   (e) $2\frac{7}{20}$.
   (f) $3\frac{4}{12} - \frac{9}{12} = 2\frac{7}{12}$.
   (g) $3\frac{5}{8}$.

Test 9

1.

9.

2.

10.

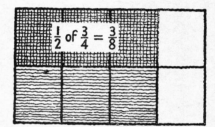

3. (a) 16.
   (b) 32.
4. 64 lb.
5.

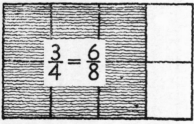

11.

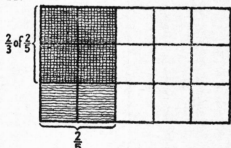

6. Where two or more answers are given, all are correct, but the last answer is the best.
   (a) $\frac{3}{6} = \frac{1}{2}$.
   (b) $\frac{3}{5}$.
   (c) $\frac{9}{12} = \frac{3}{4}$.
   (d) $\frac{8}{9}$.
   (e) $\frac{60}{75} = \frac{40}{50} = \frac{24}{30} = \frac{20}{25} = \frac{12}{15} = \frac{8}{10} = \frac{4}{5}$.
   (f) $\frac{25}{200} = \frac{5}{40} = \frac{1}{8}$.
7. (a) $\frac{17}{12} = 1\frac{5}{12}$.
   (b) $\frac{9}{10}$.
   (c) $5\frac{9}{20}$.
   (d) $4\frac{37}{30} = 5\frac{7}{30}$.
   (e) $\frac{13}{27}$.
   (f) $\frac{29}{30}$.

12. (a) $\frac{9}{20}$.
    (b) $\frac{6}{12} = \frac{1}{2}$.
    (c) $\frac{12}{45} = \frac{4}{15}$.
    (d) $\frac{5}{3} \times \frac{4}{5} = \frac{4}{3} = 1\frac{1}{3}$.
    (e) $\frac{5}{4} \times \frac{2}{3} \times \frac{9}{2} = \frac{15}{4} = 3\frac{3}{4}$.
13. (a) $\frac{2}{3} \times \frac{9}{5} = \frac{6}{5} = 1\frac{1}{5}$.
    (b) $\frac{5}{4} \times \frac{2}{7} = \frac{5}{14}$.
    (c) $\frac{5}{3} \times \frac{4}{5} = \frac{4}{3} = 1\frac{1}{3}$.
    (d) $\frac{12}{5} \times \frac{8}{15} = \frac{32}{25} = 1\frac{7}{25}$.
    (e) $\frac{10}{3} \times \frac{6}{5} = 4$.

338

Test 10

1. $\frac{3}{20}$.
2. $\frac{5}{8}$.
3. $\frac{7}{8}$.
4. $\frac{1}{4}$.
5. $\frac{3}{8}$.
6. $\frac{1}{5}$.

(d) 64 cu. in.
(e) 125 cu. in.

8. (a) $6\frac{1}{4}$ gal.
   (b) $62\frac{1}{2}$ lb.
   (c) 1,000 oz.

Test 11

1. Area 5 in. × 4 in. = 20 sq. in.
2. (Diagram and answer with exercise.)
3. (a) 45 sq. in. (d) 126 sq. ft.
   (b) 45 sq. in. (e) 28 sq. ft.
   (c) $8\frac{3}{4}$ sq. in. (f) 216 sq. yd.
4. 58 ft. × 26 ft. = 1,508 sq. ft.
5. (a) 22 in.
   (b) 12 in.
   (c) 22 in. × 12 in. = 264 sq. in.
   (d) 28 in. × 18 in. = 504 sq. in.
   (e) 504 − 264 = 240 sq. in.
6. (a) 24 ft. long; 12 ft. wide.
   (b) 24 ft. × 12 ft. = 288 sq. ft.
      (or 32 sq yd.)
   (c) 40 ft. × 24 ft. = 960 sq. ft.
      (or $106\frac{2}{3}$ sq. yd.)
   (d) 960 sq. ft. − 288 sq. ft. = 672 sq. ft.
      (or $74\frac{2}{3}$ sq. yd.)
7. (a) 28 ft. × $9\frac{1}{2}$ ft. × 2 = 532 sq. ft.
   (b) 18 ft. × $9\frac{1}{2}$ ft. × 2 = 342 sq. ft.
   (c) 532 + 342 = 874 sq. ft.
   (d) 28 ft. × 18 ft. = 504 sq. ft.

Test 12

1. (a) 6.
   (b) 12.
   (c) 12 in. = 1 ft.
   (d) 6 sq. in.
   (e) 1 cu. in.
2. 5 in. × 3 in. × 4 in. = 60 cu. in.
3. (a) 7 in. × 18 in. × 9 in. = 1,134 cu. in.
   (b) $6\frac{1}{2}$ in. × 12 in. × 15 in. = 1,170 cu. in.
   (c) $1\frac{2}{3}$ ft. × 2 ft. × 7 ft. = $23\frac{1}{3}$ cu. ft.
4. (a) 8 ft. × 7 ft. × 4 ft. = 224 cu. ft.
   (b) 224 × $6\frac{1}{4}$ = 1,400 gal.
5. (a) 1,728. (b) 1,728.
6. 2 ft. × 2 ft. × 9 ft. = 36 cu. ft.
7. (a) 1 cu. in.
   (b) 2 in. × 2 in. × 2 in. = 8 cu. in.
   (c) 27 cu. in.

Test 13

1. "Cent" in these words means "hundred."
2. 1 in 100, $\frac{1}{100}$.
3. (a) £10.
   (b) £40.
4. (a) $33\frac{1}{3}$.
   (b) $33\frac{1}{3}\%$.
   (c) 25%.
5. Half and half; equal shares between two.
6. (a) $\frac{50}{100} = \frac{1}{2}$.
   (b) $\frac{25}{100} = \frac{1}{4}$.
   (c) $\frac{75}{100} = \frac{3}{4}$.
   (d) $\frac{100}{100} = 1$ (that is, all the lot).
   (e) $\frac{12\frac{1}{2}}{100} = \frac{25}{200} = \frac{1}{8}$.
   (f) $\frac{15}{100} = \frac{3}{20}$.

Test 14

1. $3\cdot7 + 1\cdot8$ in. = $5\cdot5$ in.
2. $5\cdot3 − 1\cdot8$ in. = $3\cdot5$ in.
3. It shows which is the units figure. It is placed after the units figure.
4. (a) $27\cdot3$ in. (c) $106\cdot4$ ft.
   (b) $134\cdot4$ in. (d) $82\cdot8$ yd.
5. (a) $\cdot6$ in. (c) $\cdot25$ in.
   (b) $2\cdot3$ in. (d) $1\cdot6$ in.

Test 15

1. (a) $1,041\cdot4$ mm.
   (b) $32\cdot1869$ km., or 32 km. approx.
2. (a) 15 yd. 4 ft. $2\frac{1}{2}$ in.
   (b) 2 ft. $7\frac{1}{2}$ in.
3. (a) 44 lb. $1\frac{1}{2}$ oz.
   (b) $24\cdot7$ oz.
4. (a) $0\cdot964$ kg.
   (b) $4\cdot133$ tons
5. (a) $28\cdot16$ pints.
   (b) $3\cdot41$ litres
6. (a) $104°F$
   (b) $82\cdot2°C$

WHAT YOU SHOULD KNOW ABOUT
ENGLISH

I. HOW TO BE GOOD AT ENGLISH

You would like, I expect, to be good at English. There is one sure way of succeeding. Here it is—in four sentences:

(1) You must read lots of books and magazines.

(2) You must listen attentively to sensible people whenever you hear them talking.

(3) You must never lose an opportunity of asking them about what you do not understand when they talk to you.

(4) You must be ready at all times to try to put into words, clearly and definitely, what you have been thinking or feeling about any important matter that concerns you.

All this may sound simple enough. Anybody ought to be able to cope with it. But it calls for an alert mind; and how few of us ever manage to keep our minds alert for long? You will have to try if you want to succeed. You will need a friend to advise and help you from time to time, one who can tell you honestly how he thinks you are getting on. However, you will be able to do a great deal for yourself without outside help. If you attend closely to what we shall say you will find that you will be able to go ahead much faster and better than you ever thought you could. No doubt, your friend and others will notice it, too. Two things there are to avoid, though, when you are in company: the first thing to avoid is to be continually talking without thinking (to give way to the gift of the gab, as we say); the other thing is to avoid becoming so much wrapped up in yourself as not to want to talk to other people at all.

Your teachers and others, whose business it may be to find out how you are progressing in your attempt to master the English language, do so in various ways. For example, they may get you to read a few lines of print and then question you in order to see if you have understood what you have read. Thus, they may ask you to put into your own words what you think you have been reading about, and then engage you in conversation on the subject. Or they may content themselves with asking you the meaning of one or two of the words which you may not have found easy to pronounce. They may sometimes require you to write a sentence or two—or more, even a short letter or essay, maybe—and then note how well you are able to spell and whether you can frame good sentences.

You will find some questions to answer later on. We shall give you plenty of chances to work the kind of test or exercise often set by teachers as preliminaries to more important examinations. We shall also supply the answers, but not on the same page as the test or exercise. It you are sensible you will not allow yourself to look at the answers until you have tried to answer the questions yourself. You cannot expect always to be right, of course, and when you find that your answers do not agree with the answers which we give, and that you don't understand why this is so, then you must ask your friend to help you. But whether he can help you or not, you must not rest until you know just where and how you went wrong. This is a most important step in learning anything. Many of us, indeed, can only learn anything hard by trying to do it and then thinking about the mistakes we are bound to have made. You will be making good progress when you are able to discover where and how you made a mistake.

II. ENJOY YOUR READING

Let us begin with your reading. It is most important to bear in mind that you ought to be able to talk sense about anything you have read and understood. So be ready to talk to your friends about what you read. This helps you to find out how far you really have understood what you have read, and you can go back and make sure of any part of it which you may be unable to recall clearly. This prevents what you have read from slipping away and being forgotten. Besides, it is an excellent way of training your memory and is very useful to you later on.

There is a well-known kind of memory-training that is based almost entirely on getting children to read, just once and no more, a paragraph or a short chapter of a book, after which they are required to re-tell what they have read, or some interesting part of it, and then to add anything they may wish to say about it.

A famous Englishman who lived two hundred years ago, Dr. Johnson, told his friends that when he was a child just able to walk, his mother would often relate a story to him and then send him away to repeat it to a servant while it was still fresh in his mind. He felt quite sure, he said, that this was one of the ways in which he was helped to acquire a good memory. So you should try to re-tell stories you read in a manner that will give your friends as much pleasure as the stories have given you.

How often you must have heard others say that they have read a story and enjoyed it and yet, when asked why they thought it good, are at a loss for words—they have never bothered to be sure of what exactly it was that was described in the story which they say they enjoyed. All they can say is that it was very good, or marvellous, or exciting, or "smashing." How much better it is to be able to re-tell one or two of the incidents in it in a way that will convince another person that it really was very good, or marvellous, or exciting, or "smashing." Suppose, for instance, that you have been reading the story of Red Riding Hood for the first time, and you have been asked what you thought of it. Will you be content to say it was very good or exciting? Or will you say something like this: that you found it most interesting, particularly in the parts where the excitement is gradually worked up when a wolf, who pretended to be Red Riding Hood's grandmother, had to explain first why her ears were so long and then why her eyes were big, too, and at last why her mouth and the teeth in it were so big. ("All the better to eat you with.") To be able to do this kind of thing makes others listen to you because your pleasure becomes theirs and they, in turn, will be encouraged to read the story.

Most stories that are worth telling have been written down and printed in books. Children who make the greatest progress in English are always borrowing fresh books to read. I expect there is a public library in the district where you live. It will no doubt have a well-stocked section for children. Find the way to join it and make full use of it. So many new books are being written and published every year that it is difficult to compile a good up-to-date list of books which you may like to read, but there are scores of old favourites.

Here is a list of fifty-one books which children have usually liked to read. They may not all be of the kind you will enjoy. If you find one you don't care for, you should put it aside and try it again later on. Others will please you greatly and you will want to read them again and again.

Books to Read

(1) *The Book of Nursery Tales* (H. M. Brock)

(2) *The Story of Little Black Sambo* (Helen Bannerman)

(3) *The Tale of Peter Rabbit* (Beatrix Potter)

(4) *Milly-Molly-Mandy* (Joyce Brisley)

(5) *The Dutch Twins* (Lucy Perkins)

(6) *The Eskimo Twins* (Lucy Perkins)

(7) *Jackanapes* (Horatia Ewing)

(8) *What Katy Did* (Susan Coolidge)

(9) *The Water Babies* (Charles Kingsley)

(10) *Black Beauty* (Anna Sewell)

(11) *Dr. Dolittle* (Hugh Lofting)

(12) *Fairy Tales* (Hans Andersen)

(13) *Uncle Remus* (J. Chandler Harris)

(14) *Shadow, the Sheepdog* (E. Blyton)

(15) *Fables* (Aesop)

(16) *Stories from the Bible* (Walter de la Mare)

(17) *Just William* (Richmal Crompton)

(18) *My Bible Book* (Joyce Brisley)

(19) *Animal Stories* (Walter de la Mare)

(20) *The Tailor of Gloucester* (Beatrix Potter)

(21) *Little Women* (Louisa M. Alcott)

(22) *Just So Stories* (Rudyard Kipling)

(23) *The Wind in the Willows* (Kenneth Grahame)

(24) *Pinocchio* (Carlo Collodi)

(25) *Rip Van Winkle* (Washington Irving)

(26) *Tanglewood Tales* (Nathaniel Hawthorne)

(27) *Coral Island* (R. M. Ballantyne)

(28) *Hans Brinker and the Silver Skates* (Mary Dodge)

(29) *Rob and his Friends* (Dr. John Brown)

(30) *The Adventures of Tom Sawyer* (Mark Twain)

(31) *Puck of Pook's Hill* (Rudyard Kipling)

(32) *Robin Hood* (Carola Oman)

(33) *A Wonder Book of Old Romance* (Harvey Danton)

(34) *Call of the Wild* (Jack London)

(35) *The Young Fur Traders* (R. M. Ballantyne)

(36) *The Heroes* (Charles Kingsley)

(37) *Heidi* (Johanna Speyer)

(38) *The Jungle Book* (Rudyard Kipling)

(39) *Children of the New Forest* (Captain F. Marryat)

(40) *Tales from Shakespeare* (Charles and Mary Lamb)

(41) *The Deerslayer* (Fennimore Cooper)

(42) *Swiss Family Robinson* (J. R. Wyss)

(43) *Stories from the Arabian Nights* (Laurence Housman)

(44) *Treasure Island* (R. L. Stevenson)

(45) *A Christmas Carol* (Charles Dickens)

(46) *Robinson Crusoe* (Daniel Defoe)

(47) *David Copperfield* (Charles Dickens)

(48) *Oliver Twist* (Charles Dickens)

(49) *The Pilgrim's Progress* (J. Bunyan)

(50) *Alice in Wonderland* (Lewis Carroll)

(51) *Vice-Versa* (F. Anstey)

There are also a number of stories in the form of poems which most children discover and read with enjoyment at some time or other. Here are a half-dozen. You ought to try them.

(1) *The Pied Piper of Hamelin* (Robert Browning)

(2) *The Diverting History of John Gilpin* (William Cowper)

(3) *Hiawatha* (H. W. Longfellow)

(4) *The Hunting of the Snark* (Lewis Carroll)

(5) *Lays of Ancient Rome* (Lord Macaulay)

(6) *The Ancient Mariner* (S. T. Coleridge)

What kinds of questions are you likely to be asked about what you have read? A teacher or an examiner may ask you to tell him face to face what you have been reading and what you found the most interesting part of it, or he may ask you to write a short account of the book or describe your favourite character in it. It is more usual, however, to ask you to answer a number of questions in writing about a short passage only, that has been taken from an interesting book. This kind of test nearly always finds a place in the examination which children are expected to be able to cope with at the age of ten and a half or eleven years of age.

It's Fun to Test Yourself—1

Here is a poem from *Peacock Pie* by Walter de la Mare which a child of eight or nine should be able to manage. Read it, and then see if you can supply the answers to the questions which follow.

POOR HENRY

Thick in its glass
    The physic stands,
Poor Henry lifts
    Distracted hands;
His round cheek wans
    In the candlelight,
To smell that smell!
    To see that sight!

Finger and thumb
    Clinch his small nose,
A gurgle, a gasp,
    And down it goes;
Scowls Henry now;
    But mark that cheek,
Sleek with the bloom
    Of health next week.

Now answer these questions:
(1) Do you know another name for "physic"? What is it?
(2) Which line in the second verse tells us that Henry was a little boy and not a grown-up?
(3) How does the poet say that Henry goes pale?
(4) Whose "finger and thumb" are mentioned, do you think?
(5) Was Henry happy or not when he had swallowed the physic? Which word in the second verse tells you?
(6) Find a word in the poem which means "smooth and neat."
(7) Which lines tell you that Henry was very upset when the physic was brought to him?
(8) "To see that sight!" What sight?
(9) Find a word in the poem which means "hold tight."
(10) "A gurgle, a gasp." What caused these?

(*Answers on page* 356)

Test Yourself—2

Your teacher or your examiner may, however, ask you to choose the best answer from four (or five or six) which he will offer you. He may, for example, ask you to read the following story and then go on to the questions that follow it.

THE DOG AND THE SHADOW

A dog that had stolen a piece of meat out of a butcher's shop was crossing a river on his way home when he saw his own shadow reflected in the stream below. He thought that it was another dog with another piece of meat, so he resolved to make himself master of that also, but in snapping at the supposed treasure, he dropped the piece he was carrying and so lost all.—*Aesop.*

Pick out the best answer to the following questions:
(1) Where did the dog see a picture of himself? In the butcher's. In the

looking glass. In the water. In the treasure.

(2) Which word tells you that the dog *made up his mind*? Snapped. Reflected. Saw. Resolved.

(3) Which word tells you that the meat which the dog snapped at was not real? Supposed. Resolved. Reflected. Stolen.

(*Answers on page 356*)

III. LEARNING TO SPELL

Spelling is not a very exciting subject, but we need not make it too dull. Are you good at spelling? Some find it easy; others find it hard. Good spelling is not, of course, so

important in writing as good sense and good taste, but it is easier to learn. Many grown-ups spell certain words wrongly over and over again. They seem to have a blind spot for a particular word. I knew a very clever man who always spelt *amiable* wrongly; perhaps this was because he read a great many French books and was misled by the French word *aimable*, which has much the same meaning. The famous scientist Charles Darwin kept a diary while on a long sea voyage and several times wrote *abroard* for *abroad* and *yatch* for *yacht*.

A good deal of bad spelling comes from our not remembering our spelling rules. A few of these rules are set out below. They are easy to understand and they are well worth storing in your memory.

RULE A

I expect that you must have heard someone remind you of our first rule: it is:
   "*I before E except after C*"
Here are some words that follow this rule:
I before E: achieve, believe, brief, chief, grieve, mischief, relief, relieve, reprieve, siege, sieve, thief.

But *after C* we get: deceit, deceive, receipt, receive, perceive, ceiling.

A few words disobey the rule, such as: *forfeit, counterfeit,* and *seize*. You must be careful about *seize* and *siege*; they are frequently confused.

Test Yourself—3

An exercise which you may now be able to work quite correctly follows. Write out the sentences, filling in the missing letters marked with dots:

(1) I gr..ved to think that you meant to dec..ve me, but I was rel..ved to find that I was mistaken.

(2) The th..f s..zed the counterf..t coins and made off.

(3) The rel..f of the city ended a three months' s..ge.

(4) Did you rec..ve the stolen s..ve from Tom? If so you must forf..t your pocket money.

(5) I bel..ve you have the rec..pt for the money you gave me.

(*Answers on page 356*)

RULE B

Any word that is used as the name of a single object or thing is said to be in the *Singular*. A word used as the name of more than one thing is said to be in the *Plural*. As a rule we show the plural by adding *s* to the singular, for example: *pen, pens; boy, boys; girl, girls; boot, boots*. Some names do not obey this rule. We must deal with three groups of names that follow a different rule.

RULE C

Names of objects and things that have their singular ending with a *y* (like *daisy*). Change the *y* into *ies* for their plural (like *daisies*).

344

Here are some more examples: *army, armies; berry, berries; body, bodies; city, cities; colony, colonies; dairy, dairies; diary, diaries; duty, duties; enemy, enemies; fairy, fairies; gypsy, gypsies; melody, melodies; party, parties; penny, pennies; pony, ponies; salary, salaries; story, stories; study, studies.*

But when a vowel (that is, an *a, e, i, o,* or *u*) comes before the *y* (as in *key*), then we spell the plural with *s* and not *ies* (like *keys*). Some examples are: *day, days; essay, essays; way, ways; donkey, donkeys; monkey, monkeys; jersey, jerseys; journey, journeys; toy, toys; convoy, convoys; guy, guys; buoy, buoys.*

Two words to be careful about are *storey*, as in: "This house has two *storeys*," and *story*, as in: "Children like to have *stories* told to them"—(*storey, storeys; story, stories*).

Now see if you can get the next exercise right.

Test Yourself—4

Change the following sentences by writing the *plural* instead of the *singular* where you see a word in italic type. (You may have to leave out the words *the* or *a* sometimes.)

(1) The *gypsy* went into the *city*.
(2) I am very fond of my *donkey* and my *pony*.
(3) We like reading a *story* about an *army* fighting a strong *enemy*.
(4) The *Malay* took a *party* on a *journey* to make a *study* of the *monkey*.
(5) She gave a *penny* for her *toy*.

(Answers on page 356)

Rule D

Many names that end in *f* in the singular (like *loaf*) take *ves* in the plural (like *loaves*). Examples of these words are: *calf, calves; leaf, leaves; elf, elves; half, halves; wolf, wolves; self, selves; thief, thieves.*

But there are many other words with their singular ending in *f* that just add *s*

for their plurals. Here are some: *chief, chiefs; dwarf, dwarfs; roof, roofs; belief, beliefs; gulf, gulfs; cuff, cuffs; serf, serfs; whiff, whiffs; chef, chefs.*

Test Yourself—5

Write the following sentences, changing the words in italic type from singular to plural:

(1) The *thief* broke through the *roof*.
(2) The *wolf* killed the *calf* that belonged to the *chief*.
(3) The *serf* ate the *loaf* greedily.
(4) The *boy* threw away the *leaf*.
(5) The *elf* danced with the *dwarf* and the *fairy*.

(Answers on page 357)

Rule E

Many names that have *o* for their ending in the singular (like *hero*) take *oes* for their plural (like *heroes*). Some examples are: *echo, echoes; cargo, cargoes; motto, mottoes; negro, negroes; potato, potatoes; tomato, tomatoes; volcano, volcanoes.*

But there are others that just take *s* in the plural. Here are some of these: *banjo, banjos; curio, curios; Eskimo, Eskimos; piano, pianos; solo, solos; zoo, zoos.*

Test Yourself—6

Re-write the following sentences, changing the singular to plural where words are in italic type:

(1) The *negro* helped to carry the *curio* aboard.
(2) In the *cargo* were a *piano* and a *banjo*.
(3) Cook me a *potato* and a *tomato* to go with my meat.
(4) The *Eskimo* sang a *solo*; the *negro* played on a *banjo*.

(Answers on page 357)

Rule F

This rule covers just a few words— names that have their singular ending in *x, ch, s* or *z*. These words take *es* for the *plurals*. Examples are: *atlas, atlases; bus, buses; minus, minuses; kiss, kisses; buzz, buzzes; fox, foxes; church, churches.*

IV. SAME SOUND, BUT DIFFERENT SPELLINGS

There are lots of words that sound alike but are spelt differently and have different meanings. Here are some: *seen, scene; fair, fare; rain, rein.* The best way of learning to spell these correctly is to hold

fair *fare*

them in your memory in the form of a sentence which you can see in your mind's eye as it is printed or written down. Below there is a list of some of these troublesome words in sentences which show their meanings.

(1) The choir moved slowly up the *aisle*.
The *Isle* of Man is in the Irish Sea.

(2) Children are not *allowed* to buy cigarettes.
Cry out *aloud* and you may be heard.

(3) We played on the *beach* at the seaside.
It is shady beneath the *beech* tree.

(4) The flies settled on the *ceiling*.
We fastened the parcels with *sealing* wax.

(5) The coal is kept in the *cellar*.
This book is a best-*seller*.

(6) Do you like a *cereal* for breakfast?
I like reading the *serial* story in my weekly paper.

(7) *Coarse* oatmeal makes very good porridge.
My brother is taking a *course* at school.

(8) Is your father a member of the local *council*?
He is the kind of person to give you good *counsel*.

(9) I prefer a plain cake to a *currant* cake.

The electric *current* gave me a shock.

(10) Mother got a cold through sitting in a *draught*.
Simon was in the first *draft* for the navy.

(11) I believe in *fair* play.
The bus conductor collected my *fare*.

(12) Bread is made from *flour*.
The *flower* I like best is the rose.

(13) *Foul* play was suspected.
The chicken was a tender *fowl*.

(14) Don't leave the ashes in the *grate*.
Nelson and Wellington were *great* men.

(15) Father's photograph stood on the desk in a *gilt* frame.
The thief was overcome by a sense of *guilt*.

(16) Can't you *hear* what I say?
Come *here* at once!

(17) Misers *hoard* their wealth.
Down the valley came a *horde* of savages.

(18) Take the *key* of the door.
We waited for the ship at the wrong *quay*.

(19) Is that the *main* reason for your visit?
The lion has a fine *mane* of hair.

(20) Have you a *pain* in your stomach?
Sam broke the window *pane* with his ball.

(21) I should like a *piece* of that cake.
After war comes *peace*.

(22) Do you like to hear the church bells *pealing*?
John was *peeling* an orange just now.

(23) We saw you on the *pier* at the seaside.
Why did you *peer* at me through those opera glasses?

(24) I went to the baths to *practise* diving.
We had a good hour's *practice*.

(25) The grocer made a good *profit*.
Elijah was a *prophet* who spoke out against evil-doers.

(26) Can you *read*?
Pan made a pipe from a *reed* growing on the river bank.

(27) It always *rains* at the wrong time.
Hold the horses' *reins* tightly.

(28) Boats *sail* on the river.
Mother bought this hat at a *sale*.

(29) What a pretty *scene* the garden is now!
Have you *seen* it?

(30) Mother *sews* the shirt buttons on.
The farmer *sows* the seeds.

(31) This would make a good *site* for a new school.
Children dancing happily are a lovely *sight*.

(32) Thou shalt not *steal*.
Knife blades are made of *steel*.

peer

pier

(33) John was standing on the *stairs*.
I don't like the way she *stares* at me.

(34) Help me over the *stile* please.
Do you like her *style* of dress?

(35) Manx cats have no *tails*.
Bob told those *tales* very well.

(36) John *threw* the stone.
It went *through* the window.

(37) They went and *told* the sexton.
The sexton *tolled* the bell.

(38) A *vale* is another name for a valley.
She put on a white *veil*.

(39) How *vain* you are!
The blood came from my *vein*.

(40) Mary has a slender *waist*.
Waste not, want not.

Now for an exercise which will show at once whether you can say how to spell the words that have been given you to learn in Sections III and IV.

Test Yourself—7

Copy and complete the following sentences:

(1) I bel..ve I saw you at the sa.. buying jers..s.

(2) We bought these loa..s at a shop in a building which was four stor..s high.

(3) Both Eskim.s and negr..es live in North America.

(4) Arm..s of wol..s gave us no p..ce.

(5) We mix the fl..r with the curr.nts for the cake.

(6) The thie..s took coun..l together.

(7) I dropped the p..ces on the sta..s.

(8) Tom did not mean to break the window p... with his ball.

(9) We are not al....d to speak al..d in class.

(10) The robber who stole the g.lt candlesticks admitted his g..lt.

(*Answers on page 357*)

V. RUNNING TWO WORDS INTO ONE

In speaking we often run two words into one. For example, we say *I'll* instead of *I will*. In order to make it quite clear that we mean *I will* and not *ill* (unwell) when we write it down, we put in a comma to show that letters have been missed out. The comma is placed above the line and in this position it is called an apostrophe (a-pos-tro-fee). The following are some of the commoner forms found:

all's	(All's well.)
can't	(I can't go.)
didn't	(I didn't do it.)
doesn't	(He doesn't know.)
don't	(Don't interfere.)
hasn't	(She hasn't washed.)

haven't	(We haven't any pens.)
he'd	(He'd like to come.)
he'll	(He'll be late for school.)
he's	(He's in the playground.)
I'll	(I'll catch you.)
I'd	(I'd rather not go.)
I'm	(I'm in a hurry.)
isn't	(Isn't it hot!)
it's	(It's nearly ready.)
I've	(I've lost my purse.)
needn't	(You needn't stay.)
o'clock	(It's five o'clock.)
o'er	(for *over* in poetry.)
shan't	(You shan't come.)
she'll	(She'll be afraid.)
shouldn't	(You shouldn't tease her.)
that's	(That's the sort I want.)
there's	(There's room for all.)
they'll	(They'll catch you.)
we'll	(We'll try hard.)
we've	(We've come to stay.)
where've	(Where've you been?)
won't	(Won't you tell us?)
wouldn't	(Wouldn't you like to?)
you'll	(You'll have to look out.)
you're	(You're not trying.)

Perhaps now you will be able to say what difference there is between *ill* and *I'll; its* and *it's; well* and *we'll*. Notice the difference between *its* and *it's* in:

The tree has lost *its* leaves.

It's getting late.

ONLY when *it's* means *it is* must you put an apostrophe.

Test Yourself—8

Could you pick out the right way of writing the words in the following exercise?

(1) I hope youre we'll/you're well.

(2) Its/It's a fine day today.

(3) Dont/don't touch the fire.

(4) Wont/won't you come in?

(5) She'll/shell see me coming, I'm/Im sure.

(6) Theres/there's room for everybody in the coach.

(7) All's/alls we'll/well that ends we'll/well.

(8) Wouldnt/wouldn't you like to go at one oclock/o'clock?

(9) Don't/dont say I didnt/didn't warn you.

(10) Isnt/Isn't it hot!

(*Answers on page 357*)

VI. "I AM, I WAS, I HAVE BEEN"

Notice that you change the word after *I* in order to show whether you are speaking about something past and over, about something that now is, or about something that is still to come.

Did you notice that two ways of speaking about the past are set out above —*I was* and *I have been*? In much the same way, we say, *I began* and *I have begun*, or *I saw* and *I have seen*. Children are often puzzled whether to say *began* or *begun*, *saw* or *seen*, *broke* or *broken* after *I have*, *she has*, and *we have*, *you have*, and *they have*.

In the list which follows it is the second word that takes *have*, *has*, or *had* before it. Go through the list and make sure that you say *I have* before the second word of each pair.

beat, beaten
began, begun
bit, bitten
broke, broken
chose, chosen
drank, drunk
drew, drawn
drove, driven
ate, eaten
fell, fallen
flew, flown
forgot, forgotten
froze, frozen
gave, given
grew, grown
hid, hidden
knew, known
lay, lain
ran, run

rang, rung
rode, ridden
rose, risen
sang, sung
shook, shaken
spoke, spoken
swam, swum
tore, torn
wove, woven
wrote, written

Test Yourself—9

Copy out the following and complete the words that have missing letters.

(1) I wish I hadn't wr. . . . . that letter.
(2) A dog has bi . . . . my legs.
(3) Is this the song which the choir has just s . ng?
(4) I see that you've dr . nk all the milk.
(5) The man has sh . k . . his fist at us.

(6) The horseman had r . d . . . all day, and he f . . l asleep as soon as he had la . . down.
(7) Have you forgo . . . . what the teacher told you?
(8) Which cake have you chos . . ?
(9) The paper had been tor . into two.
(10) How far have they sw . m this morning?
(11) We dr . . k our lemonade after we had s . ng our song.
(12) By the time we had g . v . . the signal the birds had fl . . . away.
(13) The man had r . n away before I r . . g the alarm.
(14) The cloth shr . nk when it was washed.
(15) The cup had f . . . . . from the table and lay brok . . on the floor.

(Answers on page 357)

VII. DIFFERENT KINDS OF THINGS

One of the signs that a child is getting on in his English is his ability to put into a class things that are alike in some way or another and give them a name.

For example, cheese, meat, bread, and potatoes are *food*.

Peas, potatoes, cabbage, and onions are *vegetables*.

Coats, shirts, jumpers, and frocks are *clothing*.

Can you find the class word for the groups of things set out below?

Brown, Smith, Robinson and Jones.

Test Yourself—10

(1) Roses, buttercups, tulips, and dandelions are —
(2) Salmon, cod, herrings, and sprats are —
(3) Oats, barley, wheat, and rye are —
(4) Tea, coffee, and cocoa are —
(5) Beech, elm, ash, oak, and poplar are —
(6) Brown, Smith, Robinson, and Jones are —

(7) Diamond, emerald, sapphire, and ruby are —
(8) Granite, coal, slate, chalk, and limestone are —
(9) Street, road, avenue, and lane are —
(10) Turkey, goose, duck, and hen are —
(11) Bus, car, tram, and carriage are —
(12) Asia, Africa, America, Europe, and Australia are —
(13) Oxygen, nitrogen, hydrogen, and chlorine are —

(14) King, President, Emperor, and Shah are —

(15) Cloves, nutmeg, and pepper are —

(16) Ants, bees, and butterflies are —

(17) Gold, tin, copper, and lead are —

(18) Fretwork, photography, bee-keeping, and stamp-collecting are —

(19) Port, champagne, claret, and burgundy are —

(20) Bags, basins, boxes, and casks are —

(Answers on page 357)

VIII. OPPOSITES

The opposite of *friend* is *enemy* or *foe*. Here are some more opposites: *victory, defeat; fast, slow; front, back; full, empty; day, night.*

Notice that you have different words in each pair. We may also make opposites by adding a *prefix* to certain words: *obey* and *disobey* are opposites and *dis-* is a prefix as it is fixed in front of *obey*. Other prefixes are *mis-; un-; il-; im-; in-; ir-; non-; anti-*.

Here are some words whose opposites can be formed by using prefixes:

advantage	disadvantage
allow	disallow
approve	disapprove
aware	unaware
behave	misbehave
common	uncommon
considerate	inconsiderate
correct	incorrect
cyclone	anti-cyclone
direct	indirect
engage	disengage
fair	unfair
happy	unhappy
legal	illegal
loyal	disloyal
merciful	unmerciful
modest	immodest
mortal	immortal
necessary	unnecessary
noble	ignoble
order	disorder
prudent	imprudent
pure	impure

regular	irregular
sane	insane
sense	nonsense
trust	mistrust or distrust
visible	invisible
wise	unwise
worthy	unworthy

Words which are opposites may also be formed in two other ways. Some words change the prefix, for example: *ascend, descend; encourage, discourage; export, import; exterior, interior; external, internal; increase, decrease; inside, outside.*

Other words change the *suffix*, or the part added at the end of a word. For example: *careful, careless; faithful, faithless; hopeful, hopeless; cheerful, cheerless; joyful, joyless; merciful, merciless; needful, needless; tactful, tactless; useful, useless.*

Test Yourself—11

Rewrite the following sentences, adding or altering prefixes to change the words in italic type to their opposites:

(1) John was not the *obedient* child I once knew.

(2) What *encouraging* remarks we heard.

(3) Mary had a *pleasant* time at the party.

(4) Your answers are usually *intelligent*.

(5) His writing is *legible*.

(6) This stamp, I see, is *perfect*.

(7) Such *formal* treatment made the King angry.

(8) How *polite* you are!

(9) I want the *interior* of my house painted.

(Answers on page 357)

IX. COMPARISONS

I expect you have noticed how some people like to compare one thing with another when they talk, especially when it helps them to make what they say more striking or more vivid. For instance, they may tell you that you are *as mischievous as a monkey*, or, when you have not heard what they have said, that you are *as deaf as a post*. I have also heard a stubborn boy told that he was *as obstinate as a mule* and a boy who was caught doing something wrong that he turned *as red as a turkey-cock*. Perhaps you and your friends have been described as being *as thick as thieves*.

I hope you haven't been described as being *as changeable as the weather* or *as miserable as sin*, but rather that you are usually *as happy as a lark, as pleased*

As obstinate as a mule.

as Punch, and *as right as rain*. I hope your friends are *as true as steel* and *as steady as a rock*, and if you have a grown-up friend I hope he is *as wise as an owl* and *as patient as Job*. All these comparisons are called *similes* (*sim-il-iz*).

Test Yourself—12

See if you can find out which are the usual similes for ending the following sentences. Rewrite each sentence and complete it:

(1) The fellow was as slippery as —
(2) The beef was as tender as —
(3) The poor child stood there trembling like —
(4) We all laughed but John remained as sober as —
(5) The water in the spring was as clear as —
(6) She was so scared that she looked as white as —
(7) The impudent youth came up to us as bold as —
(8) I came back from my holiday as brown as —
(9) The young wrestler was as strong as —
(10) She awoke next morning as fresh as —
(11) I lifted her and she seemed as light as —
(12) The old man was half-starved and as thin as —
(13) In those days Henry was as poor as —
(14) He stood there as pale as —
(15) Mary wasn't upset; she was as cool as —
(16) Sam was ill-tempered and as sour as —
(17) He is as sharp as — and as keen as —
(18) He finds his lessons as easy as —
(19) Marmaduke was as cunning as —
(20) The baby was as good as —

(*Answers on page 357*)

X. FORMING NEW WORDS

Look at the words *succeed, strong*, and *proud* in the following sentences:

(1) I hope I shall be able to *succeed* in my task.
(2) He was a very *strong* man.
(3) She was *proud* of her children.

Could you find the words you would have to use instead of *succeed, strong*, and *proud* in the following three short sentences?

(1) I am hoping for — in my task.
(2) He was a man of great —

351

(3) She felt great — in her children.

The answers are *success*, *strength*, and *pride*.

We say that *success* and *succeed* are formed from the same "root"; so are *strong* and *strength*; and so are *pride* and *proud*.

You will find that you will frequently be asked to change some words that are given to you for other words that have been formed from them. The usual way in which you will meet with this kind of exercise is shown clearly in the following example:

VALUABLE. The watch was a thing of great VALUE. The noun (name) corresponding to *valuable* is *value*.

Test Yourself—13

Now write out the following sentences, filling in the missing words. Write clearly and spell correctly.

(1)	BRIGHT.	The — of the sun was dazzling.
(2)	PURE.	The spring water round here is renowned for its —
(3)	DEEP.	Be careful not to get out of your — when you bathe.
(4)	POOR.	In this part of the world there is a great deal of —
(5)	POPULAR.	The Prime Minister enjoyed great —
(6)	CRUEL.	The enemy gained a reputation in the last war for great —
(7)	YOUNG.	Henry V was an unusually wild —
(8)	GENEROUS.	The old gentleman was famous for his — towards everyone.
(9)	WISE.	Solomon had a great reputation for —
(10)	PUBLIC.	Whatever he did was given a full measure of —

(Answers on page 357)

All the words in capital letters in the last exercise are called *Adjectives*. We don't use them as a rule unless there is something else in our minds which they describe. If I say, "A long," you will ask, "A long what?" If I say, "Brave," you will ask, "Who is brave?" Adjectives describe; they describe *objects*, *persons*, *events*, and so on: a *round* piece of metal, a *tall* person, a *sad* event, a *poor* effort, *mischievous* conduct. Here the words *round*, *tall*, *sad*, *poor*, and *mischievous* are adjectives.

Sometimes you may meet a similar kind of exercise in this form:

GIVE. Have you a birthday — for John?

The word to write for the dash is *gift*; it is the *Noun* which is formed from the *Verb* give.

Test Yourself—14

Rewrite and complete the following examples. Where you see a dash you have to write the *Noun* formed from the *Verb* in capital letters at the beginning of the sentence.

(1)	COMPEL.	The prisoner obeyed orders only under —
(2)	BEG.	Poverty made him a —
(3)	SPEAK.	The audience listened attentively to his long —
(4)	FEED.	The hungry were filled with good —
(5)	FAIL.	The result will not, I hope, be a —
(6)	IGNORE.	You may have to remain in — of what happened.

(7) VARY. The flowers shown were many and of great —

(8) DISOBEY. I hope you will be very sorry for your —

(9) RECOGNIZE. He had changed out of all —

(10) MAINTAIN. The house cost the landlord £2 a week for —

(Answers on page 357)

XI. GRAMMAR

When we talk about the way in which words are put together or should be put together to make sentences we are talking about *grammar*. Grammar deals with the rules for putting words together to make sense. You will hear teachers, for instance, speaking about *nouns* and *verbs* and *adjectives*. These are grammatical terms, that is, words that we need in talking about how sentences are built up. Let us make it clear what these words mean.

A *noun* is a name. It is the name given to a place, or a person, or a thing. The words *John* and *diamond* are nouns; so are *Wonderland* and *happiness*. Whenever you say, "Let us talk about . . . ," then whatever you decide to talk about can be named by a noun.

Now, if you use a word to describe the particular thing or person or place you talk about, the word you use is called an *adjective*. For instance, you might speak of *big* or *little* John, *bright* diamond, *strange* Wonderland, or *great* happiness. The words *big*, *little*, *bright*, *strange*, and *great* are adjectives. You could, of course, make all these adjectives into *nouns* by adding *-ness* to them: *big*, *bigness; little*,

littleness; bright, *brightness; strange*, *strangeness; great*, *greatness*. These are *abstract* nouns; you could not point to them, or touch them, or hear them, or see them: that is why we call them abstract.

It is hard to say in words what we mean by a *verb*. Many teachers call it a "doing" word and give examples like *eat*, *drink*, *run*, *fly*, *swim*, *shout*. We will leave it at that. Now for some examples of how you will be expected to use what you know about nouns, verbs, and adjectives.

Test Yourself—15

Make three lists, one headed *nouns*, one headed *adjectives*, and one headed *verbs*. When you have done so, find words in the following sentences to write down under your headings. There will be ten of each.

When little Peter saw the poor child he waved, ran towards him, took him by the left hand and brought him to the open door to see the big buses and cars go by. The bright sun shone; smiling crowds filled the wide pavements and enjoyed the warm, summery weather.

(Answers on page 357)

XII. PRONOUNS

Have you ever read a statement like this: "I, John Smith, do hereby declare"? The word *I* means the same in this case as *John Smith*. You may often see, too, a statement beginning with the words, "We, the undersigned . . ." with the names of a number of persons at the foot of the statement. Here the word *we* means the

persons whose names are added below what is said. Now, it would be awkward if we had to say or write the names of people or things every time we had to refer to them. For instance, we do not say, "John saw a woman and the woman asked John to tell the woman the way to the Post Office." We say, "John saw a

353

woman who asked him to tell her the way to the Post Office." All these words used in place of nouns are called *pronouns*.

Some children, and some grown-ups as well, make mistakes in using pronouns. For instance, they say *I* instead of *me* in "Between you and me" and "Let you and me do it." Another kind of mistake they often make is to say "me" instead of "I" in sentences like "She is as old as I."

Test Yourself—16

See if you can complete the following sentences correctly by picking out the right pronouns in the brackets.

(1) Are you older than (he, him)?
(2) The teacher chose Tom and (I, me) to go.
(3) John is nearly as tall as (I, me).
(4) Is it (they, them) who want me?
(5) You and (she, her) must come here together.
(6) My friend and (I, me) are both scouts.
(7) Who was right? (He or I? Him or me?)
(8) You are both older than (we, us).
(9) Are you sure it was (she, her)?
(10) Jane's sister is taller than (I, me).

(*Answers on page 358*)

XIII. GOOD ENGLISH TODAY

Examiners are fond of asking you to rewrite correctly sentences that have errors in them. Some of the kinds of error they ask you to deal with follow:

Comparing Two or More Things

This one is bett*er*, bigg*er*, old*er*, grand*er*, redd*er*, green*er*, or saf*er* than another one; but if there are more than two things compared then this one may be the b*est*, bigg*est*, old*est*, grand*est*, redd*est*, green*est*, saf*est* of the lot.

Again, this one is *more* comfortable, *more* expensive, *more* convenient, *more* useful, or *more* satisfactory than the other; but if there are several things then this one may be the *most* comfortable, *most* expensive, *most* convenient, *most* useful, or *most* satisfactory of the lot.

Would you say, The *best* of the two apples or the *better* of the two apples? Would you ask, Which is the tall*est*, John or James? Would you say, Tom took the bigg*est* of the two?

What you should say is, The bett*er* of the two apples, the tall*er* of the·two boys and the bigg*er* of the two.

Double Negatives

No, Not, None, Nothing, Never are negatives. As a rule only one of these is used in a sentence. We should not say I have*n't* had *none*, but, I have*n't* had *one* (or *any*).

Would you say, She could *not* see *nothing*? No, you would say, She could *not* see *anything*.

Would you say, He can*not* try *no* harder? No, you would say, He can*not* try *any* harder.

Misplaced Words and Phrases

Suppose you were asked to say what was wrong with this sentence:
"You need to wash your face badly."
How would you rewrite it? As the sentence stands it looks as though it is a *bad wash* that is needed. That can't be right. What was meant was:
"Your face badly needs washing."

Test Yourself—17

Here is an assortment of faulty sentences for you to rewrite. When you have rewritten them and compared the new sentences with the answers, ask your friend, teacher, or parent to explain any of the answers of which you are not sure.

(1) John and Mary shared the prize among them.
(2) Arthur and me went to the pictures.

(3) The choir sung the anthem beautifully.

(4) A more pleasanter holiday I never spent.

(5) She never spent no more money after that.

(6) Between you and I, don't you think John did it?

(7) What have you forgot to bring?

(8) I bought a brush for my friend with yellow bristles.

(9) Why do you say Harry is worse than me?

(10) I can't think of nothing when you make that noise.

(Answers on page 358)

XIV. PHRASES AND CLAUSES

Look at these sentences:

(1) I found the *burnt* bread.

(2) I found the bread *burnt to a cinder*.

(3) I found the bread *that had been burnt to a cinder*.

The word *burnt* in the first sentence has been changed to *burnt to a cinder* in the second and to *that had been burnt to a cinder* in the third. *Burnt* in the first sentence is an *adjective*, a describing word that tells you about the bread. *Burnt to a cinder* in the second sentence is a *phrase;* it is different from *that had been burnt to a cinder* in the third sentence in not having a *verb*. When a *verb* is added to a *phrase* and still remains part of a sentence, the *phrase* becomes a *clause*.

Test Yourself—18

Here is a useful exercise. Re-write the following sentences, changing the under-lined *phrases* into *clauses*:

(1) The sailor in uniform stepped ashore.

(2) I lost a book of great value.

(3) After seeing the princess, the crowd dispersed.

(4) We had not been told of your arrival.

(5) Can we be sure of your help?

(6) On arriving, you should ask for Mr. Benson.

(7) Before leaving the house, be sure to shut the front door.

(8) While crossing the street, she lost her purse.

(9) Here is a coin of extreme rarity.

(10) Don't begin the game before shaking hands with your opponent.

(Answers on page 358)

XV. BUILDING LONGER SENTENCES

Who, which, whose, whom, and *that* are important words to be able to use. You might say, for example:

"We have a cat. Her name is Dinah."

Or you might say:

"We have a cat *whose* name is Dinah."

If you do this, you make a *complex* sentence out of two *simple* ones.

Here are some more examples of simple sentences being coupled to form complex sentences:

Simple. I did not win the prize. My teacher awarded it last week.

Complex. I did not win the prize *which* my teacher awarded last week.

Simple. Here is the thief. He stole my bicycle.

Complex. Here is the thief *who* stole my bicycle.

Simple. The cinema was burned down. It was the biggest in town.

Complex. The cinema, *which* was the biggest in town, was burnt down.

Simple. The boy ran to the door. The door was open.

Complex. The boy ran to the door, *which* was open.

The words *when, while, because, or, although, so,* and many others like them can be used to join simple sentences to make complex sentences. Here are some examples:

Simple. The girl slipped from the ladder. She was careless.
Complex. The girl slipped from the ladder *because* she was careless.
Simple. I like Mary. She doesn't like me.
Complex. I like Mary *although* she doesn't like me.
Simple. I saw a fire engine. I was coming to school.
Complex. I saw a fire engine *as* I was coming to school.
Simple. You can't be attending to your reading. You are listening to the radio.
Complex. You can't be attending to your reading *while* you are listening to the radio.

Test Yourself—19

Take each pair of sentences below and make them into one sentence:

(1) The referee made a mistake. It was the cause of the dispute.
(2) The winter must be approaching.

The days are getting shorter.
(3) This is the boy. They were looking for him.
(4) Matthew likes onions. They don't agree with him.
(5) It is time we were setting out. It will be dark soon.
(6) Mary had to return home in haste. She had forgotten her ticket.
(7) You are the person. You sold me the stolen goods.
(8) Can you tell me where the book is? Mother was reading from it just now.
(9) This is the door. John painted it.
(10) These chocolates have hard centres. I don't care much for them.
(11) These are my friends. Their home is near the station.
(12) This is Buckingham Palace. The Queen lives there.
(13) Please look after my dog. I am going into this shop.
(14) I was walking in the High Street. I saw an accident.
(15) They did not feel well. They did not go to the cinema.

(Answers on page 358)

ANSWERS TO THE TESTS

Test 1

(1) Medicine. (2) "Clinch his *small nose*." (3) "His round cheek wans." (4) His own—Henry's. (5) No. "Scowls." (6) Sleek. (7) "Poor Henry lifts distracted hands; his round cheek wans in the candlelight." (8) The sight of his medicine (physic). (9) Clinch. (10) Swallowing the medicine hurriedly.

The poem, *Poor Henry*, was quoted by kind permission of the author, Mr. Walter de la Mare.

Test 2

(1) In the water. (2) Resolved. (3) Supposed.

Test 3

(1) Grieved, deceive, relieved. (2) Thief, seized, counterfeit. (3) Relief, siege. (4) Receive, sieve, forfeit. (5) Believe, receipt.

Test 4

(1) The *gypsies* went into the *cities*. (2) I am very fond of my *donkeys* and my *ponies*. (3) We like reading *stories* about *armies* fighting strong *enemies*. (4) The *Malays* took *parties* on *journeys* to make *studies* of *monkeys*. (5) She gave (some) *pennies* for her *toys*.

Test 5

(1) The *thieves* broke through the *roofs*. (2) The *wolves* killed the *calves* that belonged to the *chiefs*. (3) The *serfs* ate the *loaves* greedily. (4) The *boys themselves* threw away the *leaves*. (5) The *elves* danced with the *dwarfs* and the *fairies*.

Test 6

(1) The *negroes* helped to carry the *curios* aboard. (2) In the *cargoes* were (some) *pianos* and *banjos*. (3) Cook me (some) *potatoes* and *tomatoes* to go with my meat. (4) The *Eskimos* sang *solos*; the *negroes* played on *banjos*.

Test 7

(1) Believe, sale, jerseys. (2) Loaves, storeys. (3) Eskimos, negroes. (4) Armies, wolves, peace. (5) Flour, currants. (6) Thieves, counsel. (7) Pieces, stairs. (8) Pane. (9) Allowed, aloud. (10) Gilt, guilt.

Test 8

(1) You're well. (2) It's. (3) Don't. (4) Won't. (5) She'll . . . I'm. (6) There's. (7) All's well that ends well. (8) Wouldn't . . . o'clock. (9) Don't . . . didn't. (10) Isn't.

Test 9

(1) Written. (2) Bitten. (3) Sung. (4) Drunk. (5) Shaken. (6) Ridden . . . fell . . . lain. (7) Forgotten. (8) Chosen. (9) Torn. (10) Swum. (11) Drank . . . sung. (12) Given . . . flown. (13) Run . . . rang. (14) Shrank. (15) Fallen . . . broken.

Test 10

(1) Flowers. (2) Fish. (3) Cereals. (4) Drinks or beverages. (5) Trees. (6) Surnames. (7) Precious stones, jewels, or gems. (8) Minerals. (9) Thoroughfares or highways and byways. (10) Poultry or fowls. (11) Vehicles. (12) Continents. (13) Gases. (14) Rulers. (15) Spices. (16) Insects. (17) Metals. (18) Hobbies. (19) Wines. (20) Receptacles or containers.

Test 11

(1) Disobedient. (2) Discouraging or unencouraging. (3) Unpleasant. (4) Unintelligent. (5) Illegible. (6) Imperfect. (7) Informal. (8) Impolite or unpolite. (9) Exterior.

Test 12

(1) An eel. (2) Chicken. (3) A leaf. (4) A judge. (5) Crystal. (6) A sheet or a ghost. (7) Brass. (8) A berry. (9) A lion or an ox or a horse. (10) A daisy. (11) A feather. (12) A rake. (13) A church mouse. (14) A ghost. (15) A cucumber. (16) Vinegar. (17) A needle . . . mustard. (18) Pie. (19) A fox. (20) Gold.

Other answers are possible

Test 13

(1) Brightness. (2) Purity. (3) Depth. (4) Poverty. (5) Popularity. (6) Cruelty. (7) Youth. (8) Generosity. (9) Wisdom. (10) Publicity.

Test 14

(1) Compulsion. (2) Beggar. (3) Speech. (4) Food. (5) Failure. (6) Ignorance. (7) Variety. (8) Disobedience. (9) Recognition. (10) Maintenance.

Note the spelling

Test 15

Nouns	Adjectives	Verbs
Peter	little	saw
child	poor	waved
hand	left	ran
door	open	took
buses	big	brought
cars	bright	see
sun	smiling	go
crowds	wide	shone
pavements	warm	filled
weather	summery	enjoyed

Test 16

(1) he. (2) me. (3) I. (4) they. (5) she. (6) I. (7) He or I. (8) we. (9) she. (10) I.

Test 17

(1) John and Mary shared the prize *between* them. (2) Arthur and *I* went to the pictures. (3) The choir *sang* the anthem beautifully. (4) A pleasanter holiday I never spent, or a more pleasant holiday I never spent. (5) She never spent *any* more money after that, or she spent no more money after that. (6) Between you and *me*, don't you think John did it? (7) What have you *forgotten* to bring? (8) I bought a brush with yellow bristles for my friend. (9) Why do you say Harry is worse than *I*? (10) I can think of nothing when you make that noise, or I can't think of *anything* when you make that noise.

Test 18

(1) The sailor who was in uniform stepped ashore. (2) I lost a book that (or which) was of great value. (3) After they had seen the princess, the crowd dispersed. (4) We had not been told that you had arrived. (5) Can we be sure that you will help us? (6) When you arrive, you should ask for Mr. Benson. (7) Before you leave the house, be sure to shut the front door. (8) As she crossed the street she lost her purse. (9) Here is a coin which is extremely rare. (10) Don't begin the game before you have shaken hands with your opponent.

Test 19

(1) The referee made a mistake, which was the cause of the dispute; or the cause of the dispute was a mistake which the referee made. (2) The winter must be approaching as (or because) the days are getting shorter. (3) This is the boy for whom they were looking. (4) Matthew likes onions although (or but) they don't agree with him. (5) It is time we were setting out because (or as) it will be dark soon; or it will be dark soon, so it is time we were setting out. (6) Mary had to return home in haste because she had forgotten her ticket. (7) You are the person who sold me the stolen goods. (8) Can you tell me where the book is that (or which) mother was reading from just now? (9) This is the door which John painted. (10) I don't care much for these chocolates which (or because they) have hard centres. (11) These are my friends whose home is near the station. (12) This is Buckingham Palace where the Queen lives. (13) Please look after my dog while I go into this shop. (14) I was walking in the High Street when (or where) I saw an accident. (15) They did not feel well so did not go to the cinema.

Other answers are possible

358

WHAT YOU SHOULD KNOW ABOUT
INTELLIGENCE TESTS

If somebody asks you, "What are six sevens?" or "Who was king of England in the year 1067?" your replies will be correct only if you have learnt your six-times table or if you know that William the Conqueror began his reign in England in 1066. Such questions test your knowledge. Besides knowledge, however, you have intelligence, which is something quite different.

It is rather a curious thing that nobody really knows exactly what intelligence is like, for it is impossible to see it. It is best thought of as a mental power to do things in the right way and everybody knows that this power varies greatly in different people. We express this when we say: "He is very stupid," or "He is clever," or "She is a very bright girl," and so on. We are making statements about the person's intelligence.

Now, how do we know that one child is more intelligent than another? Simply by comparing "how they go about things." The intelligent person, faced with any situation, sees at once how to tackle it and makes a successful attempt straight away, whilst the much less intelligent one will waste time wondering what to do. Suppose, for example, that a mother has left a pram outside a shop and it starts to run backwards towards the road. A really intelligent child will see at once the danger, will *first* run and stop the pram, will then put it in such a position that it cannot run away again and will, finally, go and tell the lady in the shop. A less intelligent child might stand and scream or possibly run into the shop first without thought for the immediate danger of the baby in the pram.

The fact that we can judge intelligence by the manner in which a person tackles a problem is what gives rise to intelligence tests. Makers of such tests compile a whole series of little problems requiring little knowledge and children can be placed in order of intelligence by the marks they gain, allowing for the difference in their ages. Note this, *allowing for the difference in their ages*.

This is why there is nearly always some question in such a test that you cannot solve. If every question were so easy that every child could do them all, they would no longer serve their purpose. So you can expect a proper intelligence test to include questions intended for the oldest and brightest children. A child of eight, for instance, may be *very* intelligent though he has answered fewer questions than a boy much older—and the older boy might be judged rather below average for his age.

You must remember this when doing any test and you must remember something else. Intelligence is not the whole of the story. You also need courage and perseverance. If you do not bravely face a test, no matter how difficult it looks, you will not do yourself justice. Many a child has failed to gain good marks simply because he or she has just looked at some section and, without really trying, has thought, "Oh, I can't do *that*!" On the other hand, some children make mistakes with the easiest tests—just because they *are* easy. Very simple tests are most useful in picking out the careful child from the one who is slap-dash and who gives the wrong answer through carelessness.

One final point: If you practise the tests that follow, you may not become more intelligent, but you will learn to use your intelligence to better purpose. Practise intelligence tests now—you will find them as good as a game—and you will feel less nervous and more able to tackle them quickly and clear-headedly when you are asked to do so in school. Unless you are a genius you will always miss some marks in a full test, but you can make sure now that you don't lose marks simply because the strangeness of intelligence tests is a little bewildering due to lack of practice.

I

The questions in an intelligence test are not just picked anyhow. They are very carefully chosen and arranged (and tested beforehand). There are two ways in which they differ. First of all, some are easy and some are harder; and secondly, they deal with different kinds of problems. Let us examine examples of these differences.

Example 1. You are asked to put a little cross inside the largest of certain figures.

Even quite a young child should be able to see that in this set the third figure is the largest and should be able to put a little cross inside it so as to get the correct answer, thus:

Example 2. You may be asked to put a line under the third word that comes after the word *before* the first word in this sentence that contains the letter "c."

This is probably too difficult for a little child because he or she will be unable to grasp the meaning. An older child, however, will soon spot that the important word is *comes* because it is the first word containing a *c*; that the word before *comes* is *that*; and that the third word following this is *the*. So the correct answer is: the.

Example 3. You may be asked to underline the correct word which completes a comparison:
Boy is to man as girl is to — (sister, mother, woman, child.)

Here you will see that a boy is compared to what he will be when he grows up, a man, so you have to find the word in brackets which names what a girl will be when she grows up. *Child* is obviously wrong, as is *sister*, and though she might be a *mother*, she must be a *woman*. Thus the word to be underlined is woman.

Example 4. Amongst the words on the right below there is one with the same meaning and one with the opposite meaning when compared with the word on the left. You may be asked to put a single line under a word with the same meaning and a double line under the one which has the opposite meaning.
Wealthy,   healthy, wise, poor, money, cottage, rich.
This is not so difficult, is it? *Wealthy* has the same meaning as *rich*, so you would put one line under rich. *Poor* is the opposite of rich or wealthy so you would put two lines under poor.

If you now have another look at examples 1 to 4, you will notice that 1 and 2 tell you to *do* something. They are called Instruction Tests and are meant to discover whether you can understand what is said to you and do as you are told. Number 3 asks you to compare two pairs of things but leaves you to supply one of the items. These are called Analogy Tests. Such tests ask you to use your intelligence to pick out the proper relation between two similar pairs. The 4th test is a very common one and not too difficult. It requires you to find words similar to or opposite in meaning to a given word.

Remember, all of these examples are only a very small part of an intelligence test. The test might contain quite a large number of each kind of example, some easy, some hard, but, just for the sake of practice, let us now try part of an intelligence test that deals with just these three kinds.

We will give our tests in pairs, the first of each pair being easier than the second: this will make it of special interest for the younger children. Remember this. The ones headed with even numbers—2, 4, 6, 8—will test the mettle of children up to the age of 11.

Test Yourself—1

(1) What is the third word in this sentence?

(2) How many words are there in this sentence?

(3) Pick out the figure below which has some important part missing:

(4) Draw a square about as big as a postage stamp. Draw a circle inside the square. Inside the circle put the letter *c*.

In the next three examples, find the word which completes the comparison.

(5) Boy is to girl as man is to —
(monkey, woman, baby, sky.)
Finger is to hand as toe is to —
(foot, heel, arm, ankle.)
House is to roof as box is to —
(side, bottom, lid, lock.)

(6) Pick out the word on the right which is closest in meaning to the word by itself on the left:
Dirty   tidy, soiled, face, shiny.
Basin   cup, saucer, jug, bowl.
Weeping laughing, running, crying, shouting.

In the following three, pick out the word on the right with an opposite meaning to that of the word by itself on the left.
White   grey, green, black, paper.

Wrong   action, word, ring, right.
Full   empty, book, packed, fill.
(Answers on page 375)

Test Yourself—2

(1) If this sentence has more than twenty words in it, write *Yes;* if not, write *No.*

(2) If no two of the drawings below are alike, write *None,* but if two are of the same shape but of different sizes, write *Yes.* If there are two exactly alike, write *Alike.*

(3) Since Sunday is the first day of the week, what is the day which comes third after the day before the last day of the week?

(4) What word is formed by taking in turn the first, sixth, fourteenth, third and twenty-third letters of this sentence?

(5) From the words in brackets, pick out the missing word in each of the following analogies:
Fish is to — as bird is to wing.
(scale, water, fin, net.)
Doctor is to patient as teacher is to —
(school, nurse, learn, pupil.)
Father is to — as mother is to aunt.
(wife, mother, woman, uncle.)

(6) In each case below, the word on the left has one word of the same meaning on the right and one of opposite meaning. Pick out the word having the same meaning and then the word with the opposite meaning:
Clever   lively, intelligent, mean, dull, average.

361

Dead	deceased, alive, working, buried, gone.
Begin	continue, finish, persevere, start, try.
Cruel	wicked, cheat, sinful, kind, merciless.

Damp	humid, thirsty, sandy, dry, soil.
Pleasant	taste, smell, disagreeable, attractive, sweetness.

(*Answers on page 375*)

II

One thing you will have noted in the tests you have just done, is that not all of them are word tests. Most intelligence tests include figures both in the sense of number and in the sense of drawings. Indeed, it would be possible to make a full test that was mostly filled with drawings of various shapes. To give you some practice in dealing with them, shapes and figures will be included in the tests given here.

Numbers, of course, are mostly used in what are called Number Series Tests and though some of these can be very difficult, the idea is quite simple. There are all sorts of ways in which numbers can be written in regular order. The most familiar is the order of common counting, 1, 2, 3, 4, 5, and so on. You probably also know the series, 2, 4, 6, 8, etc.; 3, 6, 9, 12, etc.; 5, 10, 15, 20, etc. If you experiment a little, however, you will find that you can think of other ways of making a series, adding and taking away, multiplying and dividing, and going both upwards and downwards. Just look at these:

123 234 345 456 567. Simple, isn't it? But note how different it can look if you are given 123234345456567 and left to find out that the numbers are in threes.

123 235 347 459. You have to examine this to find out that the third figure in each number is the *sum* of the first two. These groups too would be much more difficult if no gaps were left, thus: 123235347459.

In such tests what you are usually asked to do is to write down the next two or three or four figures that would follow the series given. There is only one possible **way of doing** this and that is by finding

just how the series ascends or descends, always remembering that *some* of the numbers may be the result of multiplying.

A good plan is to see if you can spot just one part of the series that rises and falls regularly. For example, look at the series, 192 283 374 465, and you will see that the first figures in each group if looked at separately, form the common numbers 1, 2, 3, etc., so that the next group to those given would begin with 5. You can now see that the second figures descend from 9, 8, 7 downwards, whilst the third ascends from 2. It is thus easy to see that the next group will be 556 and the one following, 647. Now try the following examples:

Example 1. What are the next two groups in the series:
1234 4321 2345 5432 3456 6543 . . . . . .
. . . . . .

Example 2. What are the missing numbers where a gap occurs in the series below?
111 224 339 . . . . 6636 7749 8864.

Example 3. What are the next two amounts in the series below?
£1·90   £2·83   £3·76   £4·69   £5·62
£6·55 . . . .

It should have taken you about one minute to do each of these. The first example is an alternating series with each group repeated in reverse so that the odd-numbered groups start with the numbers 1, 2, 3, 4 and so on. Hence, the next group to those given must be 4567 and the one following, 7654.

The second example is really only a disguised multiplication table, once one is one, twice two are four and continuing

362

like this so that the missing groups are 4416 and 5525.

The third should by now be clear and the missing items at the end are: £7·48 and £8·41.

There is another type of test similar in principle to the number series known as a Completion Test. In such questions a word or a figure is left out and you have to tell by the sense or by the order what the missing item is. Here is first an easy one and then a more difficult example:

Example 4. Complete the sentence below by using one of the words in brackets:

We have a lovely — (dog, bird, goat, cat, baby) called "Budgie." Its — (house, room, cage, box) is often — (empty, broken, sold, put) because it flies — (under, near, with, around) the room when it likes and even — (perches, falls, likes, wheels) on our heads.

In this example, if you read right through the given sentence, ignoring the blanks, you will guess that the words *Budgie* and *flies* show that the missing word in the first line is *bird*. A bird usually has a *cage*, not a *room* or a *house* or a *box*, so the second missing word is easily found whilst the only word that really fits the fourth line to make sense is *empty* as the cage must be if the bird is flying *around* the room. Finally, we talk of how a bird *perches* so that the last word is easy.

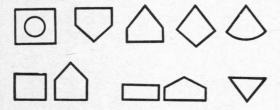

Example 5. One of the figures in the upper line of the drawing above should come at the end of the second line. Which figure is it?

This is a question of noting that the figures in the second line are in pairs with the last pair incomplete. What you have to do is to study the pairs; then look carefully at the odd one at the end of the line. The second of each pair, you will notice, has a sloping roof, so to speak, instead of a flat one, you have to look in the top line for an upside-down triangle with a "sloping roof." The only one that fits properly is the fourth. Did you get it?

Now let us try another test which includes examples of all the types so far dealt with. As before, there is an easy test for children of under eleven which older children should do quite easily, and a harder one in which even the elevens and twelves can make mistakes. The answers, as before, are printed at the end of this book but you should not look at them until you are sure you have finished. One further point. There is a time limit to all intelligence tests so that, while working carefully, you should waste no time. A full intelligence test should be finished in about forty-five minutes—though there are tests for which a longer time is allowed. This means that the following tests should not take more than about ten minutes to do. Practise working quickly, but do not panic. The time limit is usually ample for most children.

Test Yourself—3

(1) What is the letter that comes between the third and fifth letter of the alphabet?

(2) How many t's can you see in this sentence?

(3) What is the longest word in this sentence?

(4) Look at the drawings in the line below. Pick out the pair that are facing a different way from the others.

(5) In the drawing which follows, there

should be two pairs of objects to the left of the line. One object is missing from the second pair. Look at the pictures to the right of the line and pick out the object which is missing from the first group:

⚓ ⚓ ⚓ | ⚓ ⚓ ⚓ ⚓

(6) From the words in brackets find the word which best fits the space where there is a dash:
Cats have kittens and dogs have — (kennels, meat, pups.)
On chairs we sit, on beds we — (lie, sheet, read.)
Apples have pips and plums have — (skins, juice, stones.)
A box of matches and a — of cigarettes. (case, packet, bundle.)

(7) From the words on the right choose the word that is opposite in meaning to the word on the left:
Straight   crooked, right, forward, good.
Slow   running, quick, alive, frost.
Up   right, left, on, down.
Different   things, other, same, colour.

(8) In the following examples, choose the word on the right which has the same meaning as the one on the left:
Slap   punch, hurt, smack, push.
Frock   skirt, dress, coat, clothes.
Labour   hard, house, prison, toil.
Wireless   cinema, pictures, television, radio.

(9) In each line below, state the two numbers that would come next to complete the line:
2 4 6 8 10 12 — —
90 80 70 60 50 40 — —
111 112 113 114 115 116 — —
1164 1132 1116 1108 1104 — —

(10) In the little story below, pick out the word in brackets which makes sense:
Once upon a (time, place, story) there was a tiny (giant, tree, fairy) who lived in a buttercup. Like all fairies, she had a (headache, wand, ring) about as big as a small (man, chair, pin) but, though small, it was very (big, powerful, long). One day when she was asleep a cow (came, swallowed, saw) her and she woke up to find herself in the cow's (stomach, eye, shed). She was not at all (inside, hungry, afraid) for she had only to (hold, wave, tell) her wand and there she was, back in her buttercup.

(Answers on page 375)

Test Yourself—4

(1) What is the middle word of this long sentence.
(2) In question 1, does the middle letter of the sentence come in the middle word?
(3) Look at the drawings below. The first three are in their proper order but the rest are not. Choose the drawing that you think should come fourth:

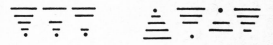

(4) If no two of the following figures are alike, write *x*. If one of them is larger than all the others, write *y*. If neither of these statements is true, write *z*.

(5) From the second line in each of the following groups, pick out the

figure that should occupy the vacant space.

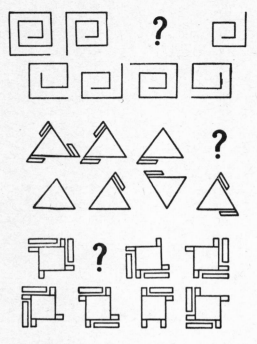

(6) Complete the analogy in each case below:

Coat is to brush as carpet is to (crumbs, nap, sweeper, dirt.)

Entrance is to exit as import is to (trade, goods, taxes, export.)

Heaviness is to scales as heat is to (thermometer, fire, radiator, coal.)

Electricity is to cable as water is to (tap, pipe, sink, bath.)

(7) Pick out the two words in each group below that have similar meanings:

Contented, overjoyed, sorrowful, satisfied, angry.

Singing, screaming, whispering, lisping, screeching.

Working, assisting, nursing, aiding, collecting.

Contract, partner, agreement, estimate, architect.

(8) In each group of words below pick out the pair that have opposite meanings:

Depart, keep, visit, remain, move.

Expanding, leaning, contracting, melting, boiling.

True, real, attractive, ordinary, repugnant.

Cautious, hurried, impulsive, sorry, apologize.

(9) What are the next two numbers in each line below?

81 64 49 36
—————————————
 9   8   7   6 — —

124 136 148 1510 — —

·0000001 ·000002 ·00003 — —

£108·47 £108·06 £107·65 £107·24 £106·83 — —

(10) Choose, from the words in brackets, the one which best fits the following passage:

We (journeyed, staggered, hopped) along, enjoying our stroll but the (sun, moon, stars) was strong enough to (make, feel, warm) us just a little too (excited, warm, breathless) in our battledress suits. It was such a (story, life, change) from the (joy, discipline, variety) of the camp, however, that we went even farther than we had (travelled, walked, intended) which made us late in getting back.

(Answers on page 375)

III

One kind of test is based on the fact that in life we find it convenient to have words for things which are normally grouped together. For example, *furniture* is a word which groups together chairs, settees, tables, sideboards and chests-of-drawers. We can even take chairs, settees, tables and so on, and use each of them as a group name, thus *chair* is a group name for easy-chair, Windsor chair, deck-chair; or *table* a group name for dining table, refectory table, gate-leg table, billiard table, kitchen table, and so on.

Classification asks you to discover to some extent the ways in which things in the same class resemble one another. If you are given the three headings, Animal, Vegetable, and Mineral, it should not be difficult to sort out the items from the following list:

peas, potatoes, mice, fish, tomatoes, iron, sugar, gold, coal, leather, brass, water, wool.

Peas, potatoes and tomatoes are easily recognized as vegetable just as mice and fish are seen to be animal; and iron, gold and brass, mineral. What of sugar, leather, wool, water? You simply ask yourself the question, Does it come from some kind of a plant? Then it is vegetable. So sugar is vegetable. Again, does it come from an animal? If so, like leather and wool, we class it as animal. If it is neither animal nor vegetable it must be mineral, like water.

Two other facts about classes you should notice. The first is that some classes *include* other classes. Thus *fruit* includes apples, pears, bananas and so on; *furniture* includes chairs, tables, beds, settees. The second fact is that certain classes may remind us of others. *Tools*, for example, brings to mind *workmen* and we know that *rabbits*, which are animal, live on *vegetables*. Tests on classification may expect you to make use of these facts. Study the examples that follow.

Example 1. Mother went to three shops, a grocer's, a butcher's and a greengrocer's. Which of these articles did she buy in each shop?

Margarine, chops, cheese, cauliflower, potatoes, Brazil nuts, oranges, bones, salt, beef, tinned salmon, sausages.

Even quite a small child will have a good idea at which shop things are sold and most children from eight upwards should be able to answer this. It will help you to check your result if you are told that there are four things bought in each shop. It's hardly necessary to tell you more, is it?

Example 2. In the list below, there are three classes which, between them, include all the rest. Pick out the three main classes and place the others under them:

Fruit, pork, toffees, clear-gums, apples, meat, beef, chocolate-drops, sweets, mutton, oranges, lamb, plums, cherries, mint humbugs.

There are two ways of doing this. You can try either to spot at once the three main classes, or you can arrange *all* the similar things in columns and then pick out the main class of each. If you do it the first way, you should quite easily pick out *fruit, meat* and *sweets*. If you do it the second way, pork, meat, beef, mutton and lamb go together and it is not hard to see that four of them are *meat*! So, too, with the others.

Example 3. Amongst the drawings below, there are three types, five of each type. Arrange the numbers of the drawings in groups of the same type.

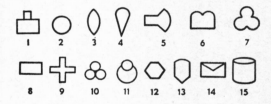

This is really a very simple test though at first sight it does not look so. Why is this? It is because many figures have no names, like figure 1, or 6, or 11, and have no special meanings that would help us to class them together. So we have to examine them to find their likenesses or differences. Remembering that we are looking for three kinds only, it will soon strike you that the figures are made of straight and curved lines, some with curved lines only, some with straight lines only and some with both curved and straight lines. Our three groups then are:

1, 8, 9, 12, 14.
2, 3, 7, 10, 11.
4, 5, 6, 13, 15.

One kind of test that can be very teasing is the jumbled word test. Of this there can be three varieties, words with the letters in the wrong order, sentences with the words in the wrong order or a combination of these two. If the order of the letters in a word is disturbed, it can be very difficult indeed to discover what the word was. This you will see if you look at the jumbled words, GRANEO, PLINCE, ESTETE. You can discover these if given plenty of time, but as there is a time-limit to a test you would be given these words in this form.

Example 4. Using the clues supplied, find the hidden words:

GRANEO   A juicy fruit
PLINCE   You write with this
ESTETE   You sit on this

The clues make a great deal of difference, don't they? It really becomes a guessing game and you quickly guess the right word if you stick to the clue. You think of juicy fruits: "Apples, pears, plums, oranges"—and you get the word ORANGE. Similarly you find PENCIL and SETTEE.

In the case of the words of a sentence being mixed up, the meanings of the words, especially of the verb or action word give you your clues. Just try these:

Example 5. Arrange the following sentences in their correct order:

John a cleverly goal scored.

And and some fish father mother bought chips.

The to off see match I'm football.

The first sentence is straightforward enough for *scored* immediately gives you "John scored a goal" so that you only have to fit in *cleverly*. Note this: if two versions are possible, both are correct. Hence "John cleverly scored a goal," or "Cleverly John scored a goal," or any other form that makes sense is right. In the second sentence the two *ands* will soon lead you to *father and mother* and to *fish and chips* so that you find the correct version, "Father and mother bought some fish and chips." The catch in the third

sentence is the difficulty of spotting a verb or action word. You soon see, however, that *I'm* must be followed by *off* and *football* by *match*. Hence: "I'm off to see the football match." Now let us try another Test.

Test Yourself—5

(1) Copy out the figures below, then place the numbers 1, 2, 3, 4 and 5, starting with the biggest and working down in order of size.

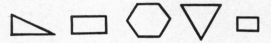

(2) How many *lines* are there in all the figures in question 1?

(3) Copy out the figure below. Place the letter "A" where it will be in the circle but not in the other two shapes; put "B" in the triangle only and "C" in the square only, "D" in triangle and square, "E" in triangle and circle.

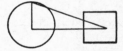

(4) Pick the item in brackets which completes the comparison in each case below:

Eye is to see as nose it to — (smell, taste, nasty, face.)

Fish is to swim as bird is to — (walk, fly, nest, air.)

Grass is to green as blood is to — (veins, body, red, hurt.)

(5) Choose the two words in each set that have the same meaning:

Story, tale, book, tell, listen.

Baby, man, policewoman, infant, doll.

Lion, donkey, tiger, snake, ass.

(6) In the following choose the words with opposite meanings:

Hard, heavy, stony, light, electricity.

367

Start, follow, stop, machine, car.
Meat, chew, tough, thick, tender.

(7) Place the following words in three columns under the headings TOOLS, TOYS, CLOTHES:

Hammer, boat, skirt, waistcoat, doll, pliers, saw, marbles, jacket.

(8) What are the next two numbers in each line below?

01 12 23 34 45 56 — —
½p 1p 1½p 2p 2½p — —
101 111 121 131 141 151 — —

(9) Find from the words in brackets the word that fits the blank:

She — (went, hurried, strolled, cried) to school because she was late.

Children shouldn't — (look, want, play, watch) in the road.

Seven — (sixes, fives, fours, threes) make twenty-one.

(10) Find the proper words from the clues given:

KLIM   We have it in our tea.
NOPOS   We also use this with our tea.
DONNOL A very famous city.
OCOHSL Where most children go daily.

Also, put this sentence in its proper order:

On to go I school bus the.

(Answers on page 375)

Test Yourself—6

(1) If all these animals are the same size in real life when full-grown, write "yes," but if not, write the names of the smallest and the largest.

(2) In which of the following words could you leave out one letter and still have a proper word left?

Trip, there, hence, faith, coke, star, mate.

(3) Complete the following analogies by choosing the correct item in brackets.

December is to winter as July is to — (spring, summer, autumn.)

SPAM is to MAPS as STOP is to — (POST, POTS, TOPS, AMPS.)

(4) In each case below, pick out the words of similar meaning:

Believe, hope, credit, relate, relieve.

Throw, catch, case, cast, might.

Thin, plump, healthy, stout, rough.

(5) Pick out the words of opposite meaning:

Describe, admire, show, despise, point.

Travel, journey, hasten, end, delay.

Performance, tragedy, play, comedy, actor.

(6) In the list below, pick out the three classes which include all the others and arrange the items in columns:

Lord, title, John, accountant, profession, James, earl, name, lawyer, George, doctor, prince, Frederick, duke, barrister.

(7) What are the next two items in each line below?

31·0 32·1 33·2 34·3 35·4 — —
AB33 CD44 EF55 GH66 — —
$\frac{1}{4}|\frac{2}{3}$ $\frac{5}{4}|\frac{2}{3}$ $\frac{5}{4}|\frac{6}{3}$ — —

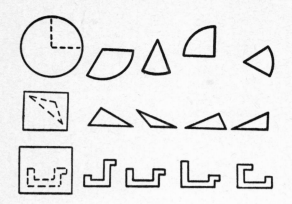

(Answers on page 376)

(8) From these drawings, find the pieces that fit into the spaces marked with dotted lines.

(9) Certain words below are given with their letters in the wrong order. Spell them correctly.

He strolled quite LWLSOY along the NORFT where there were WODCRS of people, the NDBA was playing, the sun was GRIHBT and DVRYYOEEB seemed happy.

IV

Having dealt with all the more common types of test, we now come to a kind of problem that can be quite straightforward or can be extremely difficult and can include all kinds of questions. This is the type of problem which calls upon our power to draw inferences. First of all let us see what an inference is:

"John is ten years old and Mary is John's twin." Here are two facts only, but most people will immediately see from them that a third fact can be derived: that Mary is ten years old. Again, "Mr. Sykes, who is an invalid, never goes out when it is wet. He sat out all afternoon in the garden yesterday." Once more we have two facts from which we can derive a third: that it was not wet yesterday afternoon. Now, whenever we derive a new fact from certain given ones, we are said to make an inference. We make inferences every day. When your mother says: "Take your raincoat. It's going to rain," she does so because she has made an inference from the state of the sky or perhaps from the barometer. When you say, "It's Monday today. It'll be cold meat for lunch," you are likewise making an inference. You know that you can expect cold meat from what has happened in the past.

Now, before we look at any examples at all, it is important to note that inference tests nearly always *look* more difficult than they are. Such tests have to give you a number of facts and this makes the question appear complicated. But remember that among the facts given there is always at least one, perhaps more, from which you can make a start.

Study the following examples very carefully:

Example 1. Four children, Alice, Bertha, Charles and Denis are aged 9, 10, 10, and 13, but not in this order. One boy and one girl are the same age. Bertha is four years younger than Denis.

Here you will see at once that, even in a very easy problem, it does not appear so at first. But read the facts carefully right through and it should strike you at once that the last one, "Bertha is four years younger than Denis," really is the key to the question. For Bertha must be 9 and Denis 13, leaving the other two, Alice and Charles of the same age, 10 years old.

Example 2. Arthur, Fred, James, George and Tom were the top five boys in the class, but we do not know which of them was first, second, third, fourth and fifth. James, however, was next but one below Fred. Arthur was next but one below George. Tom was next but one above Fred. What was their order?

If you remember that there were just five of them, it is clear that if any one has two boys above him and two boys below him he must be in the middle, or third. This is true of Fred, for the first and the

369

last facts prove that he was in the middle. And this makes Tom first, James last and George second, so you can write out the proper order: Tom, George, Fred, Arthur, James.

Example 3. In one innings of a cricket match, only four men batted, Robinson, Brown, Smith and Jones; Jones being 17 not out and the total scored (no extras) just 50. Smith knocked as many as Jones and Robinson together. Brown knocked twice as many as Robinson who scored 13 less than Jones. How many did each man score?

Here the key fact should be quickly spotted for the actual score of only one man is given. Jones scored 17. If so, then Robinson must have scored 4 and Brown twice as many = 8. Hence the top scorer was Smith with 21.

You must be prepared, in some tests, for much harder examples than this, but even if you do not work an inference test out fully, you do get marks for as much as you do, so if the next examples are hard to you, see if you can work at least part of them out.

Example 4. Five men, Arthur, James, James, John and Peter have the surnames Bradley, Brown, Power, Smith, Smith. Their occupations are: dentist, doctor, journalist, solicitor and teacher. You cannot tell which is which from the order here given.

Neither James earns his living by his pen. The doctor and one Smith have the same Christian name. The solicitor and the doctor have the same initials. The dentist's Christian name is Arthur. The teacher and the journalist have the same surname. Brown is one of the doctor's patients. Give the full names and occupations of each.

The best way to tackle this problem is to write on a piece of paper the three headings, CHRISTIAN NAME, SURNAME and OCCUPATION. Then work through the facts given. The full solution will not be worked out for you here but your first two steps

are: Since there are only two Christian names alike you can write:

CHRISTIAN NAME	SURNAME	OCCUPATION
James		Doctor
James	Smith	

Since the dentist's Christian name is Arthur, and since the teacher and the journalist have the same surname, you can now add to the above:

CHRISTIAN NAME	SURNAME	OCCUPATION
James		Doctor
James	Smith	Teacher
	Smith	Journalist
Arthur		Dentist

Now see if you can finish it.

You will see that if you tackle such a problem step by step, you will at least find part of the answer and, if the question is not too difficult, you can work it out in full.

As this kind of test is both important and, as a rule, not very easy, we will make the next Tests deal with inferences only. As you will see, they may vary considerably.

Test Yourself—7

(1) John is older than Ted. John and Ted are each younger than Mary. Ted's younger sister is Frances. Give the children's names in order from youngest to eldest.

(2) Mary, Anne and Helen are aged 9, 10 and 16 but not in that order. The one whose initial is nearest to Z in the alphabet is the eldest. The one whose initial is nearest to A in the alphabet is the youngest. What are their ages?

(3) "All war is wicked." After reading this statement pick out the *true* statement below:

(a) All wickedness is war.
(b) Some wars are necessary.
(c) No war is good.

(4) Read the following and again pick out the most direct inference from this:

Some children have dirty finger-nails. Dirt breeds germs and germs can make you ill. So, if you have dirty finger-nails, you may fall ill.

(a) Dirty finger-nails *can* make you fall ill.

(b) Some people have clean finger-nails.

(c) Germs are not harmful.

(5) Once more, pick out the correct statement, after reading the sentence that follows. "If you wanted the most money which would you rather have, six dozen dozen pennies or half a dozen dozen pennies?"

(a) Six dozen dozen pennies.

(b) Half a dozen dozen pennies.

(c) Both are of the same value.

(6) John doesn't like apples, pears or bananas. James won't eat any fruit with stones in it. George refuses to eat any kind of berries. Which of the following will all three boys eat?

Peaches, plums, oranges, cherries, bananas, blackberries, pears, strawberries, grapefruit, apples.

(7) There are three girls, Mary, Joan and Norah. One is dark, one fair, one ginger. Mary and Joan are friends. Joan wishes she had dark hair. The ginger one doesn't like Mary. What is the colour of each girl's hair?

(8) John is ten years old. His father said to him, "When you are five years older you will be half as old as I was five years ago." How old is John's father?

(9) Beeton is exactly half way from Aytown to Seton. Tom rides from Aytown to Beeton and back and then from Aytown through Beeton to Seton and back to Aytown. He has ridden in all thirty-six miles. How far from Aytown is Beeton?

(10) There are three married couples: the Easts, the Wests and the Norths. The wives are called Mabel, Anne and Joyce and the husbands Alfred, James and Michael, but not in this order. No husband and wife have the same initials.

Mrs. East and Joyce are great friends but Mrs. West doesn't like Mabel or Joyce. Joyce's husband is Michael. Write out the full table.

Surnames	East	North	West
Wife	—	—	—
Husband	—	—	—

(*Answers on page 376*)

Test Yourself—8

(1) At the neighbouring houses 1, 3, 5 and 7 Abel Street, live Fred, George, Tom and John. The boy with the shortest name lives at the highest number. George lives next door but one. John lives in an end house. Where does each boy live?

(2) Yorkshire, Lancashire, Surrey and Nottinghamshire played each of the others at cricket. Yorkshire won one, lost one and drew one. Lancashire drew all three. Surrey won two and drew one. Notts lost two and drew one. In the table of matches below, write out the winners. If the match was a draw, write out both teams.

Yorks *v.* Lancs   Lancs *v.* Surrey
Yorks *v.* Surrey   Lancs *v.* Notts
Yorks *v.* Notts   Surrey *v.* Notts

In each of the next three questions, a statement is given followed by three comments. Pick out the best comment in each case.

(3) He was told that if he got his feet wet he would catch a cold; and he did catch a cold; so he must have got his feet wet.

(a) Perhaps he didn't get his feet wet but caught a cold from someone else.

(b) Serves him right for not doing as he was told.

(c) You might get your feet wet and still not catch a cold.

(4) All soldiers wear uniform and all policemen wear uniform.

(a) So some soldiers must be policemen.

(b) All policemen must be soldiers.

(c) From this statement, we can't tell whether any policeman is a soldier.

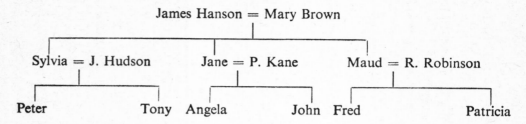

James Hanson = Mary Brown

Sylvia = J. Hudson   Jane = P. Kane   Maud = R. Robinson

Peter   Tony   Angela   John   Fred   Patricia

(5) In the family table above, the sign = means "married."

Now answer the following questions:

What is the married name of Mary Brown?

What was the maiden name of Mrs. Hudson?

What relation is Peter to Patricia? To Tony?

How many grandchildren did Mrs. Hanson have?

Who are Angela Kane's uncles?

(6) Look at the street plan on p. 373: A motorist at the point marked "A", outside the Odeon Cinema, inquires his way to *The Larches* in Ashfield Crescent. ("Z" on the plan.) He is told by a boy: "Turn right at the traffic lights; then take the first left and go as far as you can. Turn right and immediately after, turn left and go along as far as you can. Turn right and then turn first left. You'll find *The Larches* on the left at the corner of a crescent."

(a) Using the letters marked on the plan, write down what points he would pass if he followed the boy's route.

(b) Next, show which would have been the easiest route.

(7) A brother and two sisters called Brown married a sister and two brothers called Smith. The names of the three men were Arthur, Fred and Edgar and of the three wives, Doris, Bertha and Cynthia. Each couple had a son, and the youngsters were Tom, Dick and Harry. None of these names is in correct order. Tom Brown likes his uncle Fred better than uncle Edgar but his mother Doris doesn't like Fred's wife Bertha. Dick thinks Aunt Bertha is wonderful.

Who married whom? Whose sons are Tom, Dick and Harry?

(8) At the neighbouring houses 1, 3, 5, 7 and 9 Mount Street live Jones, Brown, Evans, Robinson and Smith. Their occupations are: plumber, grocer, clerk, joiner and engineer. The order of these names tells you nothing.

The joiner lives in the middle house next door but one to the grocer, Smith. Evans lives at number nine, next door to the clerk. The grocer's neighbour is Brown. Evans is not a plumber. Robinson lives next door to the joiner.

Give the name and occupation of the resident in each house.

(9) Mr. Alfred East married Miss Barbara West whose married sister, Mrs. Mary North, has a sister-in-law called Mrs. Doris South. Mr.

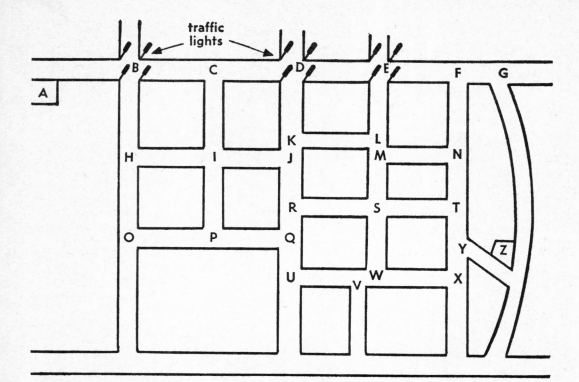

Bert West married Miss Winifred East. The Easts, the Wests, the Norths and the Souths each have one boy, in every case called Peter. Now answer these questions:

(a) What were the maiden names of the four wives?

(b) Which of them are sisters?

(c) Name the grandfathers of each of the four Peters.

(d) Which of the wives has a brother or brothers?

(*Answers on page 376*)

V

The tests used in examinations are usually standardized, that is, they are brought into a uniform pattern, in addition to being prepared with great care and themselves tested beforehand in a way that really does not concern us here.

They may vary in length according to the time it is proposed that children should be allowed to spend on them, and the time allotted is usually too short for many children. It is natural that older and unusually clever children should work more quickly than younger or less gifted children. From this fact you should learn, firstly, that there must be no delay in working through the tests, and secondly, that you need not be despondent if you have not finished. Do not, however, make the mistake of trying to rush through the tests. Go slowly enough to be clear about what you are doing. And don't waste time on some difficult question. Leave it, and come back to it when you have done the others. But *do* try it, because it may not be so difficult as it seems.

For a variety of reasons, it is not possible to give full intelligence test papers here. To give you all-round practice, here is a mixed test which differs from full tests mainly in being shorter:

Test Yourself—9

(1) Write out the first word in this sentence that contains the three letters: *h i s*.

(2) "All good children go to heaven." Write down all the letters in the above sentence that are used more than once in the sentence.

(3) Write down the second, eighteenth, ninth, third and eleventh letters of the alphabet in that order.

(4) How many letters are there before the first "y" in this sentence?

(5) Which letters of the word STRANGE would be different if reflected in a mirror?

(6) Complete the following analogies:
Garden is to gate as house is to — (room, door, path, window).
Medicine is to bottle as pill is to — (cork, box, sick, round).
Dog is to kennel as pig is to — (pork, snout, sty, swill).
Church is to parson as hospital is to — (doctor, ill, medicine, bed).
Grape is to wine as apple is to — (beer, stout, lemonade, cider).

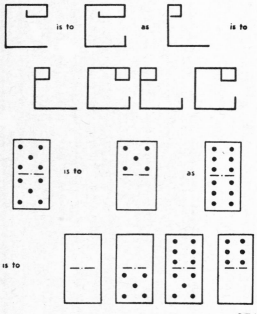

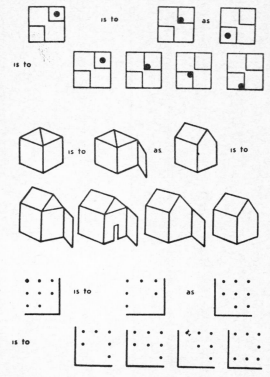

(7) Pick out the two words having opposite meanings in each of the following groups:
Blunt, shears, knife, sharp, scissors.
Lot, common, more, some, rare.
Climb, slope, valley, high, hill.
Lend, give, borrow, spend, grant.
Bedroom, height, bottom, cellar, depth.

(8) Pick out the two words having similar meanings in each of the following groups:
Sink, float, dive, plunge, swim.
Agree, imagine, reason, conform, perceive.
Away, abroad, deceased, decadent, dead.
Keep, covet, draw, hold, accept.
Threat, harsh, menace, dangerous, safe.

(9) What are the next two items in each of the following lines?
2 9 16 23 30 — —

374

36 32 28 24 20 — —
6 9 12 15 18 — —
110 121 132 143 — —
32·01 43·12 54·23 — —
AB987 BC876 CD765 — —

(10) Write out the following mixed sentences in their correct order:
The in it read I newspaper.
Hung the the on she picture wall.
Me and stop one buy.
Mouse clock ran the up the.
Ate of and butter she slice a bread.
Like woodwork do can't why boys girls?

(11) In each set below there are five objects which are in the same class. Pick them out:
Apples, potatoes, turnips, plums, pears, cherries, carrots, green-gages.

Motor-cars, taxis, trams, trains, motor-coaches, buses, lorries, horses.

Cows, horses, lions, sheep, tigers, dogs, cats, elephants.

(12) On a shelf in the chemist's shop there are six coloured bottles, red, white, yellow, green, brown and blue, all containing chemicals. In each of the following pairs one bottle is poisonous, and the other is not: green, blue; red, white; brown, yellow. In each of the following pairs, one bottle is non-poisonous: green, white; red, yellow; blue, brown. Assuming that the red bottle is non-poisonous state which of the other bottles have poison and which not.

(Answers on page 376)

ANSWERS TO INTELLIGENCE TESTS

Test 1

(1) The. (2) 8. (3) Second figure with arm missing.
(4) 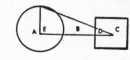 *Note:* The size of the circle does not matter—even if it touches the sides of the square.
(5) Woman, foot, lid. (6) Soiled, bowl, crying, black, right, empty.

Test 2

(1) No. (2) Yes (first and last figures). (3) Monday. (4) Woman. (5) Fin, pupil, uncle, fourth figure.
(6) Intelligent-dull, deceased-alive, start-finish, merciless-kind, humid-dry, attractive-disagreeable.

Test 3

(1) d. (2) 3 t's. (3) sentence. (4) fourth pair. (5) Third figure. (6) Pups, lie, stones, packet. (7) Crooked, quick, down, same. (8) Smack, dress, toil, radio. (9) 14, 16; 30, 20; 117, 118; 1102, 1101. (10) Time, fairy, wand, pin, powerful, swallowed, stomach, afraid, wave.

Test 4

(1) The middle word is "word." (2) Yes. (3) Second figure in right group. (4) *y*. (5) Third figure; first figure; first figure. (6) Sweeper, export, thermometer, pipe. (7) Contented, satisfied; screaming, screeching; assisting, aiding; contract, agreement. (8) Depart, remain; expanding, contracting; attractive, repugnant; cautious, impulsive. (9) $\frac{28}{5}$, $\frac{16}{4}$; 1612, 1714; ·0004, ·005; £106·42, £106·01. (10) Journeyed, sun, make, warm, change, discipline, intended.

Test 5

(1) The number 1 goes in the third figure, 2 in the fourth, 3 in the second, 4 in the first and 5 in the last. (2) 20 lines. (3)

(4) Smell, fly, red. (5) Story-tale, Baby-infant, donkey-ass. (6) Heavy-light, start-

stop, tough-tender. (7) *Tools*: hammer, pliers, saw. *Toys*: boat, doll, marbles. *Clothes*: skirt, waistcoat, jacket. (8) 67, 78; 3p, 3½p; 161, 171. (9) Hurried, play, threes. (10) Milk, spoon, London, school. I go to school on the bus.

Test 6

(1) Mouse, camel. (2) Trip, there, star, mate. (3) Summer, POTS, the third figure. (4) Believe-credit, throw-cast, plump-stout. (5) Admire-despise, hasten-delay, tragedy-comedy. (6) *Title*: lord, earl, prince, duke. *Profession*: accountant, lawyer, doctor, barrister. *Name*: John, James, George, Frederick. (7) 36·5 37·6; IJ77 KL88;

$$\frac{5 \mid 6 \quad 5 \mid 6}{4 \mid 7 \quad 8 \mid 7}$$

(8) Third piece, second piece, second piece. (9) Slowly, front, crowds, band, bright, everybody.

Test 7

(1) Frances, Ted, John, Mary. (2) Mary, 16: Helen, 10: Anne, 9. (3) (*c*) is the correct answer. (4) (*a*) is the correct answer. (5) (*a*) is correct. (6) Oranges and grapefruit. (7) Mary, dark; Joan, fair; Norah, ginger. (8) John's father is 35. (9) Aytown to Beeton is six miles.

(10) Surnames	East	North	West
Wife	Mabel	Joyce	Anne
Husband	Alfred	Michael	James

Test 8

(1) At numbers 1, 3, 5 and 7 live John, George, Fred and Tom in that order.

(2) Yorks	Lancs	Lancs	Surrey
Surrey		Lancs	Notts
Yorks		Surrey	

(3) (*a*) is the correct answer. (4) (*c*) is correct. (5) Mrs. Hanson. Sylvia Hanson. Cousin; brother. Six grandchildren. J. Hudson and R. Robinson. (6) (*a*) BHIJRSTY; (*b*) BCDEFG. (7) Arthur Brown married Doris Smith; Fred Smith married Bertha Brown; Edgar Smith married Cynthia Brown. Tom is the son of Arthur and Doris Brown; Harry is the son of Fred and Bertha Smith; Dick is the son of Edgar and Cynthia Smith.

(8) Numbers	1	3
Names	Smith	Brown
Occupations	Grocer	Plumber
5	7	9
Jones	Robinson	Evans
Joiner	Clerk	Engineer

(9) (*a*) Mrs. East was Miss Barbara West. Mrs. North was Miss Mary West. Mrs. Doris South was Doris North. Mrs. West was Miss Winifred East. (*b*) Mrs. East and Mrs. North are sisters. (*c*) Peter East, East and West: Peter North, North and West: Peter South, South and North: Peter West, West and East. (*d*) Mr. Bert West is the brother of Mrs. East and Mrs. North. Mr. North is the brother of Mrs. South. Mr. Alfred East is the brother of Mrs. West.

Test 9

(1) This. (2) ALGODHEN. (3) BRICK. (4) 6. (5) S R N G E. (6) Door, box, sty, doctor, cider, 3rd figure, 4th figure, 3rd figure, 3rd figure, 1st figure. (7) Blunt, sharp; common, rare; valley, hill; lend, borrow; height, depth. (8) Dive, plunge; agree, conform; deceased, dead; keep, hold; threat, menace. (9) 37, 44; 16, 12; 21, 24; 154, 165; 65·34, 76·45; DE654, EF543.

(10) I read it in the newspaper. She hung the picture on the wall. Stop me and buy one. The mouse ran up the clock. She ate a slice of bread and butter. Why can't girls do woodwork like boys?

(11) Apples, plums, pears, cherries and greengages are fruits.

Motor-cars, taxis, motor-coaches, buses and lorries are petrol-engined vehicles.

Cows, horses, sheep, dogs and cats are domestic animals.

(12) *Poisonous:* Blue, White and Yellow. *Non-poisonous:* Brown and Green.